Agency, Partnership and Limited Liability Companies

RICHARD J. CONVISER
Professor of Law
IIT/Kent College of Law

MICHAEL J. KAUFMAN
Dean and Professor of Law
Santa Clara University School of Law

Eighth Edition

WEST ACADEMIC

860 Blue Gentian Road, Suite 350
Eagan, MN 55121
1-877-888-1330

Published in the United States of America

ISBN: 979-8-88786-490-7

Summary of Contents

PART THREE: LIMITED LIABILITY COMPANIES

Capsule Summary

PART ONE: AGENCY

I. CREATION OF AGENCY RELATIONSHIP

A. INTRODUCTION

1. Scope and Purpose of Agency

The law of agency concerns the rights and liabilities created when one person acts for another.

2. Agency Definitions

Because of inconsistency among the courts regarding agency terminology, the Restatement of Agency definitions are generally followed in this Summary.

a. Agency

Agency is a fiduciary relationship arising from the mutual "manifestation of consent" that an ***agent*** shall act on behalf of and subject to the control of the ***principal***. An ***objective standard*** is used so that the relationship is dependent on what the agent believed the principal intended. An agency can arise even absent true mutual consent, *i.e.,* through apparent or ostensible agency.

b. Principal

A ***disclosed*** principal is one whose ***existence and identity is known*** to the person transacting business with the agent. However, if the person knows the agent is acting for another, but ***does not know the principal's identity***, the principal is an ***unidentified principal.***

(1) Undisclosed Principal

A principal is undisclosed when the third party transacting business with the agent does not know that the agent is acting for another.

c. Agent

The Restatement (Second) of Agency differentiated between general agents and special agents, and courts often use these terms. A ***general agent*** has authority to conduct a ***series of transactions*** involving a continuity of service. A ***special agent*** has authority for only a ***single transaction*** or a series of transactions ***not*** involving a continuity of service.

(1) Factor

A factor is a commercial agent employed to sell consigned merchandise in the agent's own name for the principal.

(2) Subagent

If ***authorized*** to do so, an agent may appoint a subagent to perform functions undertaken by the agent for the principal. If the agent has ***no such authority***, the appointee is the agent's agent, not a subagent of the principal.

(3) Coagent

Coagents are agents who owe duties to a ***common principal*** but not to each other. A coagent may be appointed by the principal or by another agent with authority from the principal.

(4) Gratuitous Agent

A ***gratuitous agent*** is one who acts ***without compensation*** (*e.g.,* holder of power of attorney on behalf of friends or family members).

d. Employer-Employee Relationship

This is a special type of agency relationship in which the principal ("employer") employs the agent ("employee") to perform services and ***retains control*** over the manner of performance. Note that there is ***no*** right of control over independent contractors.

B. REQUIREMENTS FOR AGENCY RELATIONSHIP

1. In General

An agency relationship is ***consensual*** but not necessarily contractual.

2. Consent

Agency relationships usually arise by prior agreement between the principal and agent because they are consensual. Consent can also occur after the fact by ratification, or the doctrine of estoppel can serve as a substitute for consent.

a. Agency by Agreement

For there to be an agency by agreement, a mutual manifestation of consent, either ***express or implied***, must be present.

b. Agency by Ratification

An agency by ratification occurs when the principal ***accepts the benefits*** or otherwise ***affirms the conduct*** of a person purporting to act on the principal's behalf. There must be some ***objective*** evidence that the principal ***knew of the act***.

(1) No Partial Ratification

A principal cannot ratify a portion of the beneficial aspects of the agent's conduct while refusing to affirm the rest.

c. Apparent Agency

When a principal causes a third party to believe one is her agent, and the third party so relies in dealing with the agent, an apparent agency will be implied by the courts. It is the ***principal's acts*** that are relevant to the agency determination.

d. Ostensible Agency

An ostensible agency arises when a principal: (i) ***intentionally or carelessly*** causes a third party to believe that the agent has authority; ***or*** (ii) upon notice of such belief by the third person, ***fails to take reasonable steps*** to notify the third party of the absence of such authority; ***and*** (iii) the third party ***detrimentally changes her position*** based on her reliance on the agent's purported authority.

3. Capacity

The principal must have capacity to perform the act that he delegates to the agent. This usually requires ***contractual capacity***. However, any person with minimal mental capacity may be an agent; *e.g.,* a minor can be an agent but not a principal.

4. No Consideration

No consideration or compensation is necessary to create an agency relationship.

5. General Rule—No Writing Required

An agency relationship may be created by conduct, or by written or spoken words. However, many states enforce the ***Statute of Frauds*** by requiring an agent's authority to be evidenced by a writing signed by the principal if the agent is to execute ***land sales contracts***. A few states have enacted ***equal dignities statutes*** that require a written agency agreement whenever the contract the agent is entering into for the principal is required to be in writing.

a. Effect of No Required Writing

If the agent's authority was not in writing when it was required to be, any contract executed by the agent is ***unenforceable against the principal***; it is voidable at the ***principal's option***.

b. Exceptions

Certain exceptions to the Statute of Frauds and equal dignities rule are available: Executives acting on behalf of ***corporations*** do not need written authority to act for the corporations, and written authority is not required when an agent acts ***mechanically***, *e.g.,* agent signs principal's name to a contract that is already drafted.

6. Proper Purpose

An agency must be for only a ***legal*** purpose. Moreover, a principal cannot delegate to an agent acts deemed personal by ***public policy*** (*e.g.,* voting) nor can ***personal services contracts*** be performed by an agent.

II. RIGHTS AND DUTIES BETWEEN PRINCIPAL AND AGENT

A. AGENT'S DUTIES TO PRINCIPAL

1. Contractual Duties and Duties Implied by Law

An agent has the duty to abide by the express and implied terms of the agency agreement. In addition, the following duties are implied by law.

a. Duty to Perform

An agent has a duty to perform—which includes the duty to perform with ***reasonable care***—to refrain from conduct that will cause damage to the principal. An agent must act within the scope of her actual authority and must obey the principal's ***lawful instructions***. There is no duty to obey instructions that will subject the agent to civil, criminal, or administrative liability.

(1) Duty of Care

An agent has a duty to carry out the agency with the ***care, competence, and diligence*** exercised by agents in similar circumstances, also taking into account any special skills or knowledge that the agent possesses.

(a) Effect of Careless Performance or Nonperformance

Non-performance of assigned duties results in agent liability only for breach of the agency contract. However, performance of the assigned duties in a careless or imperfect manner that causes loss to the principal may trigger agent liability for negligence as well as for breach of contract.

(2) Gratuitous Agent

A gratuitous (or uncompensated) agent owes to the principal the same duties owed by a compensated agent (*i.e.,* the duties of care and loyalty). The applicable standard of care is determined by what is reasonable to expect under the circumstances, taking into account the agent's skill, experience, and professional status.

(a) Effect of Careless Performance or Nonperformance

An agency relationship arises when an agent promises to perform gratuitously. However, such promise does not result in an enforceable contract. Therefore, failure to perform does not give rise to a claim for breach of contract. Nevertheless, ***improper performance*** by the agent can subject the agent to ***tort liability***. Although a gratuitous agent generally has no contractual duty to perform, if the principal ***detrimentally relies*** on the promise to perform, the principal may recover ***contract damages***.

b. Fiduciary Duties

As a fiduciary, the agent owes the principal the obligation of faithful service, the same as that of a trustee to a trust. This obligation requires the agent to ***notify*** the principal of all relevant matters affecting the agency, thus ***imputing*** the agent's knowledge to the principal.

(1) Duty of Loyalty

An agent is also charged with the fiduciary duty of loyalty, which includes the duty ***not to compete*** with his principal. However, an agent may take action during the agency relationship to compete against her principal after the agency has ended, provided such ***action is not wrongful***. ***Post-termination*** competition by the agent is ***permitted***; however, the former agent's disclosure of ***trade secrets or other confidential information*** obtained during his employment is barred.

(a) Limitation—Dishonest Principal

The agent's duty of loyalty does not obligate the agent to shield a ***dishonest principal***.

(b) Conflicts of Interest

An agent must deal fairly with the principal and disclose facts reasonably relevant to the principal's position. An agent does not breach the duty of loyalty if he acts on behalf of an adverse party in a ministerial capacity that does not involve judgment, discretion, or skill. There is a breach if an agent has an economic interest in a party with whom the principal deals or if the principal is engaged in a transaction with a party in whom the agent has an interest.

(c) Acquiring Material Benefit

Absent the principal's consent, an agent may not acquire a ***material benefit*** in connection with his position. Consequently, anything that the agent obtains as a result of his employment (*e.g.,* profits, advantages, or benefits) belongs to the principal. Similarly, a ***purchasing agent*** (*i.e.,* an agent purchasing property for the principal) cannot purchase the property for himself without the principal's consent. Neither can a ***sales agent*** buy property for sale by the principal for himself without the principal's consent. If the agent improperly buys property, the principal can rescind the sale and recover the property. If the agent has resold the property, he is liable to the principal for its value or for any profits, plus damages.

1) **Dual Agency**

When an agent is acting for more than one principal (*e.g.,* for both buyer and seller), the transaction is voidable at either principal's option unless ***both were fully informed*** of the dual representation and ***consented*** to it. Note that a ***real estate broker*** employed to sell real estate is ***not*** a dual agent merely because he counsels a buyer on sale terms. Nor is there a dual agency where a buyer represents the ***sellers of different properties*** in negotiations with a ***single buyer***.

(d) **Duties Regarding Principal's Property and Confidential Information**

An agent who possesses the principal's property or has access to confidential information must not use the property or information for his own purposes or for those of a third party. Also, the principal's property must be segregated.

2. **Duties Owed by Subagents**

If a principal authorized an agent to hire a subagent, the subagent owes the same duties to the principal as the agent owes, and the agent is liable for the subagent's breach of duty. A principal is liable to third parties for the acts of an authorized subagent. A subagent also owes to the agent the same duties he owes to the principal. If the subagent is hired without the principal's authority, he owes no duties to the principal (unless the principal ratified the appointment) as there is no agency relationship between them; the agent, however, remains liable to the principal for any losses resulting from the subagent's conduct.

3. **Remedies Available to Principal**

The following remedies may be available to a principal for an agent's breach of contractual duty, duty to perform, or fiduciary duty.

a. **Action for Damages**

A ***compensated agent*** may be liable to the principal for damages as a result of ***breach of contract***. ***All agents*** may be liable in ***tort*** for breach of fiduciary duty or for damages resulting from careless performance. ***Punitive damages*** are possible upon a showing of malice or bad faith.

b. **Action for Secret Profits**

If an agent breaches his fiduciary duty and secretly profits, the principal may recover the actual profits or property held by the agent.

c. **Rescission**

Any transaction that violates the agent's fiduciary duty is voidable by the principal regardless of any gain by the agent.

d. **Other Remedies**

If an agent obtains property in violation of his obligation to purchase, hold, or obtain it for his principal, a ***constructive trust*** may be imposed on the property. Another equitable remedy available to the principal is an ***accounting***. Moreover, when an agent has ***intentionally*** breached his fiduciary duty, the principal may, in addition to other remedies, ***withhold compensation***.

4. Rights and Benefits Flowing from Agent's Employment

Generally, everything acquired by an agent as a result of his employment (except compensation) ***belongs to his principal***, disclosed or undisclosed.

a. Inventions and Patents

This general rule extends to inventions and patents developed by an agent, absent a contrary agreement, unless the development is ***not a primary part*** of the agent's duties. But then, a principal may have a ***"shop right"*** to use the idea or invention if it was perfected on the principal's time and is related to her business.

5. Principal's Right to Indemnification

A principal has a right to indemnification against an agent for losses sustained as a result of the agent's ***tortious acts*** or ***violation of the principal's instructions***.

B. PRINCIPAL'S DUTIES TO AGENT

1. Contractual Duties and Duties Implied by Law

The following duties are ***implied by law*** in every agency or employment contract, absent a contrary provision.

a. Duty to Cooperate

A principal must assist and cooperate with the agent in the performance of his duties and do nothing wrongful to prevent the agent's performance.

b. Duty to Compensate

Unless gratuitous, an agent is to be compensated for his services as agreed upon or, if there is no agreement, for the reasonable value of the services.

(1) Sales Agents

Absent an agreement, a salesperson is entitled to his commission when he makes the sale (*i.e.*, at acceptance of offer) or when his efforts are the effective cause of the sale even though others were involved in completing the transaction.

(2) Subagents

A principal is ***not*** responsible for an authorized or unauthorized subagent's compensation, absent such an agreement. The agent alone is responsible for the subagent's compensation.

(3) State Statutes

Many jurisdictions regulate the time, place, and manner for employee compensation, as well as hours and working conditions.

c. Duty of Care

A principal generally owes an agent the same duty of care regarding torts as she would owe to a stranger, *i.e.,* ***to refrain from negligence***. However, ***workers' compensation acts*** have largely replaced common law liability regarding employees' injuries during employment. The duty to furnish ***safe working conditions*** is the main basis for a principal's common law tort liability.

d. Duty to Indemnify

A principal has the duty to indemnify the agent in accordance with the terms of the agency contract and for all expenditures or losses incurred by the agent in the discharge of authorized duties. With respect to an agent who acted without authority, the right to indemnification arises only if the principal benefited from the transaction and the agent did not act officiously.

e. **Duty to Deal Fairly and in Good Faith**

A principal must deal with the agent fairly and in good faith. This includes a duty to inform the agent about risks of physical harm or monetary loss that the principal knows, has reason to know, or should know are present in the agent's work, and that are unknown to the agent.

2. **Remedies Available to Agent**

Most contract remedies are available to an agent when the agency contract is breached by the principal.

a. **Indemnification**

An agent is entitled to indemnification pursuant to the ***terms of the agency contract*** and for all ***expenditures or losses*** incurred in performing authorized duties. An agent may also be indemnified for reasonable litigation expenses incurred in defending a lawsuit that challenges some action carried out under the agent's actual authority. Furthermore, if indemnification is otherwise proper, an ***authorized subagent*** can recover against ***either*** the principal or agent. If the subagent proceeds against the agent, the agent then has a right of indemnification against the principal. However, indemnification is not available if losses result from unauthorized acts that do not benefit the principal. Neither is there a right to indemnification if the agent acted ***illegally*** or ***negligently***. Nor is an agent entitled to be indemnified for compensation he pays to his employees absent an agreement to the contrary.

b. **Lien Against Property of Principal**

Absent a contrary agreement, the agent may place a lien on the ***principal's property*** in the agent's lawful possession up to the amount of his compensation or right to indemnity. An attorney's lien is broader than the liens of general agents (*e.g.,* an attorney may have both a retaining lien on a client's papers and a charging lien on amounts earned in securing a judgment for the client).

(1) **Lien Rights of Subagents**

A subagent has a lien against the agent's property in her possession for services and expenses, and against the principal's property in her possession to the extent of the agent's rights in such property.

c. **Other Remedies**

An agent may also withhold further performance, claim a setoff or counterclaim, or demand an accounting. An agent has ***no*** right to ***specific performance***.

III. AGENT'S POWER AND AUTHORITY TO BIND PRINCIPAL ON CONTRACTS

A. INTRODUCTION

1. **Terminology**

The terms "authority" and "power" are used interchangeably by courts, but they have distinct meanings under the Restatement.

a. **Authority**

Authority is the agent's right to bind the principal to the extent that the principal and agent have agreed. This is known as ***actual authority***.

b. Power

Power is the agent's ability to effect the legal relations of his principal, regardless of the right to do so.

B. SOURCES OF POWER

1. Introduction

Power can arise from actual authority, apparent authority, estoppel, or ratification.

2. Actual Authority

Actual (or real) authority arises from the ***manifestation of consent*** from the principal ***to the agent*** (not to a third person) that the agent should act for the principal; it is defined by the ***agent's reasonable beliefs***. Such authority may be either express or implied.

a. Express Authority

Express authority is actual authority contained within the agency agreement (*i.e.*, expressly granted). Extravagant phrases in the grant of authority can be construed as giving extremely broad powers, but courts usually limit them to the business intended by the parties.

(1) Power of Attorney

A clear example of express authority, a power of attorney, may be ***special***—to do certain acts only—or it may be ***general***—to transact all business for the principal. Sometimes such an agent is called an **"*attorney in fact.*"**

b. Implied Authority

Implied authority arises from the words or conduct between the principal and agent. It is often labeled to signify how it has arisen: (i) ***incidental to express authority***; (ii) ***implied from principal's manifestations***; (iii) ***implied from custom and usage***; and (iv) ***implied because of emergency***.

(1) Agency to Sell

An agent given the express authority to sell the principal's property has implied authority to make certain warranties, receive payment, deliver the goods, and negotiate and conclude the sale.

(a) Real Estate Brokers

A real estate broker given the authority to sell the principal's property has no actual power to convey title or to contract to convey the principal's property.

(2) Agency to Purchase

An agent given express authority to purchase property for the principal has implied authority to make warranties, pay the purchase price, accept delivery and possession, and conclude the purchase.

(3) Authority to Delegate

Generally, an agent cannot delegate her authority unless she has actual or apparent authority to do so except for ***mechanical or ministerial acts***, when the ***agent cannot perform*** the acts herself, and when ***appointment is customary or necessary***. Remember that under the majority view an authorized appointment of a ***subagent*** does ***not*** make the subagent a party to the agency agreement with the principal.

c. **Effect of Principal's Mistake in Creating Authority**

If the principal objectively manifests his intention to create authority in another, there is valid actual authority—even though the principal did not intend to grant the authority. This is true even if the ***agent fraudulently induces*** the principal into granting her authority; however, the agent will be liable to the principal in such a situation for any damages caused by the agent's acts.

d. **Limiting Instructions**

Whether certain directions of the principal to the agent are limitations on the agent's authority or merely advice is determined on a case-by-case basis.

e. **Termination of Actual Authority**

Actual authority can be terminated by expiration of the agency term or accomplishment of the agency purpose, by change of circumstances or death or incapacity of a party, or by act or agreement of the parties.

3. **Apparent (Ostensible) Authority**

The general rule states that a third party deals with an agent at his own peril and will bear the loss if the agent acts without authority. However, in practice, a principal will be bound by an agent's unauthorized acts if the principal has ***manifested to the third party*** that the agent is authorized, and the third party ***reasonably relies*** on the manifestation.

a. **Effect**

Apparent authority gives an agent the ***power, but not the right,*** to bind the principal.

b. **Relationship to Actual Authority**

Actual authority relies on the agent's power to bind the principal because of the principal's manifestations to the agent, while apparent authority is based on the ***principal's manifestations to third parties***. Apparent authority arises only when actual authority is absent.

c. **Requisites for Apparent Authority**

There must be some ***holding out by the principal*** that causes a third party to reasonably believe that the agent has authority, and the ***third party must reasonably rely*** on the principal's manifestations.

d. **Types of Apparent Authority**

(1) **Where Agent Has No Actual Authority**

Apparent authority may arise in ***imposter*** situations or where an agent's actual authority has been ***terminated without proper notification*** to a third party.

(2) **Where Agent Has Some Actual Authority**

A principal is bound by her agent's unauthorized acts when the agent's ***prior acts*** were beyond his authority and the principal does not inform interested parties of that fact.

(a) **Position**

The greatest source of apparent authority arises from appointment of an agent to a position that customarily encompasses certain authority, *e.g.*, to make some express and implied warranties.

e. Termination of Apparent Authority

Notice of the termination of apparent authority must be given to the ***third party*** to whom authority was originally manifested, and it is effective as long as it is from ***any reliable source***, not necessarily the principal. Termination also occurs on the ***expiration of a stated time or event***. The principal's death or incapacity ***does not*** automatically terminate the agent's apparent authority if the third party is without notice of the death or incapacity and reasonably believes that the agent has actual authority.

f. Distinguish—Apparent Ownership

The agent's power is much broader when the principal has given him both possession and apparent ownership of her property. The agent can deal with the property as if he were the true owner, and the principal is estopped from invalidating the agent's dealings with innocent third parties.

(1) Relevant Factors

The agent must be imbued with such ***indicia of ownership*** that a third party would reasonably believe that the agent is the owner. Merely ***transferring possession*** is ***not*** sufficient indicia, but ***delivery of a deed or document of title*** constitutes sufficient apparent ownership.

(a) U.C.C. Criteria

Under the U.C.C., personal property entrusted to a ***merchant*** who deals in goods of ***that kind*** gives the merchant apparent power to transfer title to an innocent purchaser for value. Similar power exists under state ***"factors acts"*** regarding sales on consignment.

4. Estoppel

When a principal has ***intentionally or carelessly*** caused or allowed a third party to believe his agent has authority to do an act that is actually beyond her authority, or ***fails to take reasonable steps to notify*** the third party when he has notice of the third party's belief ***and*** the third party ***detrimentally relies*** on the principal's conduct, the principal is estopped from denying the agent's authority so as to prevent unjust enrichment.

a. Distinguish—Apparent Authority

Apparent authority makes the principal a ***contracting party*** with the third party, with rights and liabilities on both sides. Estoppel only compensates the third party for ***losses arising from the third party's reliance*** on the principal's statements or omissions; the principal has no correlative rights.

5. Inherent Agency Power

The Restatement (Second) of Agency recognizes the concept of inherent agency power, by which an agent can bind a principal without power arising from actual authority, apparent authority, or estoppel. Such power is deemed to have arisen from the agency relationship itself, and is meant to protect innocent persons who have dealt with the agent. However, the Restatement (Third) of Agency does not recognize this doctrine, and few courts have adopted it.

C. TERMINATION OF AGENT'S AUTHORITY AND POWER

1. Termination of Actual Authority

a. By Expiration of Agency Term

If an agency period has been specified, expiration of the agency period terminates the agency relationship and the agent's authority. A ***reasonable time*** period is implied if no time is specified by the parties.

b. By Accomplishment of Agency Purpose

If the agent's authority was to perform a specified act, the agent's authority terminates on the accomplishment of that act, even if another person performed the necessary act. However, the agent's authority continues until he has ***knowledge or notice*** that accomplishment of the act has occurred.

c. By Change of Circumstances

A change of circumstances may terminate an agent's authority. Examples of situations in which a change of circumstances will terminate an agent's authority include a ***loss or destruction of the subject matter*** of the agency, a ***basic and unforeseen change of circumstances affecting value*** of the subject matter, and other sufficient events (*e.g.,* bankruptcy of principal or agent or change of law).

(1) Principal's Knowledge

In cases of unforeseen circumstances, the principal's knowledge is relevant in determining whether the agent's authority has been terminated, *e.g.,* if the principal knows of the change of circumstances, the agent's authority probably continues until the principal issues new instructions.

d. By Death of Either Principal or Agent

Although the prevailing view is that the death of the principal or agent automatically terminates the agent's authority, the Restatement (Third) of Agency takes a different approach: Actual authority terminates on the death of the ***agent***. The death of the principal also terminates the agent's actual authority, but ***the termination is not effective*** against the agent or a third party with whom the agent deals ***until notice of the principal's death has been received*** by the agent or third party.

e. By Cessation of Existence or Suspension of Powers

Actual authority terminates if the principal or agent ceases to exist or when its powers are suspended (*e.g.,* corporate dissolution terminates actual authority of corporate agent).

f. By Incapacity

(1) Principal's Incapacity

Under the Restatement (Third) of Agency, if a principal loses the capacity to do an act, the agent's actual authority to do the same act is terminated. However, such termination is not effective against the agent or a third party with whom the agent deals until the agent or third party has notice that the principal's incapacity is permanent or that the principal has been adjudicated incapacitated.

(2) Agent's Incapacity

An agent's authority will terminate due to mental incapacity only if her mental capacity is such that the agent ***cannot perform her required duties***. An agent also may lose capacity to act for other reasons, *e.g.,* loss of broker's license.

g. **Exceptions**

(1) **Written Instrument**

A written instrument may make an agent's actual authority effective upon a principal's incapacity, or confer it irrevocably regardless of loss of capacity.

(2) **Powers Given for Benefit of Agent**

If the agency power was given to benefit the agent, it may be irrevocable.

(3) **Banks**

A ***bank***, as its customer's agent, may pay on the customer's checks until it knows of the customer's death or adjudication of incompetency, and even if it knows of the customer's death, it may pay on the customer's checks for up to ***10 days*** after the customer's death.

h. **By Act or Agreement of the Parties**

Because of its consensual nature, an agency terminates when either party communicates an intention to terminate to the other party. An agent is said to ***renounce*** his authority while a principal ***revokes*** her authority. However, the party terminating may be liable for breach of contract.

(1) **Exception—Power Given for Benefit of Agent**

If the agency or power was created for the benefit of the agent or a third person, the agent's power may be ***irrevocable***. To be irrevocable, the power must be: (i) granted to secure performance of a duty or to protect the agent's or third person's title, and (ii) given when the duty to perform or title was created or at some other time but consideration was given in exchange for the power. Remember that such a power does not terminate upon the death or incapacity of ***either party***.

(a) **Events That Terminate Power**

Powers given for the benefit of an agent or irrevocable proxies are terminated on the ***consent*** of the person for whom the power was created, or by events that: (i) ***discharge*** the obligation or ***terminate*** the interest, (ii) make execution ***illegal or impossible,*** (iii) effectively ***surrender the power or proxy***, or (iv) have been ***agreed to*** by the principal and agent.

(b) **Distinguish—Power Coupled with an Interest**

A power coupled with an interest is narrower than a power given for benefit of the agent and requires that the agent have an interest in the subject matter of the agency.

1) **Agent's Fraud**

A principal may ***rescind*** the power if she was ***defrauded*** into giving the agent an irrevocable power.

i. **Notice Required to Terminate**

An agent's actual authority continues until she knows, or has reason to know, of the termination. No special form of notice is required.

2. **Termination of Apparent Authority**

Apparent authority continues until it is no longer reasonable for the third party with whom the agent deals to believe that the agent continues to act with authority.

a. **Specific Persons with Whom Agent Deals**

If the principal knows that the agent has been dealing with specific third parties, ***personal or individual notice*** to those third parties is required to terminate the agent's apparent authority.

b. **Public at Large**

Representations by the principal of an agent's authority to the public at large require notice of termination by ***advertisement or similar means***.

c. **Written Authority**

Authority granted in writing requires the principal to ***reclaim the writing or notify all parties*** with whom the agent may deal of the termination of the agent's authority.

d. **Death or Incapacity**

Most states hold that death or incapacity of the principal or agent ***immediately*** terminates apparent authority. The Restatement (Third) of Agency, however, provides that the termination of apparent authority due to the death or incapacity of the principal or agent is not effective until ***the third party receives notice***.

IV. RATIFICATION

A. INTRODUCTION

1. In General

Ratification is the affirmance by a person ("principal") of a ***prior act*** supposedly done on his behalf by another ("agent"), but which was ***not*** authorized. Ratification causes the agent's act to be treated as if it had been authorized by the principal at its outset.

2. Agreement Treated as Offer

Before ratification, the third party's agreement with the agent is considered merely an offer to the principal.

a. **No Ratification—No Contract**

If the principal does not ratify, there is no contract between the third party and the principal, but the agent may be liable to the third party for breach of her warranty of authority.

b. **Ratification—Acceptance of Offer**

If the principal ratifies, he has "accepted" the third party's offer and is bound by the contract. Note that the third party can rescind the contract with the agent up until the principal's ratification.

3. Effects of Ratification

Ratification may establish ***both*** the agent's authority and the agency relationship, thus making the principal liable for the agent's acts and relieving the agent of liability to the principal.

a. **"Relation Back" Theory**

The traditional rule is that the agent's act is treated as ***authorized from the outset*** upon ratification (*i.e.,* rights and liabilities "relate back" to the date of the original unauthorized act).

b. **When Ratification Is Not Effective**

Ratification is not effective if: (i) it benefits a person who engaged in ***misrepresentation or other conduct that would make a contract voidable***, (ii) the principal ***ratified the transaction to avoid a loss*** and the resulting benefit favors the agent, (iii) it would ***prejudice innocent third persons*** who acquired rights in the transaction prior to the ratification, or (iv) the principal attempts to ratify only part of the contract or alter its material terms.

B. PREREQUISITES FOR RATIFICATION

1. Act on Principal's Behalf

The act ratified must have been undertaken by a person who ***acted or purported to act on the principal's behalf.***

a. Who Can Ratify

The Restatement (Second) of Agency follows the general rule that only a disclosed or partially disclosed principal can ratify. An undisclosed principal could not ratify because the third party did not know that he was dealing with an agent. The Restatement (Third) of Agency does not distinguish between types of principals. Thus, ***any principal may ratify*** an agent's unauthorized act.

(1) Ratification Under the Restatement (Second) of Agency

In a disclosed principal situation, the majority view is that only the ***purported*** principal can ratify. If the principal is partially disclosed, only the ***person whom the agent intended to be the principal*** can ratify.

2. Delegable Act

An act that the principal ***could not have authorized*** in the first place because it would be illegal or contrary to public policy cannot be effectively ratified.

a. Illegal Acts

If the illegal act makes the contract ***void***, it cannot be ratified; however, if the contract is ***voidable*** at the principal's option, it can be ratified by the principal—*e.g.*, if the original act is ***illegal only because it was unauthorized***, ratification is effective.

3. Knowledge of Principal

Ratification is effective only if the principal has ***actual knowledge of all material facts*** at the time of ratification; if not, the principal can rescind the ratification unless the third party has detrimentally relied on it. It is immaterial whether the principal's lack of knowledge is caused by the agent's fraud or by an innocent mistake.

a. Principal's Assumption of Risk

If the principal's ignorance of the facts arises from her own failure to investigate where a reasonable person would have done so, she has assumed the risk of her lack of knowledge, and the ratification is effective.

4. Principal's Capacity

A principal can ratify an act if the principal ***existed at the time of the act*** and ***had capacity at the time of ratification***. Thus, a principal who was not in existence at the time of the agent's act cannot ratify.

a. Corporations

A corporation cannot ratify a promoter's contract because it did not exist at the time of the contract; it instead ***adopts*** the contract, but adoption ***does not relate back***, and the promoter is ***not relieved of liability***.

C. HOW TO RATIFY

1. In General

The principal must manifest his intention, by words or conduct, to be bound by the agent's act. No special formalities are required except that if the original authorization must be in writing, the ratification must also be in writing. The principal need not communicate his affirmation to anyone.

2. Express Affirmation

A principal expressly affirms the prior unauthorized act by notifying the agent or third party.

3. Implied Affirmation—Ratification by Conduct

Typically, a principal does not expressly affirm the agent's prior unauthorized act, and an examination of the principal's conduct is necessary to determine if the principal has manifested an intention to be bound by the agent's act. A principal's conduct that evidences an intention to be bound includes the ***voluntary retention of the benefits*** of the transaction, ***bringing suit or maintaining a defense*** based on the act, or, under some circumstances, a ***failure to repudiate*** the unauthorized act.

D. LIMITATIONS ON POWER TO RATIFY

1. Entire Transaction Must Be Ratified

A principal can only ratify a transaction in its entirety; he cannot ratify only the beneficial parts and reject nonbeneficial parts.

2. Intervening Withdrawal or Incapacity of Other Party

Until the principal's ratification, an unauthorized contract is considered to be merely an offer to the principal; thus, the third party is permitted to rescind the contract prior to the principal's ratification, and any subsequent ratification by the principal is ineffective. ***Death or incapacity*** of the third party will also terminate the principal's power to ratify.

3. Change of Circumstances

If ratification occurs ***after a material change*** in circumstances making it inequitable to subject the third party to liability, the third party can avoid the transaction (minority view is *contra*). A change of circumstances ***after ratification*** will not avoid a ratification.

4. Estoppel to Deny Ratification

If a principal manifests that she has ratified an act of another, and the manifestation induces a third party to detrimentally change his position, the principal may be estopped from denying the ratification.

V. NOTICE, NOTIFICATION, AND KNOWLEDGE

A. NOTICE

A person has notice of a fact if he knows of it, has reason to know of it, should know of it to fulfill a duty owed to another person, or has been given notification of it. Knowledge is a subset of notice—a person with knowledge has notice—but a person with notice will not always be charged with knowledge.

B. NOTIFICATION

1. In General

Notification usually involves an act by a third party directed to an agent intended to bring to the principal knowledge that affects the principal's rights.

2. Authority

Notification given to an agent is effective to give notice to the principal if the agent has actual or apparent authority to receive the notification, unless the person giving the notification knows or has reason to know that the agent is acting adversely to the principal.

3. Duration

Once notification is given to an agent, its legal effect continues indefinitely.

4. Agent Acting Adversely to Principal

If an agent is acting adversely to his principal, notification by or to the agent will be effective against the principal unless the person who receives or gives notification ***knows or has reason to know that the agent is acting adversely***. Also, if a third party ***knows*** that the agent is acting adversely to the principal's interests, and that the agent will not communicate the notification to the principal, the notification will not be effective against the principal.

C. KNOWLEDGE

1. In General

Knowledge is subjective and involves an ***awareness*** of the particular fact or condition in question.

2. Authority

An agent's knowledge of a fact that he knows or has reason to know will be imputed to his principal ***if*** the agent had ***actual authority*** to affect the principal's rights in the matter. Knowledge will not be imputed if the agent acts adversely to the principal or is under a duty to another not to disclose the fact to the principal.

3. When Acquired

Usually, only those facts discovered by the agent during the agency relationship will be imputed to the principal. A few cases have imputed an agent's knowledge acquired prior to employment when, because of the close connection of the transactions, the knowledge must have been present in the agent's mind when he acted for the principal. The ***Restatement*** makes the time of acquiring knowledge ***immaterial*** to imputation; rather the test is whether the agent had the knowledge ***in mind*** when it became relevant to his agency work. Notice is imputed to the principal if the fact is material to the agent's duties, regardless of whether the agent learned of the fact prior to the agency relationship, through formal education, prior work, or otherwise.

4. What Is Imputed

Only ***facts*** concerning the agency's subject matter and within the scope of the agency will be imputed. However, an agent's knowledge of factual matters will ***not be imputed*** if the principal's ***subjective, actual knowledge*** is required.

5. Duration

Because knowledge is subjective, it may become ineffective because of the passage of time.

6. Agent Acting Adversely to Principal

An agent taking a position adverse to his principal is acting outside the scope of his employment, and knowledge acquired by the agent during this time is ***not imputed*** to the principal. Many courts require that the agent's interest be ***substantially*** adverse to the principal's interest to prevent imputation of the agent's knowledge to the principal.

a. **Corporate Officers and Directors**

If a corporation's officer or director causes the corporation to enter into a contract in which the officer or director has some secret adverse interest, the corporation is generally ***not*** bound. However, some courts ***have*** imputed knowledge of such dishonest acts to the corporation, at least to bar suit against the surety on the officer's or director's fidelity bond.

b. **Exceptions to General Rule**

Even though an agent acts adversely to the principal, knowledge is imputed to the principal if: (i) knowledge is necessary to ***protect the rights of a third party*** who dealt with the principal in good faith and without knowledge of the agent's adversity, (ii) the principal has ***ratified*** the agent's actions, or (iii) the principal knowingly ***retained the benefits*** from the agent's actions.

VI. LIABILITY ON AGENT'S CONTRACTS

A. AGENT ACTING WITHOUT AUTHORITY

1. Agent's Liability

If an agent purports to act on behalf of a principal but is in fact acting without authority (or in excess of authority), the principal generally is not liable absent some other source of agency power (*e.g.,* ratification). The ***agent alone*** is liable.

a. **Agent's Liability for Breach of Warranty—Disclosed or Unidentified Principal**

An agent purporting to enter into a contract for a ***disclosed or unidentified*** principal ***impliedly warrants*** that she ***has authority*** to bind her principal. If the agent lacks such authority, she may be liable to the third party for breach of the warranty. However, the third party ***must rely*** on the warranty.

(1) **Tort Liability**

Under the warranty theory of liability, the agent is liable even though she had a good faith belief that she had authority. Moreover, ***intentional misrepresentation*** of authority may subject the agent to ***tort liability*** for ***deceit***.

(2) **Effect of Disclaimer and Warranty of Performance/Competence**

If the agent indicates to the third party that no warranty of authority is given, the warranty of authority does not usually arise. In addition, the agent's implied warranty of authority does ***not*** include a ***warranty of performance***, although it ***does include*** the agent's warranty that the principal is ***competent***.

b. **Agent's Liability on Contract—Undisclosed or Unidentified Principal**

An agent lacking sufficient authority from an ***undisclosed or unidentified*** principal is liable ***on the contract*** itself. This liability is distinct from liability for breach of warranty.

(1) **Disclosed Principal Distinguished**

An agent who purports to contract for a ***disclosed*** principal, but in fact has no authority, is ***not liable on the contract***; the parties' intent was that the principal be bound.

2. Principal's Liability—When Third Party Has Performed

If the agent exceeds her authority, but the third party has rendered part or full performance under the contract, the third party may be able to sue the principal in ***quasi-contract***, even though he cannot enforce the contract against the principal absent ratification.

B. AGENT ACTING WITH AUTHORITY

1. In General

If the agent's acts are within the scope of her authority, generally only the principal is a party to the contract and bound by it. However, the parties' rights and liabilities may vary depending on whether the principal's identity was disclosed.

2. Contract Made on Behalf of Principal (Disclosed Principal Cases)

In ***disclosed principal*** cases, the agent negotiates the contract on behalf of the principal; the agent is ***not*** a party to the contract (unless the agent and third party agree otherwise) and thus is not liable on it. The other contract party is liable directly to the principal and vice versa. If the third party ***knows*** (***or should know***) the principal's identity, the principal is considered to be "disclosed."

a. Parol Evidence Rule

An exception to the general rule that an agent is not liable on a contract that he enters into on behalf of a disclosed principal occurs when the parties intend the agent to be personally liable; however, the parol evidence rule may prohibit the use of extrinsic evidence to establish intent if a written contract is involved.

(1) Exception—Ambiguous Contracts

Extrinsic evidence is admissible when contract terms are ambiguous. To determine if a contract is ambiguous, courts look at the ***entire contract***, but often start by examining the ***form of the agent's signature***. Generally, the agent is ***personally liable*** when his signature does ***not indicate*** that he signed in a representative capacity; if the signature clearly indicates that he signed ***only in a representative capacity,*** the principal alone is liable.

3. Contract in Name of Agent Only (Undisclosed and Unidentified Principal Cases)

a. Undisclosed Principal

In undisclosed principal cases, both the ***fact of agency*** and the ***principal's identity*** are undisclosed, and the agent is generally liable as a party to the contract. However, the agent may have a right to ***indemnification*** from the principal if an agency agreement exists. If ***no*** agency agreement exists (*i.e.,* gratuitous agent), but the principal accepted the benefits of the contract, the agent may recover from the principal in ***quasi-contract***.

(1) Liability of Principal to Third Party

Once the principal's identity is made known, he may also be held liable on the contract if the agent's acts were authorized. Thus, the third party may hold ***either*** the principal or agent liable. The modern view is that the ***parol evidence rule*** does ***not*** apply to prohibit the admission of extrinsic evidence to show that one signed as an agent. The ***Statute of Frauds***, however, does apply in that if the contract the agent is entering into must be in writing, so must the agent's authority.

(a) Requirement of Election by Third Party

Although the third party normally has a right against either the principal or agent, he can recover from ***only one*** of them. The modern rule is that the third party can file suit against both, but upon objection of either party, the third party must elect ***prior to judgment*** which party he wishes to hold liable. The minority view holds that suit filed against one acts as an election to release the other party from liability.

(b) **Principal Still Undisclosed**

If the third party obtains a judgment against the agent ***without knowledge of the principal's identity***, and the judgment is unsatisfied, the third party can later sue the principal when the principal's identity is discovered.

(2) **Liability of Third Party**

Either the principal or agent can enforce the contract against the third party, but the principal is entitled to all the benefits of the contract (as if he were the assignee of the agent's rights). However, the third party has a ***right to rescind*** the contract if the agent ***fraudulently represented that she was contracting for herself*** or if enforcement by the principal ***would impose an added or different burden of performance*** on the third party. Note that fraud is involved only if the principal hides his identity because the third party would not deal with him otherwise.

(a) **Exception—Powers Given for Benefit of Agent**

If the agent's powers are irrevocable because she has some interest in the subject matter, the agent, rather than the principal, is entitled to any recovery from the third party.

(3) **Agent's Personal Performance**

The third party may refuse a tender of performance from the principal and can insist upon personal performance by the agent if the duties under the law of contracts are ***nondelegable*** (*e.g.,* credit or personal service contracts).

(4) **Liability for Agent's Dishonesty or Error**

Payment by a principal to the agent does ***not*** discharge the principal from liability to the third party if the agent does not pay the third party. The third party, however, is protected in dealing exclusively with the agent in undisclosed principal cases up until the principal's identity is disclosed.

b. **Unidentified Principal**

In certain cases, the third party knows that the agent is acting as an agent but does ***not*** know the identity of the principal. If the agent has signed or described herself as an agent of another, the agent is a party to the contract unless otherwise agreed. ***Extrinsic evidence is admissible*** to show whether the parties intended the agent to be personally bound.

VII. TORT LIABILITY FOR THE ACTS OF OTHERS

A. LIABILITY OF EMPLOYER FOR TORTS OF EMPLOYEE—RESPONDEAT SUPERIOR

1. Introduction

In an ***employer-employee relationship***, the employer (principal) hires an employee (agent) to ***perform services*** for the employer, who ***retains control*** over the manner in which the employee performs the services. Because of the retained control, the employer is liable for the torts of the employee through the doctrine of respondeat superior (*see* below). The same person may act as ***both*** an employee and an independent contractor, depending on his powers and duties (*e.g.,* store manager). ***Control*** is the essential feature of the employer-employee relationship.

a. **Independent Contractor Distinguished**

An independent contractor contracts with the employer only as to accomplishing specific ***results***. The employer has ***no right to control*** how the work is to be performed. Respondeat superior does ***not*** apply to independent contractors.

b. **Doctrine of Respondeat Superior**

Under the doctrine of respondeat superior, an employer is liable for all torts committed by her employee acting within the scope of the employment. An injured third party can proceed against ***both*** the employer and employee—the employee being directly liable for his torts while the employer is ***vicariously liable*** for the employee's torts.

(1) **Nature of Liability**

Since respondeat superior imposes ***strict liability*** on the employer, the employer ***cannot waive*** liability by contract with her employee. Respondeat superior is also a form of ***vicarious liability*** and, as such, is ***joint and several*** with the employee's liability. The victim, however, is entitled to only a ***single recovery***.

(a) **Exoneration**

If the employee is exonerated or released from liability, the employer is usually also released ***except*** if the ***employer was negligent*** or if the ***employee's immunity is not imputed to the employer*** (*e.g.*, spousal immunity bars recovery against employee).

(b) **Indemnification**

An employer held liable for an employee's torts has a right to indemnification against the employee for any damages paid ***unless*** the employee was immune from liability in the first place.

(2) **Application of Doctrine**

For the doctrine to apply, there must be an ***employer-employee relationship***, and the employee's ***wrongful act*** must have been committed ***within the course and scope of his employment***.

2. **Employer-Employee Relationship**

The first issue in respondeat superior cases is whether an employer-employee relationship existed. Liability under respondeat superior is based on the employer's ***right to control*** the physical acts of the employee—a right unique to the employer-employee relationship. Generally, a principal does ***not*** have the right to control an agent's or independent contractor's physical acts.

a. **Creation of Relationship**

The employer-employee relationship can exist only if there is an agreement manifesting assent by both parties. No formalities are required except when the Statute of Frauds applies, *e.g.*, employment for period in excess of one year. Generally, the ***employer must have capacity to contract*** but no special capacity is required for an employee. An agreement may be ***implied*** from the circumstances or the parties' conduct.

(1) **"Volunteers"**

An employee cannot foist his services upon an employer. However, an employer-employee relationship may arise if the employer ***knows*** that services are being rendered ***and accepts the benefits*** of the services.

b. **Duration of Employment**

An employee is presumed to be hired for the length of time used to compute his wages; if no time period is specified, employment is terminable at will. Many states limit time periods for personal service contracts. It is presumed that an employer's retention of an employee after an employment contract expires renews the employment under the original contract terms.

c. **Right of Employer to Recover for Injuries to Employee**

An employer's recovery for injuries to her employee is generally ***not*** permitted unless a third party ***intentionally*** injures the employee, because intentional interference with a contractual relationship is actionable—mere negligence is not.

d. **Employment by Estoppel ("Ostensible Employment")**

If a person intentionally or negligently creates the ***appearance*** that another is in her employ, and a third person ***justifiably relies*** on this appearance, the first person may be estopped from denying the employment relationship and is liable as though she were an employer.

e. **Sub-Agents**

An employer-employee relationship may be created by an ***authorized*** agent hiring an employee on behalf of the principal-employer, and the employer may be held liable under ***respondeat superior*** for the employee's torts.

(1) **Undisclosed Principal**

In an undisclosed principal case, the agent is liable to the employee ***on the contract*** (*e.g.*, for wages), but generally is ***not*** liable in ***tort*** to third persons injured by the employee. Respondeat superior imposes ***tort liability*** only on the ***true employer***.

(2) **Unauthorized Hirings**

If the agent lacked authority to employ another, the employer ordinarily is not liable to third persons for the subagent's torts ***except*** in situations where the work requires no particular skill, the subagent's services are within the scope of the agent's employment, and the services are performed ***under the agent's supervision and in his presence***.

(3) **Emergency Authority to Hire**

An ordinary employee may have authority to hire a subagent an emergency. If communication with the employer is not possible or practical, the employee is deemed to have authority to employ another to assist him, and the employer is liable for the subagent's wrongful acts.

f. **"Borrowed Employees"**

When a general or original employer loans the services of an employee to another (special) employer, either gratuitously or for compensation, the determination of which employer is liable for the employee's torts usually depends on which employer had the ***right to control*** the employee's performance.

(1) **Loan of Equipment**

A general employer who lends or leases her equipment with an operator to a special employer is presumed to ***retain the right to control*** the operator, and is liable for the operator's torts.

(a) **Exceptions**

An exception to the general rule occurs if the primary right to control has been given to the special employer—particularly when the borrowing is for an indefinite period. ***Regardless*** of who has the primary right to control, if the special employer directs the employee to perform a ***specific act***, he will be liable if the employee performs it tortiously.

(2) **Factors to Consider in Determining Who Has Right to Control**

A court may consider the following factors in determining whether the general or special employer has the right to control the employee: (i) the ***extent of control*** either employer exercises over the work; (ii) the relationship between the ***employee's work and the nature of the special employer's business***; (iii) the nature of the ***employee's work, the skills required to perform it, and the degree of supervision*** normally associated with the work; (iv) the ***length of the employee's employment*** with the special employer; (v) the ***method of payment*** for the work; and (vi) whether the ***equipment is supplied by the general or special employer***.

(3) **Distinguish—Joint Liability of General and Special Employers**

A ***division of control***, *e.g.*, when the special employer directs the performance of a specific act that is also within the scope of the employee's general employment, may render ***both*** employers liable for a tortious act of the employee.

g. **"Employees" vs. "Independent Contractors"**

Because respondeat superior applies only to employees, the employer of an independent contractor ordinarily is not liable for the independent contractor's torts. The ***test*** for whether a worker is an employee or independent contractor is whether the employer has the ***right to control*** the manner of the work performed by the worker. When an employer bargains merely for a ***result*** and retains no control over the worker's performance, the worker is an independent contractor. At times, a worker may be ***both*** an employee and an independent contractor to the same employer. In this situation, the worker's status depends on his activity at the relevant time.

(1) **Relevant Factors**

Many factors are considered in determining the status of a worker, *e.g.*, whether the worker is engaged in a business or occupation distinct from that of the employer; whether the employer supplies the tools and place of work; the method of payment for the work performed; the length of employment; etc.

(2) **Application**

General building contractors and subcontractors are clearly independent contractors. ***Truck drivers*** who own their own equipment are generally independent contractors, while one who drives his employer's trucks in the daily course of business is usually an employee.

(a) **Physicians**

Physicians engaged by an employer to treat third persons are usually considered independent contractors because of the high level of skill involved in their trade. However, a number of jurisdictions do impose liability on an employer-hospital if an employee-physician is a resident. Also, many courts hold an employer liable if a physician's services are

primarily for the benefit of the employer or if the employer authorizes the physician to make ***representations*** on her behalf. An employer may also be liable if she ***negligently selected*** a physician.

(b) Collection Agencies

An outside collection agency employed by a creditor is generally held to be an independent contractor ***unless*** the creditor ***caused or directed*** the collection agent to commit a tortious act or if the agent was not self-employed but rather was a full-time employee of the creditor.

(3) Exceptional Situations

In certain limited situations, an ***employer is liable for the torts of an independent contractor***. The employer's liability is based on her ***own negligence*** or as a matter of ***public policy***, ***not*** on respondeat superior. Such situations include those in which the contractor is to perform ***highly dangerous acts*** (*e.g.,* blasting), the employer has a ***nondelegable duty*** but engages the contractor to perform the duty, or the contractor is authorized to make ***representations*** on the employer's behalf. Employers are also liable if they are ***negligent in hiring, training, or supervising*** an independent contractor.

3. Scope of Employment

For respondeat superior to apply, the employee must have committed the tortious act ***within the course and scope of employment***, *i.e.,* the employee must have been engaged in work for the employer of a type that he was employed to perform, during working hours.

a. Relevant Factors

The Restatement sets forth factors to be considered in determining whether a particular act occurred within the scope of employment, *e.g.,* authorization of the act; time, place, and purpose of the act; whether the act was one commonly performed by employees; the extent to which the employer's interest and the employee's interest were involved; etc.

b. Authorization by Employer Not Required

It is ***not*** necessary to establish that the employer specifically authorized a particular act if the act occurred in the scope of the employee's regular duties and employment. Even acts ***specifically forbidden*** by the employer may be within the scope of employment and subject the employer to liability ***unless*** the employee ***goes beyond*** the duties for which he is hired.

c. Intentional Torts by Employee

Liability under respondeat superior extends to an intentional act by an employee if the act is related to carrying forth the employer's business, *i.e.,* the employee is acting to further the business interests of the employer (*e.g.,* bouncer in club). If the act was motivated by personal reasons of the employee, the employer is not liable. The more serious or culpable the act, the less likely it will be found to be within the scope of employment.

(1) Civil vs. Criminal Liability

Respondeat superior is a rule of ***civil*** liability. Except for violations of minor regulatory laws (*e.g.,* sale of alcohol to minor), an employer ***cannot be held criminally liable*** for an employee's act unless she somehow participated in the act. A ***corporation***, however, can be held criminally liable for the acts of its officers and employees.

d. Omissions by Employee

An employee's tortious failure to act subjects the employer to liability just as if the employee had committed an affirmative wrongful act.

e. Employee's Personal Acts

An employer may be liable for injuries caused by an employee's personal acts (*e.g.*, smoking, eating, personal hygiene) if the act is ***incidental to the employee's performance of assigned work***. Also, a personal act performed off the employer's premises and while the employee is not engaged in work is within the scope of employment if the ***employer exercises control*** over the employee's acts. Even when such an activity is outside the scope of employment, an employer will be liable if she is negligent in supervising the employee, *e.g.*, allowing smoking around flammable liquids.

f. Employee's Use of Employer's Vehicle, Equipment, Etc.

An employer is liable for injuries negligently caused by an employee's use of her vehicle, etc., only when the instrumentality is being used for the purpose of advancing the employer's business interests, rather than the employee's personal affairs.

(1) Distinguish—"Permissive Use" Statutes

Some states have "permissive use" statutes that impose limited liability on a vehicle's owner for any damages negligently inflicted by a person driving it with the owner's permission, thus making it immaterial whether an employee was driving the employer's vehicle within the scope of employment.

g. Employee's Use of Unauthorized Instrumentalities

If an employee uses some vehicle, equipment, etc., in performing the employer's business, but the employer did ***not*** authorize such use, the factor most determinative of the employer's liability for any injuries the employee caused in the use of the instrumentality is whether the instrumentality used is ***substantially different*** from that authorized. If so, the employee's use of the instrumentality is outside the scope of employment, and the employer is not liable for injuries caused by the employee's use. "Substantially different" is usually measured by determining whether ***any greater risk*** is involved.

h. Employee Going to and from Work

An employee's going to or from work or meals is usually outside the scope of employment ***unless*** the trip also includes the performance of an ***errand*** for the employer or if the employee is a ***traveling salesperson***.

i. Acts Done Entirely or Partially on Employee's Behalf

If the ***main purpose*** of the employee's activity is still the employer's business, with only incidental personal acts (***"detour"***), the employer is still liable for any injuries resulting from the employee's activity. Only a ***substantial*** deviation or departure (***"frolic"***) will take the employee outside the scope of employment. A frolic ends when the employee resumes performing work for the employer. When an employee is acting partly for his own interests and partly for his employer (***"mixed motives"***), if any substantial part of the act was done for the employer's purposes, that is sufficient to impose liability on the employer for any consequences of the act.

j. Liability to Unauthorized Passengers of Employee

The majority view holds that an employee's invitation to an unauthorized passenger to ride in the employer's vehicle (or third person riding as trespasser) is ***outside the scope*** of employment, and thus the employer is not liable for any injuries to the invitee/trespasser. A few states hold the employer liable for injuries to the invitee/trespasser if the employee's negligence occurred within the scope of employment. Other states hold the employer liable for injuries to the invitee/trespasser due to the ***wanton and willful misconduct*** of the employee.

k. Gratuitous Work of Employee

An employer can be held vicariously liable for the torts of an employee acting within the scope of employment ***even if the employee performed the work gratuitously***.

4. Exception to Respondeat Superior

An employer is not liable for the injuries inflicted by one employee upon a fellow employee. ***Exceptions*** include situations where the employer has ***negligently hired*** an employee or where an employee is injured by a ***superior*** employee acting within his authority or in protecting the employer's property.

a. Workers' Compensation Statutes

Workers' compensation statutes have generally eliminated the need for the fellow servant rule as they bar employees from suing their employers and provide fixed compensation to workers injured in the scope of employment. However, not all workers are covered by these statutes. As a result, for workers' compensation purposes, courts construe "in the scope of employment" and "employee" more liberally than in respondeat superior cases.

B. LIABILITY OF PRINCIPAL FOR TORTS OF AGENT—OUTSIDE RESPONDEAT SUPERIOR

1. In General

Outside of respondeat superior, an employer or other principal is liable for the tortious acts of an employee or other agent if the principal was directly responsible for the tort, *i.e.,* her ***own*** wrongdoing is the proximate cause of the injury.

2. Wrongful Act Directed or Authorized by Principal

If the principal directs, authorizes, or permits the agent to perform a tortious act, the principal is liable to the injured party just as if she had committed the tort herself. In most cases, the agent who commits the act is ***also*** personally liable to the injured party.

a. Fraud or Duress Exception

An agent who assists his principal in the commission of fraud or duress is not liable to the injured party if the agent had ***no knowledge*** of the fraud or duress.

3. Ratification of Tortious Conduct by Principal

A principal may be liable for injuries caused by the tortious conduct of one acting or purporting to act as her agent if she ratifies the conduct, thus becoming liable for such conduct ***as if it had been authorized by her*** at the time of commission. Note that the agent must have ***intended to act on the principal's behalf***.

a. What Constitutes a Ratification

The principal must have ***accepted or retained benefits*** obtained through a wrongful act ***with knowledge of all relevant facts***. Note that courts have split on whether an employer's ***failure to fire an employee*** who committed a tortious act is a ratification of the act.

(1) No Duty to Investigate Facts

A ratification ***cannot*** be based on the principal's ***negligence*** or failure to exercise reasonable care to ascertain what representations the agent may have made to a third party.

4. Independent Duty Owed to Injured Party

An employer may be held independently liable for breach of her duty of due care in ***hiring, training, or supervising*** the person who caused the injury. The employer is also liable if she is ***charged with the care of third persons***, *e.g.*, common carriers. Because an employer is charged with notice of all facts discovered by her employees ***within the scope of employment***, an employee's knowledge of a ***dangerous condition is imputed to the employer***.

5. Defamation

An employer in the business of disseminating information may be held liable for disseminating defamations uttered by an employee, even if the defamations were neither authorized nor within the scope of employment. Liability is based on the employer's repetition, not on respondeat superior.

C. LIABILITY OF PRINCIPAL FOR TORTIOUS REPRESENTATIONS OF AGENT

1. Introduction

The problem of liability for the misrepresentations of another generally arises when an ***agent***, rather than an employee, makes the representations. Liability depends more on ***authority*** rather than the status of the person making the representations.

2. General Rule

An employer or other principal is subject to tort liability for a third person's loss resulting from misrepresentations made by an employee or other agent ***whenever the making of representations was actually or apparently authorized***.

3. Authority to Make Representations

The injured party need not show that the agent was authorized to make false statements; rather, she must establish that the agent had authority to make ***statements concerning the subject matter involved.*** The authority may be ***express*** or ***implied*** from the circumstances, or based on the principal placing the agent in a position to deceive.

a. Implied Authority

When an agent has been authorized to deal on the principal's behalf in transactions where representations about the subject matter are customarily made, the agent has implied authority to make all such representations unless that authority was specifically withheld—the making of the representations is considered ***incidental*** to his authority to deal in the transaction.

(1) Application

Examples of agents with implied authority include ***attorneys*** (agent of client) and ***brokers and factors***. Whether a broker is the agent of the seller or an independent contractor, he is deemed to have implied authority to make representations concerning the property. The majority view considers a broker to be an ***agent*** of the person by whom he is engaged, thus imputing any misrepresentations by the broker to the principal and giving rise to an action for rescission or fraud against the principal.

(a) **No Power to Sell**

If the broker is not authorized to sell (*e.g.*, only to advertise property), there may be no authority to make representations; the defrauded purchaser could sue the ***agent only*** for fraud, but could not rescind the purchase or sue the owner for damages.

(b) **Exculpatory Provisions**

To avoid liability for misstatements by brokers, factors, etc., owners sometimes insist on exculpatory provisions in their contracts that normally absolve the principal from liability for damages for fraudulent statements made by the agent, but ***rescission*** is usually still an available remedy to the purchaser.

b. **Agent Placed in Position to Deceive**

When a third party relies on an agent's apparent authority to make representations, the principal is liable for false representations even though the agent is acting for his own purposes, because the principal placed the agent in a ***position*** to defraud. The principal need not receive any benefits from the transaction.

4. **Effect of Innocent Misrepresentations by Agent**

If an agent makes misrepresentations with no intent to deceive, the principal is generally not liable for any resultant tort damages.

a. **Exceptions**

If the principal ***knows*** that the agent is not aware of the true facts but puts him in a position to innocently misrepresent, the principal is ***directly*** responsible for any damages. If an agent makes ***negligent misrepresentations*** knowing that a third party may rely on the misrepresentations, the employer is held liable by many courts. Note that a third party may ***rescind*** a contract because of innocent misrepresentations.

PART TWO: PARTNERSHIP

VIII. NATURE AND FORMATION OF PARTNERSHIP

A. GOVERNING LAW

1. **In General**

Most states rely on the Uniform Partnership Act ("UPA") or the Revised Uniform Partnership Act ("RUPA") as a basis for partnership law. Because the majority of states have adopted the RUPA, this Summary is based on the RUPA, but the UPA provisions will be noted where they differ substantially from the RUPA.

2. **Statute vs. Agreement**

The RUPA controls ***unless*** the partners have agreed otherwise. The RUPA, however, limits partners' ability to agree to certain key terms, *e.g.*, to eliminate the duties of loyalty or of good faith.

3. **Relationship to Agency Law**

Partnership law is similar to agency law in many respects, *e.g.*, a partner is an agent of her co-partners for certain purposes, imputing of acts, etc.

B. BASIC NATURE OF PARTNERSHIP

1. Defined

A partnership is an "association of two or more persons to carry on as co-owners a business for profit." The parties need not intend to form a business entity called a partnership; they need only intend: (i) to form a for-profit business, and (ii) to own the business together.

2. Distinguish—Agency

Partners are co-owners of the business, while agents have no ownership interests in the business.

3. Distinguish—Unincorporated Association

A ***Massachusetts trust*** is an unincorporated association in which the participants transfer the association's property to trustees, receiving transferable shares in return. Because participants neither own nor manage the property, the trust is not a partnership. Similarly, ***nonprofit*** associations are not considered partnerships.

4. Distinguish—Joint Venture

Although members of a joint venture share profits and losses, it is ordinarily formed for a ***single transaction***, whereas a partnership usually engages in a continuing business for an indefinite or fixed period of time. Although it is sometimes difficult to distinguish a joint venture from a partnership, the provisions of the RUPA are often applied to a joint venture.

C. AGGREGATE VS. ENTITY CHARACTERISTICS OF PARTNERSHIP

1. Common Law View

The ***common law*** never regarded a partnership as a separate entity; rather, it was treated as an ***aggregate*** of the individual partners. Thus, each individual partner had to be sued on a partnership debt, and the partnership could not hold title to real estate in its name.

2. UPA and RUPA—Aggregate and Entity Characteristics

a. Aggregate Characteristics

Partners are jointly and severally liable for partnership obligations, regardless of whether the partnership can be sued in its own name. Under the RUPA, partners are not co-owners of partnership property. The UPA provides that partners are co-owners, but individual partners cannot transfer or encumber specific partnership property.

(1) Federal Income Tax Law

A partnership's income or losses are attributed to the individual partners because the partnership is ***not*** a taxpaying entity; however, the partnership is a ***tax-reporting*** entity.

b. Entity Characteristics

(1) Capacity to Sue or Be Sued

The RUPA permits a partnership to sue or be sued in the name of the partnership. The UPA, however, does not address this matter, and, under the UPA, a few states allow a partnership to be sued as an entity but prohibit a partnership from bringing suit in the partnership name.

(a) **Federal Courts**

In ***federal courts***, a partnership can sue or be sued in the partnership name if a federal question is involved. In ***diversity*** cases, the relevant state's law determines the capacity of the partnership to sue or be sued in its own name, and the citizenship of ***all partners*** is considered.

(b) **Effect of Judgment Against Partnership Only**

A judgment against the partnership is not a judgment against any partner. Therefore, the judgment may not be satisfied from a partner's personal assets ***unless there is also a judgment against the partner***. It is thus good practice to join all partners individually.

(2) **Bankruptcy of Partnership vs. Partners Individually**

Adjudication of a partnership as a bankrupt does not operate to declare the partners bankrupt. Nor does the bankruptcy of a partner extend to the partnership or its assets.

(3) **Capacity to Convey Property**

A partnership can hold and convey title to ***real or personal property*** without all partners joining in the conveyance.

D. FORMATION

1. In General

A partnership, as a voluntary association, must generally be based on an agreement of the partners, thus making a contract (express or implied) essential.

2. Formalities

A written agreement is usually ***not*** required. A writing ***is required*** if the partnership agreement provides that it must ***continue for more than one year*** (Statute of Frauds) or for an agreement authorizing partners to deal in ***real property*** in order to bind ***third persons***.

3. Capacity to Become a Partner

Any ***person*** having capacity to contract has capacity to become a partner. A partnership agreement with a ***minor*** is thus ***voidable*** because a minor does not have the capacity to contract. The RUPA includes ***partnerships and corporations*** within the definition of a "person" who may become a partner. Other entities, such as limited liability partnerships, limited partnerships, and limited liability companies, are also considered "persons."

4. Consent of Co-Partners

A person may become a partner only with the consent of ***all*** of the partners.

5. Rules for Determining Existence of Partnership

In determining whether the parties intended to form as co-owners a business for profit, courts examine the intent of the parties by considering certain factors. A partnership is ***not*** established merely by ***joint ownership*** of property, ***contribution of capital***, or the sharing of ***gross income***. On the other hand, the RUPA states that the ***sharing of profits*** raises a ***presumption*** of partnership (unless they were received as payment for, *e.g.*, debts, rent, wages, or retirement benefits). Similarly, under the UPA, sharing of profits is ***prima facie evidence*** of a partnership. The legal effect of a presumption is the same as that of prima facie evidence.

a. **Exception**

A sharing of profits indicates a partnership only when ***no other business reason exists*** for the sharing (*e.g.*, no presumption of partnership will arise if the sharing is as rent or salary).

b. **Parties' Designation**

The parties' designation of their relationship as a "partnership" is not conclusive. Note that partnership liability cannot be avoided even by an express negation of the relationship if the evidence establishes the essential elements of a partnership.

E. PARTNERSHIP BY ESTOPPEL

1. In General

Although a true partnership relation depends on a contract, parties who are not partners may be bound as if they were partners in dealings with third persons.

2. Liability of Purported Partner

A person who represents herself to be a partner in an actual or apparent partnership or consents to a representation that she is a partner is liable to any third person to whom the representation is made who extends credit in good faith reliance on the representation. There is generally ***no duty to deny*** partner status when, ***without consent***, one is held out by another as a partner.

a. **Extent of Liability—"Holding Out" Language**

Pursuant to the RUPA, a person who ***relies on a representation of partnership*** made in a public manner can hold the purported partner liable even if the purported partner is not aware of being held out as a partner to the person. The UPA rule is the same as the RUPA rule: When a person represents himself as a partner or consents to another so representing him, he is liable to any person to whom the representation was made, and if the representation was made in a public manner, he is liable to any person giving credit regardless of whether he was aware that the representation had been made to that person.

3. Liability of Partners Who Represent a Third Person to Be a Partner

An actual partner who represents a nonpartner to be a partner constitutes that person as her agent with the power to bind her. However, any resultant liability binds ***only those partners who made or consented*** to the representation.

IX. EFFECT OF PARTNERSHIP RELATIONSHIP

A. RELATIONS BETWEEN PARTNERS

1. Fiduciary Duty

A partner owes to the partnership and the other partners the ***fiduciary duties of loyalty and care*** and must exercise those duties ***in good faith and with fair dealing***.

a. **Duty of Loyalty**

The duty of loyalty requires a partner to: (i) ***account to the partnership*** and hold as a trustee for it any property, profit, or benefit derived by him in conducting or winding up partnership business, or in using partnership property; (ii) ***refrain from dealing with the partnership on behalf of an adverse party***; and (iii) ***not compete*** with the partnership before dissolution.

b. **Duty of Care**

Partners must refrain from engaging in grossly negligent or reckless conduct, intentional misconduct, or a knowing violation of law in the conduct or winding up of partnership business.

c. **Assets**

A partner who purchases or holds partnership ***assets*** in his own name does so as trustee for the partnership.

d. **Transacting Business with Partnership**

A partner may make loans to or transact other business with the partnership. Fiduciary duties are not violated merely because a partner's actions further his own interest.

2. **Other Rights and Duties of Partners to Each Other**

Absent provisions to the contrary in the partnership agreement, the ***law imposes*** the following rights and duties.

a. **Management**

"Each partner has equal rights in the management and conduct of partnership business." A ***majority vote*** of the partners is required to settle differences arising as to a matter in the ordinary course of business. For acts outside the ordinary course of the business and for amendments to the partnership agreement, a ***unanimous vote*** of the partners is required. By agreement, one person may be authorized to act as ***managing partner***, and as such must deal fairly on behalf of all partners.

b. **Books and Records; Information**

Each partner is entitled to access to the partnership books and records and may inspect and copy any of them. Such books and records must be kept at the partnership's chief executive office. Partners must be given, ***without demand***, information concerning the partnership that is reasonably necessary for the exercise of the partners' rights and duties. Under the UPA, partners are not obligated to provide information regarding partnership business ***unless a demand is made*** for such information. A deceased partner's personal representative has the same rights as the deceased partner would have had.

c. **Profits and Losses**

Partnership profits and losses are shared according to the partnership agreement. Absent an agreement, partners share profits equally and losses according to profits.

d. **Distributions from Partnership**

A partner is entitled to: (i) the ***return of his capital contribution*** upon dissolution, (ii) ***reimbursement*** for reasonable expenses and personal liabilities incurred while conducting partnership business and for advances beyond his agreed-upon contribution, and (iii) ***remuneration for winding up*** the business. Generally, a partner has no right to remuneration for work performed on behalf of the partnership absent an agreement by the partners.

3. **Actions Between Partners**

a. **Under the RUPA**

The RUPA specifically allows actions against other partners for either ***legal or equitable relief*** to enforce: (i) a right under the partnership agreement; (ii) a right relating to sharing profits, participation in management, indemnification, etc.; (iii) rights relating to dissociation or dissolution and winding up of the business; or (iv) any other right of the partner.

b. Under the UPA

Under the UPA, generally, a partner's principal remedy against co-partners is an equitable suit for ***dissolution*** and/or an ***accounting***. ***No action at law*** for damages is available.

(1) Exceptions

An action at law ***is*** permitted if:

(a) ***The partnership has dealt with one partner as if he were a third person***;

(b) ***The suit is not related to the partnership business***;

(c) ***The wrongful acts of one partner constitute fraud or a conversion of partnership assets***;

(d) ***One partner is wrongfully excluded from the partnership***;

(e) ***One partner negligently injures the person or property of another***; or

(f) ***Injury to a partner is caused by the negligence of a partnership employee***.

B. RELATIONS AS TO THIRD PERSONS

1. Authority of Partner to Bind Partnership

Every partner is an agent of the partnership for the purposes of its business. Rules of agency are applicable in determining whether the partnership is bound by a partner's dealings with a third person.

a. Apparent Authority

An act of a partner, ***for apparently carrying on in the ordinary course the partnership business or business of the kind carried on by the partnership*** binds the partnership ***unless***: (i) the partner had ***no authority*** to act for the partnership in the matter, and (ii) the person with whom the partner was dealing ***knew or had received notification that the partner lacked authority***.

b. Actual Authority

Actual authority can be granted in the partnership agreement or by the vote of the partners. A majority vote of the partners is sufficient to give a partner actual authority to carry on ordinary business matters, but a unanimous vote is necessary to grant actual authority for acts ***outside the ordinary course of business***. Under the UPA, a unanimous vote is required for certain extraordinary acts, *e.g.,* confessing judgment against the partnership. Cases are split on whether authority to convey real property other than in the ordinary course of business must be in writing; the prevailing view is that a writing is ***not required***.

c. Statement of Partnership Authority

A partnership may publicly file (in most states with the secretary of state) a statement of partnership authority expanding or limiting a partner's authority to act on the partnership's behalf. The statement ***must contain*** the name of the partnership, the address of its chief executive office and of an office within the state, the names and addresses of all partners (or of an agent who has such information), and the names of partners who are authorized to execute an instrument transferring partnership real property.

(1) **Effect**

A statement of authority ***granting*** a partner authority is ***conclusive evidence*** of that partner's authority. For a grant of authority to transfer partnership ***real property*** to be conclusive, in addition to being filed with the secretary of state, a certified copy of the statement must also be filed with the office for recording real property interests. A ***limitation*** on a partner's authority may be contained within a statement of authority or in another filed statement but does ***not*** give a third party constructive notice of the limitation; thus, a third party is not bound by a limitation unless he knows of the limitation.

(a) **Exceptions**

The filing of a limitation of a partner's authority will be effective as constructive notice to third parties when it limits a filed grant of authority or limits a partner's authority to transfer real property, and the limitation is filed with the secretary of state's office and the office for recording real property interests.

(2) **Statement of Denial**

The RUPA also permits a partner (or person named as a partner) to file a statement denying any fact, including denial of the person's authority or status as a partner.

d. **Distinguish—Termination Under UPA**

Under the UPA, a single partner probably cannot terminate the authority of co-partners without a dissolution of the partnership. If only two partners are involved, some courts hold that a partner's notice to a creditor regarding nonliability for a co-partner's act is effective. If more than two partners are involved, the majority vote of the partners governs all matters within the scope of the partnership business ***unless*** the act is done contrary to an ***agreement*** among the partners, and then all partners must consent.

e. **Admissions and Representations**

Agency rules also apply to charge the partnership with a partner's admissions and representations concerning partnership business made within the scope of her actual or apparent authority.

2. **Notice and Knowledge**

Notice or knowledge of any one partner regarding regular partnership business is ***imputed to the partnership*** under rules similar to those for agency.

a. **RUPA Reasonable Diligence Test**

A partnership will be deemed to have notice or knowledge of a fact when the individual conducting the transaction has notice or knowledge or would have had notice or knowledge of the fact had reasonable diligence been exercised.

b. **UPA Rules**

(1) **Notice**

"Notice" is a communication by a third person about a matter relating to the partnership business. Notice may be oral or written (sometimes a writing is required).

(2) Knowledge

"Knowledge" is information that is known or reasonably should be known by a partner. Whether the partner is a participating partner and when the knowledge was acquired are determinative factors in deciding whether the partnership should be charged with the partner's knowledge.

(a) Participant

If the partner is participating in the transaction in which the knowledge is relevant, and if the knowledge was acquired by the partner while ***she was a partner***, her knowledge will be ***imputed*** to the partnership. If the knowledge was acquired when ***she was not a partner***, the knowledge will be imputed to the partnership ***only if*** the knowledge is "present to her mind" at the time she is acting for the partnership.

(b) Nonparticipant

Information possessed by a partner not participating in the transaction will be imputed to the partnership ***if*** the partner "reasonably could and should have communicated it" to the participating partner.

c. Fraud

Notice to or knowledge of a partner will not be imputed to the partnership if the partner is acting fraudulently or adversely ***to the partnership***.

3. Partnership Liability to Third Persons

A partnership is liable to third persons for the wrongful acts of a partner committed within the scope of partnership business or with authority.

4. Partner Liability to Third Persons

The ***RUPA*** makes partners ***jointly and severally liable for all partnership obligations*** unless otherwise agreed by the claimant or provided by law. Under the ***UPA***, liability on contracts is joint, while tort liability is joint and several.

a. Joint and Several Liability

Under the ***RUPA***, partners are jointly and severally liable for ***all partnership debts and obligations*** and under the ***UPA***, partners are jointly and severally liable for ***torts and breaches of trust*** injuring third parties. An action may be brought against any single partner ***without*** joining the others. In this case, any judgment obtained against the partner is ***not*** res judicata against any other partners in subsequent suits. Each partner is deemed to assume liability for any ***tortious*** act of a co-partner ***except*** for torts requiring ***malice or intent*** where each partner must possess the malice or intent. Partners can be held liable for a co-partner's ***fraud*** if the co-partner was acting within the scope of partnership business.

(1) RUPA Exhaustion Requirement

The RUPA provides that a judgment against the partnership is ***not*** a judgment against an individual partner. A judgment may be satisfied from a partner's personal assets only if a judgment has been obtained against him. The RUPA also imposes other limitations on reaching the personal assets of a partner, *e.g.,* a judgment on the same claim has been obtained against the partnership and has not been fully satisfied.

b. Joint Liability Under UPA

The UPA makes partners ***jointly*** liable on all partnership debts and contracts. Creditors cannot proceed against any single partner, but must join all partners; of course, if the creditor is in a state that considers the partnership to be an ***entity***, the creditor may bring suit against the partnership itself without the necessity of joining all partners. Satisfaction of a judgment ***bars*** any further action. ***Release of one*** partner operates to release ***all*** partners (some states do not follow this rule). A ***silent partner*** is liable to the same extent as known partners except upon dissolution when liabilities may differ.

(1) Remedies

Partnership assets are subject to attachment and execution only upon ***partnership*** debts. A creditor's only option to recover on an individual partner's debts is a ***charging order*** against the debtor-partner's interest.

c. Distinguish—Limited Liability Partnerships

Nearly all states permit the formation of limited liability partnerships ("LLPs"). An LLP is treated as a general partnership and subject to the RUPA (or UPA), but the partners are ***not personally liable*** for all partnership debts and obligations. Laws regarding LLPs vary by state, but most require an LLP to register with the state and adopt a business name indicating its limited liability status (*e.g.,* include letters "LLP" in the name). Once registered, most states provide that an LLP partner is ***not personally liable*** for partnership debts or obligations arising ***in tort***, and many states go further and provide that an LLP partner is not liable for ***any*** partnership debts or obligations whether arising in contract or tort. Each partner, however, remains liable for her ***own wrongful acts*** (*e.g.,* torts) and for acts committed by those under her supervision. Some states require an LLP to carry liability insurance. The RUPA provisions regarding LLPs are similar to those mentioned above except the RUPA does not require an LLP to carry insurance.

5. Effect of Change in Partnership Membership

a. Liability of Incoming Partner

The RUPA provides that a person admitted into an existing partnership is ***not personally liable*** for a partnership obligation incurred before her admission as a partner. The UPA effectively reaches the same result by providing that a new partner is liable for ***all obligations*** of the partnership incurred ***before or after*** her admission to the partnership. However, her personal liability for old obligations is ***limited to her partnership contribution***, unless she agrees otherwise.

b. Liability of Retiring Partner

A retired partner remains liable on all obligations incurred by the partnership while he was a partner. He is also liable for obligations incurred after retirement unless he gives proper notice of withdrawal.

6. Liability for Crimes

Partners are ***not*** liable for the crimes of a co-partner, even if committed within the scope of partnership business, unless the partners participated in the criminal activity.

7. Third Person's Liability to Partnership for Injuries to Partner

Generally, a partnership ***cannot*** recover damages from a third person for injuries inflicted on a member—a partner is not an employee of the partnership.

X. PARTNERSHIP PROPERTY AND PARTNERS' PROPERTY RIGHTS

A. PARTNERSHIP PROPERTY

1. RUPA Rules

Under the RUPA, property is deemed to be partnership property if it is acquired: (i) ***in the name of the partnership***; or (ii) ***in the name of a partner*** and the transferring instrument ***indicates*** the named person's status as a partner ***or*** the existence of the partnership. There is a ***rebuttable presumption*** that property is partnership property if it is ***purchased with partnership assets***. If property is acquired in the name of one or more partners and the instrument transferring title indicates neither the person's capacity as a partner nor the partnership's existence, ***and*** the property is purchased without partnership assets, there is a ***rebuttable presumption*** that the property is the ***separate property*** of the named partner even if it is used for partnership purposes.

2. UPA Rules

The UPA provides that "all property originally brought into the partnership stock or subsequently acquired . . . ***on account of the partnership*** is partnership property." The critical factor is whether the partners ***intended*** to devote the property to partnership purposes. Absent clear intent, courts consider factors such as ***title*** (which is not conclusive as to ownership), purchase ***with partnership funds*** (which can be conclusive), ***improvements by the partnership***, ***relationship*** of the property to the business (the closer the association, the more likely the property is a partnership asset), ***use of the property***, and the property's ***status in the partnership books*** (this factor is given considerable weight).

3. Real Property

Under the common law aggregate theory, a partnership could not take title to real property. However, both the ***RUPA and UPA*** clearly provide that real property may be acquired and held ***in the partnership name***.

4. Insurance Policies

Partners often purchase "cross-life insurance policies" on each other's lives, the premiums for which are customarily paid out of partnership funds, but are usually charged to the draws of each partner. This raises a question as to whether the benefits of such policies are partnership assets, to be used to pay partnership debts, or the sole property of the surviving partner. Absent an agreement between the partners, many courts hold that the benefits belong outright to the surviving partner.

B. PARTNER'S PROPERTY RIGHTS

1. Rights in Specific Partnership Property

Under the ***RUPA***, a partner is not a co-owner of partnership property and has ***no transferable interest in partnership property***. Thus, a partner cannot ***voluntarily or involuntarily*** transfer partnership property. Consequently, a partner's personal creditors, spouse, and family do not have rights in partnership property. Under the ***UPA***, a partner is a ***tenant in partnership*** with her co-partners as to each partnership asset. Each partner has an ***equal right to possession*** of partnership property for partnership purposes. However, a partner's right in specific partnership property is ***not assignable*** absent assignment by all partners, and it is ***not subject to attachment*** by her individual creditors. Upon a partner's ***death***, her rights in partnership property vest in the ***surviving partners***, not in her estate. A partner's right in partnership property also is ***not subject to family allowances*** nor is it community property.

2. Interest in Partnership

A partner's interest in the partnership is his share of the profits and losses, and the right to receive distributions. This interest is considered ***personal property***.

a. Assignment of Interest

Absent a contrary agreement, a partner's partnership interest ***is assignable***, entitling the assignee to receive only the distributions to which the partner would be entitled; the assignee does not become a partner. The assignor generally retains all rights and duties of a partner other than the interest in distributions that was transferred.

(1) Effect of Assignment

The RUPA provides that a partner who transfers all or substantially all of his partnership interest may be expelled by the other partners. Under the UPA, an assignment of all of a partner's interest does not result in a dissolution of the partnership unless the partner ceases to perform his partnership duties.

b. Rights of Creditors of Individual Partners

A creditor's sole remedy against an individual partner is to obtain a judgment against the partner and thereafter obtain a ***charging order*** against his interest in the partnership.

c. Death

Rights of a deceased partner's estate in his partnership interest are discussed *infra*.

d. Family Rights

A partner's interest in the partnership ***is*** subject to family allowance and is generally treated as community property in community property jurisdictions.

3. Right to Participate in Management

Each partner has an ***equal*** right to participate in the management of the partnership.

XI. DISSOCIATION, DISSOLUTION, AND WINDING UP OF A PARTNERSHIP

A. DISSOCIATION UNDER RUPA

1. Introduction

Under the UPA, when a partner leaves the partnership, it is dissolved, even if the remaining partners continue the business (in which case, a new partnership is formed among the remaining partners). Under the RUPA, when a partner leaves the partnership it is called a "dissociation," and the term "dissolution" is used only to describe the process for actually terminating the partnership's business.

a. Effect of Dissociation

Dissociation does not necessarily terminate the partnership, but it does terminate a partner's right to participate in the business and his duty to refrain from competing with the business.

b. Events Causing Dissociation

A partner will become dissociated from the partnership on:

(1) ***The partnership's receipt of the partner's notice to withdraw*** from the partnership;

(2) ***The happening of an event agreed to in the partnership agreement***;

(3) ***The partner's expulsion pursuant to the partnership agreement***;

(4) ***The partner's expulsion pursuant to the partners' unanimous vote***;

(5) ***Judicial determination of the partner's expulsion***;

(6) ***The partner's bankruptcy, assignment of assets for the benefit of creditors, or acquiescence to the appointment of a trustee, receiver, or the like*** to take substantially all of the partner's property;

(7) ***The death*** of the partner, ***appointment of a guardian or conservator*** for the partner, or ***judicial determination that the partner has become incapable of performing his duties***;

(8) ***If the partner is a trust, distribution of the trust's interest in the partnership***;

(9) ***If the partner is an estate, distribution of the estate's partnership interest***; or

(10) ***Termination of a partner who is not an individual, partnership, corporation, trust, or estate*** (*e.g.*, limited liability company).

c. Wrongful Dissociation

A partner who wrongfully dissociates is liable for any damages caused by the wrongful dissociation. Dissociation is wrongful if: (i) it is in ***breach of an express provision*** of the partnership agreement; or (ii) the partnership is for a ***definite term or particular undertaking*** and the partner ***withdraws, is expelled, or becomes bankrupt*** before the end of the term or accomplishment of the undertaking.

2. Effect of Dissociation Where Business Not Wound Up

a. Purchase of Dissociated Partner's Interest

When the partnership continues, the partnership must buy out the dissociated partner's interest in the partnership based on the greater of the amount distributable to the partner if the partnership assets were sold at liquidation value or their value if the partnership were sold as a going concern without the dissociated partner (minus any damages if the partner wrongfully dissociated). ***Interest*** must be paid on the buyout price from the date of dissociation to the date of payment. The partnership must ***indemnify*** the dissociated partner against all partnership liabilities except for those incurred by him after dissociation that bind the partnership.

(1) Where Partner Disputes Value

If no agreement is reached as to the value of the dissociated partner's interest in the partnership within 120 days after the partner demands payment in writing, the partnership must pay the partner the value of his interest based on an estimation of the buyout price and accrued interest by the partnership. If the partner disagrees with the price, he may bring an action against the partnership (within certain time limits). Attorneys' fees and costs may be assessed against a party not acting in good faith.

(2) Dissociation Before Expiration of Term or Completion of Undertaking

If the partnership is for a definite term or particular undertaking, the dissociating partner is not entitled to payment of the buyout price before the term expires or the undertaking is completed, unless he can prove that payment will not harm the partnership.

b. Dissociated Partner's Power to Bind Partnership

A partnership will be bound by any act of a dissociated partner done within ***two years*** of dissociation if: (i) the act was ***within the partner's apparent authority***; (ii) the other party ***reasonably believed*** the dissociated partner was still a partner; and

(iii) the other party ***did not have notice or knowledge*** of the dissociation. The partnership can hold the partner liable for any losses resulting from his conduct.

c. **Dissociated Partner's Liability to Others**

The dissociated partner remains liable on partnership obligations incurred before dissociation, and on obligations incurred within ***two years*** after dissociation if the other party reasonably believed the dissociated partner was still a partner and did not have notice or knowledge of the dissociation. A ***release*** of the dissociated partner from liability will occur if a creditor knows of the dissociation and agrees with the partnership to materially alter the nature or time of payment of the obligation without the dissociated partner's consent.

d. **Constructive Notice**

To limit liability after dissociation, the dissociated partner or the partnership may file with the state a ***statement of dissociation*** that is deemed to give nonpartners notice of the dissociation ***90 days*** after the statement is filed.

e. **Continued Use of Partnership Name**

Continued use of the partnership name, even if it includes the dissociated partner's name, does not alter the liabilities discussed above.

B. DISSOLUTION

1. Introduction

The dissolution of a partnership is the change in the relation of the partners caused by any partner ceasing to be associated in the carrying on, as distinguished from the winding up, of the business. Dissolution does not terminate the partnership; it is merely a change in the legal relationship of the partners. The partnership continues until the winding up of partnership affairs is completed.

2. RUPA Approach

Dissolution leads to the termination of the partnership.

a. **Events Causing Dissolution and Winding Up**

A partnership is dissolved and its affairs must be wound up on:

(1) ***Receipt by a partnership at will of notice*** from a partner, other than a dissociated partner, of an ***express will to withdraw***;

(2) ***In a partnership for a definite term*** or particular undertaking: (i) within 90 days after a partner's death, bankruptcy, or wrongful dissociation, the ***express will of at least half the remaining partners*** to wind up; (ii) the express will of ***all partners*** to wind up; or (iii) the ***expiration of the term*** or accomplishment of the undertaking;

(3) ***Occurrence of an event that the partnership agreement states will cause dissolution*** unless ***all*** partners agree otherwise;

(4) ***Occurrence of an event making it unlawful to continue the partnership business*** (unless cured within 90 days);

(5) ***Judicial determination, on application of a partner,*** that certain circumstances make it not reasonably practical to carry on the partnership business; or

(6) ***Judicial determination, on application of a transferee*** of a partner's interest, that winding up is equitable.

b. **Right to Wind Up**

Under the RUPA, the person winding up may continue the partnership business ***as a going concern for a reasonable time***.

c. **Statement of Dissolution**

A ***statement of dissolution*** may be filed by any partner who has not wrongfully dissociated. The statement is deemed to give notice to nonpartners of the dissolution 90 days after the statement is filed.

d. **Distribution of Assets**

Under the RUPA, an account is established for each partner when a partnership is formed. The account is credited with the money and value of property contributed by the partner, plus any profits due him. The account is charged with any distributions made to the partner and also with his share of any losses. After all creditors (including partner creditors) are paid on dissolution, positive balances in the partners' accounts are paid to the partners; any partner with a negative balance must contribute that amount to the partnership. If a partner ***fails to contribute his share of partnership losses***, the other partners must pay that share in the proportion in which they share losses, but have a cause of action against the noncontributor. The estate of a ***deceased partner*** is liable for the partner's obligations to the partnership.

3. **UPA Approach**

a. **By Act of the Partners**

(1) **Per Partnership Agreement**

If the partnership agreement states that the partnership is to last for a specific period of time or until a certain project is completed, the expiration of the period or completion of the project dissolves the partnership.

(2) **By Will of Partner**

Any or all of the partners can effect a dissolution of the partnership ***at any time*** merely by expressing a will to dissolve. If the partnership is for a fixed term or particular undertaking, a partner's election to dissolve prior to the term's expiration or accomplishment of the undertaking is a violation of the agreement, and the partner may be liable for any losses caused by the dissolution.

(3) **Mutual Assent of Partners**

A partnership may be dissolved by the mutual assent of all of the partners who have not assigned their interests or had them charged for their separate debts.

(4) **Expulsion of Partner**

A bona fide expulsion of a partner done pursuant to a power reserved in the partnership agreement will cause a dissolution of the partnership, and the expelling partners are not liable for any resulting losses.

b. **By Operation of Law**

Dissolution also occurs on the happening of an event that makes it ***illegal*** for the partnership to continue. In addition, absent an agreement to the contrary, the partnership is dissolved on the ***death or bankruptcy*** of any partner.

c. **By Decree of Court**

On application of a partner, a court can decree a dissolution of the partnership. Grounds for judicial dissolution include a partner's ***incompetency, incapability*** of performing partnership duties, or ***improper conduct***. Judicial dissolution is also available when the business can be carried on only ***at a loss*** or when there are other circumstances rendering a ***dissolution equitable.*** The judicial action is generally for dissolution and an ***accounting***.

d. **Rights of Partners in Dissolution**

(1) **When Dissolution Does Not Violate Partnership Agreement**

When dissolution does not violate the partnership agreement, no partner has a claim or cause of action against any other partner for any loss sustained because of the dissolution. Each partner has the right to have partnership assets applied to discharge partnership liabilities and the balance distributed to the partners in accordance with their respective interests.

(2) **When Dissolution Violates Partnership Agreement**

The "innocent" partners have the right to ***damages*** from the partner who dissolves the partnership in violation of the partnership agreement; the right to ***purchase the business***, provided they pay the wrongfully dissolving partner the value of his interest (minus damages); and the right to ***wind up partnership affairs***.

(3) **Rights and Duties of Surviving Partner(s)**

On the death of a partner, the surviving partner is entitled to possession of the partnership assets and is charged with winding up partnership affairs. She acts as a ***fiduciary*** and must account to the deceased partner's estate for the value of the decedent's interest in the partnership. If the surviving partner ***continues the business without consent*** of the estate, she is liable for interest on the amount owed to the estate, ***or*** an appropriate share of any profits she earned following the decedent's death, whichever is greater. If an ***unjustified delay diminishes*** the value of the partnership business, the surviving partner may be liable to the decedent's estate for the value of the decedent's interest as of the date of death. The surviving partner is entitled to ***compensation*** for her services in winding up.

e. **Effects of Dissolution**

(1) **General Rule—Termination of Actual Authority**

Dissolution ***terminates the actual authority*** of any partner to act as an agent for either the partnership or the other partners, except for winding up partnership affairs; however, termination of a partner's actual authority is not effective until he knows of the dissolution.

(a) **Termination of Apparent Authority**

Even though a partner's actual authority is terminated by dissolution, he still has apparent authority as to all who knew of the partnership prior to dissolution. ***Creditors*** must be given ***actual notice*** (*e.g.,* a letter) of dissolution for termination of a partner's apparent authority. A partner's apparent authority as to other third parties can be terminated by newspaper notice. The liability of ***silent partners*** for post-dissolution transactions when notice was not given is ***limited to partnership assets***.

(2) Liability for Existing Partnership Debts

The partners' joint liability ***remains*** after dissolution until partnership debts are discharged unless there is a ***novation***.

(3) Liability of Partners Continuing Business

When the business continues after a dissolution, the new partnership remains liable for all debts of the previous partnership. ***Incoming partners'*** liability is limited to their respective partnership interests.

f. Winding Up

"Winding up" is the process of settling partnership affairs after dissolution. During the process, actual authority exists to carry out necessary acts to wind up the business. Generally, ***only transactions*** designed to ***terminate***, rather than to carry on, the business are within the scope of a partner's actual authority; *i.e.,* "old business" can be wrapped up; if "new business" is entered into, the partner who continues to carry on the business assumes sole liability for her actions and is liable for losses.

(1) "Old Business" vs. "New Business"

Old business includes assigning claims, selling assets, performing contracts made prior to dissolution, collecting debts due, compromising claims, paying off creditors, and distributing the remainder of the business's assets. New business includes extending time on a debt, entering into new contracts, and increasing any partnership obligation, except for necessary contracts.

(2) Who May Wind Up

All partners may wind up the partnership if the partners agree to wind up, the partnership term expires, or the partnership undertaking is accomplished. If a partner dissolves the partnership by bankruptcy, the remaining partners may wind up, and if the partnership is dissolved by the death of a partner, the surviving partners or the executor of the last surviving partner's estate may wind up the partnership. A partner who ***wrongfully dissolves*** the partnership ***cannot*** wind up.

g. Distribution of Assets—Final Accounting

After a dissolution of the partnership and a reduction of its assets to cash, partnership liabilities are paid first to ***outside creditors*** and then to partners (first partner creditors are paid, then partners are paid for the return of their capital contributions); lastly, any cash remaining is distributed to the partners according to their share of profits or surplus.

(1) When There Are Losses

If there is a partnership loss, each partner must contribute her share of the loss, usually in the same proportion as her share of the profits. When a partner is insolvent or refuses to pay her share of the loss, the remaining partners must pay her share proportionately, and they will then have a right of action against the defaulting partner.

(a) Dual Insolvency

If both a partnership and a partner are insolvent, under bankruptcy law, partnership creditors have priority in partnership assets and parity with the partner's separate creditors with respect to the partner's individual assets.

Bankruptcy law preempts the UPA, which provides that the partner's separate creditors have priority in the partner's individual assets.

(2) **Termination of Partnership**

A partnership is terminated when all partnership affairs have been wound up, including liquidation and distribution of assets.

C. CONVERSIONS AND MERGERS UNDER RUPA

1. Introduction

The RUPA contains provisions for converting a partnership into a limited partnership, converting a limited partnership into a partnership, and merging partnerships.

2. Conversion of Partnership to Limited Partnership

Converting a partnership into a limited partnership requires the ***unanimous consent*** of the partners (or the vote specified in the partnership agreement), and the filing of a certificate of limited partnership with the state.

a. Contents of Certificate

In addition to other mandatory provisions, the certificate must contain the partnership's former name, a statement of conversion, and the number of votes cast for and against the conversion.

b. Liability

A general partner who becomes a limited partner because of a conversion remains liable as a general partner on obligations incurred before the conversion, but has no personal liability on obligations incurred after the conversion except for those incurred within 90 days after the conversion if the other party believed that the limited partner was still a general partner.

3. Conversion of Limited Partnership to Partnership

All partners must consent to a conversion of a limited partnership into a partnership. Conversion is accomplished by canceling the certificate of limited partnership. A limited partner remains liable only as a limited partner for obligations incurred by the partnership before the conversion, but is liable as a general partner for all post-conversion obligations.

4. Merger

A partnership may merge with one or more partnerships or limited partnerships upon approval of a merger plan: (i) in a partnership, by all partners or the number set in the partnership agreement; or (ii) in a limited partnership, by the vote required by statute, or if none, by the consent of all partners, notwithstanding a contrary provision in the partnership agreement.

a. Contents of Plan

The plan must state: (i) the name of each partnership or limited partnership that is a party to the merger; (ii) the name of the surviving entity, its status as a partnership or limited partnership, and the status of each partner; (iii) the terms and conditions of the merger; (iv) the basis for converting each party's interests; and (v) the street address of the surviving entity's chief executive office.

b. Liabilities

A partner of the surviving partnership is liable for all obligations of the merging entity that she was liable for before the merger, and to the extent of partnership property, all other obligations of the surviving entity incurred before the merger, and all obligations of the surviving entity incurred after the merger.

XII. LIMITED PARTNERSHIPS

A. IN GENERAL

1. Nature

A limited partnership is a hybrid business organization that has a business structure similar to a partnership, but provides the limited partners with limited liability similar to a shareholder in a corporation. Profits and losses of a limited partnership flow directly to the partners, thus avoiding the "double tax" on corporate profits, and unlike an S corporation, a limited partnership is not limited in size. A limited partnership must have at least one general partner who is personally liable for all partnership obligations, and (in most states) the limited partners cannot participate in the management or control of the limited partnership.

2. Governing Law

There were no limited partnerships at common law; they are created by statutes. Nearly every state has adopted the 1976 Revised Uniform Limited Partnership Act ("RULPA"), and a majority of states have also adopted the 1985 amendments. The RULPA was revised in 2001 and the revision is named the Uniform Limited Partnership Act of 2001 ("ULPA"); however, few states have adopted it. This Summary discusses the RULPA as amended in 1985. The rules of the jurisdiction's general partnership act govern where the RULPA does not contain an applicable rule. The ULPA, on the other hand, is a stand-alone act de-linked from any partnership act.

3. Structure

A limited partnership must have one or more general partners and one or more limited partners.

a. General Partner

A general partner manages the partnership and has full personal liability for the partnership's debts. (Under the ULPA, general partners are jointly and severally liable.) A general partner may be a natural person, partnership, limited partnership, trust, estate, association, or corporation.

b. Limited Partner

A limited partner is a partner who makes a contribution to the partnership and obtains an interest in the partnership's returns, but who is inactive in management and generally is not liable for partnership debts beyond her contribution. A limited partner may be a natural person or any of the entities named above for a general partner.

4. Permitted Activities

The RULPA contains no restrictions on activities in which a limited partnership may engage, although many jurisdictions forbid some undertakings, *e.g.*, banking and insurance. The ULPA states that a limited partnership can be formed for ***any lawful purpose***.

B. FORMATION OF LIMITED PARTNERSHIP

1. Certificate of Limited Partnership

A certificate of limited partnership must be signed by all of the general partners and filed with the secretary of state, upon which the limited partnership comes into existence if there has been substantial compliance with certificate requirements. Absent substantial compliance, all partners may be held liable as general partners for partnership obligations.

a. Contents

The certificate need only contain the name and address of the limited partnership and of an agent for service of process, the name and address of each general partner (***not*** limited partners), and the latest date upon which the limited partnership is to dissolve.

(1) Distinguish—Partnership Agreement

The certificate of limited partnership does not control the relations among the partners. That job is performed by a document called the partnership agreement. The partnership agreement must include the amount of cash or value of property contributed by each partner, the times or events upon which future contributions are to be made, any right of a partner to receive distributions, and any events that will cause dissolution.

b. Amendment of Certificate of Limited Partnership

An amendment must be filed if there are errors in the certificate or significant changes concerning required information. It must be signed by ***at least one general partner***, and if it reflects the admission of an additional general partner, that partner must sign it. Only general partners are liable for failure to amend, and not even then if an amendment is filed within 30 days after the event necessitating amendment.

(1) Liability for False Statements

Anyone suffering a loss by relying on a false statement in the certificate or amendment may recover damages from any person who signed the certificate (including agents) ***knowing*** that it contained a false statement, and any general partner who ***knew or should have known*** that a false statement was included.

2. Records Office

A limited partnership must maintain a records office with certain records, *e.g.,* names and addresses of all partners, copies of the partnership's tax returns and partnership agreements for the three most recent years.

C. NAME OF LIMITED PARTNERSHIP

1. Requirements

The limited partnership name must include the words "limited partnership," not be the same as or deceptively similar to any corporate or limited partnership name registered in the state, and not include the name of a limited partner unless it is also the name of a general partner or the business had been carried on in the limited partner's name prior to her becoming a limited partner.

2. Liability for Use of Limited Partner's Name

A limited partner who ***knowingly permits*** her name to be used in the partnership name in violation of the RULPA is liable as a general partner to creditors who did not know that she is not a general partner. The ULPA ***allows a limited partnership to use the name of any partner in its name***. The ***name chosen should be distinguishable*** from the name of other business entities unless authorized by the secretary of state.

D. CHANGES IN MEMBERSHIP

1. Admission of Additional General and Limited Partners

An additional general or limited partner may be admitted to the partnership in any manner provided in the partnership agreement or, if not provided for, upon the written consent of all partners. Under the ULPA, an additional ***limited partner*** may be admitted as provided in the partnership agreement, as the result of a conversion or merger, or with the consent of all the partners. An additional ***general partner*** may be admitted in the same manner and also after the dissociation of the last general partner.

2. Assignment of Partner's Interest

A partner's interest in the partnership may be assigned in whole or in part absent a contrary provision in the partnership agreement. Assignment does not dissolve the partnership; however, unless stated differently in the agreement, a partner ceases to be a partner upon the assignment of ***all*** of his interest. Note that if a ***general*** partner assigns all of his interest, the assignment can be of such significance as to require the dissolution of the partnership.

a. Assignee's Rights

Unless an assignee becomes a substitute partner, he is entitled to receive only the assignor's share of profits or return of contribution; he does not have the rights of a limited partner.

b. Creditor's Right to Charge Partner's Interest

A creditor of a partner may ***charge the partner's interest***; she does not become a partner.

3. Death, Incompetency, or Withdrawal of a Partner

a. Limited Partners

The death, incompetency, or withdrawal of a limited partner does ***not*** dissolve the partnership. If a limited partner dies or becomes incompetent, her legal representative may exercise all of her rights for purposes of settling her estate and administering her property. A limited partner ***may withdraw*** pursuant to the conditions stated in the partnership agreement. If no conditions are stated, she may withdraw on six months' prior written notice to each general partner.

b. General Partners

The death, incompetency, or withdrawal of a general partner is an "event of withdrawal" dissolving the partnership unless there is at least one other general partner and the partnership agreement permits the business to continue, or within 90 days after the event, all partners consent in writing to continue the business and to appoint a general partner if necessary.

(1) Right to Withdraw

A general partner may withdraw from the partnership at any time on written notice to the other partners; however, if the withdrawal violates the partnership agreement, he is liable for any resultant damages.

(2) Other "Events of Withdrawal"

Other events that may cause the dissolution of the partnership include the bankruptcy of a general partner and the assignment by a general partner of all of his interest.

4. Dissociation Under ULPA

The ULPA uses the term ***"dissociation"*** when discussing the withdrawal of a limited or general partner from the partnership. As with withdrawal under the RULPA: (i) dissociation can be voluntary or involuntary, and (ii) general and limited partners have the ***power*** to dissociate at any time, but not necessarily the ***right***. If a dissociation is ***wrongful***, the partner may be liable to the limited partnership for damages caused by the breach.

a. Continuation of Limited Partnership After Dissociation

As in the case of withdrawal under the RULPA, under the ULPA, if at least one general partner remains after dissociation, there is no dissolution unless within 90 days after the dissociation partners owning a majority of the rights to receive distributions consent to dissolution. If no general partner remains after the dissociation, dissolution occurs after 90 days unless the limited partners consent to continue and admit at least one new general partner.

E. NATURE OF PARTNER'S CONTRIBUTION

1. In General

A partner's contribution to the partnership may be in cash, property, or services, or a promise to contribute such in the future.

2. Liability for Unpaid Contribution

A partner is obligated to make any promised contribution even if she is unable to perform because of death, disability, or other reason. If a partner does not make a promised contribution of property or services, she is liable to the partnership for its cash equivalent. Note that a ***limited partner's*** promise to contribute is not enforceable unless it is in a writing and signed by him.

3. Compromise of Liability

A partner's contribution obligation may be compromised by the consent of ***all*** of the partners. Even when there has been a compromise, it does not affect a partnership creditor who extends credit after the partner signs a written promise to contribute and before an amendment of the writing to reflect the compromise.

4. Liability for Return of Contribution

Generally, a partner may not receive the return of any part of her capital contribution unless there are sufficient partnership assets to pay liabilities (excluding liability for partners' interests). Otherwise, the receiving partner may be liable for the returned contribution for one year thereafter for the discharge of prereturn creditors. A partner remains liable to the partnership for a ***wrongful return*** for six years under the RULPA and for two years under the ULPA.

F. RIGHTS AND LIABILITIES OF PARTNERS

1. Rights of General and Limited Partners

a. Right to Share in Profits and Losses

A partner's share of the profits and losses is determined by the partnership agreement; if the agreement is silent, profits and losses are allocated on the ***basis of the value of each partner's contributions***.

b. Right to Distributions

Absent a provision in the partnership agreement, distributions are made on the basis of the value of the partner's contributions. A partner obtains ***creditor status*** when she becomes entitled to a distribution and is thus entitled to any nonpartner creditor remedy. The partnership may not pay a distribution unless it is solvent—*i.e.,* its assets are sufficient to satisfy all partnership liabilities (other than those reflecting the partners' interests).

(1) ULPA View

Under the ULPA, a distribution by a limited partnership must be shared among the partners on the basis of the value of the contributions the limited partnership has received from each partner. A partner has no right to any distribution (i) before the dissolution and winding up of the limited partnership ***unless the partnership decides to make an interim distribution***, or (ii) upon dissociation.

c. Other Rights

A partner has the right to ***transact business with the partnership***, ***assign*** his partnership interest, and ***withdraw*** (or dissociate, under the ULPA) from the partnership. Upon withdrawal, a partner has the right to receive in cash any ***distribution*** provided for in the partnership agreement. If there is no such provision, he is entitled to receive the value of his interest as of the date of withdrawal, based on his right to share in partnership distributions. Property in kind may be returned but the withdrawing partner cannot be forced to accept an asset that exceeds the value of his share of the distributions.

2. Rights Specific to General Partners

Except as provided by statute or in the partnership agreement, a RULPA ***"catch-all" provision*** grants a general partner all of the rights and powers of a partner in a general partnership, the most important of which is the right to manage the limited partnership. A general partner's ***right to compensation*** is governed by the RUPA because the RULPA does not address the issue, and under the RUPA, a partner is not entitled to compensation for services rendered absent an agreement to the contrary.

a. Rights of General Partners Under ULPA

Under the ULPA, general partners have explicit ***rights to information*** without having any particular purpose for seeking the information. General partners have the right to maintain a ***derivative action to enforce the partnership's rights*** if the person first makes a demand on the general partners requesting to bring an action to enforce the right and the general partners do not do so within a reasonable time, or if a demand would be futile.

3. Rights Specific to Limited Partners

A limited partner has the right to ***bring a derivative action*** to enforce the partnership's rights when the general partners refuse to do so. The limited partner must have been a limited partner when the complained-of transaction occurred (or must have so devolved from a limited partner). Each limited partner has the ***right to information***, which includes the right to inspect and copy any partnership records required to be maintained, and to obtain from a general partner, upon demand, full information regarding the state and financial condition of the business, income tax returns, etc.

a. Right to Vote

The RULPA provides that a limited partner who participates in control of the limited partnership can be held personally liable as a general partner for the partnership's obligations. However, the RULPA allows limited partners to vote on certain issues (generally regarding fundamental changes in the partnership) without being deemed to have participated in control of the business. Similarly, the ULPA specifically gives limited partners the right to be asked for consent to undertake fundamental changes, *e.g.*, the admission of a new partner or the amendment of the partnership agreement.

4. Liabilities of General Partners

A general partner has all of the liabilities of a partner in a general partnership, thus being ***personally*** liable for the limited partnership's debts.

5. Liabilities of Limited Partners

Generally, a limited partner is not liable for partnership debts beyond her contribution. Under the RULPA four ***exceptions*** exist: (i) the limited partner ***signs the partnership certificate knowing*** of a falsity; (ii) the limited partner ***knowingly permits her name to be used*** in the partnership's name; (iii) the limited partner ***is also a general partner***; and (iv) the limited partner ***participates in control*** of the business.

a. Participates in Control

A limited partner is liable as a general partner if she participates in control of the business and ***the person dealing*** with the limited partnership ***reasonably believes***, based on the partner's conduct, that she is a general partner. A number of states retain the pre-1985 RULPA amendment rule that the creditor must have had ***actual knowledge*** of the limited partner's controlling acts regardless of whether the creditor reasonably believed the limited partner was a general partner.

(1) "Safe Harbors"

The RULPA lists certain activities that are not considered "participation in control of the business," *e.g.,* being an employee, agent, or independent contractor for the partnership; acting as surety for the partnership.

(2) ULPA—No Similar Rule

The ULPA does away with this so-called control rule and provides a ***full liability shield for limited partners***. Thus, an obligation of the limited partnership, whether arising in contract, tort, or otherwise, does not become the obligation of a limited partner, ***even if the limited partner participates in the management and control of the limited partnership***.

G. RIGHTS OF ONE ERRONEOUSLY BELIEVING HERSELF TO BE A LIMITED PARTNER

1. General Rule—Not Liable as General Partner

A contributor to a business enterprise who, in good faith, erroneously believes that she is a limited partner can avoid liability as a general partner if, upon discovering the mistake, she: (i) causes an ***appropriate certificate of limited partnership*** (or amendment) to be filed with the secretary of state; or (ii) ***withdraws from future equity participation*** in the enterprise by filing a certificate of withdrawal with the secretary of state.

2. Exception

A person who erroneously believes herself to be a limited partner will be liable as a general partner to third parties who reasonably believe her to be a general partner ***and*** transact business with the enterprise before she withdraws or before her true status is reflected in the certificate.

H. DISSOLUTION AND DISTRIBUTION

1. Methods of Dissolution

a. Nonjudicial Dissolution

A limited partnership will be dissolved whenever any of the following occurs: (i) the occurrence of the ***time for or events of dissolution*** specified in the certificate of limited partnership; (ii) ***all of the partners consent in writing***; or (iii) ***a general partner withdraws or dissociates***, no provision is made for continuation, and the partners do not consent to continue.

b. Judicial Dissolution

Any partner can seek judicial dissolution whenever it is not reasonably practicable to carry on the business in conformity with the partnership agreement. It is most commonly granted because of a general partner's misconduct.

2. Winding Up Partnership Affairs

The winding up process is similar to that of a general partnership. Any general partner who has not wrongfully dissolved the partnership can wind up. If no such partner is available, the limited partners may wind up or, upon a partner's application, the court may wind up.

3. Distribution of Assets

Assets are distributed in the following order:

(i) ***To creditors, including general and limited partners who are creditors*** (excepting interim distributions and distributions to partners on withdrawal);

(ii) Except as provided in the partnership agreement, ***to general and limited partners and former partners in satisfaction*** of liabilities for interim distributions and to former partners to satisfy withdrawal distributions owed to them; and

(iii) Except as provided in the partnership agreement, ***to general and limited partners first for the return of their contributions and second for partnership profits and property***, in the proportions that distributions are shared.

a. ULPA

Under the ULPA, the assets of the limited partnership must be applied to satisfy the limited partnership's obligations ***to creditors, including partners who are creditors***. Any surplus remaining after the obligations are paid will be paid ***to the partners as a distribution***. If a limited partnership's assets are insufficient to satisfy all of its obligations, each person who was a general partner when the obligation was incurred must contribute to satisfy the debt.

4. Cancellation of Certificate

Upon completion of dissolution and winding up, a certificate of cancellation must be filed with the secretary of state.

I. CONVERSIONS AND MERGERS UNDER ULPA

1. Conversions

An organization other than a limited partnership may convert to a limited partnership, and a limited partnership may convert to another organization. A conversion involves only ***one entity*** and must be consented to by all of the partners.

2. Mergers

A merger involves at least ***two separate entities***. When a merger becomes effective, the surviving organization continues or comes into existence and each constituent organization that merges into the surviving organization ceases to exist as a separate entity. A merger requires the consent of the partners.

J. FOREIGN LIMITED PARTNERSHIPS

A foreign limited partnership may register with the secretary of state to do business in the state. The state of organization governs the internal organization of the partnership. Absent registration, the partnership cannot maintain a court action, but can defend an action filed against it.

PART THREE: LIMITED LIABILITY COMPANIES

XIII. LIMITED LIABILITY COMPANIES

A. INTRODUCTION

1. History

Wyoming was the first state to enact legislation permitting the formation of limited liability companies ("LLCs"). Since then, every state has adopted an LLC statute. There is much variance among the states' laws regarding LLCs. A growing number of states have adopted the Revised Uniform Limited Liability Company Act ("RULLCA"). The major highlights of the state statutes and the RULLCA will be discussed in this Summary.

2. Main Features

An LLC provides its owners (called "members") with: (i) the ***limited liability enjoyed by corporate shareholders***, and (ii) the ***tax advantages that partners enjoy***.

3. Controlling Law—Statute vs. Operating Agreement

Generally, members can adopt an ***operating agreement*** with provisions different from the LLC statute, with the agreement usually controlling. A majority of states require the agreement to be in writing.

B. FORMATION

1. Filing Articles

Articles of organization (or under the RULLCA, certificate of organization) must be filed with the secretary of state. Many states and the RULLCA permit an LLC to have ***one or more members***; some states require at least two members. Articles of organization may be required to include such information as the name of the LLC (including an indication that it is an LLC); the street address of its registered office; the specified term of the LLC, if any; a statement that management is vested in managers if that is to be the case; whether any member(s) are to be liable for all or certain LLC debts; and any other provisions that the members elect to include. (Under the RULLCA, a certificate of organization need include only the name of the LLC and its address and the name and address of its registered agent.)

2. Capital Contributions

All states allow members' contributions to be in cash, property, or services already performed. Many states also permit promissory notes and other binding obligations as contributions.

C. BASIC CHARACTERISTICS OF AN LLC

1. Distinct Legal Entity

An LLC is an entity distinct from its members and can hold property in its own name, sue or be sued, etc. Unless the articles provide otherwise, an LLC generally has the same ***power to carry out its business affairs*** as a corporation.

2. Taxation

An LLC is automatically taxed as a ***partnership*** unless it makes an election to be taxed as a corporation. However, treasury regulations do not allow partnership tax treatment for a single-member LLC; rather, it will be treated as a sole proprietorship.

3. Fiduciary Duties

Most statutes provide that members owe duties of loyalty and care to each other. In some states, the duty of care is to refrain from grossly negligent or reckless conduct, intentional misconduct, or knowing violation of law. Under the RULLCA, members owe each other the duty of ordinary care and have the benefit of the business judgment rule (*i.e.,* they cannot be liable for making good faith business decisions that turn out poorly). Some state statutes provide that the duties of loyalty and care may not be eliminated in the operating agreement, but allow the agreement to prescribe reasonable standards for measuring performance. The RULLCA allows the operating agreement to eliminate these duties (but may not authorize intentional misconduct or knowing violations of law).

4. Distributions

Under most statutes, unless the articles or an operating agreement provides otherwise, distributions of an LLC are allocated to the members ***on the basis of the value of the members' contributions***. The RULLCA provide that distributions are to be ***shared equally*** by members.

a. Profits and Losses

Statutes generally provide that profits and losses of an LLC are allocated among members in the same way as distributions. The RULLCA is silent on the allocation of profits and losses.

5. Management

An LLC can be managed by members or management may be centralized in one or more managers, as in a corporation. If members are managing, each member is an ***agent*** of the LLC and has the power to bind the LLC. If management is by managers, only the managers are agents of the LLC and have the power to bind the LLC.

a. Voting

In manager-managed LLCs, a ***majority vote*** of the managers is usually required to approve most decisions. In member-managed LLCs, all members have a right to participate in management decisions, but the members' voting strength generally follows how profits and losses are shared.

6. Limited Liability

Similar to shareholders and directors of a corporation, LLC members and managers are not personally liable for the LLC's obligations unless they have contracted to become personally liable. They are, however, liable for their own torts.

a. Exception—Piercing the Veil

Courts will "pierce the veil" of an LLC and impose personal liability on its members to prevent fraud or other inequity (*e.g.,* when an LLC is formed to avoid existing personal obligations of the members; but failure to observe corporate formalities is not a ground because LLCs can be run with fewer formalities than a corporation).

7. Transfer of Ownership

A member may assign, in whole or in part, his interest in the LLC. An assignment only transfers the member's ***right to receive distributions***. An assignee can become a member only with the consent of ***all*** members.

8. Information Rights

Each state statute grants members certain access to the LLCs books and records. Generally, each member of an LLC is entitled to inspect and copy the books and records of the LLC during regular business hours.

9. Derivative Action

Most state statutes and the RULLCA permit members to bring derivative actions on the LLC's behalf based on a breach of fiduciary duties. A member may bring a derivative action if she first makes a demand on the controlling members or managers to enforce the right and they do not bring an action within a reasonable time, unless demand would be futile.

10. Withdrawal of Members

Generally, the events that will cause dissociation of a partner in a partnership will also cause dissociation of a member of an LLC. Under most statutes and the RULLCA, a member has the power to dissociate as a member of an LLC at any time by expressing the will to withdraw, although a wrongfully dissociating member may be liable to the LLC for damages.

a. Obligation to Buy out Interest

Following the rule for general partnerships, some statutes provide that an LLC is obligated to buy out the interest of a dissociating member. To provide LLCs with greater stability, the RULLCA has declined to impose such an obligation.

11. Events Causing Dissolution

The events giving rise to dissolution vary widely among the states. Under the RULLCA, an LLC will be dissolved upon: (i) the occurrence of an event or circumstance that the operating agreement states causes dissolution; (ii) the consent of all the members; (iii) the passage of 90 consecutive days during which the LLC has no members; or (iv) a judicial decree or administrative order dissolving the LLC.

a. Grounds for Judicial Dissolution

The grounds for judicial dissolution vary by state. The RULLCA provides that an LLC may be dissolved by a court upon application by a member when: (i) the conduct of all or substantially all of the LLC's activities is unlawful; (ii) it is not reasonably practicable to carry on the company's activities in conformity with the certificate of organization and the operating agreement; or (iii) the managers or controlling members have acted, are acting, or will act in a manner that is illegal or fraudulent, or have acted or are acting in a manner that is oppressive and directly harmful to the member applying for dissolution.

Gilbert Exam Strategies

A. AGENCY

Agency problems concern the liability of one person (the purported principal) for the acts of another (the purported agent) allegedly done on the principal's behalf. Generally, the issue is liability to a third party, but rights and liabilities between the principal and agent may also be involved.

When analyzing agency problems, the following approach may be helpful:

1. Are There Problems Between the Principal and Agent?

Determine first that an ***agency relationship in fact exists*** (*i.e.*, look to see if there is consent and capacity of the parties, a writing if required by the Statute of Frauds or an equal dignity statute, and a proper agency purpose). If so, consider:

a. Has the ***agent breached*** any duty owed to the principal—*e.g.,* improper performance, breach of fiduciary duty, breach by subagent?

b. Is the principal entitled to any ***property or benefits*** acquired by the agent during the relationship (patents, inventions, etc.)?

c. Can the ***principal*** obtain ***indemnification*** from the agent when she is liable to a third party (*see* below)?

d. Has the ***principal breached*** any duty owed to the agent—*e.g.,* compensation, cooperation, etc.?

e. Can the ***agent*** obtain ***indemnification*** from the principal for losses or damages sustained in performing for the principal?

2. Is the Principal (and/or Agent) Contractually Liable to a Third Party Based on the Agent's Acts?

This is the most frequent type of agency problem, and requires analysis of several factors:

a. Does the agent have the ***power*** to bind the principal?

b. If so, what is the ***source*** of the agent's power?

(1) Look for ***actual authority***: Has there been a ***manifestation of consent*** (express or implied) ***from the principal to the agent*** that the agent should act for the principal?

(2) If there is no actual authority, is there ***apparent or ostensible authority***; *i.e.*, has the ***principal manifested to a third party*** that the agent has authority to act on the principal's behalf?

(3) If there is no actual or apparent authority, did the principal (i) ***intentionally or carelessly cause a third party to believe that the agent had authority*** to act on the principal's behalf; or (ii) ***fail to take reasonable steps*** to notify the third party who detrimentally relies on the appearance of authority, such that the principal is ***estopped*** from denying the agent's authority?

c. If the agent had authority, was it ***terminated***—*e.g.*, by expiration of the agency term, death or incapacity of the principal or agent, etc.? If so, is ***notice*** of the termination required to be given to third parties?

d. Even if the agent had no original authority to act, has there been a subsequent ***ratification*** of his act by the principal? Consider whether the act is capable of ratification, and whether the ratification is effective to establish liability (*i.e.*, consider the "relation back" theory, no partial ratification, etc.).

e. What is the ***nature of liability*** on the contract?

(1) If the agent acted ***without authority*** (so the agent alone is ordinarily liable), is the agent liable for breach of warranty and/or on the contract itself? Can a third party recover against the principal in quasi-contract?

(2) If the agent acted ***with authority***, was the principal named in the contract?

(a) If there is a ***"disclosed" principal***, are ***both*** the agent and principal liable on the contract? Is extrinsic evidence admissible to establish the intent of the parties?

(b) If there is an ***"undisclosed" principal***, are ***both*** the agent and principal liable on the contract? Can the principal and/or agent enforce the contract against the third party? Can the third party insist on personal performance by the agent?

(c) If there is an ***"unidentified" principal***, are ***both*** the agent and principal liable on the contract? Is extrinsic evidence admissible to establish the intent of the parties?

3. Is There an Issue of Tort Liability to a Third Party Because of the Acts of Another?

Distinguish tortious acts generally (where an employer-employee relation is usually required to impose liability) from misrepresentations (usually made by an agent, rather than an employee).

a. For tortious acts ***other than misrepresentations,*** consider:

(1) Is there an employer-employee relationship between the actor and the employer—*i.e.*, does the employer have the ***right to control*** the physical acts of the employee? Consider whether actor is an independent contractor.

Also note possible liability for acts of subservants or "borrowed employees"; and possible liability even when the employer has ***no*** right to control (*e.g.*, highly dangerous acts).

(2) Was the tortious act within the ***course and scope of the employee's employment***? Consider the various relevant factors—*e.g.*, authorization by employer, motivation (including "mixed motive" acts), "fellow servant rule," liability ***apart from*** respondeat superior (common carriers, independent duty to third party, etc.).

b. For ***misrepresentations by an agent***, consider:

(1) Was the misrepresentation ***tortious***—*i.e.*, are the requisite elements of scienter, reliance, etc., present?

(2) If so, was the agent ***actually (expressly or impliedly) or apparently authorized*** to make representations?

TEMPLATES FOR THREE LIKELY AGENCY EXAM ISSUES:

I. Liability of Principal to Third Parties for *Torts* of an Agent

II. Liability of Principal to Third Parties for *Contracts* Entered into by an Agent

III. Duties Which Agents Owe to Principals

I. LIABILITY OF PRINCIPAL FOR TORTS OF AGENT—RESPONDEAT SUPERIOR OR VICARIOUS LIABILITY

A. Issue: Whether the principal will be vicariously liable for torts committed by its agent.

B. Two-Part Test: Principal will be liable for torts committed by its agent if:

(1) there is a principal-agent relationship and

(2) the tort was committed by the agent within the SCOPE of that relationship.

1. **The Principal-Agent Relationship**

a. **Principal-agent relationship requires:**

ASSENT (an informal agreement between the principal and the agent), BENEFIT (the agent's conduct is for the principal's benefit), AND CONTROL (the principal has the RIGHT to control the agent by having the power to supervise the manner of its performance)

b. **Contrast Agents with Independent Contractors**

1) The key distinction between an agent and an independent contractor is:

<u>CONTROL: POWER TO SUPERVISE THE MANNER OF PERFORMANCE</u>

2) Vicarious liability rule for independent contractor torts:

<u>THERE IS NO VICARIOUS LIABILITY FOR TORTS OF AN INDEPENDENT CONTRACTOR</u>

3) Exceptions:

a) <u>ULTRAHAZARDOUS ACTIVITIES, AND</u>

b) <u>ESTOPPEL</u>

4) **<u>Exam Hypo:</u>** Tory Victus went to "E-Stop-L Chimney Repair and Demolition" to have her chimney replaced. E-Stop-L had an independent contractor arrangement with its Chimney Demolition Expert. The Demolition Expert, while wearing an E-Stop-L uniform, tortiously demolished Tory's chimney, resulting in serious injuries to Tory. Is E-Stop-L liable?

<u>YES, ALTHOUGH AS A RULE THERE IS NO VICARIOUS LIABILITY FOR THE TORTS OF AN INDEPENDENT CONTRACTOR, BOTH EXCEPTIONS ARE PRESENT HERE: DEMOLITION IS ULTRA-HAZARDOUS AND E-STOP-L IS ESTOPPED FROM DENYING VICARIOUS LIABILITY BECAUSE IT HELD OUT ITS EXPERT AS ITS AGENT BY GIVING THE EXPERT ITS UNIFORM</u>

2. **Scope of Principal-Agent Relationship Factors**

a. Was conduct "of the kind" agent was hired to perform?

b. Did the tort occur "on the job"? Frolic v. Detour:

FROLIC—A NEW AND INDEPENDENT JOURNEY

DETOUR—A MERE DEPARTURE

c. Did the agent intend to benefit the principal?

Exam Hypo: Employer instructs Employee to drive across town to deliver files to a branch office. On the way back, Employee stops to pick up shirts at the dry cleaner for work the next day. In the parking lot of the dry cleaner, Employee hits a pedestrian. Is Employer liable?

YES. THE PRINCIPAL IS LIABLE FOR ITS AGENT'S TORTS IN THE SCOPE OF EMPLOYMENT. IN THIS CASE, THE EMPLOYEE WAS ON A DETOUR BECAUSE THE TORT HAPPENED ON THE WAY BACK TO WORK. THEREFORE, THERE IS VICARIOUS LIABILITY.

3. **Intentional Torts**

a. Rule:

INTENTIONAL TORTS ARE GENERALLY OUTSIDE THE SCOPE

b. Exceptions: Intentional torts are within the scope if the conduct was:

1) AUTHORIZED BY THE PRINCIPAL or

2) NATURAL FROM THE NATURE OF EMPLOYMENT or

3) MOTIVATED TO BENEFIT THE PRINCIPAL

II. LIABILITY OF PRINCIPAL FOR CONTRACTS ENTERED BY AGENTS

A. Issue: Whether the principal is liable for contracts entered into by its agent

B. One Test: Principal is liable for contracts entered into by its agent only if the principal **authorized** the agent to enter the contract.

C. There are four types of **authority**: actual express, actual implied, apparent, and ratification.

1. **Actual Express Authority**: Principal used words to express authority to agent. It can be ORAL except for CONTRACTS INVOLVING THE CONVEYANCE OF LAND

2. **Actual Implied Authority**: Authority which the principal gives the agent through conduct or circumstance, including

NECESSITY, CUSTOM, OR PRIOR DEALINGS.

3. **Apparent Authority**: Two-Part Test: (i) Principal "cloaked" agent with the appearance of authority, and (ii) third party reasonably relies on appearance of authority.

Exam Hypo: Charles owns an antique store. A shipment of antique clocks arrives from London. Charles tells his employee Dufus not to sell a special grandfather clock. Charles goes to lunch. Dufus sells the clock. Is Charles bound on the sales contract?

YES. PRINCIPAL IS LIABLE FOR THE AGENT'S AUTHORIZED CONTRACTS. IN THIS CASE, THERE WAS NO ACTUAL OR IMPLIED AUTHORITY. NONETHELESS, CHARLES IS LIABLE BASED ON

APPARENT AUTHORITY BECAUSE HE CLOAKED DUFUS AND THE BUYER MAY REASONABLY RELY.

4. **Ratification:** Authority can be granted after the contract has been entered, if:

   a. Principal has knowledge of all material facts regarding the contract, and

   b. Principal accepts its benefits.

   c. Exception: Ratification cannot alter the terms of the contract.

   Exam Hypo: Priscilla gives Agnes a power of attorney only to purchase steel drums. Agnes enters a contract to purchase 11,000 wooden barrels. Priscilla tells Agnes, "Great job! I love wooden barrels, but I only need 10,000." Is Priscilla bound?

   NO. THE PRINCIPAL IS LIABLE ONLY ON ITS AUTHORIZED CONTRACTS. THERE WAS NO EXPRESS, IMPLIED, OR APPARENT AUTHORITY TO BUY WOODEN BARRELS, ONLY STEEL DRUMS. NONETHELESS, PRISCILLA ARGUABLY RATIFIED THE CONTRACT TO PURCHASE WOODEN BARRELS THROUGH KNOWLEDGE AND ACCEPTANCE OF ITS BENEFITS. BUT, RATIFICATION HERE WAS NOT VALID BECAUSE PRISCILLA TRIED TO ALTER THE CONTRACT'S TERMS.

D. The Rules of Liability on the Contract

1. **General Rule**: The principal is liable on its authorized contracts, and therefore as a rule: THE AGENT IS NOT LIABLE ON ITS AUTHORIZED CONTRACTS

2. **Exception**: The undisclosed principal—If principal is partially disclosed (only the identity of the principal concealed) or undisclosed (fact of principal concealed), authorized agent may nonetheless be liable at the election of the third party.

III. DUTIES AGENT OWES TO PRINCIPAL

A. In return for reasonable compensation and reimbursement of expenses, agents owe principal the duty of **care, obedience**, and

LOYALTY

The agent may never do any of the following:

a. Self-dealing: Agent cannot receive a benefit to the detriment of the principal,

b. Usurping the principal's opportunity, or

c. Secret profits: making a profit at the principal's expense without disclosure.

B. **Exam Hypo:** Priscilla authorizes Agnes to buy diamonds. Agnes spots choice diamonds and secretly buys them for herself for $1 million. Agnes then resells the diamonds for $2 million.

1. What duties, if any, has Agnes breached?

   LOYALTY BY SELF DEALING, USURPING, AND SECRET PROFITING

2. What remedies, if any, does Priscilla have against Agnes?

   LOSSES CAUSED BY THE BREACH AND INDEMNITY, PLUS DISGORGING PROFITS

B. PARTNERSHIP

Partnership problems may involve the effect of the partnership relation itself, the effect of a dissolution of the partnership, or the effect of a partner's dissociation from the partnership under the Revised Uniform Partnership Act ("RUPA").

1. If the Effect of the Partnership Relation Is an Issue, Consider:

a. ***Is there a partnership***—*i.e.,* an "association to carry on as co-owners a business for profit"? Remember that intent is *not* necessary. Note whether the partnership agreement must be in writing, whether all purported partners have the capacity to be partners, and whether there are sufficient indicia of partnership status (*i.e.,* joint ownership of property, sharing of profits, etc.).

   (1) If there is no partnership by agreement, is there one ***by estoppel***?

b. If a partnership exists, are any of its ***general characteristics*** relevant to the facts at hand?

   (1) ***Aggregate characteristics***—joint and several liability, taxing of income?

   (2) ***Entity characteristics***—capacity to sue or be sued, conveyance of property, bankruptcy?

c. Is there an issue concerning relations ***between the partners***? Consider:

   (1) Has there been a ***breach of duty*** (*i.e.,* fiduciary obligations, management and inspection rights, etc.) by any partner?

   (2) If so, ***what remedies*** are available to the injured partner(s)? Dissolution? Accounting? Action at law?

d. Is there an issue regarding ***liability to third persons*** (creditors)? Recall that partners function as agents for the partnership, and consider:

   (1) Did the partner(s) have ***authority*** to bind the partnership (*i.e.,* any limitations on, or termination of, authority)?

   (2) Is ***contract*** liability involved so partners are jointly and severally liable under the RUPA and jointly but not severally liable under the UPA?

   (3) Is ***tort*** liability at issue so partners are jointly ***and*** severally liable under both the RUPA and UPA?

   (4) Did the partners form a limited liability partnership so that the partners are ***not personally*** liable for all of the partnership's debts and obligations?

e. Is there an issue concerning the ***partnership property or partners' property rights***? Consider:

   (1) Is the property in question ***partnership property***? If so, what are the partners' rights in the property?

   (2) If a partner has an interest in the partnership, of what does that interest consist?

      (a) Can a partner assign his interest?

      (b) If so, what are the rights of the assigning partner and the assignee?

2. If the Partnership Is Formed Under the RUPA, and the Effect of a Partner's Dissociation Is an Issue, Consider:

a. Is a ***cause*** for the partner's dissociation shown—*i.e.*, partner provides the partnership with notice to withdraw, partner expelled per partnership agreement, etc.?

b. If a partner is dissociated, what is the ***effect of the dissociation*** on that partner and the partnership? Consider:

(1) Has an event occurred that requires the ***dissolution and winding up*** of the partnership (*e.g.*, receipt by partnership at will of partner's notice to withdraw, event making it unlawful to carry on the partnership business)?

(2) If not, what are the rights and liabilities of the ***dissociated partner*** after her dissociation?

3. If the Effect of a Dissolution of Partnership Is an Issue, Consider:

a. Is a ***cause for dissolution*** shown—*i.e.,* expiration of partnership term, at the will of partner (at any time), etc.? If there is an attempted judicial dissolution, are proper grounds shown?

b. If the partnership is dissolved, what are the ***partners' rights***? Distinguish rights where there is no violation of the partnership agreement from rights where the agreement is violated. If relevant, what are the rights and obligations of the surviving partner(s) regarding a deceased partner's estate?

c. If there is a dissolution, what is the ***effect on creditors*** of the partnership? Note liability for existing debts (not discharged without novation), and liability of partners who continue the business.

d. If there is a ***winding up*** of the partnership, who may wind up? What transactions may be entered into by those entitled to wind up?

e. If ***assets are available after the partnership is dissolved,*** to whom are they distributed and in what order?

4. If the Partnership Is Possibly a Limited Partnership, Consider:

a. Has a limited partnership been ***properly formed***—*i.e.*, has a certificate of limited partnership been filed?

b. Does the ***name*** of the partnership comply with statutory provisions?

c. Has there been a ***change in partnership membership***? Consider:

(1) Have ***all*** partners consented to the admission of any new partners?

(2) If a partner has ***assigned his interest*** in the partnership, what are the rights of the assigning partner and the assignee?

(3) If a general or limited partner has ***withdrawn*** from the partnership, what effect does the withdrawal have on the partnership?

d. What are the rights and liabilities of the ***general and limited partners***? Did a limited partner do anything to lose her limited liability, *e.g.*, permit her name to be used improperly in the name of the partnership, or participate in control of the business?

e. Has an event occurred that requires the partnership to be ***dissolved and wound up***? If so, may ***both*** the general and limited partners wind up?

f. If ***assets are available after the partnership is dissolved***, to whom are they distributed and in what order?

C. LIMITED LIABILITY COMPANIES

Limited liability company ("LLC") problems may concern the formation of the LLC or any of the basic characteristics of the LLC.

1. **If Formation Is an Issue, Consider:**

   a. Has the ***appropriate filing*** been made—*i.e.,* have articles of organization been filed?

   b. If so, do the articles contain the information ***required by statute***?

2. **If the Basic Characteristics of the LLC Are in Issue, Consider:**

   a. How will the LLC be ***taxed***?

   b. How will LLC ***profits and losses*** be shared?

   c. Is management vested in the members or in managers? Distinguish the voting of ***manager-managed*** LLCs and ***member-managed*** LLCs.

   d. What are the ***liabilities*** of the members and/or managers for LLC obligations?

   e. Can a member ***transfer*** his interest in the LLC?

   f. What events will cause an LLC to ***dissolve***?

TEMPLATES FOR FIVE LIKELY PARTNERSHIP EXAM ISSUES

I. General Partnership Formation

II. Liabilities of General Partners to Third Parties

III. Rights and Liabilities Between General Partners

IV. General Partnership Dissolution

V. Alternative Unincorporated Business Organizations

I. GENERAL PARTNERSHIP FORMATION

A. Formalities

GENERALLY, THERE ARE NO FORMALITIES TO BEING A GENERAL PARTNERSHIP (UNIQUE AMONG BUSINESS ORGANIZATIONS).

B. Definition

ASSOCIATION OF TWO OR MORE PERSONS WHO ARE CARRYING ON AS CO-OWNERS OF A BUSINESS FOR PROFIT.

C. Sharing of Profits is the Key Factor. Therefore:

PARTNERS CONTRIBUTE MONEY OR SERVICES FOR A SHARE OF PROFITS, IF ANY. THE CONTRIBUTION OF MONEY OR SERVICES IN RETURN FOR A SHARE OF THE PROFITS, IF ANY, CREATES A **PRESUMPTION** THAT A GENERAL PARTNERSHIP EXISTS.

II. LIABILITIES OF GENERAL PARTNERS TO THIRD PARTIES

A. Agency Principles Apply

   1. Partners are agents of the partnership for apparently carrying on usual partnership business.

   2. Therefore, the general partnership is liable for each partner's torts in the scope of partnership business and for each partner's authorized contracts.

B. Each General Partner Is Personally Liable for All Debts of the Partnership and for: EACH CO-PARTNER'S TORTS

1. Incoming partner's liability for pre-existing debts

   NO DIRECT PERSONAL LIABILITY. BUT CAPITAL CONTRIBUTED CAN BE USED FOR THAT PURPOSE.

2. Dissociating (withdrawing) partner's liability for subsequent debts

   PARTNER RETAINS LIABILITY UNTIL ACTUAL NOTICE OF DISSOCIATION IS GIVEN TO CREDITOR, OR UNTIL 90 DAYS AFTER FILING "NOTICE OF DISSOCIATION" WITH STATE.

C. General Partnership Liability by Estoppel: One who represents to a third party that a general partnership exists will be liable as if a general partnership exists.

III. RIGHTS AND LIABILITIES BETWEEN GENERAL PARTNERS

A. General Partners are **Fiduciaries** of Each Other and the Partnership.

1. Therefore, general partners owe to each other and the partnership:

   THE DUTY OF LOYALTY which means that general partners may never engage in SELF-DEALING BY RECEIVING A BENEFIT TO THE DETRIMENT OF THE PARTNERSHIP OR A CO-PARTNER;

   may never USURP partnership opportunities;

   and may never make a SECRET, UNDISCLOSED PROFIT AT THE PARTNERSHIP'S EXPENSE.

2. Action for Accounting

   PARTNERSHIP MAY NOW BRING ACTION TO RECOUP LOSSES, OR TO ACCOUNT FOR PROFITS MADE BY BREACHING PARTNER (DISGORGE)

B. **Exam Hypo:** Priscilla and Agnes are partners in a diamond business. Agnes spots choice diamonds and secretly buys them for herself for $1 million. Agnes then resells the diamonds to the partnership for $2 million.

1. What duties, if any, has Agnes breached?

   AGNES HAS BREACHED THE DUTY OF LOYALTY BY: (1) SELF-DEALING because SHE DID BENEFIT HERSELF TO THE PARTNERSHIP'S DETRIMENT (2) USURPING THE PARTNERSHIP'S DIAMONDS, AND (3) MAKING A SECRET PROFIT AT PARTNERSHIP EXPENSE.

2. What remedies, if any, does Priscilla have against Agnes?

   PARTNERSHIP MAY BRING AN ACTION FOR AN ACCOUNTING AND MAY RECOVER: (1) LOSSES CAUSED BY BREACH INCLUDING INDEMNITY, AND (2) DISGORGE PROFITS MADE BY THE BREACHING PARTNER.

C. Partners' Rights in Partnership Property and Liquidity

1. Specific Partnership Assets

   LAND, LEASES, EQUIPMENT, TRUCKS, CARS OWNED ONLY BY PARTNERSHIP, AND CANNOT BE TRANSFERRED BY ANY INDIVIDUAL PARTNER.

2. Share of Profits

   PERSONAL PROPERTY OWNED BY INDIVIDUAL PARTNER, AND CAN BE TRANSFERRED (I.E. INHERITED).

3. Share in Management

<u>NOT PERSONAL PROPERTY, AND CANNOT BE TRANSFERRED. PARTNERSHIP INTEREST IS RELATIVELY ILLIQUID. ONLY PROFITS ARE TRANSFERRABLE, LIQUID, PERSONAL PROPERTY.</u>

4. In order to determine whether the fact pattern involves property owned by the partnership or personal property owned by an individual partner, the test is:

<u>WHOSE MONEY WAS USED TO BUY THE PROPERTY. IF PARTNERSHIP MONEY WAS USED, THE PROPERTY IS PARTNERSHIP PROPERTY. IF PERSONAL FUNDS WERE USED, IT BECOMES PERSONAL PROPERTY.</u>

D. Management: Absent an agreement, each partner is entitled to **EQUAL** control (vote).

<u>Exam Hypo:</u> A, B and C agree to contribute money and share profits 60-30-10. How do they vote?

<u>ABSENT AN AGREEMENT, *EQUAL CONTROL* (ONE PARTNER/ONE VOTE) AND MAJORITY VOTE GOVERNS ORDINARY MATTERS, BUT UNANIMOUS CONSENT IS REQUIRED FOR FUNDAMENTAL PARTNERSHIP MATTERS</u>

E. Salary: Absent an agreement, partners get **NO SALARY**.

<u>Exam Hypo:</u> A and B are partners. A works 96 hours a week. B sleeps all day. Does A get any salary?

<u>NO!</u>

Exception:

<u>COMPENSATION FOR HELPING TO "WIND UP"</u>

F. Partner's Share of Profits and Losses

1. Absent an agreement, **PROFITS ARE SHARED EQUALLY**
2. Absent an agreement, **LOSSES ARE SHARED LIKE PROFITS**

<u>Exam Hypos:</u>

a. If an agreement is silent on profits and losses?

(1) <u>PROFITS ARE SHARED EQUALLY</u>

(2) <u>LOSSES ARE SHARED LIKE PROFITS, WHICH MEANS SHARED EQUALLY AS WELL</u>

b. If an agreement states that "profits are shared 60/40" but is silent on losses. Losses shared?

<u>LOSSES, LIKE PROFITS, ARE SHARED 60/40 AS WELL</u>

c. If agreement states that "losses are shared 60/40" but is silent on profits. Profits shared?

<u>PROFITS ARE SHARED EQUALLY</u>

d. Partner A puts up all of the money. Partner B does all of the work. Partner C gives the partnership its fine name. Partner D does nothing. How are profits shared?

<u>EQUALLY</u>

IV. GENERAL PARTNERSHIP DISSOLUTION

A. Key definitions

1. Dissolution

   <u>IN THE ABSENCE OF AN AGREEMENT THAT SPECIFIES EVENTS OF DISSOLUTION, A GENERAL PARTNERSHIP DISSOLVES UPON NOTICE OF THE EXPRESS WILL OF ANY ONE GENERAL PARTNER TO DISSOCIATE.</u>

2. The Real End of the Partnership Is Called:

   <u>TERMINATION</u>

3. Winding Up

   <u>REMAINING PARTNERS LIQUIDATE THE ASSETS TO SATISFY CREDITORS</u>

B. Partnership's Liability

1. Old business. The partnership and therefore its individual general partners retain liability on:

   <u>ALL TRANSACTIONS ENTERED TO WIND UP OLD BUSINESS BY SATISFYING CREDITORS WHO EXISTED WHEN WINDING UP BEGAN</u>

2. New business. The partnership and therefore its individual general partners retain liability on brand new transactions during winding up until:

   <u>NOTICE OF DISSOLUTION IS GIVEN. BUT LIABILITY TERMINATES 90 DAYS AFTER FILING "STATEMENT OF DISSOLUTION" WITH THE STATE</u>

C. Priority of Distribution

1. Each level of priority must be fully satisfied before beginning the next level. Order of priority:

   a. First, the partnership must pay ALL creditors. Creditors include:

      (1) <u>TRADE CREDITORS AND SUPPLIERS AND (2) PARTNERS WHO LOANED MONEY TO THE PARTNERSHIP</u>

   b. Second, the partnership must repay all capital contributions paid into the partnership by partners.

      <u>MONEY PAID IN BY PARTNERS (NOT LOANS) AND NOT FOR ANY FIXED RATE OF INTEREST, BUT NOW MUST BE REPAID. IT'S A PARTNERSHIP OBLIGATION OR LIABILITY.</u>

   c. Third, profits or losses, if any:

      <u>ANY MONEY REMAINING, IS SHARED EQUALLY AMONG PARTNERS IN THE ABSENCE OF AN AGREEMENT.</u>

2. <u>Rule:</u> Each partner must be repaid his or her loans and capital contributions, plus that partner's share of any profits, or minus that partner's share of any losses.

V. ALTERNATIVE UNINCORPORATED BUSINESS ORGANIZATIONS

A. **Limited Partnerships**

1. Defined: <u>A PARTNERSHIP WITH AT LEAST 1 GENERAL PARTNER AND AT LEAST 1 LIMITED PARTNER. DUAL LIABILITY/LIMITED LIABILITY FORM</u>

2. Formation: LIMITED LIABILITY FORMS MUST FILE WITH THE STATE. A LIMITED PARTNERSHIP MST FILE A "LIMITED PARTNERSHIP CERTIFICATE" THAT INCLUDES THE NAMES OF ALL GENERAL PARTNERS

3. Liability and Control:

   a. General Partners: HAVE GENERAL (SUBSTANTIAL MANAGERIAL) CONTROL, AND GENERAL LIABILITY

   b. Limited Partners: HAVE LIMITED LIABILITY. THEY ARE NOT LIABLE FOR OBLIGATIONS OF THE OTHER PARTNERS OR PARTNERSHIP. UNDER THE NEWEST REVISED UNIFORM LIMITED PARTNERSHIP ACT, THEY MAY MANAGE AND STILL NOT BE LIABLE. BUT IN SOME STATES, A LIMITED PARTNER WHO MANAGES THE BUSINESS BECOMES LIABLE TO THIRD PARTIES WHO REASONABLY BELIEVE THAT THEY WERE GENERAL PARTNERS. THE LIMITED PARTNER IS ESTOPPED FROM DENYING PARTNERSHIP LIABILITY.

B. **Registered Limited Liability Partnerships (RLLP)**

1. Formation: MUST FILE "STATEMENT OF QUALIFICATION" AND ANNUAL REPORTS

2. Liabilities: NO PARTNER IS LIABLE FOR PARTNERSHIP OBLIGATIONS. BUT THEY ARE LIABLE FOR OWN WRONGDOING, OR WRONGDOING OF THOSE UNDER THEIR DIRECT SUPERVISION.

Agency, Partnership and Limited Liability Companies

Eighth Edition

Part One: Agency

Chapter One: Creation of Agency Relationship

CONTENTS	PAGE

Key Exam Issues

This chapter introduces you to the concept of agency, the parties involved, and the creation of the agency relationship.

A basic issue of any exam question involving agency is whether an agency relationship exists. Agency is generally defined as the relationship that arises when one person, the ***principal***, manifests an intention that another person, the ***agent***, shall act on the principal's behalf. The manifestation can occur by ***express or implied agreement*** between the principal and the agent, or after the fact by the principal's ***ratification*** of the agent's act. Even if there is no agreement or ratification, an agency can arise from the principal's conduct toward third parties that causes them to believe that the principal has appointed someone to be his agent (***apparent*** or ***ostensible agency***).

There are a few other requisites for the creation of an agency: The principal must have the ***capacity*** to contract (the agent need not have such capacity), and although ***no consideration*** is required and generally ***no writing*** is required (except where the Statute of Frauds or an equal dignities rule applies), the agency must be formed for a ***legal purpose***.

A. Introduction

1. Scope and Purpose of Agency

Agency is a device that allows one person to appoint another person to act for him in such a way as to effect legal acts and liabilities. While agency is not limited to commercial settings, it is there that agency is most often encountered. Most of the world's business is done by agents—corporate directors, partners, and employees are agents in the broad sense of the word, as are attorneys, factors, and brokers. Regardless of the setting, the law of agency concerns the rights and liabilities created when one person "acts for another." Agency law encompasses several distinct areas: (i) when one person may act for another and to what extent; (ii) the various duties that the parties to the agency relationship owe to each other; (iii) the contractual rights and liabilities of third parties who have dealt with the agent; and (iv) the various circumstances in which one person may be liable in tort for the wrongful acts of another in his employ.

2. Agency Definitions

Often, liability of a party to an agency relationship will depend on the classification assigned to that party. Unfortunately, the courts have not been entirely consistent in their terminology concerning agency. Indeed, a single court decision may use a number of terms to describe the same concept. The Restatements of Agency have been a unifying force in the field, and the Restatement definitions will generally be followed in this Summary.

a. Agency

"Agency" is defined as the fiduciary relationship that results from the mutual manifestation of consent that one person (the ***agent***) shall act on behalf of and subject to the control of another person (the ***principal***). [*See* Restatement (Third) of Agency ("Rest. 3d") § 1.01] However, agency is broader than this simple definition implies. As will be seen (*infra*, p. 29), the "manifestation of consent" standard is ***objective***—it does not matter what the principal truly intended; rather, the agency relationship depends on what the agent believed the principal intended. Thus, an agency relationship can arise even if the principal subjectively intended no such relationship. Moreover, agency power (*i.e.*, an agent's power to bind the principal to a contract with a third party) can arise even absent true mutual consent under the doctrine of apparent or ostensible agency (*see infra*, p. 9).

b. Principal

Certain rights and liabilities under agency law depend on whether a third party knew of a principal's existence and/or identity. To this end, principals are described as follows:

(1) Disclosed Principal

A principal is disclosed if the third party with whom the agent is transacting business knows that the agent is acting for a principal ***and knows the principal's identity.*** [Rest. 3d § 1.04(2)(a)]

(2) Unidentified Principal

A principal is unidentified if the third party with whom the agent is transacting business knows that the agent is acting for a principal but does ***not know the principal's identity***. [Rest. 3d § 1.04(2)(c)]

(3) Undisclosed Principal

A principal is undisclosed if the third party with whom the agent is transacting business does not know that the agent ***is acting for a principal.*** [Rest. 3d§ 1.04(2)(b)]

TYPES OF PRINCIPALS	
DISCLOSED	Third party knows ***existence and identity*** of principal.
UNIDENTIFIED	Third party knows ***existence but not identity*** of principal.
UNDISCLOSED	Third party does ***not know of existence*** of principal.

c. Agent

Certain aspects of agency law depend on the type of agent involved. The Restatement (Second) of Agency ("Rest. 2d") differentiated between general agents and special agents, and courts often use these terms. Types of agents include the following:

(1) General Agent

A general agent is an agent authorized to conduct a ***series of transactions*** involving a ***continuity of service.*** [Rest. 2d § 3(1)]

e.g. **Example:** P is the owner of a grocery store. P hires A to manage the grocery store. A will hire employees, order produce and other merchandise, etc. A is a general agent of P.

(2) Special Agent

A special agent is an agent authorized to conduct only a ***single transaction*** or a series of transactions ***not*** involving a continuity of service. [Rest. 2d § 3(2)]

e.g. **Example:** P is a collector of Chinese art. A 15th century Ming dynasty vase that P has wanted for years has been put up for auction. P and A agree that A will attend the auction and purchase the vase for P's collection. A is a special agent of P.

(3) Factor

A factor is a commercial agent employed by a principal to sell consigned merchandise in the agent's own name on behalf of the principal.

(4) Subagent

Sometimes an agent will appoint another to perform functions undertaken by the agent for the principal. The appointee is a ***subagent*** if the appointing agent acted with the ***authority of the principal*** in making the appointment. The appointment of a subagent involves the delegation of power by the appointing agent; thus, the ***subagent has two principals***—the appointing agent and the principal. The appointing agent is primarily liable for the acts of the subagent, and the principal is secondarily liable. [Rest. 3d §§ 1.04(8), 3.15] *But note:* If the agent is ***not authorized*** to appoint a subagent, but nevertheless appoints a person to perform a function for the principal, the appointee is not a subagent, but rather the agent's agent, and the principal is not liable for the acts of the appointee.

EXAM TIP

Whenever an exam question presents an agent who appoints another to do his work, be sure to check the facts to see if the principal expressly or impliedly authorized the agent to do so. Remember that an agent's appointee is *not a subagent of the principal* (and the principal is not liable for the appointee) *unless* the principal gave the agent the authority to appoint a subagent.

(5) Coagent

Coagents are two or more agents who owe duties to a ***common principal*** but not to each other (unlike the subagent, who owes duties to both the principal and the appointing agent). A coagent may be appointed by the principal or by another agent with authority from the principal. [Rest. 3d § 1.04(1)] If the coagent is directed by another agent, then the directing agent is the ***superior coagent*** and the other agent is the ***subordinate coagent.*** [Rest. 3d § 1.04(9)] Because coagents are not agents of each other, they are not vicariously liable for wrongs committed by the other. [Rest. 3d § 1.04, comment a]

EXAM TIP

Do not confuse a subagent with a coagent. A subagent is appointed by an agent to assist with tasks *that the appointing agent has agreed to perform* for the principal. The appointing agent is primarily liable for the subagent. A coagent is *one of several agents who has agreed to perform tasks for the principal* and for whom the principal is primarily liable (even if he was appointed by another agent).

SUBAGENT VS. COAGENT		
	SUBAGENT	**COAGENT**
APPOINTMENT	By agent with principal's authority	By principal or agent with principal's authority
PRINCIPAL	Two—appointing agent and her principal	One common principal
DUTY OWED TO PRINCIPAL?	Yes	Yes
DUTY OWED TO APPOINTING AGENT?	Yes, acts as agent of appointing agent	No
PRINCIPAL'S LIABILITY	Secondary	Primary
APPOINTING AGENT'S LIABILITY	Primary, if agent acted with authority	None
DELEGATION OF POWER BY APPOINTING AGENT?	Yes	No
EXAMPLE	Principal hires an accounting firm to prepare its tax returns. The firm hires a CPA to prepare the forms. The firm is the agent and the CPA is the subagent.	Manager of a corporation hires subordinate employees. The manager and the employees are coagents of the corporation.

(6) Gratuitous Agent

A gratuitous agent is one who acts ***without compensation.*** [Rest. 3d § 1.04(3)] Examples of gratuitous agents are holders of powers of attorney on behalf of friends or family members or when one person agrees to do some service for another that will affect the other's legal position.

d. Employer-Employee Relationship

The employer-employee relationship (traditionally called a "master-servant" relationship) is a special type of agency relationship in which the principal ("employer" or "master") employs the agent ("employee" or "servant") to perform services and ***retains control*** over the manner in which the employee performs the services. (*See infra*, p. 91 *et seq.*) An employee is to be distinguished from an independent contractor, *i.e.*, a worker over whom the principal retains ***no right of control.***

EXAM TIP

The difference between whether a person is an employee or an independent contractor is significant in determining whether a principal will be liable for the person's tortious conduct. As will be discussed in detail later in this Summary (*infra*, p. 101), the key to determining whether a person is an employee or independent contractor is whether the principal has *control over the person's performance.*

B. Requirements for Agency Relationship

1. In General

The agency relationship is ***consensual***, but not necessarily contractual; therefore, not every contractual formality is required for its creation.

2. Consent

Agency relationships ordinarily arise by prior agreement between the principal and the agent because they are consensual in nature. However, consent also can occur after the fact by ratification, and estoppel can serve as a substitute for consent (*i.e.*, an "apparent" or "ostensible" agency case).

a. Agency by Agreement

An agency by agreement must be based on some indication by the principal to the agent that the principal consents to have the agent act on her behalf. A similar manifestation of consent by the agent to act for the principal must be indicated as well. [**Eitel v. Schmidlapp,** 459 F.2d 609 (4th Cir. 1972)]

(1) Express vs. Implied Consent

The agency agreement may be express or it may be implied from the conduct of the parties (*e.g.*, if Farmer habitually leaves her crops with Produce Broker she has impliedly appointed Produce Broker as her agent for the purpose of selling the crops at the market price).

b. Agency by Ratification

An agency also may be created by ratification. This results whenever the principal ***accepts the benefits*** or otherwise ***affirms the conduct*** of one ***purporting to act on the principal's behalf***, even though there is no agency agreement and no authority was given for the act. Ratification retroactively creates the effects of actual authority. [Rest. 3d §§ 4.01, 4.02]

(1) Objective Determination

Ratification is deemed to supply the consent required for the principal-agent relationship. Thus, to find such consent or affirmance of the agency, there must be some objective evidence that the principal ***knew*** of the act in question. The principal will not be bound if the ratification is made without knowledge of the material facts, although knowledge may be inferred from the facts. Ratification does not apply to future acts. [Rest. 3d § 4.06]

(a) Express vs. Implied Ratification

Of course, an express approval of the transaction is the clearest evidence of consent. However, consent will also be found whenever the principal *accepts the benefits* of the transaction (*e.g.*, by electing to take title to property purchased by an unauthorized agent), or otherwise obtains an advantage from the transaction with knowledge of it.

e.g. **Example:** A, without authority to do so, buys property "on behalf of my employer, P." P discovers what A has done, decides that the purchase is advantageous, and indicates approval. P's conduct constitutes a ratification, and P is bound by the purchase.

(2) No Partial Ratification

A principal cannot ratify the beneficial aspects of an agent's conduct while refusing to affirm the rest. If she ratifies at all, she ratifies the entire transaction. [Rest. 3d § 4.07; **C.Q. Farms, Inc. v. Cargill Inc.,** 363 So. 2d 379 (Fla. 1978)] In other words, ratification is an ***all or nothing*** proposition.

(3) Tort Liability

As discussed *infra* (p. 117), ratification may also expose the principal to ***tort liability*** for the agent's misrepresentations, etc.

c. Apparent Agency

The general rule requires that an agency relationship be based on actual consent between the principal and agent. However, if the principal ***causes a third person to believe*** another to be her agent, and the ***third person so relies*** in dealing with the supposed agent, at least as between the principal and the third person, the court will act as if an agency existed. In such a case, there is an "apparent" agency. [Rest. 3d § 3.03] The acts relied upon to establish the apparent agency must be the acts of the principal and not those of the agent alone. Also, to recover against the principal, the third person's ***reliance must be reasonable.*** [**Adamski v. Tacoma General Hospital,** 579 P.2d 970 (Wash. 1978)]

e.g. **Example:** P operated a hotel and employed one night clerk. Late one evening when the night clerk was away from the hotel desk, a stranger went behind the desk and posed as the clerk. The stranger accepted valuables from a registering guest for placement in the hotel safe. The stranger then absconded with the valuables. The guest sought to hold P liable as the stranger's principal. The court held that P was estopped from denying the stranger's agency because by P's voluntary act or negligence, P placed the stranger in the position where it would appear to P's customers that the stranger was P's agent. [**Kanelles v. Locke,** 12 Ohio App. 210 (1919)]

d. Ostensible Agency

An "ostensible" agency (also called "agency by estoppel") arises if the principal: (i) ***intentionally or carelessly causes a third person to believe*** that the agent has authority; ***or*** (ii) upon notice of such a belief by the third person, ***fails to take reasonable steps*** to notify the third person that the agent does not have authority; ***and*** (iii) the third person makes a ***detrimental change in position*** (*e.g.*, expends money or labor or incurs a loss) based on reliance on the agent's purported authority. [Rest. 3d § 2.05 and comments] (*Note:* Some state statutes use the terms "apparent" and "ostensible" agency synonymously.)

EXAM TIP

Note the distinguishing factor differentiating apparent agency from ostensible agency: In the apparent agency situation, *the principal manifests that the agent has authority.* In the ostensible agency situation, the principal makes no such manifestation, but instead *fails to use reasonable care* in preventing a third party from relying on an agent's erroneous assertion of power or *fails to notify the third person* that the agent has no authority.

3. Capacity

A principal must have the capacity to individually perform the act that he delegates to the agent. This usually requires ***contractual capacity.*** [Rest. 3d § 3.04] On the other hand, ***any person may ordinarily act as an agent*** provided she has the ability to perform the actions. Minimal mental capacity is sufficient; contractual capacity is not required. [Rest. 3d § 3.05]

a. Minors

Because a minor generally does not have the capacity to contract, she cannot validly appoint another as her agent, except to the limited extent of contracting for her necessities of life. [**Casey v. Kastel,** 237 N.Y. 305 (1924)] However, a minor can be appointed as another's agent.

b. Incompetent Persons

Similarly, a person who is legally incompetent does not have the capacity to contract and cannot appoint an agent. However, it is possible that if the incompetent person is in fact capable of performing the necessary agency functions, he might be appointed as the agent of another.

EXAM TIP

Notice the different capacity requirements: A *principal* must have *contractual capacity* but an *agent need not.* Remember that whenever an exam question involves a minor or incompetent person, that person generally may be an agent but cannot be a principal.

4. No Consideration

No consideration is necessary for either party to create an agency relationship. [**Groh v. Shelton,** 428 S.W.2d 911 (Mo. 1968)] Thus, a person may act as an agent without receiving any compensation or other benefit.

5. General Rule—No Writing Required

Ordinarily, no writing is required to create an agency relationship. Hence the principal-agent relationship may generally be created by written or spoken words or by conduct. [Rest. 3d § 1.03]

a. Statute of Frauds—Land Contracts

In many states, however, the Statute of Frauds requires an agent's authority to be evidenced by a writing signed by the principal if the authority conferred is ***to execute contracts for the sale of land.***

b. "Equal Dignities" Statutes

A few states go farther and require the agency to be evidenced by a writing whenever the law requires the contract that the agent is to enter into on behalf of the principal to be in writing. [*See* Cal. Civ. Code § 2309] This would include every contract falling within the Statute of Frauds, not just those involving the sale of land.

c. Effect of Not Having Required Writing

If the agent's authority is required to be evidenced by a writing, but it is not, any contract executed by the agent is ***unenforceable against the principal***, even though the contract itself is in writing.

(1) Principal's Option

The contract is voidable ***at the option of the principal***, not the other party to the contract. Thus, if the principal decides to accept the contract, she can subsequently ***ratify*** it in writing. [**Moore v. Hoar,** 27 Cal. App. 2d 269 (1938); *and see infra,* p. 63]

Example: P orally authorizes A to sell P's house. A then enters into a contract on behalf of P to sell the house to X. X cannot enforce the contract because A's authority to sell the land had to be evidenced by a writing. However, if P wishes to enforce the contract, she can ratify it in writing—whereupon it becomes enforceable by ***both*** parties.

d. Exceptions

Even if a writing is required by the Statute of Frauds or an equal dignities statute, exceptions are available.

(1) Corporate Executives

An executive officer of a corporation need not have written authority from the corporation to act on its behalf. This is said to be justified by the necessities of modern business practice. [**Jeppi v. Brockman Holding Co.,** 34 Cal. 2d 11 (1949)] The same is true of general partners of a partnership.

(2) Mechanical Acts

Written authority usually is not required if the agent acts mechanically, *i.e.*, if the agent does not have discretionary authority to enter into a contract, but is merely authorized to sign the principal's name to a contract already made.

Example: P negotiates a contract with X, but leaves town before the agreement has been drawn up. If P authorizes A to sign P's name to the agreement, the authority is valid even though oral. [**Murphy v. Munson,** 95 Cal. App. 2d 306 (1949)]

6. Proper Purpose

An agency may be created only for a ***legal*** purpose. If the purpose is illegal or contrary to public policy, the purported agency will be disregarded.

a. Public Policy Requires Principal to Perform

A principal cannot delegate to an agent acts that public policy requires the principal to perform ***personally*** (*e.g.*, voting in a public election). [**Mansfield v. Scully,** 29 A.2d 444 (Conn. 1942)]

b. Personal Services

Similarly, performance in a ***personal services contract*** with a third person cannot be delegated to an agent (*e.g.*, singer hired to sing at a concert cannot delegate her duty to another singer). [**Trenouth v. Mulroney,** 227 P.2d 590 (Mont. 1951)]

CREATION OF AGENCY—ELEMENTS CHECKLIST

FOR A VALID AGENCY RELATIONSHIP TO EXIST, CHECK FOR THE FOLLOWING:

☑ ***Consent***	of ***both parties***
☑ ***Capacity***	Principal must have ***contractual capacity*** Agent needs ***only minimal mental capacity,*** not capacity to contract
☑ ***Writing seldom required***	Check ***Statute of Frauds*** and/or ***equal dignities statute;*** most likely required for land sale contracts
☑ ***Proper purpose***	***not illegal*** or ***against public policy***

Note: Consideration is ***not*** required.

Chapter Two:

Rights and Duties Between Principal and Agent

CONTENTS	PAGE

Key Exam Issues

An exam question may ask you to identify the rights and duties that arise among the parties to an agency transaction. This chapter addresses the rights and duties between the principal and agent. If your exam question involves the breach of a duty by an agent or principal, you should consider the following:

1. Duties of Agent/Rights of Principal

A compensated agent owes the principal the ***duty to perform*** with reasonable care. If the agent does not so perform, he may be held liable for breach of duty in both contract and tort (negligence). An uncompensated agent generally does not have a duty to perform, but once he performs, he may be subject to tort liability if he improperly performs. Additionally, every agent is a fiduciary, whether or not he is compensated. As such, he has a duty to: (i) ***notify*** the principal of all matters that come to his knowledge affecting the subject of the agency; and (ii) ***be loyal*** to the principal, which includes ***avoiding conflicts of interest.*** If an agent breaches his duties, the principal may, among other things, seek damages, recover the agent's ill-gotten profits, and withhold the agent's compensation (if any).

2. Duties of Principal/Rights of Agent

A principal also owes duties to her agent. Generally, the principal must deal with the agent ***fairly and in good faith*** and act ***in accordance with the terms of the agency*** contract. Unless it appears that the agency was intended to be gratuitous, the principal has a ***duty to compensate*** the agent. The principal must also ***reimburse*** the agent for all expenses incurred by the agent in the discharge of the agent's duties. Furthermore, the principal has a duty to ***cooperate*** with the agent in the performance of his duties and to do nothing to prevent such performance. If the principal breaches these duties, the agent may seek ***indemnification*** from the principal, put a ***lien*** on the principal's property in his lawful possession, or obtain most other ***breach of contract relief.*** However, the agent cannot obtain specific performance.

A. Agent's Duties to Principal

1. Contractual Duties and Duties Implied by Law

Because the agency relationship is consensual, the agent has the duty to abide by the express and implied terms stated in the agency agreement. [Rest. 3d § 8.07] In addition, the following duties are implied by law from the agency relationship and exist whether or not the principal is known or disclosed to any third party.

a. Duty to Perform

An agent has a duty to perform—which includes the duty to perform with reasonable care—and to refrain from conduct that will cause damage to the principal. [Rest. 3d § 8.10] An agent must act within the scope of her actual authority and has the duty to obey the principal's ***lawful instructions***, even if the agent believes that another course of action would be better for the principal. However, there is no duty to abide by instructions that will subject the agent to civil, criminal, or administrative liability. [Rest. 3d § 8.09 and comments]

(1) **Duty of Care**

An agent has the duty to carry out his agency with the ***care, competence, and diligence*** exercised by agents in similar circumstances. If the agent has any special skills or knowledge, he must act with the care, competence, and diligence normally exercised by agents with similar skills or knowledge. [Rest. 3d § 8.08]

(a) **Effect of Careless Performance or Nonperformance**

If the agent fails to perform all duties assigned to him, he is generally liable only for breach of the agency contract. However, if he performs the assigned duties, but in a *careless or imperfect manner* and thereby causes loss to the principal, he may be liable for negligence (tort) as well as for breach of contract. [Rest. 3d § 8.08, comment b; **Darman v. Zilch,** 186 A. 21 (R.I. 1936)]

e.g. **Example:** An insurance agent who fails to obtain coverage ordered by the principal and places orders for wrong insurance is liable for negligence as well as for breach of the agency contract. [**Colpe Investment Co. v. Seeley & Co.,** 132 Cal. App. 16 (1933)]

(2) **Gratuitous Agent**

A gratuitous (or uncompensated) agent owes to the principal the same duties owed by a compensated agent (*i.e.*, the duties of care and loyalty). The standard of care owed by the gratuitous agent is based on what is reasonable to expect under the circumstances, taking into account the agent's skill, experience, and professional status. [Rest. 3d § 8.08, comment e]

(a) **Effect of Careless Performance or Nonperformance**

An agency relationship arises when an agent promises to perform gratuitously. However, failure to perform *does not give rise to a claim for breach of contract* because the promise does not give rise to an enforceable contract. Nevertheless, if the agent performs improperly, he can be subject to *tort liability.* [Rest. 3d § 1.01, comment d; **Estes v. Lloyd Hammerstad, Inc.,** 503 P.2d 1149 (Wash. 1972)]

e.g. **Example:** If real estate broker A gratuitously offers to act as P's agent in the sale of Blackacre, P has no cause of action against A if A fails to attempt to sell the property. However, if A procures T as a buyer but neglects to get a signed sales contract, and T later changes his mind and refuses to proceed, P might have a cause of action in tort (negligence) for T's failure to exercise the degree of care reasonably expected of a real estate broker.

1) **Exception—Detrimental Reliance**

Even though a gratuitous agent generally has no contractual duty to perform, if the principal ***detrimentally relies*** on a gratuitous agent's promise to perform, the principal may recover ***contract damages*** sustained by the agent's refusal to perform. [Rest. 2d § 378]

e.g. **Example:** P asks A to sell his stock in Acme Company when it drops to $50 per share. A gratuitously promises to do so. Acme stock drops to $50 per share, and A does not sell P's stock. P does not find out that A did not sell his stock at $50 per share until the stock has dropped to $35 per share, at which point P sells his stock himself. P may recover contract damages from A because P detrimentally relied on A's promise to sell his stock at $50 per share.

EXAM TIP

On an exam, pay attention to the status of the agent. Remember that a *paid agent* can be subject to *both contract and tort liability*, whereas an *unpaid agent* is generally subject *only to tort liability* unless the principal can show that he *detrimentally relied* on the agent's promise.

---

b. Fiduciary Duties

In addition to the basic duty to perform the contract and render services with reasonable care, every agent is deemed a fiduciary; *i.e.*, he owes the principal the obligation of faithful service. [Rest. 3d § 8.01] An agent's obligation to the principal with respect to the subject matter of the agency is the same as that of a ***trustee*** to a trust.

(1) Duty to Notify

The fiduciary obligation requires an agent to notify the principal of all facts that the agent knows, has reason to know, or should know affecting the subject of the agency. [Rest. 3d § 8.11] The effect of this rule is that notice of all such matters coming to the attention of the agent is ***imputed*** to the principal. [Rest. 3d § 5.03] (*See infra*, p. 68 *et seq.*)

(2) Duty of Loyalty

As a fiduciary, the agent owes a duty to be loyal to the principal on all matters connected with the agency. [Rest. 3d § 8.01]

EXAM TIP

Pay particular attention to the duty of loyalty because it is one of the most important duties an agent owes to a principal and, thus, is a likely exam topic. Be sure to discuss the duty whenever you see an agent who is *using information* he obtained from the principal *for his own benefit*, when an agent is getting some *personal benefit* from the agency *that the principal is unaware of*, or when an agent tries to *represent two principals who have adverse positions*. In all of these cases, the duty is breached unless the principal is aware of the situation and consents.

(a) Competing with Principal

It follows that the agent is under a duty not to compete with his principal or to assist or act on behalf of persons who are in competition with his principal, unless he has the consent of the principal. An agent may, however, take action during the agency relationship to compete against his principal after the agency has ended as long as *the action is not wrongful*. [Rest. 3d § 8.04 and comment a]

e.g. **Example:** P, a local office supply business, employs A to coordinate shipments to P's customers. As agent, A becomes familiar with P's customers and suppliers. Without P's knowledge, A establishes a home-based office supply business and conducts business with some of P's customers. A's business competes with P's business and he has violated the duty not to compete.

cf. **Compare:** Same facts as above, except A does not establish the home-based business. He does, however, take steps to establish such a business in anticipation of the termination of the agency relationship with P, and in doing so has created marketing materials and business cards. A has not engaged in competition with P and his actions are not wrongful; therefore, he has not violated the duty not to compete.

1) Post-Termination

After termination of his employment, the agent ***can compete*** with the principal or accept employment from a competitor, unless he has agreed otherwise and the agreement is valid. [Rest. 3d § 8.04, comment b; **Karpinski v. Ingrasci,** 28 N.Y.2d 45 (1971)]

2) Trade Secrets

On the other hand, a former agent cannot use or disclose ***trade secrets or other confidential information*** obtained during his employment. [**Holiday Food Co. v. Munroe,** 426 A.2d 814 (Conn. 1981); *and see infra*, p. 19]

a) Customer Lists

In this respect, customer lists may be protected trade secrets if substantial time and money of the principal were involved in compiling the lists. [**Arnold's Ice Cream Co. v. Carlson,** 330 F. Supp. 1185 (E.D.N.Y. 1971)—breach of fiduciary duty for present or former employees to use customer lists in setting up competing business]

(b) Limitation—Dishonest Principal

Note, however, that the duty of loyalty does not obligate an agent to shield a dishonest principal.

e.g. **Example:** A discovered that his principal, P, had been cheating a third person, T, on various contracts. A disclosed P's actions to T, who then obtained a judgment against P for damages. *Held:* A's duty of loyalty did not extend to concealing P's dishonest acts from persons affected by them. [**Willig v. Gold,** 75 Cal. App. 2d 809 (1946)]

(c) Conflicts of Interest

The agent's fiduciary duty likewise dictates that he may not take a *position adverse to that of his principal* without the principal's consent. [Rest. 3d § 8.03] The principal's consent, however, does not relieve the agent of his duty of loyalty. He must deal fairly with the principal and disclose facts reasonably relevant to the principal's position. [Rest. 3d §§ 8.03, comment b; 8.06]

1) Breach of Duty

An agent does not breach the duty of loyalty if he acts on behalf of an adverse party in a ministerial capacity that does not require the exercise of judgment, discretion, or skill. He does breach the duty if he has an economic interest in a party with whom the principal deals or if the principal is engaged in a transaction with a party in whom the agent has an interest (*e.g.*, a relative or close friend of the agent). [Rest. 3d § 8.03, comment b]

(d) Acquiring Material Benefit

An agent must not acquire a material benefit in connection with his position or through transactions on behalf of the principal without the principal's consent. An agent acts to further the interests of the principal; therefore, anything the agent obtains by virtue of his employment (*e.g.*, profits, advantages, or benefits) belongs to the principal. [Rest. 3d §§ 8.02, 8.06]

e.g. **Example:** P employs A to purchase certain goods for P on the open market. A places P's order with T. T agrees to give A a rebate under the table. Unless P knows of and consents to the rebate, A's acceptance violates his fiduciary duty to P, and P may recover the secret profits obtained by A. [**Kinert v. Wright,** 81 Cal. App. 2d 919 (1947)]

1) Personal Purchase by Purchasing Agent

An agent authorized to purchase certain property for his principal cannot purchase the property for himself without his principal's consent. If the agent purchases the property for himself without consent, the principal is entitled to whatever property the agent purchased, at the same price, and on the same terms as the agent received—the agent being deemed to hold the property as ***constructive trustee*** for his principal. (*See infra*, p. 21.)

a) Right of First Refusal

Even if the agent has not been given specific authority or instructions to purchase certain property, many court decisions hold that the agent owes the principal the ***right of first refusal*** if he knows that the principal would be interested in purchasing this type of property; *i.e.*, the agent must inform his principal that such property is available and offer it to the principal on the same terms he was offered. [*See* 20 A.L.R.2d 1140]

2) Personal Purchase by Sales Agent

An agent authorized to sell property on behalf of his principal cannot buy that property himself unless the principal consents. This is true even if the transaction is fair and the price is reasonable, because the agent might have obtained a better price from someone else. [**Groh v. Shelton,** *supra*, p. 10]

EXAM TIP

Remember that sometimes the duty of loyalty is breached even though the agent *doesn't seem to have damaged the principal* in any way. Consider the case above, where the agent purchases the property he was to sell for the principal. The duty is so broad that even though the principal got the price she asked for, the duty has been breached by the agent's self-dealing.

a) Purchase Through a Nominee

Of course, the agent may not avoid this rule by purchasing the property indirectly through a nominee or dummy.

b) Principal's Remedies

On discovering the agent's interest, the principal can rescind the sale and recover the property. If the property has been resold by the agent, the principal can hold the agent liable for its value or collect any profits realized by the agent from the sale, plus damages for any harm. [Rest. 3d § 8.02, comment e]

c) **Exception**

The rule against self-purchase generally does not apply if the agent is authorized to sell property for a ***certain net price and to keep any excess*** as his commission. In this situation, no injury to the principal can result from a purchase by the agent. [**Allen v. Dailey,** 92 Cal. App. 308 (1928)]

3) **Dual Agency**

An agent acting for more than one principal (*e.g.*, for both buyer and seller) in negotiations between them may well be representing conflicting interests, and such situations clearly present the possibility of fraud. Hence, unless it clearly appears that ***both*** principals are ***fully informed*** of the dual representation ***and consent*** to it, the transaction is voidable at the option of either principal, and the agent may not recover commissions from either, regardless of the fairness of the contract in the particular case. [Rest. 3d § 8.06(2); 48 A.L.R. 917]

a) **Real Estate Brokers**

A broker employed to sell real estate does not become an agent of the buyer ***merely because he counsels*** the buyer on terms in procuring an offer. The broker is still the agent of the seller, and no dual agency exists. Nor is there a dual agency when a broker ***represents the sellers of different properties in negotiations with a single buyer.*** [**Foley v. Mathias,** 233 N.W. 106 (Iowa 1930)] *Rationale:* The sellers in this situation are not principals in the same transaction. If the law were otherwise, a broker could list only one property at a time.

(e) **Duties Regarding Principal's Property and Confidential Information**

An agent with possession of the principal's property or with access to confidential information *must not use the property or confidential information for his own purposes or for those of a third party.* Additionally, the principal's property must be segregated, and the agent must maintain an accounting of money or other property received or paid out on the principal's behalf. [Rest. 3d §§ 8.05, 8.12]

2. Duties Owed by Subagents

a. Authorized Subagent

If the principal has authorized the agent to hire a subagent (*see supra*, p. 6), the ***subagent owes the same duties*** to the principal as the agent would owe. In addition, the ***agent*** is responsible to the principal for any violation of duty by the subagent, even if the agent exercised good faith in selecting the subagent. [Rest. 3d § 3.15 and comments; **Phillips v. JCM Development Corp.,** 666 P.2d 876 (Utah 1983)]

(1) **Duty of Subagent to Agent**

Likewise, the subagent owes the agent who hired her substantially the same duties as she owes to the principal, and she is liable to the agent for any loss sustained because of her improper performance. [Rest. 3d § 3.15, comment d]

(2) Principal's Liability to Third Parties for Acts of Subagent

A principal is liable to third parties for the acts of an authorized subagent to the same extent as if the act had been performed by the appointing agent. This is known as the "***principle of transparency.***" [Rest. 3d § 3.15, comment d]

b. Unauthorized Subagent

If the subagent is employed ***without*** authority from the principal, there is no agency relationship between the principal and subagent ***unless*** the principal ***ratified*** the appointment. [Rest. 3d § 3.15, comment c] The principal is not liable to third persons for acts of the unauthorized subagent; conversely, the unauthorized subagent owes no duties to the principal.

(1) Duty of Agent to Principal

The agent, of course, remains responsible to his principal for performance of the duties involved in his agency, and is liable for any loss sustained by the principal because of the subagent's conduct. [Rest. 3d § 3.15 and comments]

EXAM TIP

Whenever you see an agent appointing someone else to perform one or more of his tasks, check to see whether the principal *authorized the hiring* of a subagent, because this will affect the duties and liabilities of the parties. Only an *authorized subagent* owes duties to the principal; an unauthorized subagent does not. Likewise, the principal is liable to third parties only for the acts of an authorized subagent.

3. Remedies Available to Principal

If an agent breaches a specific contractual duty, breaches his duty to perform, or violates a fiduciary duty, the following remedies may be available to the principal:

a. Action for Damages

(1) Breach of Contract

A ***compensated agent*** may be held liable for damages suffered by the principal as a result of a breach of contract. All of the remedies and methods of calculating damages that apply in normal breach of contract situations apply here. (*See* Contracts Summary.) However, an ***uncompensated*** agent generally cannot be held liable for breach of contract damages because he has made no contract. (*See supra*, p. 15.)

(2) Tort

All agents, whether compensated or gratuitous, may be held liable in tort for damages resulting from careless performance or breach of fiduciary duty. [*See* Rest. 3d § 8.08, comment b]

(3) Punitive Damages

If malice or bad faith is established, punitive damages may also be awarded against the agent. [**Ward v. Taggart,** 51 Cal. 2d 736 (1959)]

b. Action for Secret Profits

If an agent breaches his fiduciary duty and secretly profits, the principal may recover the actual profits or property held by the agent.

c. Rescission

Regardless of whether the agent derived any personal gain, any transaction that violates the agent's fiduciary duty is voidable by the principal. Thus, if the principal discovers that the agent who was employed to sell property actually purchased it for himself, the principal may ***rescind*** the sale if she chooses. [**Slusher v. Buckley,** 174 Cal. App. 2d 324 (1959)]

d. Constructive Trust

If the agent has obtained property from third persons in violation of his fiduciary duty to purchase, hold, or obtain the property for the principal, equity may impose a ***constructive trust*** on the property (or, if it has been resold, on the profits obtained from the sale). A constructive trust is an equitable remedy imposed by the courts, and it is used to prevent unjust enrichment of a person who has gained title to property through misappropriation. (*See* Remedies Summary.)

e. Accounting

The principal may bring an action in equity in complicated situations to have the court determine the exact amount of funds that the agent must return to the principal. [**Farr v. Southern Supply Co.,** 44 So. 2d 247 (Ala. 1950)]

f. Withhold Compensation

If the agent has committed an ***intentional*** breach of fiduciary duty, the principal may, in addition to any other remedy, refuse to pay the agent for any unapportioned compensation.

4. Rights and Benefits Flowing from Agent's Employment Belong to Principal

a. General Rule

An agent must not acquire a material benefit from a third party in connection with actions taken on behalf of the principal or through use of the agent's position. (*See supra*, p. 17.) Thus, everything acquired by an agent by virtue of his employment (except for his compensation) belongs to the principal. All rights, property, or claims that the agent receives or obtains must be held for and on behalf of the principal, and the agent owes the principal a duty to account for such rights, property, and claims. [Rest. 3d § 8.02 and comments]

b. Undisclosed Principal Cases

So far as the agent's duties to his principal are concerned, it is ordinarily immaterial whether the agent discloses the identity of his principal to the person with whom he is dealing; *i.e.*, all rights and claims acquired under a contract with a third person belong to the principal, even if undisclosed, and the principal is entitled to enforce the contract. (*See infra*, p. 82.)

(1) Note—Identity of Principal Discovered

There are exceptional situations in which the third person may refuse to proceed with the contract when the identity of the principal is discovered—*e.g.*, when the agent fraudulently concealed the principal's identity. (*See infra*, p. 82.)

c. Inventions and Patents

If the agent is hired to develop inventions or patents, any and all rights to such developments belong to the principal absent an agreement to the contrary. However, if developing such items is ***not a primary part*** of the agent's duties (*i.e.*, the agent was not hired to invent or solve a particular problem), any patent or invention is the ***property of the agent*** rather than the principal. [**Scott System, Inc. v. Scott,** 996 P.2d 775 (Colo. 2000)]

(1) "Shop Right" Doctrine

Nonetheless, if the patent or invention was perfected on the principal's time (or using the principal's materials or money) and is related to the principal's business, the principal is deemed to have a "shop right" to the patent, *i.e.*, an irrevocable right to use the idea or invention which does not terminate when the employment ends. [**Aero Bolt & Screw Co. v. Iaia,** 180 Cal. App. 2d 728 (1960)]

5. Principal's Right to Indemnification

a. Tortious Acts of Agent

A principal has a right to indemnification against an agent for any loss sustained on account of the agent's tortious acts. Thus, if the principal is held liable for damages to a third party because of the negligent conduct of her agent, she can sue the agent for the amount of the damages. (*See infra*, p. 95.)

b. Violation of Principal's Instructions

Similarly, a principal has a cause of action against her agent for any loss sustained by the principal as a result of the agent's violation of her instructions. For example, the principal may be held liable for breach of warranty made by the agent, even though she specifically instructed the agent not to make warranties. (*See infra*, p. 40.) Under such circumstances, the principal has a cause of action against the agent for indemnification.

B. Principal's Duties to Agent

1. Contractual Duties and Duties Implied by Law

A principal owes her agent the duty to act in accordance with the express and implied terms of the agency contract. [Rest. 3d § 8.13] The following duties on the part of the principal are ***implied by law*** in every agency or employment contract, absent a provision to the contrary.

a. Duty to Cooperate

A principal must assist and cooperate with the agent in the performance of his duties and do nothing wrongful to prevent performance. [Rest. 3d § 8.13, comment b]

e.g. **Example:** If an agent is given an exclusive sales territory, and the principal later invades the territory and makes sales, some courts have held that the agent may recover from the principal the profits he would have made on the sales. [*See* **Hacker Pipe & Supply Co. v. Chapman Valve Manufacturing Co.,** 17 Cal. App. 2d 265 (1936)]

(1) But Note

Other courts hold that while a principal may not interfere with an exclusive agent by appointing another agent to compete, the principal herself ***can*** compete with the agent. [**Stahlman v. National Lead Co.,** 318 F.2d 388 (5th Cir. 1963)]

b. Duty to Compensate

Unless it appears that the agent's services were intended to be gratuitous, a principal must compensate the agent for the agreed value of those services (or, in the absence of a specific agreement, for the reasonable value of the services). [Rest. 3d § 8.13, comment d]

(1) Sales Agents

The most frequent problem involving compensation of an agent involves the time at which a salesperson is entitled to a commission. In the absence of an agreement on this point, a salesperson is entitled to recover a commission when he makes the sale (*i.e.*, when the offer is accepted), even though the sale is not actually consummated or performed. Furthermore, a salesperson is entitled to a commission if his efforts are the effective or procuring cause of the sale, even if others were involved in completing the transaction. [12 A.L.R.2d 1360; *see also* Rest. 3d § 8.13, comment c]

(2) Subagents

A principal is clearly not responsible for compensation to a subagent if there was no authority to hire the subagent. Nor is the principal liable for compensation to a subagent merely because the agent was authorized to hire subagents. The subagent must look to the agent for compensation. [**McKnight v. Peoples-Pittsburgh Trust Co.,** 61 A.2d 820 (Pa. 1948); Rest. 3d § 8.13, comment d]

e.g. **Example:** P hired interior decorator A to decorate her home. P authorized A to hire subagents. A hired carpet layers, who carpeted the home and tried to recover compensation from P. The carpet layers are performing the work of A and must look to A for payment. [*See* **Yates v. Bernard's Carpet & Draperies, Inc.,** 481 So. 2d 515 (Fla. 1985)]

cf. **Compare—additional agents:** The principal is liable for compensation to additional agents (or coagents) hired by her agent because the additional agents are not hired to do all or part of the work of the agent, as is a subagent. Instead, the additional agents have their own tasks to perform and are considered agents (not subagents) of the principal. For example, if P authorizes her store manager to hire clerks, the clerks are hired to perform tasks separate from those of the manager and are considered additional agents of P. Thus, P is liable for their compensation.

(3) State Statutes

If an agent is an ***employee***, the principal may have to abide by state statutes regulating the employee's compensation. Statutes in many jurisdictions regulate the time, place, and manner of paying wages to employees, as well as their hours and working conditions. [*See, e.g.*, Cal. Labor Code §§ 201 *et seq.*]

c. Duty of Care

In general, a principal owes an agent the same duty of care with regard to torts as the principal would owe a stranger—*i.e.*, the principal must ***refrain from negligence.*** As to an employer, however, the common law liability for personal injuries to employees while performing the duties assigned to them has been largely superseded by workers' compensation acts in effect in most states. Only in cases specifically exempted under such acts (*e.g.*, certain domestic servants), or where an employer fails to maintain the required workers' compensation insurance, do common law liabilities still exist.

(1) Duty to Furnish Safe Working Conditions

The main basis for common law liability is a breach of the employer's duty to furnish and maintain safe premises, equipment, and conditions for her employees. This includes the duty to inspect the premises or equipment for defects, and to warn of any such defects. (*See* Torts Summary.)

d. Duty to Indemnify

The principal has the duty to indemnify the agent in accordance with the ***terms of the agency contract*** and for all ***expenditures or losses*** incurred by the agent in the discharge of his authorized duties. If the agent acted without authority, then his right to indemnification arises only if the principal benefited from the transaction and the agent did not act officiously. [Rest. 3d § 8.14 and comment b; *see infra*, pp. 24–25]

e. Duty to Deal Fairly and in Good Faith

A principal has the duty to deal with the agent fairly and in good faith, including a duty to provide the agent with the information about risks of physical harm or pecuniary loss that the principal knows, has reason to know, or should know are present in the agent's work but which are unknown to the agent. [Rest. 3d § 8.15]

2. Remedies Available to Agent

If there is a breach of the agency contract by the principal, the agent has most of the remedies available to a contracting party.

a. Indemnification by Principal

The agent is entitled to indemnification from the principal pursuant to the ***terms of the agency contract*** and for all ***expenditures or losses*** incurred in performing authorized duties on behalf of the principal. [Rest. 3d § 8.14 and comment b; *see supra*, p. 24]

(1) Scope of Indemnification

The scope of this right is often defined in the agency agreement. If not, the courts will indemnify the agent if it appears just to do so, considering the nature of the business, losses incurred, etc. [**Long v. Vlasic Food Products Co.,** 439 F.2d 229 (4th Cir. 1971)]

(2) No Right to Indemnity for Unauthorized or Illegal Acts

The agent generally is not entitled to indemnity for losses resulting from acts that are unauthorized and do not benefit the principal. [***In re* Lathrop Haskins & Co.,** 216 F. 102 (2d Cir. 1914)] If the agent acted without authority, then his right to indemnification arises only if the principal benefited from the transaction and the agent did not act officiously. [Rest. 3d § 8.14 and comment b] Additionally, there is no right to indemnification if the agent acted illegally or negligently. [**Erlich v. First National Bank,** 505 A.2d 220 (N.J. 1984)]

(3) Compensation Paid by Agent to Employees and Other Subagents

The agent does not have the right to be indemnified for compensation that he pays to his employees or other subagents ***unless the principal has agreed*** otherwise. [Rest. 3d § 8.14, comment b]

(4) Litigation Expenses

A principal must indemnify the agent for reasonable expenses and losses incurred in defending himself against actions brought by third parties ***if the action challenged by the third party was carried out pursuant to the agents actual authority.*** The principal has no duty to indemnify the agent for defending against unauthorized actions or for losses caused by his wrongful acts. [Rest. 3d § 8.14, comment d]

(5) Recovery by Subagents

If indemnification is otherwise proper, an ***authorized subagent*** can recover against ***either*** the principal or the agent, because the subagent is a fiduciary of both. If the subagent proceeds against the agent, the agent has a right of indemnity in turn against the principal. [Rest. 3d § 8.14, comment b; **Admiral Oriental Line v. Atlantic Gulf & Oriental Steamship Co.,** 88 F.2d 26 (2d Cir. 1937)]

b. Lien Against Property of Principal

Absent an agreement to the contrary, the agent has a right to a lien on the principal's property in his lawful possession up to the amount of his compensation (or right to indemnity). [**McGregor Co. v. Heritage,** 620 P.2d 488 (Or. 1980)]

(1) Attorney's Liens

With respect to the client-principal, an attorney has broader lien rights than the average agent. For example, the attorney may have both a ***retaining lien*** on all of the client's papers, securities, etc., in his possession as the result of his position as attorney, and a ***charging lien*** on amounts earned in securing a judgment in specific cases. [***In re* Heinsheimer,** 214 N.Y. 361 (1915)]

(2) Lien Rights of Subagents

The subagent has a lien against the agent's property in her possession for services and expenses, and against the principal's property in her possession to the extent of the agent's rights in such property. [**Korns v. Thomson & McKinnon,** 22 F. Supp. 442 (D. Minn. 1938)]

c. Other Remedies

In addition to the above rights, an agent may be entitled to withhold further performance under the agency contract, to claim a setoff or counterclaim in any action brought by the principal, or to demand an accounting by the principal.

(1) No Right to Specific Performance

However, the agent is ***not*** entitled to specific performance of the agency contract because the principal-agent relationship is deemed to be consensual in nature. [**McMenamin v. Philadelphia Transportation Co.,** 51 A.2d 702 (Pa. 1947)]

DUTIES OF PRINCIPAL AND AGENT	
DUTIES	**CORRESPONDING REMEDIES FOR BREACH OF DUTIES**
AGENT • Express and implied contractual duties • Reasonable care in performance • Obedience • Notification • Loyalty • Segregation and accounting of property • Confidentiality	**PRINCIPAL** • Contract remedies (if agent compensated) • Tort remedies (if agent negligent) • Punitive damages (for malice or bad faith) • Action for secret profits • Recession • Constructive trust • Accounting • Withhold compensation • Indemnification
PRINCIPAL • Express and implied contractual duties • Cooperation • Compensation • Indemnification • Avoidance of negligence • Deal fairly and in good faith	**AGENT** • Contractual remedies • Indemnification • Possessory lien • Withhold further performance • Setoff • Accounting

Chapter Three:

Agent's Power and Authority to Bind Principal on Contracts

CONTENTS	PAGE

Key Exam Issues

Often, an exam question will focus on whether a principal is contractually bound by the acts of his agent. Your answer will depend on whether the agent had the ***power to bind*** the principal. Such power can arise from the following sources:

1. Actual Authority

This is the best source of power because it is the cornerstone of the agency relationship. It includes all powers ***expressly granted by the principal*** to the agent and any powers that can be ***implied from the principal's manifestations***, as interpreted from the ***agent's*** point of view. If actual authority is not present in your exam fact pattern, you then must determine whether some other source of power is available to bind the principal.

2. Apparent Authority

This is the power that the principal manifests ***to third parties*** that the agent has. Inasmuch as agency is based on the objective theory of contract, a principal will be bound by an agent's acts if a third party ***reasonably believes***, based on the principal's manifestations ***to the third party***, that the agent has authority.

3. Estoppel

This source of power is closely related to apparent authority and arises when the principal ***intentionally or carelessly*** causes a third party to believe another to be his agent, and the third party ***detrimentally relies*** on the belief. Whereas apparent authority contractually binds the principal, estoppel merely makes the principal liable for the third party's resulting losses.

Note that power from the above sources is not everlasting. Once you have found a source of power, you must then examine ***whether the power had expired before the agent's act. Actual*** authority can terminate in a number of ways: (i) by expiration of the agency term; (ii) by accomplishment of the agency purpose; (iii) by change of circumstances, such as destruction of the subject matter or other change affecting value; (iv) by death or incapacity of the principal or agent (upon notice); (v) by agreement of the parties; or (vi) by cessation of existence of or suspension of powers. Even if an agent's actual authority has terminated, recall that any ***apparent*** authority continues until third parties are ***notified*** of the termination.

A. Introduction

1. Overview

Agency is a device that allows an agent's acts to effect a principal's legal liabilities. (*See supra*, p. 4.) However, not every act of an agent affects the principal, even if the act was purportedly undertaken on the principal's behalf. This chapter focuses on which acts of an agent will have an effect on the principal's legal liabilities.

2. Terminology

Terminology concerning agency law is not consistent, and this is especially true regarding the authority and power of agents. (*See supra*, p. 4.) Many courts and commentators use the terms "authority" and "power" interchangeably, but they have distinct meanings under the Restatement.

a. Authority

Agency usually arises consensually, with the principal and agent agreeing that the agent shall act on the principal's behalf. (*See supra*, p. 4.) [Rest. 3d § 1.01] In such a case, the agent has the right to bind the principal to the extent that the principal and agent have agreed. Such a right is known as "***authority.***" [Rest. 3d § 2.01] If the agent has authority to do the act in question, the principal will be bound by the agent's act regardless of the knowledge of the third party with whom the agent deals (*i.e.*, the principal will be bound even if the third party does not know that the agent has authority or that the agent is acting as an agent).

(1) Actual Authority

Most courts use the term "actual authority" to denote "authority." This common terminology will be used herein to more readily distinguish it from other sources of power, such as apparent authority (*see infra*, p. 37 *et seq.*).

b. Power

A principal can also be bound in certain situations where the agent does not have actual authority. In such a situation, a true agency relationship may or may not exist (*i.e.*, there may or may not be a mutual agreement between the principal and agent), but as between the principal and the third party with whom the agent dealt, the court will act as if the agent had authority by finding that the agent had the power to bind the principal. Power is simply the ability to effect the legal relations of the principal, regardless of the right to do so. [*See* Rest. 3d § 1.01, comment c]

B. Sources of Power

1. Introduction

When confronted with the question of whether a principal will be bound by his agent's acts, the first matter to be determined is whether the agent had the power to bind the principal. If the agent had actual authority, power is presumed and the principal will be bound. If the agent did not have actual authority, it then must be determined whether some ***other source of power*** is available. Power can arise from apparent authority, estoppel, or ratification. [*See* Rest. 3d § 1.01, comment c]

2. Actual Authority

Actual (or real) authority arises from the ***manifestation of consent*** from the principal ***to the agent*** (not to a third person) that the agent should act for the principal. It includes the power to do whatever the principal has engaged the agent to accomplish [**Makousky, Inc. v. Stern,** 172 N.W.2d 317 (Minn. 1969)] and is controlled by the ***agents*** reasonable beliefs; *i.e.*, the agent has actual authority to act in any manner that a reasonable person in the agent's position would believe was authorized by the principal's words or conduct. [Rest. 3d § 2.02] Courts have referred to two principal types of actual authority: express and implied.

a. Express Authority

Express authority is actual authority contained within the "four corners" of the agency agreement between the principal and the agent, *i.e.*, authority expressly granted by the principal to the agent.

WILL AGENT'S ACTS BIND THE PRINCIPAL TO CONTRACT?

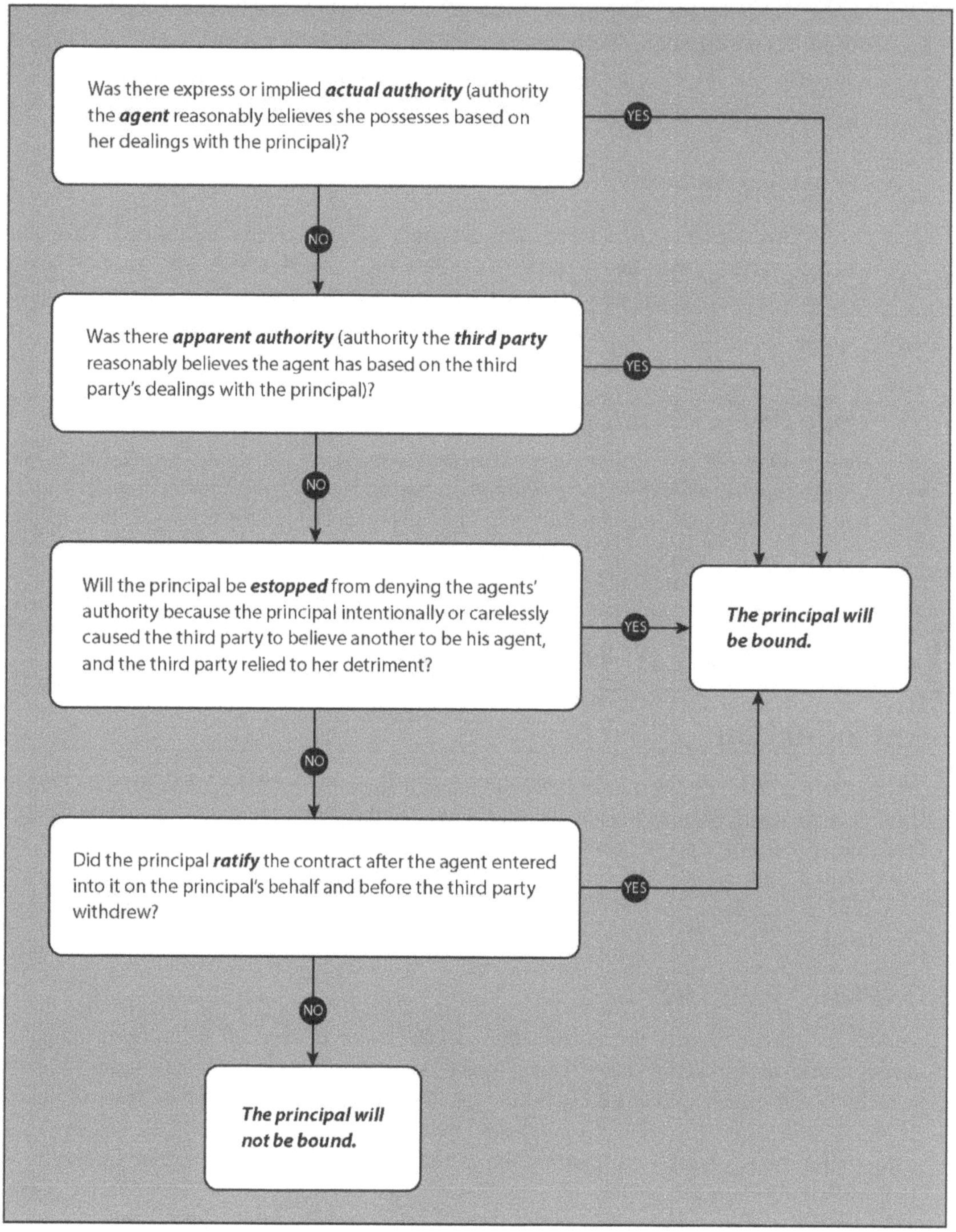

(1) **Extravagant Phrases**

Often, grants of authority contain extravagant phrases that could be construed as giving the agent extremely broad powers, *e.g.*, "to conduct any business." Courts generally will limit such broad language to what appears to be the business actually intended by the parties. [*See, e.g.*, **Brantley v. Southern Life Insurance Co.,** 53 Ala. 554 (1875)—authority to sign principal's name to transact business does not include authority to sign note for penal bond unrelated to the business]

(2) **Power of Attorney**

Perhaps the clearest example of express authority is a power of attorney, which is a written instrument that states an agent's authority. [Rest. 3d § 1.04(7)]

(a) **Scope of Authority**

The power may be "*special*"—to do certain acts only—or it may be "*general*"—to transact all business for the principal. Any vagueness or uncertainty as to the scope of a power of attorney is normally construed against the principal.

(b) **Proper Signature**

An agent acting under such a grant of authority is sometimes called an "*attorney in fact*" for the principal, and the normal form of signature for such an agent is: "John Jones (principal) by Mary Smith, his attorney in fact." However, deviations from this form are usually immaterial; as long as the agent had authority to sign, the principal will normally be bound.

EXAM TIP

If you have an exam question where you have to determine whether an agent had actual authority, first check for actual *express* authority. If express authority to do a particular act exists, there is no need to examine if the agent had actual implied authority (*see* below) to do that act.

b. **Implied Authority**

An agent's actual authority includes not only the authority expressly granted by the principal to the agent, but also any authority implied by the agent from the words or conduct between the principal and the agent. [Rest. 3d § 2.02(1); **Arkansas Valley Feed Mills, Inc. v. Fox De Luxe Foods, Inc.,** 171 F. Supp. 145 (W.D. Ark. 1959)] Implied authority may arise in a number of ways and is often labeled as follows to signify how it has arisen (note, however, that these labels are merely for convenience, and the categories may overlap).

(1) **Incidental to Express Authority**

In most cases, the principal does not expressly grant detailed authority to the agent. Instead, the agent is given a general authority or objective—*e.g.*, to sell the principal's goods or to purchase on the principal's behalf. Such an express grant includes the implied authority to act in any way that is a natural and general consequence of the express authority granted. It also includes the power to do all acts ***reasonably necessary*** to accomplish the given objective. [Rest. 3d § 2.02, comment d; **Fidelity & Casualty Co. v. Continental Illinois National Bank & Trust Co.,** 25 N.E.2d 550 (Ill. 1940)] Such implied authority is often called incidental authority or inferred authority.

Example: If authority is conferred on an agent to "collect" an account owing to the principal, the agent is deemed to have express authority not only to negotiate with the debtor for payment, but also to institute suit, enforce any judgment obtained, and incur reasonable expenses and costs (including attorneys' fees) to this end. However, mere authority to "collect" an account would probably ***not*** authorize compromising, discounting, or settling the account for less than what is due the principal.

(2) Implied from Principal's Manifestations

Actual authority may be impliedly conferred by the manifestations of the principal (through words or conduct) indicating his intention to confer it, or by otherwise causing the agent to believe that she possesses it. [Rest. 3d § 2.02]

Example: For many years, P has delivered his cattle to A, a cattle sales agent, and A has sold the cattle for the best price then available. Upon P's current delivery of cattle, and in the absence of contrary instructions, A has implied authority to sell the cattle.

Example: P's secretary, A, without previous authorization, has purchased office supplies, and P has paid for them without objection. A has implied authority to continue to purchase necessary office supplies for P.

(3) Implied from Custom or Usage

Unless directed otherwise, an agent also has implied authority to act in accordance with general custom or usage, provided the agent has knowledge of the custom or usage. [Rest. 3d § 1.03, comment e]

Example: P appoints A as manager of his business. A has implied authority to carry out all of the normal operative functions of a manager in that type of business.

(4) Implied Because of Emergency

In an unforeseen emergency where the agent cannot contact the principal to obtain additional authority, the agent is impliedly deemed to have the authority to do all acts reasonably necessary to protect or preserve the property or rights of the principal (including the right to delegate authority and appoint subagents). [**Jacobsma v. Goldberg's Fashion Forum,** 303 N.E.2d 226 (Ill. 1973)]

Example: P ships his crops to a factor, A. Upon arrival, A notes that the crops are infested and must be treated immediately to prevent their entire loss. If A cannot reach P, A has implied authority to order the necessary treatment on P's behalf, and P is liable for the cost. [Rest. 3d § 2.02, comment b]

EXAM TIP

If your exam question requires you to determine whether an agent had actual authority to act, remember that the agent is not limited to the "four corners" of the document granting authority (express authority). The agent also has actual authority to do anything that a reasonable person in the agent's position would presume was authorized based on the communications or conduct between the principal and agent (*i.e., implied authority*). (*See also* Implied Authority Checklist, below.)

IMPLIED AUTHORITY CHECKLIST
IMPLIED AUTHORITY TO ACT MAY ARISE:
☑ Incidentally from ***express authority***
☑ From principal's ***manifestations*** (words or conduct)
☑ From ***custom or usage***
☑ From an ***emergency situation***

(5) Specific Examples of Implied Authority

(a) Agency to Sell

An agent who is given the express authority to sell the principal's property is deemed to have the following implied authority:

1) Making Warranties

An agent authorized to sell property on behalf of the principal is empowered to make such warranties concerning the property as are ***implied by law or customary*** in the community in connection with sales of such property. [**Lindow v. Cohn,** 5 Cal. App. 388 (1907)—agent authorized to sell merchandise can warrant quality of goods sold]

a) Real Property

Customary warranties in the sale of real property include description, size, character of soil, boundary lines, and title.

b) Personal Property

Customary warranties in the sale of personal property include size, weight, grade, etc.

c) Sale of Business

In the sale of a business, warranties concerning income, expenses, assets, and liabilities are customary.

d) Power to Warrant Narrowly Construed

Because the power to warrant may increase the principal's liabilities, courts generally construe narrowly the agent's authority to warrant, finding no power in doubtful cases.

2) Receiving Payment

An agent with authority to sell the principal's property has authority to receive payment of the purchase price in accordance with the terms authorized by the principal. [**Tysk v. Griggs,** 91 N.W.2d 127 (Minn. 1958)]

a) Cash Only

Unless otherwise specified, the authority to sell permits a sale for cash only; the agent is not empowered to accept goods, etc., as payment. [**Wilier v. Railway Express Agency,** 86 A.2d 104 (D.C. 1952)]

3) **Delivering Goods**

If personal property is involved, a selling agent has authority to deliver the goods on receipt of the purchase price.

4) **Negotiating**

If the terms of sale are specified by the principal, the agent generally has the authority to negotiate and conclude a sale on those terms.

a) **Additional Terms**

However, an agent is not necessarily prevented from making additional terms (especially where personal property is involved), as long as such terms are more advantageous than—or at least not inconsistent with—the specified terms. [**Myers v. Stephens,** 233 Cal. App. 2d 104 (1965)]

5) **Concluding Sale**

If the terms of sale are not specified by the principal or are incomplete, authority to sell might ***not*** include the actual power to negotiate and conclude a sale. Particularly where land is involved, the courts treat a mere authority to sell as authority only to find a purchaser to whom the principal may sell. [**Forbis v. Honeycutt,** 273 S.E.2d 240 (N.C. 1980)]

a) **Real Estate Brokers**

If the authority to sell is given to **a *real estate broker***, it is almost always held that the broker has no actual power to convey title to the principal's property, or even to contract to convey the property. This is true even if the agent is given the "exclusive right to sell" on specific terms; such language is deemed only to protect the agent's right to a commission, not to authorize the agent to convey title. [**Mason v. Mazel,** 82 Cal. App. 2d 769 (1947)]

(b) **Agency to Purchase**

An agent who is given the express authority to purchase property on behalf of the principal likewise has certain implied authority:

1) **Making Warranties**

An agent authorized to purchase property on behalf of the principal is generally deemed to be empowered to make warranties regarding the principal's credit, assets, and liabilities—*i.e.*, to qualify the principal as a purchaser.

2) **Paying Purchase Price**

An agent authorized to purchase property for the principal has the authority to pay the purchase price from the principal's funds, or if no funds have been given by the principal, to purchase on the principal's credit. [**Pan American World Airways, Inc. v. Local Readers Service, Inc.,** 240 N.E.2d 552 (Ind. 1968)]

3) Accepting Delivery and Possession

An agent with authority to purchase also has the power to accept delivery and possession of goods (where personal property is involved) or a conveyance of title (in the case of real property).

4) Concluding Purchase

Note that an agency "to purchase" may be interpreted merely as authority to find property and procure an offer of sale. The less complete the terms of authority, the more likely the agent will be deemed to have power only to solicit an offer to sell.

(c) Authority to Delegate

Because an agency involves a consensual relationship between the principal and agent, the general rule is that the agent cannot delegate her authority to another unless she has actual or apparent authority to do so. [Rest. 3d § 3.15(2)] There are certain situations, however, in which the agent is deemed permitted to delegate her authority to another:

1) Mechanical or Ministerial Acts

An agent has authority to delegate when the act delegated is purely mechanical or ministerial. [**Loftus v. American Realty Co.,** 334 N.W.2d 366 (Iowa 1983)]

e.g. **Example:** P authorizes A to inventory P's incoming merchandise and issue receipts. These acts are purely mechanical, and A can delegate the task to a subagent. [**Kadota Fig Association v. Case-Swayne Co.,** 73 Cal. App. 2d 815 (1946)]

2) Agent Cannot Perform Act Herself

When the principal has notice that the act exceeds the agent's individual capability, or that the agent cannot lawfully perform it herself, the agent has authority to delegate the act to a subagent who can perform it. [Rest. 3d § 3.15, comment c]

e.g. **Example:** P engages A to auction off P's goods, knowing that only a licensed auctioneer is permitted to conduct such a sale. If A has no such license, she can delegate the authority to conduct the sale to any licensed auctioneer. [**Cleaveland v. Gabriel,** 180 A.2d 749 (Conn. 1962)]

3) Custom or Necessity

The agent has authority to appoint subagents whenever it is customary or necessary to do so. [Rest. 3d § 3.15, comment c]

e.g. **Example:** If P employs broker A to sell his property, and it is customary for brokers to appoint each other as subagents to procure buyers for listed properties, A has authority to appoint any other broker as her subagent. Any broker so appointed has the same authority as A to negotiate a sale. [*See, e.g.*, **Barker v. Mosby,** 118 S.W.2d 946 (Tex. 1938)]

4) Subagent Not Party to Agency Agreement

Even though an agent has the power to delegate her authority to another, the subagent is not a party to the principal-agent agreement; *i.e.*, the subagent, X, generally has no right to sue the principal for the compensation that the principal agreed to pay the agent for performance of the agency services, X's claim being against the agent who hired her. (*See supra*, p. 23.)

a) Minority View

Some courts ***have*** allowed the subagent to sue the principal directly in quasi-contract for the reasonable value of the services rendered.

EXAMPLES OF IMPLIED AUTHORITY

SELLING AGENT	PURCHASING AGENT	DELEGATION
• Make warranties • Receive payment • Deliver goods • Negotiate terms	• Make warranties • Pay purchase price • Accept goods	• Mechanical/ministerial acts • Agent cannot perform • Custom or necessity

c. Effect of Principal's Mistake in Creating Authority

As long as the principal objectively manifests his intention to create authority in another, there is valid, actual authority—even though the principal did not intend to grant the authority. [Rest. 3d § 3.01]

e.g. **Example:** P goes to an office where several stockbrokers have desks and leaves a note on A's desk, believing it is X's desk. The note states, "I authorize you to sell my 100 shares of Acme Manufacturing stock at the market price." If A finds the note, A has actual authority to effect the sale, even though P intended to give the authority to X, not A.

(1) Agent's Fraud

The above rule has also been applied when the agent deceives the principal into granting her authority. For example, if A falsely represents her qualifications as a sales agent to P, and in reliance P authorizes A to sell certain goods, A has valid authority and any sale effected by A is binding on P.

(a) Discovery of Fraud by Principal

If P discovers the fraud *before* any sale, he may rescind (revoke) the authority even if the authority would otherwise be irrevocable (*see infra*, p. 51).

(b) Damages

In any case, P can hold A liable for any damages he sustains that result from his granting A authority (*e.g.*, if A's lack of qualifications results in P's property being sold for less than its fair market value).

d. Instructions—Limitations on Actual Authority

A frequent and difficult issue is whether particular directions given by the principal to the agent constitute a limitation on the agent's authority or mere advice to the agent.

e.g. **Example:** P owns a factory running at 50% capacity due to a lack of orders. Before leaving for his vacation, P tells his manager A not to order more than 100 tons of coal for power and heating at the factory. An order comes in the following day which would require more than 100 tons of coal to process promptly. Can A purchase the additional fuel, or is P's directive a limitation on A's authority?

(1) Result

There is no automatic answer in this type of situation. It depends on what the principal intended (or can be assumed he intended). The courts will consider the principal's purposes, whether or not he could be reached to give further directions, and any other relevant circumstances. Thus, in the example above, P's accessibility for advice, the importance of filling the order promptly (customer involved, etc.), and the like, would have to be determined.

(2) Note

Instructions may also be an issue in apparent authority situations. (*See infra*, p. 40.)

e. Termination of Actual Authority

An agent's actual authority can be terminated in a number of ways: (i) by expiration of the agency term or accomplishment of the agency's purpose, (ii) by change of circumstance or the death or incapacity of a party, or (iii) by act or agreement of the parties. (For detailed analysis, *see infra*, pp. 45–51.)

3. Apparent (Ostensible) Authority

There is a general rule in agency law that a third party deals with an agent at his own peril; *i.e.*, the third party has the duty of determining the scope of the agent's authority and will bear the loss if the agent acts outside that scope. [*See* **Wing v. Lederer,** 222 N.E.2d 535 (Ill. 1966)] However, this maxim is perhaps overstated, for a principal will be bound by his agent's unauthorized acts if the principal has ***manifested to a third party***, through words or conduct, ***that the agent has authority***, and the third party ***reasonably relies*** on this manifestation. This is the concept of apparent (sometimes called ostensible) authority. [*See* Rest. 3d § 3.03]

a. Basis for Apparent Authority

There is debate over whether apparent authority arises from estoppel (the principal is estopped from denying the agency because of his actions) or as a corollary of the objective theory of contract (if one objectively holds out another as having the power to contract for him, that objective manifestation will control despite subjective intent to the contrary). Most authorities seem to favor the objective contract theory because true estoppel would require a change of position by the third party, and no such change has been required under agency law. However, estoppel may still provide agency power in some circumstances (*see infra*, p. 43 *et seq.*).

b. Effect of Apparent Authority

Apparent authority gives the agent the ***power*** to bind the principal, ***but not the right***, which can be derived only from a grant of actual authority. Thus, although a principal will be bound by an agent who acts with apparent authority, the principal usually can hold the agent liable for breach of duty.

c. Relationship to Actual Authority

While actual authority focuses on the agent's power to bind the principal by virtue of the principal's manifestations to the agent, apparent authority is based on the ***principal's manifestations to third parties.*** It is often said that an agent's apparent authority is usually consistent with her actual authority because the principal's manifestations to the third party are often similar to his manifestations to the agent. However, the two are independent concepts. Indeed, an agent with apparent authority might have no actual authority whatsoever. [**System Investment Corp. v. Montview Acceptance Corp.,** 355 F.2d 463 (10th Cir. 1966)]

e.g. **Example:** P writes to A, directing her to act as P's agent for the sale of Blackacre. P sends a copy of this letter to T, a prospective purchaser. A has actual authority to sell Blackacre to anyone, and as to T, A has apparent authority as well.

e.g. **Example:** P leaves his car with A, directing A to find a buyer for the car but not to accept any offers without P's approval. Subsequently, X asks P about the car, and P tells X that she should "work out a deal" with A. In this situation, A has no actual authority to sell, but she does have apparent authority as to X, and P is therefore bound if A sells the car to X.

(1) Note

Technically, apparent authority arises only in the absence of actual authority (*i.e.*, if the agent had actual authority, a true agency relationship is established and there is no need to look to apparent authority, which creates only an ostensible agency; *see supra*, p. 9).

EXAM TIP

Be sure to remember that in an apparent authority situation, you need to discuss what transpired between the *principal and the third party*. This differs from an actual authority situation, where you would be discussing what transpired between the principal and the agent. In discussing apparent authority, ask yourself what the principal did to indicate *to the third party* that the agent had authority.

---

d. Requisites for Apparent Authority

(1) Holding out by Principal

There must be some act by the principal that causes the third party to reasonably believe that the agent has authority. [*See* **Gizzi v. Texaco, Inc.,** 437 F.2d 308 (3d Cir. 1971)] However, in most jurisdictions the principal's act may be very slight, and even inaction may suffice. [*See, e.g.,* **Kanelles v. Locke,** *supra*, p. 9—principal voluntarily or negligently allowed imposter to pose as agent; *but see* **Hoddeson v. Koos Bros.,** 135 A.2d 702 (N.J. 1957)—insufficient evidence to conclude that person posing as furniture salesman in store and who took plaintiff's money had apparent authority] An agent cannot create apparent authority by her own acts. [**Home Owners' Loan Corp. v. Thornburgh,** 106 P.2d 511 (Okla. 1940)]

(2) Reliance by Third Party

Regardless of whether apparent authority is based on estoppel or the objective theory of contract, the principal will be bound only if the third party ***reasonably relied*** on the principal's manifestation of authority. If the third party knew or had reason to know that the principal was in error, no apparent authority will arise. [**S.S. Silberblatt, Inc. v. Seaboard Surety Co.,** 417 F.2d 1043 (8th Cir. 1969)]

(a) Test for Reliance

The test for reliance is what a *reasonable person under the circumstances* would have believed—a test that is sometimes difficult to apply.

e.g. **Example:** Customer C calls P's office and asks for the price of P's products. P's secretary answers the phone and supplies erroneous prices. If C relies on the prices to her detriment in bidding on a construction contract, is P bound by the erroneous quotation? This depends on whether a reasonable person in C's position would have believed that P's secretary was authorized to supply such information (perhaps so, for a small subcontractor; probably not, if the supplier is a large corporation).

(3) Writing

If the creation of the agency relationship is required to be in writing (*see supra*, pp. 10–11), the principal's holding out on which the apparent authority is based must be in writing.

EXAM TIP

If an apparent authority situation presents itself on an exam, you must look for (and discuss) the two requirements for apparent authority: (i) the principal *held the agent out* to a third party as having authority, and (ii) the third party in fact *reasonably relied* on the holding out.

---

e. Types of Apparent Authority

(1) Where Agent Has No Actual Authority

Apparent authority may arise in certain circumstances even though the agent has ***no actual authority.***

(a) Imposters

If the principal negligently permits an imposter to be in a position where the imposter appears to have authority to act for the principal, the imposter may have apparent authority. [*See, e.g.,* **Kanelles v. Locke,** *supra*, p. 38; *but see* **Hoddeson v. Koos Bros.,** *supra*, p. 38]

(b) Lingering Authority

An agent whose actual authority has been terminated will have apparent authority as to persons who knew of the agent's prior authority but were not properly notified of the termination of actual authority. [Rest. 3d § 3.11, comment c; *and see infra*, p. 51]

(2) Where Agent Has Some Actual Authority

(a) Prior Acts

If the principal has previously allowed the agent to act beyond her authority and the principal knows that a third party is aware of this fact, the principal is bound by the agent's unauthorized act.

e.g. **Example:** A, a janitor in P's employ, has no authority to employ other people. On two prior occasions, A hired T to do some painting in P's building. P paid T's invoices without protest. If A hires T to do more painting, P will be liable to T for his services because of A's apparent authority; *i.e.*, it appeared to T that A had authority to hire him. [**Colyer v. Vanderbilt Hotel Co.,** 4 S.E.2d 436 (N.C. 1939)]

(b) Position

Perhaps the greatest source of apparent authority arises from position. [Rest. 3d § 3.03, comment b] When a principal appoints an agent to a position (or allows her to occupy a position) that customarily in the locality carries with it certain authority, a third party who knows of the agent's position may reasonably assume that the agent has such authority. If the principal has denied the agent some aspect of this customary authority, the agent will still have apparent authority to perform the customary act as long as the third party does not know of the curtailment of authority.

1) Illustration—Warranties

If the rights of third persons dealing with an agent are concerned, the agent is deemed to have apparent authority to make warranties concerning the subject matter of the agency whenever the making of such warranties is customary in connection with the agent's actual authority. (For typical warranty powers, *see supra*, pp. 33, 34.)

a) Types of Warranties

1/ Express Warranties

Any affirmation of a present fact regarding the subject matter in question is an express warranty of that fact. For example, an agent's statements of identification, description, quantity, or quality of the subject matter are express warranties (*e.g.*, "This barrel contains 50 gallons of pure Pennsylvania S.A.E. #30 motor oil"). Statements that the principal "guarantees" or "warrants" satisfaction or performance (*e.g.*, "We warrant these tires against blowouts for 30,000 miles") are also express warranties, as are statements that the goods are returnable if unsatisfactory to purchaser.

a/ Liability for False Factual Warranties

If the warranty is a representation of an existing fact subsequently proved false, the principal may be liable under either a tort theory of misrepresentation or a contract theory of breach of warranty.

1] Tort

Tort liability requires proof of scienter (*i.e.*, knowledge of falsity or reckless disregard of truth) by either the principal or agent (*see infra*, p. 121).

2] Contract

However, no such intent or guilty knowledge need be established for contractual liability, which exists even if the representation was made in good faith and without knowledge of its falsity by either the principal or agent.

2/ Implied Warranties

In addition to express warranties, the agent's acts on behalf of the principal may give rise to certain implied warranties. For example, a store clerk's sale of goods can give rise to the implied warranty of merchantability. (*See* Sale & Lease of Goods Summary for a discussion of how the warranty arises.)

f. Termination of Apparent Authority

Apparent authority is not terminated merely by giving notice to the agent. Rather, notice of the termination of apparent authority must be given to the ***third party*** to whom authority was originally manifested. [Rest. 3d § 3.11; **Tucker v. Atkinson,** 245 S.W.2d 388 (Ark. 1952); *and see infra*, p. 51]

e.g. **Example:** P appoints A his agent for the sale of Blackacre, and so advises T. If P were to write to A, revoking her authority, this would effectively terminate A's ***actual*** authority. However, unless and until P communicates the revocation to T, A's ***apparent*** authority would continue as to T, and T would be protected in dealing with A (*i.e.*, any contracts entered into between T and A, on behalf of P, would be binding).

(1) Source of Notice

Notice need not come to the third party directly from the principal. Notice of termination will be effective as long as it is from ***any reliable source.*** [Rest. 3d § 3.11, comment e]

(2) Expiration of Stated Limitation

If the apparent authority is originally ***conditioned*** as to time or events, an expiration of the time period (or occurrence of the event) will terminate the authority.

e.g. **Example:** If P advises T that A is his agent in selling Blackacre "for the next 60 days," A's apparent authority ceases as to T after that period of time.

(3) Death or Incapacity

The death or incapacity of a principal ***does not*** automatically terminate the agent's apparent authority if the third party has no notice of the death or incapacity and reasonably believes that the agent is acting with actual authority. [Rest. 3d § 3.11, comment b—this is contrary to the position taken in Rest. 2d § 120, comment c, that the death or incapacity of the principal terminates apparent authority]

g. Distinguish—Apparent Ownership

An apparent agent merely has authority to deal with third parties to the extent that the principal, by his statements to those persons, indicates that the agent is authorized. However, if the principal has clothed the agent with both possession and ***apparent ownership*** of the principal's property, the agent's power is much broader: The agent can deal with the property as if she were the true owner, and the principal (the real owner) is estopped to assert the invalidity of his agent's dealings where the rights of innocent third parties are concerned.

e.g. **Example:** To deceive his creditors, P deeds his home to A, it being verbally agreed between P and A that A will surrender the premises and reconvey the property on P's demand. If A sells the property to T, an innocent purchaser, P is estopped to assert his title. On the other hand, P can always assert his rights to the property against A.

(1) Relevant Factors

"Apparent ownership" requires that the principal clothe the agent with such ***indicia of ownership*** that a reasonable person would conclude that the agent actually owned the property involved. [**Lamb v. General Associates, Inc.,** 374 P.2d 677 (Wash. 1962)]

(a) Transferring Possession

In general, merely transferring possession of tangible real or personal property to the agent is not enough. Possession is *not a sufficient indicia* of ownership, because the possessor may be a tenant, adverse possessor, manager, etc. [**Carter v. Rowley,** 59 Cal. App. 486 (1922)]

(b) Delivery of Deed

However, if the owner delivers to the agent a bill of sale or deed to the property in addition to possession of the property, this *is* a sufficient indicia of ownership. [**Carter v. Rowley,** *supra*]

(c) Document of Title

Similarly, if the property involved is represented by a *document of title* or is a negotiable instrument indorsed in blank by the principal, mere delivery to the agent constitutes sufficient apparent ownership. [**Phillips v. Clifford F. Reid, Inc.,** 3 Cal. App. 2d 304 (1934)]

(d) U.C.C. Criteria

If personal property is entrusted to a *merchant* who deals in goods of *that kind,* this is sufficient to vest the merchant with the power to transfer title to the goods to an innocent purchaser for value. [U.C.C. § 2–403; *and see* Sale & Lease of Goods Summary]

1) Factors Acts

Under state "factors acts," if goods are consigned for sale to one in the business of selling goods for others (a factor), the factor has power to transfer title to an innocent purchaser for value.

4. Estoppel

Estoppel is a remedy applied to prevent a principal who has ***misled*** another from profiting from his own misconduct. Estoppel may be invoked whenever the principal has ***intentionally or carelessly*** caused or allowed a third party to believe that his agent has authority to do that which in fact the agent is not authorized to do, or ***fails to take reasonable steps to notify*** the third party when he has notice of the third party's belief, ***and*** the third party ***detrimentally relies*** so that it would be unjust to allow the principal to deny the agent's authority. [Rest. 3d § 2.05]

e.g. **Example:** P learns that A, who has no authority to sell P's skiing equipment, is negotiating for its sale with T on the representation that A is P's agent. P does nothing, although he could easily notify T, and T pays A for the goods. P is bound to deliver the equipment to T at the agreed price, and he is also liable to T for breach of any warranty customary in such a sale; *i.e.*, P is bound to perform as if A were in fact authorized to sell the goods, being estopped to deny such authority.

a. Distinguish—Apparent Authority

Like apparent authority, estoppel is based on the principal's manifestations to, or withholding information from, a third party. [Rest. 3d § 2.05, comment c] However, whereas apparent authority makes the principal a ***contracting party*** with the third party, with rights and liabilities as to both sides, estoppel only compensates the third party for ***losses arising from the third party's*** reliance on the principal's statements or omissions and does not create rights in the principal.

(1) Note

In most cases, this distinction is academic, because the courts tend to treat cases of apparent authority and estoppel interchangeably. This is particularly true when the principal makes actual representations to third parties (as opposed to withholding information, as in the example above). [*But see* **Hoddeson v. Koos Bros.**, *supra*, p. 38—dicta suggested that estoppel could be applied where an imposter posed as a salesman in plaintiff's store and the facts were insufficient to support an action at law based on apparent authority]

(2) But Note

In certain cases there simply is no apparent authority, and thus the presence or absence of the elements of estoppel determines whether the third party has a right to relief.

e.g. **Example:** Without authority, A offers to sell T ***real property*** that in fact belongs to P. T asks P whether A is authorized to act on his behalf, and P (either intentionally or carelessly) leads T to believe that A is so authorized. Thereafter, T pays the purchase price to A, who absconds with the funds, and T demands a deed from P. Although any actual or apparent authority to sell the land would have to be in writing under the Statute of Frauds (*see supra,* p. 10), the fact that P misled T, coupled with T's detrimental reliance, is sufficient to invoke an estoppel against P, and the estoppel bars P from denying A's authority *or* from asserting the Statute of Frauds as a defense. [Rest. 3d § 3.02]

SOURCES OF AGENCY POWER		
TYPE OF POWER	**HOW CREATED**	**EFFECT**
ACTUAL AUTHORITY:		
• **EXPRESS**	Expressly granted by P to A (Between P and A)	A has the ***power and right*** to act for P (P is bound)
• **IMPLIED**	Implied by A from P's words or conduct (Between P and A)	A has the ***power and right*** to act for P (P is bound)
APPARENT AUTHORITY	Holding out by P and reliance by Third Party (Between P and Third Party)	A has the power to act (P is bound) ***but not the right*** (A may be liable to P)
ESTOPPEL	P's intentional or careless causing of detrimental reliance by Third Party (Between P and Third Party)	A has ***no power*** to act (P is not bound) but P must compensate Third Party for losses
Note: In some cases P may also be found by ***ratification*** (*see* Chapter IV, *infra*).		

5. Inherent Agency Power

The Restatement (Second) of Agency recognizes the concept of inherent agency power, which allows an agent to bind the principal even though the ***agent has no power*** from actual authority, apparent authority, or estoppel. The power is said to arise from the agency relationship itself and is to protect persons who have innocently dealt with the agent. [Rest. 2d § 8A] The Restatement (Third) of Agency, however, does not recognize this doctrine. In fact, few courts have adopted the doctrine of inherent agency power [*see* Fishman, *Inherent Agency Power—Should Enterprise Liability Apply to Agent's Unauthorized Contracts?* 19 Rutgers L.J. 1 (1987)], probably because they can usually rely on the more definite doctrine of apparent authority. A few courts have even rejected the doctrine. [*See* 3 Am. Jur. 2d, *Agency* §§ 73, 76]

EXAM TIP

One of the most important and frequently tested questions on an exam is whether the agent had the *power* to act on behalf of the principal. In answering such a question, you should use the approach suggested in the chart at the beginning of this chapter; that is, look first for *actual authority,* then for *apparent authority.* If neither exists, don't overlook the other three ways that a principal can be held liable for his agent's acts. Consider: (i) whether the principal acted inappropriately and as such will be *estopped* from denying the agent's power; or (ii) whether the principal *ratified* the agent's act (*see* Chapter IV, *infra*). Finally, keep in mind that the principal will *not be bound* by the agent's act if the agent's authority (if based on actual or apparent authority) to act was *terminated* (*see* below).

C. Termination of Agents Authority and Power

1. Termination of Actual Authority

The agency relationship, as well as the authority of the agent, may be terminated in any of several ways:

a. By Expiration of Agency Term

Authority conferred for a specified period of time terminates upon expiration of the period. [Rest. 3d § 3.09, comment b; **Shelton v. Lemmon,** 268 S.W. 177 (Tex. 1924)]

(1) "Reasonable Time"

If no time is specified by the parties, a reasonable time is implied, and the authority terminates at the end of a reasonable period. [**Beaucar v. Bristol Federal Savings & Loan Association,** 268 A.2d 679 (Conn. 1969)] What constitutes a "reasonable time" depends on all of the circumstances, including the nature of the agency, the likelihood of a change in purposes, etc. [Rest. 3d § 3.09, comment d]

e.g. **Example:** P authorizes A to sell P's car. If 10 years elapse without any communication between P and A, the agency would probably be deemed terminated—*i.e.,* A would no longer have authority to sell the car. [*See* Rest. 3d § 3.09, comment d]

b. By Accomplishment of Agency Purpose

If the agent's authority was to perform a specified act or to accomplish a specific result, the agent's authority terminates upon the accomplishment of that act or result—even if the authorized performance was by another agent or the principal himself. [Rest. 3d § 3.09, comment b; **Echaide v. Confederation of Canada Life Insurance,** 459 F.2d 1377 (5th Cir. 1972)]

e.g. **Example:** P engages A and B as real estate brokers to sell Blackacre for her. If A sells Blackacre to X, and B learns of this, both agents' authority is terminated. Thus, neither A nor B is then authorized to rescind the transaction with X or make a new deal with X or anyone else.

(1) But Note

As discussed *infra,* p. 51, the agent's authority would continue until she has ***knowledge or notice*** that the act, result, or event has occurred. Thus, in the example above, B's authority may continue until B acquires notice that A has sold Blackacre—unless P had originally made it clear to B that others were also being engaged to sell the property. [*See* Rest. 3d § 3.06, comment b]

c. By Change of Circumstances

(1) Loss or Destruction of Subject Matter

If the subject matter of the agency is lost or destroyed, the agent's authority to deal with that subject matter is terminated. (A ***partial*** destruction would likewise terminate the authority if further actions by the agent would not be in the best interests of the principal.)

e.g. **Example:** P authorizes A to sell P's house. Prior to any sale, the house is destroyed by fire (or lost through mortgage foreclosure, eminent domain proceedings, etc.). A's authority to sell is thereby terminated.

(2) Change of Circumstances Affecting Value

Similarly, if there is a ***basic and unforeseen change*** of circumstances that substantially affects the value of the subject matter, or otherwise makes it apparent that the principal would not wish the agent to proceed, the agent's authority is terminated. [*See* Rest. 3d § 3.06, comment b]

e.g. **Example:** If P authorizes A to sell his land for a certain amount and then minerals are discovered on the land which triple its value, A's authority to sell for the original amount is terminated.

e.g. **Example:** Similarly, if P hires A to charter a ship to transport certain goods that P was planning to purchase, and A subsequently learns that P did not purchase the goods, A's authority to charter the ship terminates.

(a) Other Sufficient Events

Other "unforeseen events" that have been held sufficient to terminate an agent's authority include the outbreak of war, the bankruptcy of the principal or agent, changes of law, and embezzlement or other disloyalty of the agent. [*See, e.g.,* **McKey v. Clark,** 233 F. 928 (9th Cir. 1916)—bankruptcy a sufficient "unforeseen event"]

(b) Principal's Knowledge Relevant

In any case of unforeseen circumstances, the *principal's* knowledge and actions are obviously relevant in determining whether an agent's authority has been terminated. For example, if P and A are in close contact, and P is aware of the change of events, A's authority probably continues absent new instructions from P.

d. By Death of Either Principal or Agent

Under the prevailing view, the death of the principal or agent ***automatically terminates*** the agent's authority. However, the Restatement (Third) of Agency adopts a new approach: Actual authority terminates on the ***agent's*** death. [Rest. 3d § 3.07(1)] The death of the principal also terminates the agent's actual authority, ***but the termination is not effective*** against the agent or any third party with whom the agent deals ***until notice of the principal's death has been received*** by the agent or third party. [Rest. 3d § 3.07(2)]

e. By Cessation of Existence or Suspension of Powers

The actual authority of an agent terminates if the agent or principal ceases to exist (or commences a process that will lead to cessation of existence) or when its powers are suspended. [Rest. 3d § 3.07(3), (4)] For example, the dissolution of a corporation terminates the actual authority of any agent that was acting on behalf of the corporation.

f. By Incapacity

(1) Principal's Incapacity

As in the case of the death of the principal or agent (*see supra,* p. 46), the Restatement (Third) of Agency departs from the general view that incapacity of the principal or agent automatically terminates the agent's authority. Under the Restatement (Third) of Agency, if a principal loses the capacity to do an act, then the agent's actual authority to do the same act is terminated. The termination is effective against the agent or third party with whom he deals when the agent or third party has notice that the principal's incapacity is permanent or that the principal has been adjudicated incapacitated. [Rest. 3d § 3.08(1)]

EXAM TIP

Remember that, at least under the Restatement (Third) of Agency, *apparent authority* may apply even if *actual authority has been terminated.* If the agent's actual authority has been terminated because of the principal's death or incapacity, check to see whether any third party has notice of the death or incapacity. If the agent has notice but the third party does not, then the agent is acting with apparent authority and the third party is protected. The rationale is that it is unjust to penalize third parties dealing with an agent because of the unknown death or incapacity of the principal. [*See* Rest. 3d § 3.08, comment b]

---

(2) Agent's Incapacity

Because an agent need only possess minimal mental capacity to act on a principal's behalf (*see supra,* p. 10), an agent's authority to act for a principal is not necessarily terminated when the agent becomes mentally "incapacitated." An agent's authority will terminate only if her mental capacity is such that she cannot do the particular act authorized. If she can do the act, then she is not technically "incapacitated."

(a) Note

In addition to mental incapacity, an agent may lose the capacity to act for other reasons. Thus, if a real estate broker loses her license, she may lose her capacity to act in a real estate transaction, and her authority to represent the principal is terminated.

EXAM TIP

If on an exam you have to determine whether an agent's authority to act for a principal is terminated due to incapacity, ask yourself if the agent can still perform the act authorized by the principal *even though she is incapacitated.* If so, the agent's authority will not terminate.

---

g. Exceptions

(1) Written Instrument

A written instrument may make an agent's actual authority effective upon a principal's incapacity or confer it irrevocably regardless of loss of capacity. [Rest. 3d § 3.08(2)]

e.g. **Example:** A principal executes a written durable power of attorney which provides that the agent (or attorney in fact) has authority to act on behalf of the principal and that the authority to act will not be affected by the principal's subsequent incapacity. If the principal does subsequently become incapacitated, the agent's authority to act on his behalf continues as provided in the written instrument. The principal may, however, revoke the agent's authority at any time that he has capacity. [*See* Rest. 3d § 3.08, comment c; Uniform Probate Code §§ 5–501, 5–504]

(2) **Powers Given as Security**

As will be discussed later (*infra,* pp. 49–51), agency powers may be held to be ***irrevocable*** by the principal because the agency is really for the benefit of the agent. Such powers do ***not terminate*** on the death or incapacity of the principal or agent, and their exercise therefore binds the principal's estate. [*See* Rest. 3d § 3.13]

(3) **Banks**

To the extent that a bank is its customer's agent for the payment of checks, the bank may pay on its customer's checks unless it knows of its customer's death or adjudication of incompetency. Even after the bank knows of its customer's death, it may pay on its customer's checks for up to ***10 days*** after the customer's death. [U.C.C. § 4–405; *and see* Commercial Paper & Payment Law Summary]

EXAM TIP

On an exam, it may seem unfair to hold the principal (or his estate) liable for the agent's act if the principal was dead or incapacitated when the agent exercised authority. For example, while the agent was en route to France to purchase an original Monet painting on the principal's behalf, the principal died but the agent received no notice of the death. When the agent arrived in France she purchased the Monet for the principal on the principal's credit. Under the Restatement (Third) of Agency, the *termination of authority was not effective* because the agent had no notice of the death. Consequently, the agent acted with actual authority and the principal's estate is liable to the third party for payment of the purchase price for the Monet. Note, however, that under the Restatement (Second) of Agency, the agent's authority terminated on the principal's death. Thus, the estate would not be liable pursuant to that view.

h. By Act or Agreement of the Parties

Because the principal-agent relationship is consensual in nature, it terminates when either or both parties agree (or otherwise act) to end the relationship. This is true regardless of any previous agreement that the agency or authority would be "irrevocable," or would last for a specified time; *i.e.,* the agency ends whenever either party communicates to the other an intention that the authority shall end. Such a communication effectively terminates the rights, duties, and powers of the relationship. [Rest. 3d §§ 3.09, 3.10]

(1) **Renunciation by Agent**

Where the agent terminates the relationship, there is said to be a renunciation of her authority. The renunciation is effective when the principal receives notice. The fact that the agent is contractually bound to perform, and that her renunciation thus constitutes a breach of contract and exposes her to liability in damages, does not prevent the renunciation from being effective to terminate her authority and duties as an agent. [Rest. 3d § 3.10; **Century Refining Co. v. Hall,** 316 F.2d 15 (10th Cir. 1963)]

e.g. **Example:** P hires A as the manager of his business for a period of one year. After six months, A resigns. A may be liable to P for the cost of finding a replacement, but her resignation effectively terminates her authority and relieves her of the duties of the principal-agent relationship.

(2) Revocation of Authority by Principal

(a) General Rule

An agency is deemed to be created for the benefit of the principal, and it follows that the principal is usually free at any time to terminate the agency relationship or any authority granted to the agent. The termination is effective when the agent receives notice. [Rest. 3d § 3.10]

1) Agent's Contract Rights

Of course, the principal's revocation may well constitute a breach of contract with the agent. If the principal revokes the agent's authority notwithstanding a contractual provision to the contrary, the revocation is nonetheless effective, and the actual authority of the agent terminates, but the principal may be liable to the agent for breach of contract. [Rest. 3d § 3.10; **McDonald v. Davis,** 389 S.W.2d 494 (Tex. 1965)—principal liable for breach of contract because principal had the power, but not the right under an exclusive listing contract, to revoke the agent's authority]

(b) Exception—Power Given for Benefit of Agent

Notwithstanding the general rule permitting revocation, there are certain situations in which an agent's authority *cannot* be revoked, *i.e.,* the agent's powers are deemed to be *"irrevocable"* These are cases in which the agency or power was created *for the benefit of the agent or a third person,* rather than for the principal. The power is given *as security* or is an *irrevocable proxy.* In such situations, it is not proper to permit the principal to terminate it at will. [Rest. 3d § 3.12]

1) Requirements

A mere recital that a power is irrevocable is insufficient to create an irrevocable power. [**Todd v. Superior Court,** 181 Cal. 406 (1919)] For the power granted to be held irrevocable, it must appear that:

(i) ***The power or authority was granted to secure the performance of a duty*** or to protect the title of the agent or some third person; ***and***

(ii) ***It was given when the duty or title was created,*** or it was ***supported by consideration.***

In addition, a power to exercise voting rights associated with securities or a membership interest may be conferred on a proxy through a manifestation of actual authority. The power may be given as security as discussed above and may be made irrevocable. [Rest. 3d § 3.12]

e.g. **Example:** P owns Blackacre and wants to operate a restaurant on the property. A loans to P money to finance construction. The written agreement between P and A provides that, as security for the loan, A has the irrevocable authority to transfer ownership of Blackacre to himself in the event P defaults on the loan. A has a power given as security—the power was granted to secure the performance of P's payment on the loan and it was supported by consideration. [Rest. 3d § 3.12, comment b]

cf. **Compare:** P owns a restaurant and hires A to manage the restaurant for a period of 10 years and expressly agrees to not terminate A's authority during that period. The agreement states that P's promise is irrevocable and is given as security to A for A's interest in receiving the management fee as specified in the agreement. A does not have a power given as security. If P terminates A's authority before the expiration of 10 years, A will not have a specifically enforceable right to continue to manage the restaurant. He may seek only contract damages. [Rest. 3d § 3.12, comment b]

cf. **Compare:** P and A, who own Blackacre as tenants in common, agree to sell the property for $20,000 and further agree that A shall have the "exclusive right to sell." P's authority to A is ***revocable***—*i.e.*, not "a power given as security"—because it did not arise at the time that A's title to the property was created.

2) Termination

Because a power given as security is not held for the benefit of the grantor of the power (*i.e.,* the "principal"), it is not really an "agency power" in the usual sense. Accordingly, the power generally does not terminate on the death or incapacity of the grantor ("principal") or its holder ("agent"). [Rest. 3d § 3.13; **Pan American Petroleum Corp. v. Cain,** 340 S.W.2d 93 (Tex. 1960)]

a) Events That Terminate Power

Powers given as security or irrevocable proxies are terminated on the ***consent*** of the person for whom the power was created (*i.e.,* the agent or the beneficiary) or by events that: (i) ***discharge*** the obligation or ***terminate*** the interest, (ii) make execution ***illegal** or **impossible,*** (iii) effectively ***surrender the power or proxy*** by the person for whose benefit it was created, or (iv) have been ***agreed*** to by the principal and agent. [Rest. 3d § 3.13]

3) Distinguish—Power Coupled with an Interest

A power coupled with an interest is narrower than a power given as security and requires that the agent have an interest in the subject matter of the agency. The agent must be vested with an interest that accompanies the power (as opposed to a power given as security, where the agent can hold the power but has no interest—the interest can be in favor of a third-party beneficiary). [Rest. 3d § 3.12, comment c; *and see* **Hunt v. Rousmanier,** 21 U.S. (8 Wheat.) 174 (1823)]

e.g. **Example:** P and A agree that if A lends P $5,000, A shall have a one-half interest in P's property and authority to sell the property for $20,000, A's loan to be repayable out of the sale proceeds. A's power (to sell the property) is coupled with an interest (one-half ownership) and is irrevocable.

cf. **Compare:** P engages attorney A to represent him in certain litigation, and it is agreed that A's fee will be a percentage of the recovery. A's authority is revocable because her interest is merely in the ***proceeds*** resulting from the exercise of her power (*i.e.,* A has no beneficial interest in the subject matter of the agency). [**Fields v. Potts,** 140 Cal. App. 2d 697 (1956)]

cf. **Compare:** P owns Blackacre and wants to operate a restaurant on the property. A loans to P money to finance construction. The written agreement between P and A provides that as security for the loan, A has the irrevocable authority to transfer ownership of Blackacre to himself in the event P defaults on the loan. As discussed above, A has a power given as security. He does not, however, have a power coupled with an interest because he has no interest in Blackacre until P defaults on the loan. [Rest. 3d § 3.12, comment c]

a) Effect of Attempt to Revoke Powers Coupled with an Interest

Because such powers are truly irrevocable, any attempt by the principal to revoke a power coupled with an interest is regarded as a ***nullity***. The agent is entitled to an order for specific performance of the principal's promise not to revoke.

b) Agent's Fraud

If the principal was ***defrauded*** by the agent into giving the agent an irrevocable power, or if there is some other failure of the consideration that the principal was to receive for giving the power, the principal has the right to ***rescind*** the power, provided no innocent third parties are involved.

i. Notice Required to Terminate

The general rule is that an agent's actual authority continues until she knows, or has reason to know, of the change relied on to terminate the authority. Thus, the principal must notify the agent, or the agent must otherwise have discovered the principal's revocation, the loss or destruction of the subject matter, other unforeseen happening, etc. [Rest. 3d § 3.10; **Robertson v. Cloud,** 47 Miss. 208 (1872)]

(1) Form

No particular form of notice is required. Hence, notice is equally effective if the principal informs the agent directly or if the agent independently learns of the event that terminates her authority. Notice may be oral or written. [Rest. 3d § 3.10, comment c]

2. Termination of Apparent Authority

Whenever the principal represents to a third party that another person is his agent and is authorized to act on his behalf on certain matters, and the third party reasonably relies on the representation, the agent has apparent authority (*see supra,* p. 37 *et seq.*). Such apparent authority continues, despite the termination of actual authority, until it is no longer reasonable for the third party with whom the agent deals to believe that the agent continues to act with actual authority. [Rest. 3d § 3.11]

a. Specific Persons with Whom Agent Deals

If the principal knows that the agent has been dealing with particular third parties, personal or individual notice to those third parties is usually required to terminate the agent's apparent authority. [**Holdam v. Middlesex Supply, Inc.,** 355 F.2d 122 (1st Cir. 1966)]

b. Public at Large

In cases where the agent's apparent authority arose from representations by the principal to the public at large, notice by advertisement or similar means is generally sufficient to terminate the agent's apparent authority.

c. Written Authority

If the principal has given the agent ***written*** authority (*e.g.*, a power of attorney), he must reclaim the writing or notify all parties with whom the agent may deal that the authority has been revoked. In other words, the principal is charged with knowledge that the agent may show the writing to third parties. [Rest. 3d § 3.11, comment d]

(1) Recorded Writing

If the writing granting the agent authority has been recorded, the principal must record a revocation of the authority.

(2) Limits Within Writing Itself

However, if a written authorization indicates specific conditions upon which the agent's authority will terminate, and a third party learns that the conditions have occurred, no further notice of termination to the third party is required.

e.g. **Example:** Broker A shows prospective purchaser B the power of attorney to sell P's house. If the power states that it expires on a certain date, no further notice to B is necessary to terminate A's apparent authority after that date.

d. Termination at Death or Incapacity

Most states hold that the death or incapacity of the principal or agent terminates apparent authority. The Restatement (Third) of Agency provides that apparent authority terminates on the death or incapacity of the principal or agent ***when the third party receives notice.*** [Rest. 3d § 3.11, comment b; *and see supra,* pp. 46–48]

EXAM TIP

On an exam, if you find that the agent had the actual or apparent authority to act for her principal, recall that the principal will not be bound by the agent's act *if the agent's authority was terminated.* Therefore, before answering that the principal will be bound by the agent's act, check the facts of your question to see if the agent's authority was somehow terminated, such as by the principal's death (accompanied by notice under Restatement (Third) of Agency) or expiration of the agency term. Remember that only if the agent's authority had not been terminated will the principal be bound by the agent's act.

METHODS OF TERMINATING AGENT'S AUTHORITY

ACTUAL AUTHORITY	APPARENT AUTHORITY
• Expiration of agency term • Accomplishment of agency purpose • Destruction of subject matter or change of circumstances affecting value • Death of incapacity of agent • Death or incapacity of principal (except for powers given as security and durable powers of attorney) — Majority view: Authority terminates automatically — Restatement (Third) of Agency: Authority terminates but is not effective against third parties until notice is given • By agreement or by act of one or both parties • Cessation of existence of suspension of powers	• Notification of termination to third parties — Parties with whom agent dealt usually must receive personal or individual notice — If apparent authority was created by public representation, public notice (*e.g.*, in newspaper) is generally required — If principal gave agent a written authority, principal must reclaim the writing or notify all parties with whom agent may deal. (If the writing was recorded, principal must record revocation.) • Death or incapacity of principal or agent — Majority view: Authority terminates automatically — Restatement (Third) of Agency: Authority terminates when third party receives notice

Chapter Four: Ratification

CONTENTS	PAGE

Key Exam Issues

Occasionally, in an exam question you may run into a situation where one person (the agent) purports to be acting on behalf of another (the principal) when entering into a transaction with a third party, but the agent in fact has ***no authority*** to act (indeed, an agency relationship might not exist at all). Under ordinary agency rules, the principal cannot be bound by the agent's act because the agent lacked authority. But what happens if the principal wants to be bound? The doctrine of ratification allows the principal to give authority ***after the fact,*** and the authority is treated as having existed at the time the agent acted.

For exam purposes, the important points to remember are:

(i) ***Only the principal may ratify,*** and the act being ratified must be one that ***can be performed by an agent*** (*i.e.,* illegal acts cannot be ratified).

(ii) ***The principal must have actual knowledge of all material facts*** of the transaction at the time of ratification; otherwise, the ratification can later be rescinded.

(iii) The principal can ratify an act only if ***the principal was in existence when the agent acted*** and ***the principal had capacity at the time of ratification*** (generally only relevant for artificial entities such as corporations).

(iv) The principal must ***manifest an intention to be bound by the agents' acts.***

(v) ***Only the entire transaction*** can be ratified. The principal may not adopt beneficial parts of the transaction and reject the rest. It is an "all or nothing" proposition.

(vi) Finally, ***ratification must occur before the third party revokes*** (the contract between the third party and the agent is treated as an offer, and the offer must be accepted by the principal before it is revoked).

Remember, ratification can both establish the agency relationship and provide authority for the agent at the same time. If your exam question involves an agent's previously unauthorized act that the principal wishes to adopt, go through the above steps to determine whether the agency can be established through ratification.

A. Introduction

1. In General

Ratification is the affirmance by a person of a *prior act* supposedly done on his behalf by another, but which was ***not*** authorized (and hence would otherwise not be binding upon him). [**Higgins v. D & F Electric Co.,** 140 S.E.2d 99 (Ga. 1964)] The essence of ratification is that the prior unauthorized act is treated as if it had been authorized by the "principal" at the outset. [Rest. 3d § 4.01]

2. Agreement Treated as Offer

Before the ratification, the relation of the third party to the principal is similar to that of an offeror to an offeree—*i.e.,* the third party's agreement with the agent is deemed to be no more than an offer to the principal.

a. No Ratification—No Contract

It follows that if the principal never ratifies, there is no contract between the third party and the principal. The agent, however, can be held liable to the third party for breach of her warranty of authority. (*See infra,* pp. 74–75.)

b. Ratification—Acceptance of Offer

If the principal ratifies, however, he is deemed to have "accepted" the third party's offer and becomes bound by the contract. As a corollary, the third party is generally free until ratification to rescind the contract with the unauthorized agent—*i.e.,* to "revoke" the offer to the principal. [Rest. 3d § 4.05]

3. Effects of Ratification

Ratification may establish ***both*** the agent's authority and the agency relationship. Thus, after ratification, the principal becomes liable for the agent's act and the agent is relieved of liability to the principal. [Rest. 3d § 4.02, comment b; *and see* **Rakestraw v. Rodrigues,** 8 Cal. 3d 67 (1972)]

Example: P, the owner and publisher of a small newspaper, is taken ill. Without being asked to do so, his friend A takes charge of the paper and publishes several issues, in the course of which A libels T and incurs certain debts for printing supplies furnished by X. If P subsequently affirms A's actions, he has made A his agent (no such relationship previously existed) and has bound himself by A's conduct during his absence. P's affirmation may subject him to ***tort*** liability for T's libel (*see infra,* pp. 117–118).

a. "Relation Back" Theory

The traditional rule is that once an agent's act is ratified, it is treated as though it had been ***authorized from the outset.*** All rights and liabilities are therefore said to "relate back" to the date of the original unauthorized act. [Rest. 3d § 4.02, and comment b] In other words, ***ratification is retroactive.***

Example: Without authority, A negotiates a loan purportedly on P's behalf on January 1, the agreement providing that interest is payable from that date. The funds are received by P on February 1, and P decides to affirm the transaction. Interest is payable by P from January 1, the date the loan was originally negotiated by A.

b. When Ratification Is Not Effective

Ratification is not effective if: (i) it benefits a person who engaged in ***misrepresentation or other conduct that would make a contract voidable;*** (ii) the principal ***ratified the transaction to avoid a loss*** and the resulting benefit is in favor of the agent (*i.e.,* if the agent's unauthorized act forces the principal to take action to avoid a loss, the agent is not exonerated and the principal's act in avoiding the loss does not operate as a ratification of the agent's act); or (iii) it would ***prejudice innocent third persons*** who acquired rights in the transaction prior to the ratification. [Rest. 3d § 4.02(2)]

Example: Without authority, A purports to sell Blackacre to T on P's behalf for $10,000. Without knowledge of A's transaction, P subsequently sells the land to B for $8,000. Upon learning of the sale to T at a higher price, P attempts to ratify that transaction. *Result:* The ratification will not "relate back" against B; B can compel specific performance of the contract with P, and P may also be liable to T for damages because of his ratification. [**Pettis v. State Farm Mutual Automobile Insurance Co.,** 239 So. 2d 772 (Ala. 1970)]

e.g. **Example:** P offers to sell Blackacre to T for $10,000. Later, A (who is P's real estate agent) finds someone willing to pay more for the property and, although A has no authority to do so, she notifies T that P has revoked the offer to sell. T ignores A's notice and advises P that he accepts P's offer to sell. By this time, P has learned of the higher offer and "affirms" A's unauthorized notice of revocation. Under the general view, A's unauthorized revocation is deemed invalid because P's ratification would prejudice T, a third person; hence there is no "relation back" to cut off T's acceptance. [Rest. 3d § 4.02] *Note:* A few courts hold differently, however, asserting that the agent's notice of revocation—even though unauthorized—would deprive the other party of the power to accept P's offer.

B. Prerequisites for Ratification

1. Act on Principal's Behalf

The act ratified by the principal must have been undertaken by a person who ***acted or purported to act on the principal's behalf.*** Thus, ratification may create a relationship of agency where none existed before. When the actor is not an agent and does not purport to be one, neither agency law nor ratification applies. Other bodies of law govern the circumstances under which such consequences might occur. [Rest. 3d § 4.03 and comments]

e.g. **Example:** A poses as the owner of Blackacre and sells it to T. Later, P, the real owner, discovers what A has done and decides to affirm the sale to T. No ratification results—and T is not bound to purchase from P—because A was not purporting to act as P's agent.

a. Who Can Ratify

The Restatement (Second) of Agency follows the general rule that only a disclosed or partially disclosed principal can ratify. (*See infra*, pp. 58–61.) An undisclosed principal could not ratify because, by definition, the third party did not know that he was dealing with an agent; thus, the agent did not purport to be acting on a principal's behalf. The Restatement (Third) of Agency does not distinguish between disclosed, unidentified, or undisclosed principals; therefore ***any principal may ratify*** an agent's unauthorized act. [Rest. 3d § 4.03, comment b; **Acuri v. Figliolli,** 398 N.Y.S.2d 923 (1977)]

e.g. **Example:** P authorizes A to negotiate a lease agreement with T for P's home. A negotiates the terms but also agrees to lease the home to T without P's authority and without disclosing P's identity or existence to T (*i.e.*, P is an undisclosed principal). P subsequently learns of the lease agreement and is informed that T wants to make renovations to the home. P agrees to the renovations. Later that day, P agrees to lease the home to R. Under the Restatement (Third) of Agency, P's acquiescence of the lease and his approval of the renovations constitute a ratification of the lease to T. Under the Restatement (Second) of Agency, however, there is no ratification because P was an undisclosed principal.

(1) Ratification Under the Restatement (Second) of Agency

(a) Disclosed Principals

In a disclosed principal situation, the majority view is that only the *purported* principal can ratify. This is a consequence of contract law: The contract the agent made is treated as an offer to the principal and only the offeree (the purported principal) has the power to accept. [**Gillihan v. Morguelan,** 186 S.W.2d 807

(Ky. 1945)] It would be unfair to allow someone else to accept because it would change the bargain that the third party thought he was making.

e.g. **Example:** Purporting to act on P's behalf (but without authority to do so), A contracts to purchase a rare antique from T at a very reasonable price. X, a stranger to the transaction, who wants the antique, pays A $500 for an assignment of all rights under the contract and then notifies T that he "affirms" A's purchase. This affirmation is ineffective because the original A-T contract was purportedly made on P's behalf, so only P can ratify it.

APPROACH TO RATIFICATION

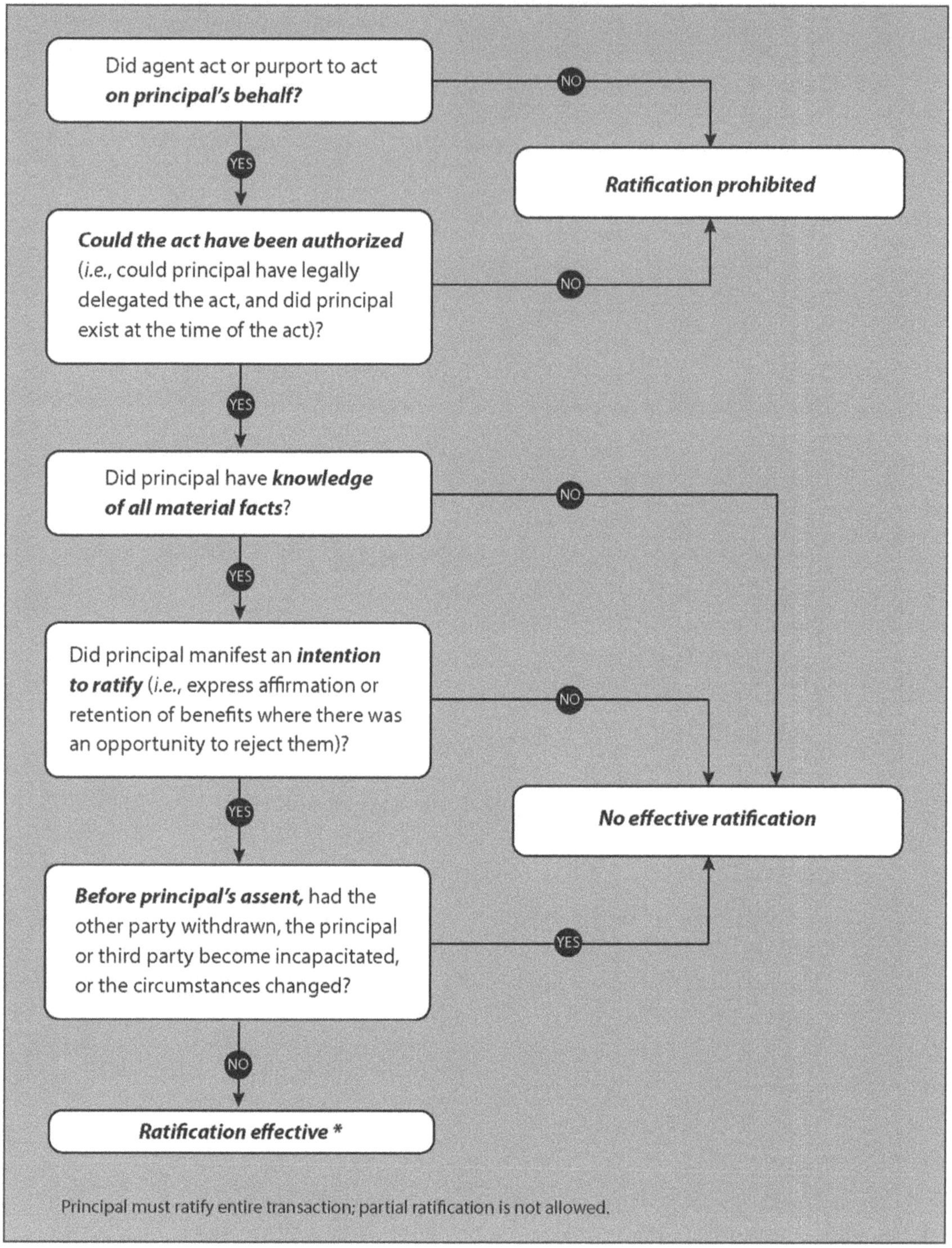

1) Minority View

Some courts have held that the unauthorized agent, A, or the new party, X, ***can*** "affirm" the contract and enforce it against the third party. *Rationale:*

As long as the third party receives the price he contracted for and his performance to A or X is no more onerous than his performance to P, he has no basis for being excused from performing. [**Barnett Bros. v. Lynn,** 203 P. 389 (Wash. 1922)]

(b) Partially Disclosed Principals

If the agent discloses the fact that she is acting as an agent for some principal but *does not disclose the identity* of the principal, the Restatement (Second) provides that only the *person whom the agent intended to be the principal* can ratify. [Rest. 2d § 87]

1) Comment

This view creates an evidence problem: Only the agent will know whom she intended to be the principal; so there is little to keep her from principal-shopping. Therefore, the rationale of *Barnett Bros., supra,* is even stronger here.

EXAM TIP

Watch for a situation on your exam where a third party does not know he is dealing with an agent, but the undisclosed principal wants to ratify the unauthorized act of her agent. In this situation, ratification would be ineffective under the Restatement (Second) of Agency: An *undisclosed* principal *cannot ratify* the unauthorized act of her agent because one of the requirements of ratification is that the agent purport to act *on the principal's behalf.* If the agent did not disclose the principal's existence to the third party, the agent did not purport to be acting on the principal's behalf, and thus the principal may not ratify the agent's act. (*Note:* Under the Restatement (Third) of Agency, however, the ratification is *effective.*)

---

2. Delegable Act

Only acts that can be performed by agents may be ratified. An act that the principal ***could not have authorized in the first place*** because it was illegal or contrary to public policy (*see supra,* p. 11) does not become effective by ratification. [**Andrews v. Claiborne Parish School Board,** 189 So. 355 (La. 1939)] Similarly, an act cannot be ratified if it is ***currently*** illegal or contrary to public policy.

e.g. **Example:** Without authority, A purports to represent P in a gambling wager in a state where such a wager is illegal. Later, P finds out and affirms the wager. Since the wager could not have been authorized originally, it is not made enforceable by the subsequent affirmation. Similarly, if the wager were legal when entered, but the state subsequently made such a wager illegal, P could not ratify.

a. Illegal Acts

If the illegality makes the contract ***void,*** it cannot be ratified. However, if the contract is merely ***voidable*** at the option of the principal, the principal can ratify it. (*See* Contracts Summary for a discussion of what makes a contract void versus voidable.) If the original act is illegal ***only because it was unauthorized*** (*e.g.,* an agent forged principal's name on contract), a subsequent ratification will be effective (the act then being treated as legal). [*See, e.g.,* Rest. 3d § 4.03, comment c]

3. Knowledge of Principal

There can be no effective ratification unless the principal has ***actual knowledge of all material facts*** at the time of the ratification. If he did not—or if he was mistaken as to any such fact—he can later rescind the ratification unless the third party has changed his position in reliance thereon (*see infra,* p. 65). *Rationale:* The unauthorized agent-third party contract is merely an "offer," and there can be no valid "acceptance" by ratification unless all of the terms of the offer are known. It is immaterial whether the principal's lack of knowledge is caused by the agent's fraud or is an innocent mistake on his part. [Rest. 3d § 4.06; **Templeton Construction Co. v. Kelly,** 296 A.2d 242 (Vt. 1972)]

e.g. **Example:** Without authority, A executes a promissory note on P's behalf, payable to T. Mistakenly believing that the note was one of a number of which he had previously authorized A to execute, P tells T that the note is good. P then discovers his mistake and advises T accordingly, repudiating his affirmation. If T has not changed his position in reliance on the ratification, P is not liable on the note. [**Menveg v. Fishbaugh,** 123 Cal. App. 460 (1932)]

e.g. **Example:** Falsely purporting to be P's agent, A sells Blackacre to T. P does not know that oil has just been discovered on Blackacre and affirms the sale. When he learns about the oil, P can retract his affirmation of the sale (assuming no detrimental reliance by T). *Note:* There is some authority, however, that a mere mistake as to the ***value*** of the subject matter is ***not*** sufficient to justify repudiating a ratification.

a. Principal May Assume Risk of Lack of Knowledge

If the principal's ignorance of the facts arises from his own failure to investigate, under circumstances in which a reasonable person would have made an investigation, he is held to assume the risk of his lack of knowledge—*i.e.,* the ratification is effective despite the fact that the principal did not know certain material facts. [Rest. 3d § 4.06, comment d; **See-Tee Mining Corp. v. National Sales, Inc.,** 417 P.2d 810 (N.M. 1966)]

e.g. **Example:** Without authority, A purports to sell Blackacre to T on P's behalf. When informed of this, P—without inquiring about the terms of sale—writes T that he will stand by anything A has done. This probably constitutes a ratification which P cannot later repudiate upon learning of the actual terms of the sale.

4. Principal's Capacity

A principal can ratify an act if the principal ***existed at the time of the act*** and ***had capacity at the time of ratification.*** Thus, a principal who was not in existence at the time of the agent's act cannot ratify. [Rest. 3d § 4.04]

EXAM TIP

When determining whether the principal has capacity to ratify, remember that capacity is determined at the time of ratification—the principal need *not* have had capacity to ratify *at the time of the act.* Thus, the principal can ratify an act even if there is no capacity until after the act. (*See supra,* p. 10, for capacity.)

a. Corporations "Adopt"

A corporation cannot ratify the contract of a promoter (one who sets out to create the corporation; *see* Corporations Summary) entered into before the corporation was formed because at the time of the promoter's act the corporation did not exist. Nevertheless, courts allow corporations to ***adopt*** a promoter's contract, which has the effect of binding the corporation, but unlike ratification, the adoption ***does not relate back*** to the date the promoter made the contract, and the ***promoter is not relieved*** of liability on the contract by reason of the adoption. [Rest. 3d § 4.04, comment c]

b. Partial Incapacity—Contracts Voidable

If the principal's incapacity makes his contracts voidable, he ***may*** ratify after the incapacity is removed. [Rest. 3d § 4.04, comment b]

e.g. **Example:** A, without authority, purchases a car for P, who is an infant. P affirms. The contract is ongoing, but is voidable as long as P is an infant, because he is incapable of consenting. If P ratifies after coming of age, he will be bound. [*See* Rest. 3d § 4.04, comment b]

C. How to Ratify

1. In General

As indicated previously (*see supra,* pp. 8–9), ratification requires that the principal in some way manifest his intention to be bound by the prior unauthorized act of the agent, *i.e.,* to become a party to the transaction.

a. Principal Must Manifest Intention to Be Bound

Ratification requires some words or conduct ***by the principal*** that manifests his intention to be bound by the agent's act. Statements or conduct by the agent or some other third person will not suffice. [Rest. 3d § 4.01]

b. Generally No Formalities

A ratification need merely be made in a form and manner proper for an original authorization—which means that usually no special formalities are required (*see supra,* pp. 8, 10). In the few cases where the original authorization must be in writing (*see supra,* p. 10), the ratification must also be in writing.

e.g. **Example:** Without authority, A contracts to sell Blackacre to T on P's behalf. Any subsequent affirmation by P must be in writing, since the original authorization would have had to have been in writing. [**Moore v. Hoar,** *supra,* p. 11]

(1) Ratification Need Not Be Communicated

It is ***not*** necessary that the principal notify or otherwise communicate affirmation to the agent, the third party, or anyone else. Of course, direct communication is the clearest way of manifesting the intent to ratify. Nevertheless, there are other ways to ratify, such as accepting the benefits of the agent's actions with knowledge of all material facts (*see infra),* and there is no requirement that the principal notify anyone of such acceptance. [*See* Rest. 3d § 4.01, comment d]

2. Express Affirmation

If the principal expressly affirms the prior unauthorized act—*e.g.,* by notifying the agent or third party thereof—this is sufficient to establish ratification. [**Rakestraw v. Rodrigues,** *supra,* p. 57]

3. Implied Affirmation—Ratification by Conduct

Typically, however, the principal does not specifically express his intention to "become bound" or "go ahead" with the transaction. In such cases, the question is whether there is conduct by the principal that sufficiently evidences the intent to affirm the transaction. [**Shimonek v. Nebraska Building & Investment Co.,** 191 N.W. 668 (Neb. 1922)]

a. Retaining Benefits

Voluntary acceptance or retention by the principal of the benefits of a transaction purportedly entered into on his behalf will generally establish a ratification by the principal. [Rest. 3d § 4.01, comment g; **Compuknit Industries, Inc. v. Mercury Motors Express, Inc.,** 72 Misc. 2d 55 (1972)]

e.g. **Example:** Without authority, A contracts to sell Blackacre to T on P's behalf. T advises P of the contract and tenders the purchase price to P. If P accepts the tender, he will be held to have affirmed the sale.

(1) Exception—Involuntary Retention

Of course, if the retention is involuntary—*e.g.,* the "benefits" have been consumed or made an inseparable part of the principal's property—there is no ratification.

e.g. **Example:** Without authority, A purchases fertilizer for P and spreads it on P's ground. P knows nothing of the transaction until after the fertilizer is absorbed. P's retention of the benefits under these circumstances is not a ratification. [**Pacific Bone, Coal & Fertilizer Co. v. Bleakmore,** 81 Cal. App. 659 (1927)]

b. Bringing Suit or Maintaining Defense

If the principal institutes an action or sets up a defense to any action ***in reliance on some prior unauthorized act,*** he will be deemed to have affirmed that act. [Rest. 3d § 4.01, comment h; **Strawn v. Jones,** 285 A.2d 659 (Md. 1972)]

e.g. **Example:** Without authority, A purports to sell Blackacre to T on P's behalf. Knowing the facts, P brings an action against T for the purchase price. P thereby ratifies the transaction. The same result would follow if T had sued P on some other matter, and P had set up the unpaid purchase price as a defense or setoff in T's suit. [*See* **La Salle National Bank v. Brodsky,** 201 N.E. 2d 208 (Ill. 1964)]

(1) Distinguish—Principal Asserts Defense That Act Was Unauthorized

If a suit is brought by a third party and the principal asserts as a defense that the agent's act was unauthorized, there is no ratification. [*See* Rest. 3d § 4.01, comment h]

c. Failing to Act When Duty to Act

Under certain circumstances, the principal's failure to repudiate an unauthorized transaction may constitute a ratification of the transaction. [*See* Rest. 3d § 4.01, comment f; **NAACP v. Overstreet,** 142 S.E.2d 816 (Ga. 1965)] In this type of case, the principal is in effect ***estopped*** from denying his affirmation. (*See infra,* p. 66.)

e.g. **Example:** Without authority, A places an order with T for advertising on behalf of P. P learns of A's act, knows that T is spending time and money to prepare copy, but does nothing to repudiate the transaction. P would be deemed to have ratified the order.

cf. **Compare:** However, an employer's failure to discharge an employee who committed a tortious act with respect to a ***third person*** does not in itself constitute a ratification by the employer of the employee's conduct. (*See infra,* p. 118.)

EXAM TIP

If the issue in an exam question is whether the principal has indicated an intention to be bound by his agent's unauthorized act, remember that the principal does not have to expressly affirm the agent's act (*e.g.,* by notifying the agent or third party that he wants to accept the deal) to be bound by it. In fact, the usual case does not involve such an obvious affirmation. Rather, the principal often *impliedly affirms* the act. Therefore, be sure to check the facts to see if the principal *retained the benefits* of the act, *brought suit or maintained a defense* based on the act, or *failed to repudiate* the act when he had a duty to do so. If so, the principal has ratified the agent's act.

D. Limitations on Power to Ratify

1. Entire Transaction Must Be Ratified

A contract or other single transaction must be ratified *in its entirety* to have an effective ratification; *i.e.,* the principal cannot ratify only the beneficial parts and refuse to ratify the rest. [Rest. 3d § 4.07; **Lewis v. Martin,** 492 P.2d 877 (Colo. 1971)]

2. Intervening Withdrawal or Incapacity of Other Party

As noted previously, until ratification, the unauthorized contract between the third party and agent is treated merely as an "offer" to the principal. It follows that until ratification the third party is free to rescind—to "revoke" the offer—and that any ratification by the principal thereafter will be ineffective. [Rest. 3d § 4.05, comment c]

e.g. **Example:** A purports to buy goods from T on P's behalf, both parties believing that A is authorized when in fact she is not. T then discovers that A was not authorized and notifies A that he withdraws from the transaction. If P subsequently affirms, his ratification is ineffective to bind T. [**Salfield v. Sutter County Land Improvement & Reclamation Co.,** 94 Cal. 546 (1892)]

a. Note

The above holds true even if T has ***contracted*** that he will not withdraw from the contract, or if he rescinds on grounds that would not be adequate to discharge him from the contract had A been authorized.

b. Death or Incapacity

The death or incapacity of the third party will also terminate the principal's power to ratify.

3. Change of Circumstances

Finally, if the principal's ratification occurs ***after a material change*** in the basic circumstances such that it would be inequitable to subject the third party to liability thereon, the third party can avoid the transaction despite the ratification. [**Pape v. Home Insurance Co.,** 139 F.2d 231 (2d Cir. 1943); Rest. 3d § 4.05, comment d]

e.g. **Example:** Without authority, A purports to sell Blackacre to T on P's behalf. The next day the house on Blackacre burns down. P's subsequent ratification of the sales contract will not bind T.

a. Minority View Contra

Some jurisdictions hold that ratification merely substitutes the principal as a party to the contract; hence rights and liabilities should be decided on the basis of the original agreement. If the original agreement was fair when made, the ratification binds the third party despite the change of circumstances.

b. After Ratification

Of course, a change of circumstances occurring ***after*** ratification by the principal will not be sufficient to avoid the ratification.

EXAM TIP

A ratification issue that is often overlooked is whether the principal's power to ratify has been limited in some way. Recall that the principal's *ratification will be ineffective* if the principal does *not ratify the entire transaction,* the third party *revokes the offer before the principal ratifies,* or the *circumstances change before ratification* so that it would be inequitable to hold the third party liable on the transaction. If the principal's ratification is ineffective, he cannot, of course, hold the third party liable on the transaction.

---

4. Estoppel to Deny Ratification

If a principal manifests that she has ratified an act of another, and the manifestation induces a third party to detrimentally change his position, the principal may be estopped from denying the ratification. [Rest. 3d § 4.08]

Chapter Five:

Notice, Notification, and Knowledge

CONTENTS	PAGE

Key Exam Issues

Notice is an important agency concept because, under agency law, facts of which an agent has notice will be imputed to the principal and vice versa. However, it is not always clear whether an agent has notice of a fact. To answer an examination question concerning notice of a fact, you will need to be familiar with the following:

Notice is a broad concept that includes several lesser components, perhaps the two most important of which are notification and knowledge.

Notification involves an act intended to bring to the principal knowledge that affects her legal rights. If notification is involved, the key points to remember are that:

(i) If the agent receives notification, the principal will be deemed to have notice if the agent had ***actual or apparent authority*** to act regarding the subject matter of the notification; and

(ii) Notification will ***not become ineffective*** because of the passage of time.

Knowledge, on the other hand, involves facts subjectively known. On your exam, if a principal's rights or liabilities depend on knowledge of a certain fact, the key points to remember are that:

(i) An agent's knowledge will be imputed to the principal only if it ***concerns the subject matter*** of the agency and is ***within the scope*** of the agent's ***actual*** authority; and

(ii) Because knowledge is subjective, it ***may become ineffective*** because of the passage of time.

A. Notice

1. In General

The Restatement treats notice as a broad concept. A person has notice of a fact if he knows of it, has reason to know of it, should know of it to fulfill a duty owed to another person, or has been given notification of it. [Rest. 3d §§ 1.04(4), 5.01(3)] Legal relationships often turn on whether a person had notice of a fact.

a. Distinguish—Knowledge

Sometimes, however, legal relationships turn on whether a person had knowledge of a fact (*e.g.*, under the attractive nuisance doctrine, a principal can be held liable only if he can be charged with knowledge that children frequent the area of the dangerous condition). As is readily apparent, knowledge is a subset of notice; a person with knowledge has notice, but a person with notice will not always be charged with knowledge.

B. Notification

1. In General

Notification is a juristic act calculated to give information to another that affects the legal relationship between the parties. Within agency law, notification usually involves an act by a third party directed to an agent intended to bring to the principal knowledge that affects the principal's rights (*e.g.*, a tenant delivers to the building's managing agent a notice intended to inform the landlord of the tenant's desire to terminate his lease with the landlord).

2. Authority

Notification given to an agent is effective to give notice to the principal if the agent had actual or apparent authority to receive the notification, unless the person giving the notification knows or has reason to know that the agent is acting adversely to the principal. [Rest. 3d § 5.02(1)]

e.g. **Example:** P owns an apartment building in which T is a tenant. T notifies A, the manager, that he intends to move. T's notification is imputed to P because A had authority to receive it. Moreover, the notification would be effective even if P had fired A as manager—assuming T was not aware of this fact—because A would have apparent authority.

3. Duration

Once notification is given to the agent, its legal effect will continue indefinitely (*i.e.,* it will not become ineffective because of the passage of time and will operate against all interested parties who come at a later time). Thus, in the example above, if T gave the apartment manager timely notification of his intent to end his lease, and if P subsequently sells the building to X, the notification will be effective against X. (*Compare* "knowledge," *infra,* p. 71.)

4. Agent Acting Adversely to Principal

Generally, as long as the agent had authority, notification by or to the agent will be effective against the principal regardless of whether the agent was acting adversely to the principal ***unless*** the person who receives or gives notification ***knows or has reason to know that the agent is acting adversely.*** [Rest. 3d § 5.02 and comment c]

e.g. **Example:** In the example above, T's notification to A, the apartment building manager, would be effective even if at the time A received the notification he was planning to misappropriate the tenants' security deposits and leave for parts unknown and had no intention of informing P of the notification, ***unless*** T knew or had reason to know of A's plans.

a. Exception

If the third party knows that the agent is acting adversely to the principal's interests, and that the agent will not communicate the notification to the principal, the notification will not be effective against the principal. [Rest. 3d § 5.02(1) and comment c]

EXAM TIP

If on an exam you have to determine if notification given to an agent will be imputed to the principal, check to see if the agent *had actual or apparent authority* to act for the principal. If the agent had authority, *notification will be imputed* to the principal unless the agent was acting adversely to the principal and the third party knew that the agent was acting adversely. Remember that when notification is given to an agent, its legal effect will continue *indefinitely.*

C. Knowledge

1. In General

Knowledge is subjective and involves an ***awareness*** of the particular fact or condition in question.

2. Authority

As a general rule, an agent's knowledge of a fact that he knows or has reason to know will be imputed to his principal ***if*** the agent had ***actual authority*** to affect the principal's rights in the affairs at hand. However, knowledge will not be imputed if the agent acts adversely to the principal (*see infra,* p. 71) or is under a duty to another (*e.g.*, attorney-client confidentiality) not to disclose the fact to the principal. [Rest. 3d § 5.03]

Example: Buyer entered into an agreement to purchase a piece of property. The owner of the property later conveyed the property to T. Although Buyer's purchase agreement was unrecorded, T's attorney knew of it but failed to inform T. T will be charged with the knowledge of his attorney and so takes the property subject to Buyer's interest. [**Farr v. Newman,** 14 N.Y.2d 183 (1964)]

a. Rationale

An agent has a duty to inform the principal of all matters in connection with the agency that the principal would desire to know. If the agent breaches this duty, and the principal is not informed of facts relevant to a transaction with a third party, it is the principal who will have to accept the consequences of the agent's breach and not the innocent third party, because the principal chose the (unreliable) agent. Thus, as to innocent third parties, the principal is deemed to know all that the agent should have told him.

EXAM TIP

On an exam, be sure to remember the difference in authority required to impute an agent's knowledge to the principal versus imputing to the principal notification given to an agent. For an agent's *knowledge* to be imputed to the principal, the agent must have *actual authority* to act for the principal. Less authority is required to impute *notification* to the principal: Notification given to an agent will be imputed to the principal if the agent had *actual or apparent authority* to act for the principal.

---

3. When Acquired

Ordinarily, only those facts discovered by the agent during the period of the agency will be imputed—*i.e.,* the principal is not charged with knowledge of facts learned by the agent before (or after) his employment. [**Cooke v. Mesmer,** 164 Cal. 332 (1912)]

a. Exception

A few cases have imputed knowledge acquired by the agent prior to employment when, because of the close connection of the transactions, the knowledge must have been present in the agent's mind when he acted for the principal. [**Blue Diamond Plaster Co. v. Industrial Accident Commission, 188 Cal. 403** (1922)—knowledge of managing officer of corporation, gained while serving with predecessor corporation, held imputed to corporation]

b. Restatement View

Under the Restatement, it is ***immaterial*** to imputation when the agent acquired his knowledge. The issue is whether he had the knowledge ***in mind*** when it became relevant in his work for the principal. Notice is imputed to the principal if the fact is material to the agent's duties, regardless of whether the agent learned of the fact prior to the agency relationship through formal education, prior work, or otherwise. [Rest. 3d § 5.03, comment e]

4. What Is Imputed

Only ***facts*** concerning the subject matter of the agency and within the scope thereof will be imputed. [Rest. 3d § 5.03]

a. No Imputation of Agent's Knowledge When Principal's Actual Knowledge Required

An agent's knowledge will not be imputed when the principal's subjective, actual knowledge is required.

e.g. **Example:** P ships certain goods to T, who finds them unsatisfactory and so notifies P's general manager, A. A forgets to notify P, and P files a lawsuit against T for failure to pay for the goods. Later, T sues P for abuse of process, which requires a showing that the action for the purchase price was filed in bad faith. T cannot prevail merely by showing that he gave A notification of rejection—*i.e.,* P's alleged bad faith cannot be based on imputed knowledge; rather, the actual knowledge of P must be shown. [**Snook v. Netherby,** 124 Cal. App. 2d 797 (1954)]

5. Duration

Because knowledge is subjective—what was on the agent's mind when he acted—unlike notification, it may become ineffective because of the passage of time. [Rest. 3d § 5.03, comment b; *and see* **Graham v. White-Phillips Co.,** 296 U.S. 27 (1935)]

6. Agent Acting Adversely to Principal

An agent who takes a position adverse to the principal is acting outside the scope of his authority, and knowledge acquired by him while acting in this fashion is, therefore, ***not imputed*** to the principal. *Rationale:* If an agent is acting in derogation of his employer's interest, there is no reason to suppose that he will keep his employer properly informed, and it would be extremely unfair to impute his knowledge to the principal. [Rest. 3d § 5.04]

e.g. **Example:** X, unable to procure auto insurance, conspires with insurance agent A to obtain a policy for his car in Y's name from A's principal, P Co. If P Co. later seeks to have the policy declared void, A's knowledge will not be imputed to P Co. (because A was colluding to defraud P). [**Southern Farm Bureau Casualty Insurance Co. v. Allen,** 388 F.2d 126 (5th Cir. 1967)]

a. Interest Must Be Substantially Adverse

Many courts have held that the agent's interest must be ***substantially*** adverse to the principal's interest in order to prevent imputation of the knowledge. [*See, e.g.,* ***In re* Mifflin Chemical Corp.,** 123 F.2d 311 (3d Cir. 1941)]

b. Corporate Officers and Directors

If an officer or director of a corporation causes the corporation to enter into contracts in which the officer or director has some secret adverse interest, the corporation is generally ***not*** bound (*i.e.,* knowledge of the officer's or director's adverse interest is not imputed to the corporation). [**Mylander v. Chesapeake Bank,** 159 A. 770 (Md. 1932)] However, some courts ***have*** imputed knowledge of dishonest acts by corporate officers or directors to the corporation, at least to bar suit against the surety on fidelity bonds of the dishonest officers or directors.

c. Exceptions to General Rule

Knowledge is imputed to the principal, despite the fact that the agent acted adversely to the principal, if: (i) knowledge is necessary to ***protect the rights of a third party*** who dealt with the principal in good faith and without knowledge of the agent's adversity; (ii) the principal has ***ratified*** the agent's actions; or (iii) the principal knowingly ***retained the benefits*** from the agent's actions. [Rest. 3d § 5.04; *and see* ***In re*** **Brainard Hotel Co.,** 75 F.2d 481 (2d Cir. 1935)—embezzling hotel cashier stole guests' money to replace prior embezzlements from hotel]

NOTIFICATION VS. KNOWLEDGE—A COMPARISON

	NOTIFICATION	KNOWLEDGE
DEFINED	An ***act calculated to give information*** to another that affects the legal relationship between the parties	Subjective ***awareness*** of a particular fact or condition
AUTHORITY REQUIRED FOR IMPUTATION	Principal will be charged with notification given to agent if agent had ***any actual or apparent authority*** in the transaction to receive notification	Principal will be charged with agent's knowledge only if agent had ***actual authority*** in the transaction to affect principal's rights
DURATION	Continues indefinitely—does ***not become ineffective*** because of the passage of time	***May become ineffective*** because of the passage of time
EFFECT OF ADVERSE AGENT	Notification still imputed to principal unless third party knew agent was acting adversely	Knowledge not imputed to principal because agent was acting outside the scope of actual authority

Chapter Six: Liability on Agent's Contract

CONTENTS PAGE

Key Exam Issues

A common exam issue is who may be held liable on a contract entered into by an agent on a principal's behalf. If you get such a question, remember that the basic rules are relatively simple:

1. The ***principal*** can be held liable if the agent acted ***with authority or some other form of agency power.***

2. ***The agent*** can be held liable in a number of circumstances:

   a. ***If the agent lacked authority,*** the third party can hold the agent liable on a ***breach of warranty theory*** (*i.e.*, an agent warrants that she is acting with authority) ***and/or on the contract itself.***

   b. ***Even if the agent acted with authority*** (and the principal, therefore, can be held liable), the agent might still be held liable by the third party:

      (1) If the principal is ***disclosed,*** the agent can be held liable but ***only if her name appears on the contract as a party*** (and not merely as an agent); and

      (2) If the principal is ***unidentified or undisclosed,*** the agent may be held liable in most cases.

3. The ***third party*** generally can be held liable only by the principal. However, note that in some cases, not even the principal will be able to enforce the contract, *e.g.*, if the agent ***fraudulently*** conceals the principal's identity.

A. Agent Acting Without Authority

1. Agent's Liability

If the agent purports to act on behalf of a principal when entering into a contract with a third party but is in fact acting without authority or in excess of her authority (*e.g.,* by making unauthorized representations), the principal generally cannot be held liable to the third party absent some other source of agency power. In such cases, ***the agent alone*** is liable. [*See* Rest. 3d § 6.10] Depending on the situation, the agent's liability may be based on breach of warranty, on the contract, or both.

a. Agent's Liability for Breach of Warranty—Disclosed or Unidentified Principal

An agent who purports to enter into a contract with a third party on behalf of a principal ***impliedly warrants*** that she ***has authority*** to bind her principal. If the agent was not authorized or exceeded her authority, so that the principal is not bound, the agent may be liable to the third party for breach of the warranty of authority. [Rest. 3d § 6.10; **First National Bank v. Jefferson Mortgage Co.,** 576 F.2d 479 (3d Cir. 1978)]

CONTRACT LIABILITY TO THIRD PARTIES—AN APPROACH

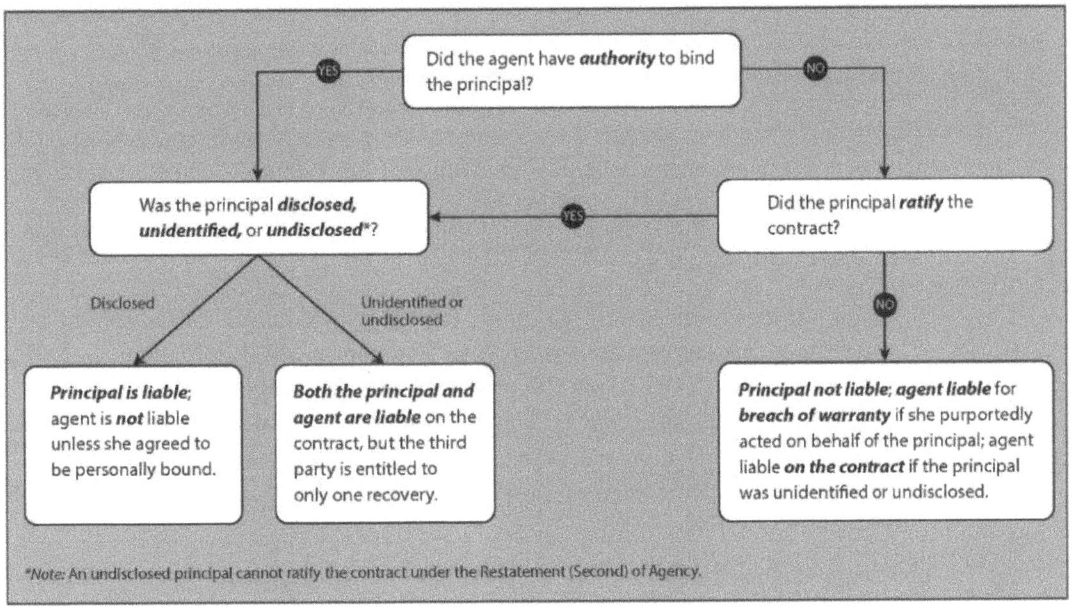

(1) Nature of Liability

Note that the agent's liability to the third party in this situation is ***not*** on the contract itself; rather, the agent's liability is based on her ***breach of the warranty*** of authority.

EXAM TIP

Obviously there can be no breach of warranty liability in an *undisclosed principal* case (*see supra,* p. 5). In that case, the agent does not warrant that she has any authority to act for another (in fact the third party doesn't even know that there is a principal). Thus, you should consider the warranty theory only in a *disclosed or unidentified* principal situation.

(2) Reliance Required

It is essential that the third party ***rely*** on the warranty; *e.g.,* an agent is not liable if the third party ***knows*** that the agent was mistaken as to her authority. [*See* **R.D. Johnson Milling Co. v. Brown,** 196 A. 100 (Md. 1938)]

(3) Tort Liability

Under this warranty theory of liability, the agent is liable even though she believed in good faith that she was authorized. Moreover, if the agent ***intentionally misrepresents*** that she has the requisite authority, she may also be held liable in ***tort*** for ***deceit.*** [**R.D. Johnson Milling Co. v. Brown,** *supra*]

(4) Effect of Disclaimer

If the agent clearly indicates to the third party that no warranty of authority is given, this will usually prevent any warranty of authority from arising, and, hence, will protect the agent from liability based on breach of warranty if it turns out that she was not in fact authorized. [Rest. 3d § 6.10(2)]

(5) No Warranty of Performance

The agent's implied warranty of authority does ***not*** include a warranty that the principal will perform the contract, or even that he is capable of performing it (*e.g.,* has the money to perform). [**Greenlee v. Beaver,** 79 N.E.2d 822 (Ill. 1948)]

(a) Distinguish—Warranty of Competence

The implied warranty of authority, however, *is* deemed to include the agent's warranty that the principal is not legally incompetent. [**Goldfinger v. Doherty,** 153 Misc. 826 (1934)] (If the principal were incompetent, he would not have capacity to appoint an agent or grant authority to the agent in the first place; *see supra,* p. 10.) If a person acting as an agent makes a contract on behalf of a nonexistent or incapacitated principal, the agent becomes a party to the contract. [Rest. 3d § 6.04]

(b) Agent's Liability on Contract—Undisclosed or Unidentified Principal

Distinct from an agent's liability for breach of warranty is the agent's liability ***on the contract*** itself. An agent who without authority enters into a contract with a third party is liable to the third party ***on the contract*** if the principal is undisclosed or unidentified. If the principal is ***undisclosed,*** the agent is the only party to the contract (*i.e.,* she is the promisor) and therefore she is liable on the contract. Courts follow the same rule when the agent purports to act on behalf of an ***unidentified*** principal (*see supra,* p. 5). [**Unger v. Travel Arrangements, Inc.,** 25 A.D.2d 40 (1966)]

1) Distinguish—Disclosed Principal

However, if an agent purports to act on behalf of a ***disclosed*** principal (*see supra,* p. 5) when contracting with a third party, and the agent in fact acts without authority or in excess of her authority, the agent is ***not liable on the contract.*** The agent was not intended to be personally liable; the agent purported to be acting on the principal's behalf, and the parties' intent was that the principal be bound. Recall, however, that the agent can be liable for breach of warranty. (*See supra,* p. 74.)

EXAM TIP

On an exam, if you see an agent contracting without authority or in excess of authority, be sure to consider both possible ways for the agent to be liable to the third party: *breach of warranty and on the contract.* Remember that if the principal's *existence has not been disclosed,* the agent can be liable *only* on the contract. If the principal's *existence and identity have been disclosed,* the agent can be liable *only* for breach of warranty. If the principal's *existence has been disclosed but not his identity,* the agent can be liable *both* for breach of warranty and on the contract. (*See* the chart *infra,* for a summary of these rules.)

AGENT'S LIABILITY TO THIRD PARTY WHEN ACTING WITHOUT AUTHORITY		
	FOR BREACH OF WARRANTY	ON CONTRACT
DISCLOSED PRINCIPAL SITUATION	Agent Liable	Agent ***Not*** Liable
UNIDENTIFIED PRINCIPAL SITUATION	Agent Liable	Agent Liable
UNDISCLOSED PRINCIPAL SITUATION	Agent ***Not*** Liable	Agent Liable

2. Principal's Liability—When Third Party Has Performed

As noted *supra*, p. 74, a principal is generally not liable on a contract entered into by an agent acting without authority or in excess of authority. However, if the agent exceeds her authority, but the third party renders full or part performance under the contract, the third party may be entitled to sue the principal in ***quasi-contract*** for the value of any benefits conferred on the principal, even though the third party cannot enforce the contract itself against the principal absent the principal's ratification.

e.g. **Example:** P hires A to sell certain property. To induce X to purchase the property, A represents that P will give X a "kickback" on the purchase price. X pays the purchase price to P and obtains delivery of the property. If P later refuses X's demand for the "kickback," X can obtain a rescission of the sale. *Rationale*: Even though A's representations were entirely unauthorized, P cannot repudiate A's representations and still retain X's payment because there is no enforceable contract, and X is entitled to restitution of benefits paid in the mistaken belief that there was an enforceable contract. [33 A.L.R. 90]

B. Agent Acting with Authority

1. In General

If the agent's acts are within the scope of her authority (or are subsequently ratified), generally only the principal is a party to the contract and bound by it. [**Lux Art Van Service, Inc. v. Pollard,** 344 F.2d 883 (9th Cir. 1965)] However, the rights and liabilities of the parties may vary depending on whether the identity of the principal was disclosed.

EXAM TIP

Pay particular attention to the rules that follow regarding liability of the parties on contracts entered into by agents acting with authority because this is one of the most important and frequently tested issues on an exam. Your exam will likely have an agent enter into a contract with a third party for a principal and ask you to determine if the agent and/or principal is liable to the third party and to whom is the third party liable. In this situation, you will have to be prepared to discuss the *type of principal* (disclosed, unidentified, or undisclosed) involved in the transaction, because the agent's liability depends on the type of principal. You also should consider the intent of the parties when determining their liability, because the parties' intent controls.

2. Contract Made on Behalf of Principal (Disclosed Principal Cases)

If the agent negotiates a contract on behalf of the principal, the agent is ***not*** a party to the contract unless the agent and third party agree otherwise. [Rest. 3d § 6.01(2)] Thus, she is not liable on the contract and is not entitled to enforce it against any other party or to otherwise assert any rights under it. The other party to the contract is liable directly to the principal and vice versa. [Rest. 3d § 6.01]

e.g. **Example:** A executes a contract that makes clear that A is executing the contract solely on P's behalf. If A's acts are authorized, she is not liable for P's nonperformance of the contract, nor is she entitled to assert any rights under the contract. [**H & B Construction Co. v. James R. Irwin & Sons, Inc.,** 198 A.2d 17 (N.H. 1964)]

a. Need Not Specify Principal if Already Known

If the third party knows (or should know) the identity of the principal, the principal is "disclosed" even though his name does not appear on the contract or the agent does not specifically state that she is acting for a principal. Thus, if the third party knows that the person with whom he is dealing is acting on behalf of another specific person, the agent is not a party to the contract. [Rest. 3d § 6.01, comment c]

e.g. **Example:** T knows that P is A's employer and the owner of a horse that A is offering to sell. If T buys the horse from A, he cannot hold A as a party to the sale. [*See* **Hannin v. Fisher,** 5 Cal. App. 2d 673 (1935)]

b. Parol Evidence Rule

Although the general rule is that an agent is not liable on a contract that the agent enters into on behalf of the principal, there is an exception when the parties intend the agent to be personally liable. [Rest. 3d § 6.01, comment d] In oral deals, what the parties intended generally can be proved by the surrounding circumstances. However, if a written contract is involved, the parol evidence rule may apply and prohibit the introduction of extrinsic evidence, *i.e.,* evidence of intent from any source other than the written contract itself.

(1) General Rule

Generally, the parol evidence rule prohibits the introduction of prior or contemporaneous oral or written statements that conflict with a written contract that appears to be the complete agreement between the parties. Thus, a complete contract that reflects that the agent is acting in a representative capacity, and not personally, cannot be contradicted. Similarly, a complete contract that appears to include the agent as a party generally may not be contradicted.

(2) Exception—Ambiguous Contracts

There are a number of exceptions to the parol evidence rule, and one exception in particular often arises in agency cases—*i.e.,* parties may bring in extrinsic evidence if the terms of the contract are ambiguous. In determining whether a contract is ambiguous, a court will look at the ***entire contract*** [*see* **Stroll v. Epstein,** 818 F. Supp. 640 (S.D.N.Y. 1993)], but the starting point often is the ***form of the agents signature.*** *Note:* In most litigated cases, the third party usually is arguing that the agent's signature unambiguously shows that the agent was meant to be a party, and the agent usually is arguing that the signature is ambiguous, so that the agent can bring in extrinsic evidence to show that she was not meant to be bound on the contract. Sometimes, however, the third party will argue that the contract is ambiguous so that he may bring in extrinsic evidence that the parties intended the agent to be personally bound.

(a) When Agency Is Not Indicated

If the signature does not indicate that the agent signed in a representative capacity (*e.g.*, agent signed a contract, "Peter Smith, Andrea Jones"), the signature generally is treated as unambiguously indicating an intent that the agent be a party to the contract and be *personally liable;* extrinsic evidence to the contrary is not permitted. [*See* **London v. Zachary,** 92 Cal. App. 2d 654 (1949)] However, the rest of the contract may render such a signature ambiguous, so that extrinsic evidence may be permitted. [*See, e.g.,* **Puckett v. Codisco, Inc.**, 440 So. 2d 596 (Fla. 1983)—terms of the contract indicated that the parties were looking to solely hold the principal corporation liable on the contract, rather than its agent]

(b) When Agency Is Indicated

If the contract clearly indicates that the agent signed *only in a representative capacity,* the principal alone will be liable and extrinsic evidence to the contrary will be prohibited. [**Carlesimo v. Schwebel,** 87 Cal. App. 2d 482 (1948)] Most courts hold that the following are sufficient to indicate that the agent was not intended to be bound: "[the principal's name] 'by,' 'for,' or 'per' [the agent's name]." Again, however, the terms of the contract may cast doubt on whether the agent is excluded from liability, in which case, the third party may be allowed to bring in extrinsic evidence to show that the agent was intended to be liable as a party to the contract.

1) "Ambiguous" Signatures

a) Case Law

Perhaps surprisingly, a number of older cases held an agent's signature "John Smith, agent of Principal Co." or "Penny Principal, John Smith, Agent" to be ambiguous, and the parties were allowed to bring in extrinsic evidence of intent. *Rationale:* The signature does not clearly indicate whether the parties intended the agent to be personally bound; it merely is descriptive of the person signing (the *descriptio personae* doctrine). The same rule was applied to a signature that merely designated the agent's office (*e.g.,* "Principal Co., Paula Perez, President"). [*See, e.g.,* **Stroll v. Epstein,** *supra,* p. 78] This remains the majority view. [*See, e.g.,* 113 A.L.R. 1364]

b) Restatement View

The Restatement departs somewhat from the above rule, but the Restatement view has not been widely embraced. It provides that if ***both the principal's and the agent's names appear on a contract,*** any indication that the agent was acting as an agent (such as the word "agent" after the agent's signature) unambiguously indicates that the agent was not meant to be a party absent a contrary provision in the contract. If ***only the agent's name appears on the contract,*** the Restatement view is that the term "agent" (and the like) is deemed only to indicate that the agent is a fiduciary of another; *i.e.,* it is merely descriptive of the person signing (*see* above). The Restatement treats designations of office (*e.g.,* "president") the same as the term "agent," and the above rules apply. [Rest. 3d, § 6.01, comment d]

(3) Extrinsic Evidence

Extrinsic evidence is admissible only if there is ***ambiguity.*** Extrinsic evidence includes the acts, declarations, and relationships of the parties, and the circumstances surrounding execution of the contract.

EXAM TIP

Before you determine on your exam that an agent contracting on behalf of a disclosed principal is not liable on the contract, you must first examine the *intent of the parties.* You can examine the intent of the parties by looking at the contract and the surrounding circumstances (*i.e.,* extrinsic evidence). But remember that if the contract is in writing, the parol evidence rule may prohibit the admission of extrinsic evidence of intent—in which case you must look solely to the contract. But note that if the contract is ambiguous (*e.g.,* form of agent's signature not clear whether agent signed as agent or party), you may look to extrinsic evidence in determining the parties' intent.

---

3. Contract in Name of Agent Only (Undisclosed and Unidentified Principal Cases)

a. Undisclosed Principal

In the "undisclosed principal" case, the agent's name alone appears on the contract, with no statement regarding the fact of agency or the name of the principal; *i.e.,* both the ***fact of agency*** and the ***principal's identity*** are undisclosed. [Rest. 3d § 1.04(2)(b)]

(1) Liability of Agent to Third Party

In an undisclosed principal case, the general view is that the agent is liable as a party to the contract. Following the objective theory of contracts (*i.e.,* the third person is entitled to hold liable the person with whom he apparently deals), the agent is deemed personally obligated under the contract, because the third party was obviously relying on the agent's credit and reputation. Also the agent was responsible for such reliance if she failed to advise the other party that she was acting only as an agent for another. [Rest. 3d § 6.03 and comments; **Jensen v. Alaska Valuation Service, Inc.,** 688 P.2d 161 (Alaska 1984)]

(a) Agent's Rights Against Undisclosed Principal

If the agent is held liable by a third party, the agent may have a right against the undisclosed principal.

1) Indemnification

If an agency agreement existed between the principal and agent, there is deemed to be an implied promise that the principal will perform any contract that the agent is authorized to execute on the principal's behalf, so as to prevent the agent from being held liable on the contract. The principal's failure to perform would therefore be a breach of his agreement with the agent, and the principal would be required to indemnify the agent against any loss she incurred in having to perform on the contract. [*See Rest.* 3d § 8.14]

2) Quasi-Contract

If ***no*** agency agreement exists (*i.e.,* the agent was acting gratuitously on behalf of the principal) but the principal accepted the benefits of the agent's contract with the third party, the principal may be held liable to the agent in quasi-contract, in order to prevent unjust enrichment.

(2) Liability of Principal to Third Party

Once the principal's identity is made known, he may also be held liable under the contract. [Rest. 3d § 6.03] Provided the agent's acts were authorized, the agent ***had*** the power to bind the principal. The third party may therefore hold ***either*** the principal or the agent liable on the contract. [**N.K. Parrish, Inc. v. Southwest Beef Industries Corp.,** 638 F.2d 1366 (5th Cir. 1981); *but see infra,* pp. 81–82]

(a) Parol Evidence Rule

Allowing the third party to hold either the principal or agent liable arguably changes the terms of the written contract by adding a party (the principal). Some earlier cases thus held that if the contract was in writing it would violate the parol evidence rule to allow extrinsic evidence to show that one of the signatories was acting as the agent for another. [**Ferguson v. McBean,** 91 Cal. 63 (1891)] However, the modern view is that the parol evidence rule does *not* apply; *i.e.,* the extrinsic evidence is being admitted not to contradict the writing, but merely to "explain" the capacity in which the party (agent) signed. [Rest. 3d § 6.03, comment c; **Chapman v. Java Pacific Line,** 241 F. 850 (9th Cir. 1917)]

(b) Statute of Frauds

Remember, however, that if the contract is required to be in writing under the Statute of Frauds, the agent's *authority* to execute the contract may also have to be in writing. [*See* **Mitchell v. Locurto,** 79 Cal. App. 2d 507 (1947); *and see* discussion *supra,* pp. 10–11] If it is not, the contract may be unenforceable against the principal.

(c) Requirement of Election by Third Party

Although the third party normally has a right against either the undisclosed principal or the agent, he can obtain satisfaction from *only one* of them.

1) Minority View

The early rule (and a minority view today) held that the third party's ***filing suit*** against either the principal or the agent constituted an election that operated to release the other from liability—*i.e.,* the third party could not file suit against both at the same time. [**Kayton v. Barnett,** 116 N.Y. 625 (1889)]

2) Majority View

The modern rule, however, is that the third party can file suit against ***both*** the principal and the agent, but that—upon objection of either defendant—the third party must elect ***prior to judgment*** which party he wishes to hold liable. In other words, the third party cannot obtain judgment against both (unless the defendants fail to object). [**Conner v. Steel, Inc.,** 470 P.2d 71 (Colo. 1970)]

a) **Single Recovery**

Even if the principal and agent fail to object, and a joint judgment is rendered against them, the third party is still limited to a ***single recovery*** on the judgment. [**Grinder v. Bryans Road Building & Supply Co.,** 432 A.2d 453 (Md. 1981)]

3) **No "Election" if the Principal Is Still Undisclosed**

Of course, if the third party obtains a judgment against the agent ***without knowledge of the principal's identity*** and the judgment is not satisfied, the third party can later sue the principal when the principal's identity is discovered. [**Hugener v. Greider's Wooden Shoe, Inc.,** 246 N.E.2d 323 (Ill. 1969)]

EXAM TIP

In determining who is liable to the third party on a contract entered into by an agent for an undisclosed principal, remember that the third party may sue *both* the principal and agent, but the third party is entitled to only *one recovery* (*i.e.,* the third party may not satisfy a judgment against both the principal and the agent).

(3) **Liability of Third Party**

Either the principal or the agent can enforce the contract against the third party. However, as between the principal and agent, the principal is entitled to all benefits of the contract; the agent acquires no beneficial interest in it. In this respect, it is immaterial that the third party thought he was contracting only with the agent and knew nothing of the principal's existence. [Rest. 2d § 302; **American Enameled Brick & Tile Co. v. Brozek,** 231 N.W. 45 (Mich. 1930)]

(a) **Effect**

The principal is treated as if he were an assignee of all the rights under the contract; thus, the rights and benefits nominally flowing to the agent are deemed to go to the principal. [**Buckley v. Shell Chemical Co.,** 32 Cal. App. 2d 209 (1939)—contract provision waiving any warranty by "seller" held to bar any claim for breach of warranty not only against agent who effected sale, but also against undisclosed principal (manufacturer)] Note that even if the agent sues on the contract, any recovery must be held by the agent in trust for the benefit of the principal. [**Clifton v. Litchfield,** 106 Mass. 34 (1870)—recovery would not pass to agent's receiver in bankruptcy because it was in trust for principal]

(b) **Exception—Fraudulent Concealment of Principal's Identity**

If the agent fraudulently represents to the third party that she is contracting on her own behalf (or on behalf of someone other than the real principal), the third party has a *right to rescind; i.e.,* upon discovering the agent's fraud, the third party has the option to go ahead with the contract or be relieved of it entirely. [**Casteel v. King**, 269 P.2d 529 (Or. 1954)]

e.g. **Example:** P knows that T will never sell Blackacre to him and for this reason employs A to purchase the property. A buys the property in her own name and represents that she is acting for no one else (or that she is acting for X). Upon discovering P's interest, T has the right to rescind the contract entirely, and unless T waives this right to rescind, neither P nor A can enforce the contract.

1) Affirmative Misrepresentation

It is not clear whether an affirmative misrepresentation about the principal's identity is required to grant rescission. [*See* **Kelly Asphalt Block Co. v. Barber Asphalt Paving Co.,** 211 N.Y. 68 (1914)—right to rescind only when agent made some positive misrepresentation; *but see* **Barnes v. Eastern & Western Lumber Co.,** 287 P.2d 929 (Or. 1955)—right to rescind whenever principal or agent had notice that third party would not deal with principal] If the third party has already refused to deal with the principal, rescission is more likely even absent positive misrepresentation. [*See* **Coast Fisheries Co. v. Linen Thread Co.,** 269 F. 841 (D.C. Mass. 1921)] The Restatement does not appear to require a positive misstatement. [*See* Rest. 3d § 6.11, comment a]

a) Motive Relevant

It is not considered to be fraud for the principal to hide his identity merely to avoid paying a premium because of his identity (*e.g.*, famous restaurateur wants to purchase family restaurant and is afraid the present owner will raise the selling price if she knows who the purchaser is). Fraud is involved only when the principal hides his identity because the third party would not want to deal with him at all.

(c) Exception—Performance to Principal Would Impose Greater Burden

An undisclosed principal will be denied the right to enforce the contract (and the third party will have the right to rescind) when enforcement by the principal would impose an added or different burden of performance on the third party.

e.g. **Example:** A signs a contract with T whereby T is to provide "all coal requirements" for A. T did not know that A was in fact contracting on behalf of P, whose coal requirements are much greater (or otherwise different from A's). P cannot enforce the contract and T has the right to rescind.

e.g. **Example:** Acting for an undisclosed principal, A engages T as a butler. The rendering of such personal services may involve different burdens as between P and A. Thus, P cannot enforce the contract and T has the right to rescind.

(d) Exception—Powers Given for Benefit of Agent

If the agent's powers are held irrevocable because she has some interest in the subject matter (*see supra,* pp. 49–51), the agent's rights are considered paramount to those of the principal so that she, rather than the principal, is entitled to any recovery from the third party.

e.g. **Example:** A loans $5,000 to P, and as security P gives A the authority to sell Blackacre to collect the debt. A contracts to sell Blackacre to T, without disclosing the agency. A's authority to sell Blackacre was "coupled with an interest" and thus irrevocable, because the benefits of the agency were really intended for A. Therefore only A, and not P, is entitled to sue under the contract and to obtain its benefits.

EXAM TIP

Watch out for a situation on your exam where a third party refuses to perform on a contract entered into by an agent for an undisclosed principal. Although the general rule is that the third party is liable to the principal on the contract—because the rights and benefits of the contract flow from the agent to the principal—there are exceptions to the rule. Remember that the third party does *not* have to perform if: (i) the agent *fraudulently concealed* the principal's identity, (ii) the performance to the principal would impose a *greater burden* on the third party, or (iii) the agent's authority is *coupled with an interest.* Before concluding that the third party has to perform on the contract for the principal, check to see if any of the above exceptions applies. If so, the third party is not liable to the principal.

(4) Third Party's Right to Insist on Agent's Personal Performance

As already indicated, the third party can hold the agent liable for performance of a contract on behalf of an undisclosed principal. Moreover, if the duties involved are ***nondelegable*** under the law of contracts (*see* Contracts Summary), the third party can ***refuse*** a tender of performance from the principal and insist upon the agent's personal performance. [Rest. 3d § 6.03, comment d] *Examples:*

(a) Credit Contracts

Whenever the contract involves an extension of credit, the third party can insist on the credit of the agent.

e.g. **Example:** A, acting on behalf of undisclosed principal, P, buys T's car for $1,000, the terms of sale being a $250 down payment and the balance secured by a promissory note executed by A. T can refuse a promissory note tendered by P. [**Lansden v. McCarthy,** 45 Mo. 106 (1869)]

(b) Personal Service Contracts

Similarly, if the performance to be rendered by the agent consists of nondelegable personal services, the third party may refuse a tender by the undisclosed principal.

e.g. **Example:** A, acting on behalf of undisclosed principal, P, advertises that she will conduct an art tour through Europe. T signs up for the tour in reliance on A's reputation in the field. T can rescind the contract if P seeks to conduct the tour. [*See* **Walton v. Davis,** 22 Cal. App. 456 (1913)]

(5) Liability for Agent's Dishonesty or Error

When an agent is dishonest or makes a mistake in handling payments, a question arises as to who must bear the burden of the loss—the principal or the third party.

(a) Payment by Undisclosed Principal

Suppose A enters into a contract with T, under which A is to pay T $5,000. P gives the money to A, and A absconds with it. Can T sue P for the $5,000? Under the great weight of authority, payment to the agent does *not* discharge the principal from his liability to the third party. *Rationale:* Having created the agent's authority, the principal must assume any loss resulting from the agent's violation of duty. [**Senor v. Bangor Mills,** 211 F.2d 685 (3d Cir. 1954)]

(b) Payment by Third Party

As long as the third party does not know or have reason to know that the agent was acting as the agent for another, the third party is protected in dealing exclusively with the agent (and in making whatever payments are required under the contract to the agent). Thus, the third party would not be liable to the principal for a required contract payment if the third party gave the payment to the agent, but the agent never gave the payment to the principal.

1) Distinguish—After Agency Revealed

Once the third party learns that the agent was acting as agent for the principal, the third party must render performance to the principal, ***if so requested.*** Should the third party continue making payments to the agent, the third party will be liable to the principal. [**Darling-Singer Lumber Co. v. Commonwealth,** 195 N.E. 723 (Mass. 1935)]

b. Unidentified Principal

In certain situations, the third party may have notice that the agent is acting as an agent, but does ***not know the identity of the principal*** (*e.g.,* agent signs contract, "A agent"). The Restatement characterizes such cases as involving an "unidentified principal." [Rest. 3d § 1.04(2)(c)] Historically, this has been referred to as a "partially disclosed principal" situation.

(1) Liability of Agent to Third Party

If the agent signs or describes herself as the agent of another, but does not set forth the name of the principal in the contract, the agent is a party to the contract, unless otherwise agreed between the agent and third party. [Rest. 3d § 6.02(2)]

e.g. **Example:** A offers to sell goods to T, stating that she is a representative of the manufacturer but not otherwise identifying the manufacturer. If T accepts, A is liable as a party to the contract. *Rationale:* Under the objective theory of contracts, T must be held to have relied on A's reputation and credit unless it clearly appears that T was relying on that of the unidentified principal. [**Beck v. Suro Textiles, Ltd.,** 612 F. Supp. 1193 (S.D.N.Y. 1985)]

(2) Rights and Liabilities of Principal

The principal also is a party to the contract and is entitled to all the rights and benefits under the contract. [Rest. 3d § 6.02]

AGENT ACTING WITH AUTHORITY—KEY POINTS TO REMEMBER

TYPE OF PRINCIPAL	DISCLOSED	UNDISCLOSED	UNIDENTIFIED
WHAT INFORMATION DOES THIRD PARTY HAVE?	***Knows or should know*** principal's identity	***None***—neither fact of agency nor principal's identity disclosed	Notice that agent is ***acting as agent*** but does not know ***principal's identity***
WHO ARE PARTIES TO CONTRACT?	***Principal*** only, ***unless agreed*** that agent is also party	Principle ***and*** agent	Principal ***and*** agent, ***unless*** agent and third party agree agent is not a party
WHAT ARE CONTRACT RIGHTS OF PRINCIPAL?	***Enforcement*** of terms	***Compel third party's performance unless*** agent fraudulently concealed principal's identity; performance would impose a greater burden on third party; or agent's authority is coupled with an interest (only agent can compel performance)	***Enforcement*** of terms
WHAT ARE CONTRACT RIGHTS OF AGENT?	***None,*** unless agent is also a party	***Indemnification*** or relief based on ***quasi-contract***	***Enforcement*** of terms
IS PAROL EVIDENCE ADMISSIBLE?	***No,*** unless there is an ambiguity	***Yes,*** to show agent was acting on behalf of principal	***Yes,*** to show parties intended agent to be bound

(3) Parties' Intent Governs

Of course, the parties may indicate their intention that the agent ***not*** be bound. In such a case, the agent does not become a party to the contract (*e.g.,* A tells T that she cannot guarantee the performance of the principal who she represents and who remains unidentified). [Rest. 3d § 6.02(2)]

(a) Parol Evidence Admissible

If the contract discloses the agency but not the principal's identity, extrinsic evidence generally *is* admissible to show the intentions of the parties as to whether the agent is personally bound, unless the contract clearly resolves this issue. [Rest. 3d § 6.02, comment b]

Chapter Seven:

Tort Liability for the Acts of Others

CONTENTS	PAGE

Key Exam Issues

The preceding chapter discussed whether a principal can be bound in contract by an agent's acts. Exam questions often ask about tort liability too. The general rule under agency law is that a principal will ***not be liable*** for the tortious acts of her agent. However, there are several ***exceptions*** to this rule, and you must be prepared to apply the exceptions on an exam.

1. Respondeat Superior

The doctrine of respondeat superior provides the biggest exception. Under the doctrine, an employer—a special principal who retains ***control*** over the manner in which the agent performs his duties—will be liable for the tortious acts of her employee—a special type of agent hired by the employer to provide service in her affairs and over whom the principal retains control—if the act occurred ***within the scope of employment.***

a. ***The first step*** in applying the doctrine is to determine ***whether the agent is an employee*** as opposed to an independent contractor. The key is ***control***: Does the employer retain control over the manner in which the agent performs? If so, the agent is an employee; if not, he is an independent contractor.

b. ***The next step*** is to determine whether the employee was ***acting within the scope of employment.*** If the employee is acting to benefit the employer, performing the type of work that he was employed to perform, and performing during hours within which he was supposed to perform, the act is clearly within the scope of employment. However, your exam will probably not be that easy. It will ask you to determine whether deviating from this model makes a difference. The rule to remember is that the more drastic the deviation, the less likely it is that the employee was acting within the scope of employment.

c. ***Finally,*** you may be asked to determine ***who*** among several people ***is the employer.*** This issue will arise when an employer lends an employee to another (a special employer) and the employee negligently injures someone. In determining whether the general (original) employer or the special employer is liable, the key again is ***control***: Who had control over the employee's acts? Usually, you will find the general employer liable, but note that in some cases both the general employer and the special employer may be held liable.

2. Other Exceptions

You should also remember that nonrespondeat superior liability may exist for an agent's torts in some situations. If, on your exam, it turns out that the tortfeasor-agent was not an employee, or did not act within the scope of his employment, check to see whether the principal can be held liable for her ***own negligence in hiring, training, or supervising*** the agent; *e.g.*, did the principal appoint an unqualified employee or independent contractor? The principal will also be liable if she appoints an independent contractor to perform ***nondelegable acts*** or a ***highly dangerous activity.*** Finally, remember that a principal will be liable for an agent's ***misrepresentations*** whenever the making of such representations by the agent was ***actually or apparently authorized*** by the principal.

A. Liability of Employer for Torts of Employee—Respondeat Superior

1. Introduction

a. Employer-Employee Relationship

The employer-employee relationship (traditionally called a "master-servant" relationship) is a special type of agency relationship. Generally in agency, the agent is hired ***to contract*** for the principal. In the employer-employee relationship, the agent is generally hired ***to perform services*** for the employer, and the employer ***retains control*** over the employee as to the manner in which the employee performs the services. Because of this retained control, courts allow an employer to be held liable for the torts of the employee through the doctrine of respondeat superior (*see infra,* p. 93).

(1) "Employer"

The Restatement (Second) of Agency defines "employer" as a specific type of principal, namely one who employs an agent to perform services in her affairs and who has the right to control the physical conduct of the agent in performing the services. [Rest. 2d § 2(1)]

(2) "Employee"

Similarly, an employee is a specific type of agent, namely one who is employed to render services of any type, other than the pursuit of an independent calling, and who remains under the control of the employer in performing such services. [*See* Rest. 3d § 7.07(3)(a)]

(3) May Be Both Employee and Independent Contractor

The same person may act as both an employee and an independent contractor, depending on the duties and powers assigned to him (*See infra*, p. 93).

(4) Control Is Key

The essential feature of the employer-employee relationship is that at all times the employer ***controls or has the right to control*** the physical conduct of the employee in the performance of his duties of employment. The employee is entirely under the control of the employer and has no independent discretion. [Rest. 3d § 7.07(2)] A regular agency relationship can be distinguished by its ***representative character and derivative authority,*** which give the agent a degree of discretion in carrying out the purposes of the principal that an employee would not have. [**Wallace v. Sinclair,** 114 Cal.App. 2d 220 (1952)]

(5) Distinguish—Independent Contractor

An independent contractor, like an employee, is hired for physical services and not in a representative capacity. However, the independent contractor contracts with the employer only as to the specific ***results*** to be accomplished, not as to the means by which the work is to be performed. Also, the independent contractor renders services in the course of an independent occupation or calling.

LIABILITY OF EMPLOYER/PRINCIPAL FOR AGENT'S TORTS

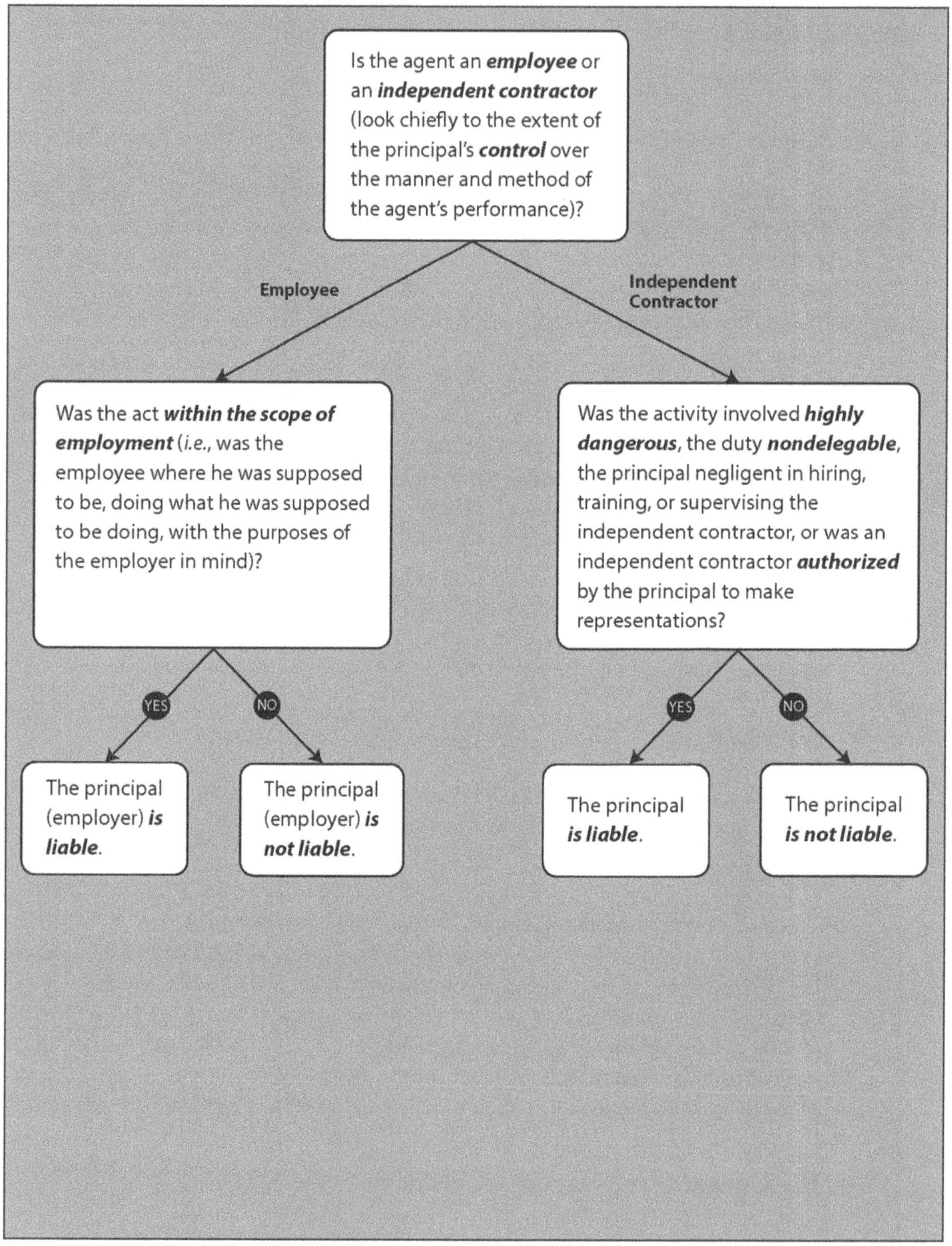

(a) No Right to Control

The primary characteristic of an independent contractor is that the employer has *no right to control* how the work is to be performed. [Rest. 3d § 7.07, comment f]

(b) Significance

The main reason for distinguishing between an employee and an independent contractor is that the doctrine of respondeat superior, upon which the tort liability of employers for employee conduct is usually based, does *not* apply to independent contractors. The distinction between an "employee" and "independent contractor" is also important in determining rights to benefits under unemployment insurance laws, workers' compensation laws, etc.

(c) Dual Function

In certain cases, the same person may function as *both* an employee and an independent contractor for the same employer, and his status therefore will depend on his activity at the particular time in question.

e.g. **Example:** P hires X as a distributor of P's goods and also requires that X help unload all shipments as they arrive. X would be an independent contractor while acting as a distributor but an employee when unloading shipments. [**Clough v. Estate of Malley,** 11 A.2d 398 (Conn. 1940)]

EXAM TIP

A fairly common exam question is one that raises the issue of employer liability for the torts of an employee. Your first step in analyzing this issue is to determine whether the "employee" is really an "independent contractor." The way to do this is to look at the facts for the *key factor of control* (or the right to control), because with control comes liability for the employee's torts. Note too that the right to control will be important for determining whether a general employer or special employer is liable for a borrowed employee's torts (*see infra,* p. 100 *et seq.*).

b. Doctrine of Respondeat Superior

Under the doctrine of respondeat superior ("let the master answer"), an employer will be liable for all torts committed by her employee acting within the scope of the employment. [Rest. 3d § 2.04] Any third person injured by the employee's tortious act can, therefore, proceed against ***both*** the employee and the employer—the employee being directly liable for his wrongful act, and the employer being ***vicariously liable*** for the act. [Rest. 3d §§ 7.01, 7.07]

(1) Background

The doctrine developed at early common law when the employee was considered the "property" of the employer. The employer was deemed to have absolute control over the employee's acts so that she might properly be held to answer for them. [*See* Rest. 3d § 2.04, comment b]

(2) Present Rationale

An employee is obviously no longer viewed as being the property of the employer, but the doctrine of respondeat superior has been retained in our modern law on either or both of the following theories:

(a) "Entrepreneur Theory"

Even though the employee is not the property of his employer, the employer does have the right to control the employee's acts. Having created the risk that some third person may be injured if the employee acts wrongfully, and having the right to control the employee, the employer must assume full responsibility for any damages caused by the employee, including acts beyond the employer's actual or possible control, but inherent in or created by the enterprise. [**Rodgers v. Kemper Construction Co.,** 50 Cal. App. 3d 608 (1975)]

(b) "Deeper Pocket Theory"

Public policy requires that the person injured by the employee's wrongful act be afforded the most effective relief. Because the employer is more likely than the employee to be able to respond in damages, she should be held liable. [*See* 70 Yale L.J. 499]

(3) Nature of Liability

Respondeat superior imposes ***strict liability*** ("liability without fault") on the employer. Therefore, the employer is responsible for the employee's wrongful acts, notwithstanding the employer's exercise of due care in hiring the employee or supervising his acts.

(a) Waiver Ineffective

Because this liability is imposed for the protection of third persons, the employer *cannot* contract with her employee to insulate herself from liability.

e.g. **Example:** E hires I in what is clearly an employment relationship, but has I agree in writing that he is serving as an "independent contractor," and that "in no event shall E be liable for Fs tortious acts." The contract between E and I will *not* affect E's liability to third persons injured by I's wrongful acts.

(b) Vicarious Liability

Respondeat superior is likewise a form of *vicarious liability,* because the employer is held accountable for the acts of another. [Rest. 3d §§ 7.03(2), 7.07, comment b] Such liability is *joint and several* with that of the employee for his own acts: The employer can be sued alone, or she can be sued together with the negligent employee.

1) Single Recovery

However, the victim is entitled to only one recovery, and a recovery against either party will bar recovery against the other.

2) Exoneration

Moreover, if the employee is exonerated or released from liability, this generally operates to release the employer from vicarious liability as well. [**Holcomb v. Flavin,** 216 N.E.2d 811 (Ill. 1966)]

a) Exception—Employer's Own Negligence

If the employer was guilty of some negligence or breach of duty to the injured party, ***independent of the acts of her employee,*** she could be held liable even if the employee was exonerated. [**Barsoom v. City of Reedley,** 38 Cal. App. 2d 413 (1940); *and see infra,* pp. 118–119]

b) Exception—Employee's Immunity Not Imputed to Employer

An employer may be held liable for torts committed by her employee ***even if the employee is immune from liability***; *e.g.,* H negligently injures his wife, W, while acting in the course and scope of his employment. In this situation, the employer ***can*** be held liable by W, even though no judgment could be obtained by her against H if interspousal tort immunity applied. [*See* **Fields v. Synthetic Ropes, Inc.,** 215 A.2d 427 (Del. 1965)]

1/ Rationale

H's immunity is ***personal*** and does not cover the enterprise by which he is employed. There is no realistic threat to "family harmony" in allowing W to recover against H's employer, particularly because insurance exists in most cases. [**Schubert v. August Schubert Wagon Co.**, 249 N.Y. 253 (1928)]

3) Employer's Right to Indemnification

If the employer is held liable for an employee's torts, the employer can hold the employee liable in turn—*i.e.,* the employer has a right of ***indemnification*** against the employee for any damages the employer must pay to a third person because of the employee's wrongful acts. [**Solar-West, Inc. v. Falk,** 687 P.2d 939 (Ariz. 1984)]

a) Exception—Employee Immune from Liability

Indemnity is denied if the employee was ***immune*** from liability in the first place (*see supra,* p. 95).

(4) Application of Doctrine

In determining whether the doctrine of respondeat superior applies, two basic elements must be established:

(a) Employer-Employee Relationship

For the doctrine to apply there must be an employer-employee relationship between the party who caused the injury and the person sought to be held liable for the injury; and

(b) Act Within Scope of Employment

The employee's wrongful act must have been committed within the course and scope of his employment.

EXAM TIP

Don't forget that if an employee commits a tort within the scope of employment, *both* the employer and employee are liable to the injured person. The *employee is directly liable* for his tort, and the *employer is vicariously liable* for the employee's tort under the doctrine of respondeat superior. Thus, the injured person can sue both the employer and employee or the employer alone. *But note:* If the injured person sues both the employer and employee, she is entitled to *only one recovery,* and if that recovery is against the employer, the employer usually may seek indemnification from the employee.

2. Employer-Employee Relationship

As mentioned, the first issue in respondeat superior cases is whether an employer-employee relationship actually existed between the person who committed the tortious act and the person sought to be held vicariously liable.

a. Right to Control Physical Acts of Employee

Liability under the doctrine of respondeat superior is based on the employer's right to control the physical acts of the employee, a right unique to the employer-employee relationship. [Rest. 3d § 2.04, comment b; **Gifford-Hill & Co. v. Moore,** 479 S.W.2d 711 (Tex. 1972)] As will be seen, a principal ordinarily does ***not*** have the right to control the physical acts of a nonemployee agent or of an independent contractor in her employ; accordingly, respondeat superior generally does not apply in regular principal-agent or employer-independent contractor relationships.

e.g. **Example:** P engages real estate broker A, an independent contractor, to sell P's land. While driving a prospective purchaser to the land, A negligently injures X. P has no right to control the physical acts of A and, therefore, is not liable to X for A's negligence.

b. Creation of Relationship

The employer-employee relationship (like that of principal and agent) is consensual in nature and can exist only if there is an agreement manifesting assent by each of the parties to the creation of the relationship. [**Oleksinski v. Filip,** 30 A.2d 912 (Conn. 1943)]

(1) Formalities

The employment contract may be oral, except when required to be in writing under the Statute of Frauds (*e.g.,* employment for period in excess of one year from the date the contract was made).

(2) Capacity of Parties

(a) Employer

Generally, any person having the *capacity to contract* may employ an agent or employee. Thus, *minors and incompetents,* lacking contractual capacity, ordinarily cannot appoint employees or agents to act on their behalf and, hence, cannot be held vicariously liable. [Rest. 3d § 3.04]

(b) Employee

However, no special capacity is required to *be* an employee or agent. Therefore, an employer *can* be held vicariously liable for the negligent acts of employees who are minors. [Rest. 3d § 3.05]

(3) Implied Agreement

While the employer-employee relationship is usually created by an express agreement (whether oral or written), it may also be ***implied*** from the circumstances or conduct of the parties. [Rest. 3d §§ 1.03; 3.01]

e.g. **Example:** At harvest time each year, E has hired F as a farmhand. F returns at the current harvest and places his belongings in the employees' bunkhouse. If E knows of and permits this, an employment relationship arises by implication.

(4) "Volunteers"

Because the employment relationship is consensual, the employee cannot foist his services on the employer without her consent. However, the mere fact that one party has not requested the other to render services does not prevent an employer-employee relationship from arising if the employer ***knows*** that services are being rendered ***and accepts the benefits*** of the services. [**Copp v. Paradis,** 157 A. 228 (Me. 1931)] Note that consideration is ***not*** essential to the creation of an employer-employee relationship. [Rest. 3d § 3.01, comment b]

e.g. **Example:** E's employees are loading merchandise on a truck in front of her store. X, a passerby, gratuitously helps them. At this point, X is not an employee of E. However, if E observes X's act and allows X to continue (thereby accepting the benefits of X's work), an employer-employee relationship may be held to exist between E and X, at least so far as to impose liability on E for any wrongful act by X injuring a third party.

c. Duration of Employment

An employee is presumed to be hired for the length of time adopted for computing his wages (hourly, weekly, monthly, etc.). If no time period is specified, the employment is presumed to be terminable at will.

(1) Statutory Limitations

Many states have statutes limiting the length of personal service contracts. [*See, e.g.,* Cal. Labor Code § 2855—specifies that such contracts may not exceed seven years]

(2) Expiration and Renewal

If the employee remains employed by the employer after the original employment agreement expires, it is presumed that the employment has been renewed on the same terms as those under the original employment agreement.

d. Right of Employer to Recover for Injuries to Employee

The early common law held that one who injured an employee was liable to the employer for the loss of the employee's services, the employee being regarded as a "chattel" of the employer and the injury being to the employer's property interest. Modern cases uniformly reject this notion, because the relationship between employer and employee is now considered strictly one of ***contract*** and not property.

(1) Recovery in Tort

If a third party ***intentionally*** injures an employee, the employer may be able to recover for the loss of the employee's services because the intentional interference with a contractual relationship is an actionable tort. (*See* Torts Summary.)

(2) Distinguish—No Recovery for Negligence

There will be no recovery if the injury is merely the result of ***negligence*** by the third party. [**Snow v. West,** 440 P.2d 864 (Or. 1968)]

(a) Note—Partnership

Similar rules apply in *partnership* cases; *i.e.,* the partnership generally cannot recover against third parties for negligent injuries to one of the partners. [**Sharfman v. State,** 253 Cal. App. 2d 333 (1967); *and see infra,* p. 158]

e. Employment by Estoppel ("Ostensible Employment")

As noted previously, the general rule is that the employer-employee relationship must be founded on an agreement between the parties. However, if a person intentionally or negligently creates the ***appearance*** that another is in her employ, and a third person ***relies*** on this appearance, the first person may be estopped from denying the employment relationship and would be liable to the third person for any injuries as though she in fact were the employer. This is known as ***ostensible employment.*** [**Standard Oil Co. v. Gentry,** 1 So. 2d 29 (Ala. 1941)]

(1) Requirements

Because this relationship is based on estoppel, it must clearly appear that (i) the "employer" in some way created the ***appearance*** that the "employee" was in her employ, and (ii) the injured person ***justifiably relied*** on the appearance of employment in dealing with the "employee." If either element is lacking, the ostensible employer cannot be held liable for the torts of the "employee." [**Councell v. Douglas,** 126 N.E.2d 597 (Ohio 1955)]

e.g. **Example:** A department store advertises that it employs skilled chiropractor X, offering X's services to the public at nominal rates. Relying on the ad, P engages the services of X. If P is injured through X's negligence, the store may be estopped from denying that X was its employee (*e.g.,* it cannot assert that X was in fact an independent contractor). Having created an appearance of employment by its representations, the store would be vicariously liable for P's injuries.

(2) Acts by Employer Required

Note, however, that the appearance of employment must be created ***by the purported employer*** and not by the purported employee. Thus, if S holds himself out as M's employee, and M neither knows of nor consents to the representation, M would not be liable to a third person injured through S's negligence. [**McMurry v. Pacific Ready-Cut Homes, Inc.,** 111 Cal.App. 341 (1931)]

(3) Injury in Reliance

The third person's injury must be sustained in ***reliance*** on the appearance of employment.

e.g. **Example:** D Department Store engages independent contractor I to deliver its parcels. D requires I's trucks to carry signs advertising D Department Store. If one of I's trucks hits P, D is ***not*** estopped from showing that I was actually an independent contractor because P was ***not*** injured in reliance on D's sign.

f. Subservants

To create an employer-employee relationship, it is not necessary that the employer or principal herself hire the employees. Such status can be created by an authorized agent acting on behalf of the principal. [**Dickerson v. American Sugar Refining Co.,** 211 F.2d 200 (3d Cir. 1954)]

(1) Respondeat Superior

If an agent is ***authorized*** to hire an employee for his principal, the employee is placed in direct relation to the employer, and the employer is therefore liable for the employee's tortious acts. [**Smith v. Rutledge,** 163 N.E. 544 (Ill. 1928)]

e.g. **Example:** E authorizes her agent A to hire truck drivers to work in E's business. A hires X as an employee. X subsequently injures a pedestrian while driving one of E's trucks. E is liable for X's negligence notwithstanding the fact that A hired by X, rather than E.

(a) Undisclosed Principal

If the agent does not disclose that he is hiring on behalf of another, and the employee is not otherwise aware of this, the employer is said to be an undisclosed principal (*see supra,* p. 5). In such a case, the agent remains liable to the employee *on the contract (e.g.,* for wages due and owing the employee). [**Pierce v. Johnson,** 34 Conn. 274 (1867)] However, the agent is generally *not* liable in *tort* to third persons injured by the wrongful acts of the employee. *Rationale:* Respondeat superior imposes liability only on the *true employer,* and as between the principal and the agent, the principal must be held the employer of the employee.

(2) Unauthorized Hirings

If the agent was ***not*** authorized to employ another, there is no relationship between the employer and the subservant hired, and ordinarily the employer would not be liable to third persons for the subservant's torts. [**White v. Consumers Finance Service, Inc.,** 15 A.2d 142 (Pa. 1940)]

(a) Exception

Nevertheless, if the work in question requires no particular skill or discretion (so that the employer had attached no special significance to the identity of the employee), *and if the* services of the subservant are within the scope of the agent's employment for the employer and are performed *under the agents' supervision and in his presence,* the employer may be held liable to third persons if the subservant performs the services tortiously. *Rationale:* This situation is tantamount to the agent having rendered the services himself. [**Calhoun v. Middletown Coca-Cola Bottling Co.,** 332 N.E.2d 73 (Ohio 1974)]

e.g. **Example:** E hires F to flag traffic for E's paving business. Without authority, F permits a friend to flag cars in F's presence and under her supervision. E may be held liable for injuries caused by the friend's negligent actions at the job site.

(3) Emergency Authority to Hire

Even an ordinary employee may have authority to hire and employ a subservant in an emergency. If an unanticipated situation requires immediate action to preserve or protect the employer's interests, and communication with the employer is impossible or impractical, the employee is deemed to have the authority to employ another to assist him. In such an event, the employer becomes liable for the wrongful acts of the subservant.

e.g. **Example:** While delivering perishable merchandise for E, D becomes ill. D is unable to contact E and asks a passerby to deliver the merchandise. If the passerby negligently injures someone while attempting to make the delivery, E may be liable. [**Kirk v. Showell, Fryer & Co.,** 124 A. 84 (Pa. 1924)]

g. "Borrowed Employees"

Frequently, an employer may lend the services of her employee to another, either gratuitously or for compensation. A common example is when the employer lends or leases a piece of equipment to a third party and sends along her employee to assist in the operation of the equipment. If the employee commits a tortious act while operating the equipment, who is liable? Who is the "employer"?

(1) Right to Control Determinative

Liability in these situations usually turns on whether the general employer or the special employer had the right to control the employee. [Rest. 3d § 7.03, comment d(2)]

(a) Loan of Equipment

Normally, a general employer who lends or leases her equipment with an operator to a special employer is presumed to *retain the right to control* the operator. Hence, the general employer (rather than the special employer) would be liable for the operator's torts unless the operator must take orders from the special employer. [**L.B. Smith, Inc. v. Mar-Van Equipment, Inc.,** 67 A.D.2d 751 (1979)]

1) Exceptions

However, if the primary right to control has been given to the special employer (particularly when the borrowing is for an indefinite period), liability for the employee's actions also passes to the special employer. [**Meyer v. All-Electric Bakery, Inc.,** 271 Ill. App. 522 (1933)] And ***regardless*** of who has the primary right to control, if the special employer directs the employee to perform ***a specific act,*** he will be liable if the employee performs it tortiously. [Rest. 3d § 7.03, comment d(2); **Hilgenberg v. Elam,** 198 S.W.2d 94 (Tex. 1947)]

(b) Factors to Consider in Determining Who Has Right to Control

The court may consider the following factors in determining whether the general or special employer has the right to control the employee:

(i) The ***extent of control*** either employer exercises over the employee's work;

(ii) The relationship between the ***employee's work and the nature of the special employer's business*** (does the employee provide a unique service?);

(iii) The nature of the ***employee's work, the skills required to perform it, and the degree of supervision*** normally associated with the work (who has primary control over the employee's work?);

(iv) The ***length of the employee's employment*** with the special employer (is there a stated duration for the employment?);

(v) The ***method of payment*** for the work (*e.g.*, whether the employee is paid a salary or paid a certain sum for a particular task); and

(vi) Whether the ***equipment is supplied by the general or special employer.***

[Rest. 3d § 7.03, comment d(2)]

EXAM TIP

The borrowed employee issue is a likely exam topic, and usually arises when a general employer loans a piece of equipment, vehicle, etc., to a special employer along with the services of an employee. Remember that the key to liability depends on which employer has the *right to control* the employee. Normally the *general employer retains the right to control* the employee and will be liable for the employee's torts. However, the *special employer* will be liable for the torts of the employee if (i) the general employer *gives* the special employer the right to control the employee; or (ii) the special employer *directs* the employee to do a specific act, and the employee performs it tortiously.

---

(2) Distinguish—Joint Liability of General and Special Employers

If there is a ***division of control*** over the employee—as where the special employer directs the employee to perform a specific act which is also within the scope of the employee's employment by the general employer—***both*** the general employer and the special employer may be liable for the tortious performance of the act. [Rest. 3d § 7.03, comment d(2)]

e.g. **Example:** E loans her truck and driver, D, to T. T orders D to load dirt on the truck and haul it to T's construction project. D loads the truck in a negligent manner, and as a result the truck overturns en route to the construction site, injuring P. If loading was within the scope of D's employment by E, both E and T may be liable to P. [Rest. 3d §§ 7.03, comment d(2), 7.07; 17 A.L.R.2d 1388]

h. "Employees" vs. "Independent Contractors"

The doctrine of respondeat superior is limited to the employer-employee relationship and does not apply when the tortious acts are committed by an independent contractor (or ***his*** employees). [Rest. 3d § 2.04, comment b] Thus, an employer ordinarily is not liable for injuries caused by the negligent acts of an independent contractor, even though the contractor is acting for the employer's benefit. [**Green v. Independent Oil Co.,** 201 A.2d 207 (Pa. 1964)] (Of course, the employer may still be liable for the ***results*** she ordered from the independent contractor; *see infra,* pp. 116–117.)

(1) Test Is Right to Control

The chief criterion for whether a given party is an employee or independent contractor is whether the employer has the right to control the party's conduct in the performance of the work. As noted previously, the employer-employee relationship requires that the employer have the right to control the employee's services and means of doing the work. Thus, if the employer is merely bargaining for a ***result*** and retains no such control, the relationship is that of employer-independent contractor. [**Stockwell v. Morris,** 22 P.2d 189 (Wyo. 1933)—employer not liable for commissioned salesperson's (agent's) auto accident when employer had no control over how agent drove and agent used own car]

(a) Note—Dual Capacity as Employee and Independent Contractor

In certain cases, the same person may be *both* an employee and an independent contractor to the same employer; in such cases his status will depend on his activity at the particular time in question. (*See supra,* p. 93.)

EXAM TIP

Remember that the first step in determining whether a principal can be held liable for the torts of an agent under *respondeat superior* is finding that an *employer-employee relationship* existed. When discussing the existence of an employer-employee relationship, you must discuss the principal's right to control the agent's physical acts. If the principal has no right to control the agent, the agent is not an employee and the principal cannot be found liable for the agent's acts under respondeat superior. Conversely, liability under respondeat superior can be imposed in cases where the principal has the right to control the agent, even if it is never exercised.

---

(2) Relevant Factors

The legal distinction between an employee and an independent contractor is easy to state but more difficult to apply in practice. Frequently, the extent of control by the employer is disputed or unclear, and the distinction between employee and independent contractor may be a matter of degree. The following factors are relevant in determining the status of the person performing the work [Rest. 3d § 7.07, comment b; *and see* **Community for Creative Non-Violence v. Reid**, 490 U.S. 730 (1989)]:

(a) ***The agreed extent of control*** that the employer may exercise over details of the work; the more control exercised by the employer, the more likely it is that the person is an employee.

(b) Whether the ***employer is in business,*** if the employer is in business, it is more likely the person performing the work is an employee.

(c) Whether the person employed is engaged in an ***occupation or business distinct from that of the employer,*** if the person is engaged in a distinct occupation or business, he is more likely an independent contractor.

(d) Whether the work is ***part of the regular business*** of the employer; if the work is part of the regular business of the employer, the person is more likely an employee.

(e) Whether the work is ***usually done under the employer's direction, or by a specialist*** without supervision; if the work is performed under the employer's direction, the person performing the work is more likely an employee.

(f) Whether the employer ***supplies the tools and place of work,*** if the employer supplies the tools and place of work, the person is more likely an employee.

(g) ***The length of time*** for which the person is employed; the longer the length of time a person is employed, the more likely the person is an employee.

(h) ***The method of payment*** (whether by time or by completed job) for the work performed by the person; if payment is by time, the person is more likely an employee.

(i) ***The degree of skill*** required by the person employed; if great skill is required, the person is more likely an independent contractor.

(j) ***Belief of the parties*** as to their creating an employer-employee relationship.

FACTORS TENDING TO SHOW STATUS AS EMPLOYEE OR INDEPENDENT CONTRACTOR		
	EMPLOYEE	**INDEPENDENT CONTRACTOR**
CONTROL	Employer has ***right to control how work is performed***	Employer has ***no right to control*** how work is performed
EMPLOYER'S STATUS	Employer ***is in business***	Employer is ***not in business***
TYPE OF OCCUPATION OR BUSINESS	Engaged in ***employer's occupation*** or business	Engaged in occupation or business ***distinct from employer***
TYPE OF WORK	Performs work that is part of ***employer's regular business***	Performs work that is ***not part of employer's regular business***
SUPERVISION	Employer ***supervises*** work	Employer does ***not supervise*** work
TOOLS AND PLACE OF WORK	Employer ***supplies tools and place of work***	Employer does ***not supply*** tools and place of work
LENGTH OF EMPLOYMENT	***Long length*** of employment	***Short length*** of employment
COMPENSATION	Compensated ***by time***	Compensated ***by job***
LEVEL OF SKILL	***Average skilled***	***Highly skilled***

(3) Application

(a) Building Contractors

A general contractor who erects a building is clearly an independent contractor, and so is a *subcontractor* who contracts to furnish materials and services for a particular part of the job. Each usually has his own organization and employees, and the property owner generally has no right of direct control over the manner and means used to accomplish the job. [**Moriarty v. W.T. Grant Co.,** 155 N.Y.S.2d 218 (1956)]

(b) Truck Drivers

A truck driver who owns his own equipment and is hired out for specific jobs is generally an independent contractor [**Skelton v. Fekete,** 120 Cal. App. 2d 401 (1953)]; whereas one who drives his employer's trucks in the daily course of business is usually an employee [**Amyx v. Henry & Hall,** 79 So. 2d 483 (La. 1955)].

(c) Physicians

A frequent problem arises when physicians are engaged by an employer to treat third persons—*e.g.,* the "company doctor," or the resident physician employed by a hospital. If the physician negligently injures a patient, can the employer be held liable under respondeat superior?

1) General View

Most courts hold that highly skilled persons such as physicians or lawyers are independent contractors, even though employed on a retainer basis. *Rationale*: Medicine is a skilled and learned art, and it would be incompatible to say that a physician is subject to the "complete control" of another, without which there can be no employer-employee relationship. [**Giannelli v. Metropolitan Life Insurance Co.,** 29 N.E.2d 124 (Mass. 1940)] Thus, an employer is generally not liable for the torts of a physician.

a) Minority View

However, a number of jurisdictions ***do*** impose liability on the employer, at least in the case of a physician employed by the hospital where she is a resident. [*See* **Bowers v. Olch,** 120 Cal. App. 2d 108 (1953)] There is also a trend to hold hospitals liable under apparent agency principles (*see supra,* p. 9). [*See, e.g.,* **Arthur v. St. Peters Hospital,** 405 A.2d 443 (N.J. 1979)]

2) Distinguish—Physician's Services Primarily for Benefit of Employer

If the physician's services were primarily for the benefit of the employer—rather than for treatment of a third person—many courts have held that the physician should be considered an "employee," and the employer held liable for the physician's negligent injury of the third person.

e.g. **Example:** E hires a doctor to give a physical examination to P, whom E is considering employing. The examination results are to be used by E in determining P's fitness as an employee. In such a case, the examination is primarily for the benefit of E rather than P, and hence E may be liable for any injuries that the doctor negligently inflicts on P in the course of the examination. [**Pearl v. West End Street Railway,** 57 N.E. 339 (Mass. 1900)]

a) Representations

A similar result would follow when the employer authorizes the physician to make ***representations*** to third persons on the employer's behalf.

e.g. **Example:** E hires a doctor to treat an injured employee, P, and for the purpose of minimizing P's claim against him, E directs the doctor to assure P that her injuries are not serious. Relying on the doctor's assurances, P returns to work too soon and greatly aggravates the injury. E may be liable for the false representations by the doctor. (*See infra,* p. 121.)

3) Distinguish—Employer Negligent in Hiring Physician

Even under the general rule that a physician is an independent contractor whose employer is not liable for his negligence, the employer may be liable if it appears that the employer was negligent in ***hiring*** the physician (*see infra,* p. 106).

e.g. **Example:** Hospital hires D as a resident physician, knowing that D is an alcoholic. While intoxicated, D negligently treats and injures P. Hospital is liable to P for its negligence in hiring D. *Rationale:* This is ***not*** an application of respondeat superior, but rather is a case of ***liability for the employer's own direct negligence.***

(d) Collection Agencies

An outside collection agency employed by a creditor to collect a debt is generally held to be an independent contractor, because the agency is usually engaged in a distinct occupation, and the creditor reserves no control over the methods of collection. As a result, the creditor generally is not liable for any torts committed by the agency in attempting to collect the claim (*e.g.,* assault, defamation, invasion of privacy).

1) Exceptions

Of course, the creditor would be ***liable*** if the creditor were shown to have ***caused or directed*** the collection agent to commit the tort, or if the agent was not self-employed but rather was a full-time employee of the creditor. [*See* **Loughan v. Harger-Haldeman,** 184 Cal. App. 2d 495 (1960)]

(4) Exceptional Situations in Which Employer Is Liable for Torts of Independent Contractor

There are certain limited situations in which an employer may be held liable for the tortious acts of an independent contractor in her employ. As will be seen, however, these are ***not*** applications of respondeat superior—which is limited to the employer-employee relationship. Rather, liability is imposed on the employer because of her ***own*** negligence or wrongdoing, or the act of the independent contractor is attributed to the employer as a matter of ***public policy.***

(a) Highly Dangerous Acts

When the work to be performed is of a highly dangerous nature, the employer will be liable for any injuries caused by that work. The employer cannot avoid or delegate such liability by arranging to have it done by an independent contractor. [**Giem v. Williams,** 222 S.W.2d 800 (Ark. 1949)]

1) Abnormally Dangerous Activities

This exception is usually limited to cases in which the activity in question amounts to an "ultrahazardous activity"—*i.e.,* one in which ***strict liability***

("liability without fault") would be imposed as a matter of law. (*See* Torts Summary.) It is therefore immaterial whether the independent contractor was negligent in causing the injury.

e.g. **Example:** E hires I, an explosives expert, to blast some boulders on E's land. The blast is set off carefully, but a piece of rock is unforeseeably hurled onto P's land, injuring P. E would be liable, even though I was not negligent. (Of course, E would be liable as well if I had actually been negligent.)

e.g. **Example:** Other abnormally dangerous activities include transporting highly volatile chemicals, using poisonous gases in fumigation or crop-spraying, drilling of oil wells, etc. (*See* Torts Summary.)

(b) Nondelegable Duties

Similarly, if the employer is under a duty that is nondelegable as a matter of law or public policy, but nevertheless engages an independent contractor to perform the duty, *the employer remains fully liable* for the independent contractor's conduct. [Rest. 3d § 7.06]

e.g. **Example:** E, who is required to provide a safe place of employment for her factory workers, engages I to make repairs on the place of employment. I is negligent and, as a result, one of the workers sustains injuries. E would be liable for the injuries.

1) Automobile Cases

Because of the substantial risk of harm involved, a number of cases hold that the owner of an ***automobile*** is liable for injuries caused by its defective condition, even though the owner employed a reputable garage to repair the automobile; *i.e.,* the owner's duty to maintain her automobile in a safe condition is considered nondelegable. [**Maloney v. Rath,** 69 Cal. 2d 442 (1968); *and see* Torts Summary]

(c) Employer Negligence in Hiring, Training, or Supervising Independent Contractor

An employer may be charged with liability for injuries caused by an independent contractor if the employer is negligent in hiring, training, or supervising the independent contractor or permitting him to undertake the activity in question. [Rest. 3d § 7.05]

(d) Representations

Finally, if the independent contractor is authorized to make representations on behalf of his employer, the employer may be liable for any misstatements made by the contractor. (*See infra,* p. 121.)

SITUATION IN WHICH EMPLOYER LIABLE FOR TORTS OF INDEPENDENT CONTRACTOR
AN EMPLOYER IS LIABLE FOR THE TORTIOUS ACT OF AN INDEPENDENT CONTRACTOR WHEN:
☑ The act to be performed by the independent contractor is ***highly dangerous*** (*i.e.*, it is an abnormally dangerous activity).
☑ The employer had a ***nondelegable duty*** to perform the act herself.
☑ The employer is ***negligent in hiring, training, or supervising*** the independent contractor.
☑ The employer ***authorized*** the independent contractor to make representations on her behalf, and the independent contractor made ***misrepresentations.***

3. Scope of Employment

Once it is established that an employer-employee relationship exists between the employer and the person employed, one must also determine whether the employee committed the tortious act ***within the course and scope of employment*** in order to hold the employer liable. Basically, this means that the employee must have been engaged in work for the employer of a type that he was employed to perform, during working hours.

EXAM TIP

Before you discuss scope of employment on your exam, you first must have discussed the employer-employee relationship. Remember that an employer's liability under respondeat superior is a *two-step process*: (i) an *employer-employee relationship must exist*, and (ii) the employee must have committed *a tort within the scope of employment.* If you don't find that an employer-employee relationship existed, there cannot be any liability under respondeat superior, and consequently there is no need to discuss scope of employment.

a. Relevant Factors

Under the Restatement (Second) of Agency, section 229, the following general factors should be considered in determining whether a particular act occurred within the scope of employment:

(1) ***Whether the act was authorized*** (or incidental to any act authorized) by the employer;

(2) ***The time, place, and purpose*** of the act;

(3) ***Whether the act was one commonly performed by employees*** on behalf of their employers;

(4) ***The extent to which the employer's interests were advanced*** by the act;

(5) ***The extent to which the private interests of the employee were involved;***

(6) ***Whether the employer furnished the means or instrumentality*** (truck, machine, etc.) by which the injury was inflicted;

(7) ***Whether the employer had reason to know that the employee would do the act*** in question; and

(8) ***Whether the act involved the commission of a serious crime.***

b. Authorization by Employer Not Required

Very few employers knowingly authorize tortious acts by their employees. Hence, it is ***not*** necessary to show that the employer authorized or permitted the particular act that caused the injury if the act occurred in the scope of the employee's regular duties and employment. [**Tucker v. United States,** 91 F. Supp. 527 (Alaska 1950)]

e.g. **Example:** E employs D to deliver merchandise for her, using E's truck. Instead of driving E's truck, D uses his own private car, and while negligently driving on a delivery, injures P. Even though the particular act (driving his own car) was not authorized, the negligence occurred within the scope of the duties assigned to D (delivering merchandise), and E may therefore be liable.

(1) Forbidden Acts

On the same theory, even acts that are ***specifically forbidden*** by the employer may be within the scope of employment; *i.e.,* an employer cannot avoid responsibility for an employee's negligence by telling the employee to act carefully, or never to commit some particular tortious act. [**National Premium Budget Plan Corp. v. National Fire Insurance Co.,** 234 A.2d 683 (N.J. 1967)]

e.g. **Example:** E, the owner of a sporting goods store, directs her salesperson, S, never to insert a cartridge while exhibiting a gun to a customer. Nevertheless, S does so and causes injuries to P. Because S's act was directly related to his assigned duties (selling guns) and hence within the scope of his employment, E would be liable to P.

(a) Violations Affecting Authorization

However, when the employee—in violating the employer's instructions—goes *beyond the duties for which he is hired,* his act may be outside the scope of his employment, and the employer is relieved of liability for the tortious consequences.

e.g. **Example:** E hires C to collect for goods sold by E to third parties. C is specifically instructed not to attempt repossession of any goods, even peaceably. If C uses force to repossess goods previously sold by E to someone, C has exceeded the scope of his employment (*i.e.,* collecting monies). Therefore, E is not liable for any tort committed by C during the repossession.

1) Analysis

Decisions in this type of case are a matter of ***degree.*** Minor deviations from assigned orders generally do not take the act out of respondeat superior, whereas major departures would. [Rest. 3d § 7.07, comment c]

2) Distinguish—Representations

Authorization is of ***crucial*** importance when liability for the ***representations*** of another are concerned. (*See infra,* p. 122.)

c. Intentional Torts by Employee

Liability under respondeat superior extends to intentional acts by the employee only if the acts occur within the scope of employment. If the employee's intentional act is related to carrying forth the employer's business, the employer may be liable. [Rest. 3d § 7.07, comment c; **Carroll v. Kencher, Inc.,** 491 So. 2d 1311 (Fla. 1986)]

(1) Motivation

Again, the factual issue is whether the intentional act is related to carrying forth the employer's business. Probably the most important factor in these cases is whether the infliction of injury was motivated by the employee's personal reasons or whether he was acting to further the business interests of his employer. The more serious or culpable the act, the less likely it will be found to be within the scope of the employment. [**Nelson v. AmericanWest African Line, Inc.,** 86 F.2d 730 (2d Cir. 1936)]

Example: E hires R to repossess goods sold to P. P refuses to give up the goods, and R obtains them by the use of excessive and unlawful force. Because the excessive force was in furtherance of E's business interests, E is civilly liable for R's battery upon P. [*See* **Magnolia Petroleum Co. v. Guffey,** 102 S.W.2d 408 (Tex. 1937)—forcible detention of customer by gas station attendant]

Compare: E sends D to deliver a package to T. When D sees T, he recognizes him as a longtime enemy and strikes T. Even though E's business happened to lead D to the spot where he attacked T, the act was not related to the duties of D's employment; hence E would not be liable.

(2) Nature of Employment

Certain types of employment may authorize the use of some force. Intentional torts committed during this type of employment are likely to be considered related to the employer's business and often result in the employer's liability.

Example: E hires B as a bouncer to maintain order in E's tavern. When B attempts to evict P, a noisy patron, a fight ensues, and B becomes unreasonably excited and kills P. Even though B's reaction may have been abnormal, and even though B clearly used excessive force, the act was related to E's business, and E may be held liable. [34 A.L.R. 2d 372]

Compare: A bartender's shooting of a customer who made advances toward another patron was held to be ***outside the scope*** of the bartender's employment. A bartender's job is to serve beverages, not to maintain order, evict patrons, etc. [**Howard v. Zaney Bar,** 85 A.2d 401 (Pa. 1952)]

(3) Civil vs. Criminal Liability

Respondeat superior is a rule of ***civil*** liability. Except as to minor regulatory laws (*e.g.,* sale of impure food or sale of alcoholic beverages to minors), the doctrine does not apply in criminal law. Thus, even when the employee acts within the scope of employment, the employer ***cannot be held criminally liable*** for the employee's act unless she somehow participated in the act.

(a) Distinguish—Corporations

A corporation can be held criminally liable for the acts of its officers and employees—the rationale being that the corporation can act *only* through its officers, etc. (*See* Corporations Summary.)

EXAM TIP

On your exam, if an employee commits an intentional tort, remember that you can hold an employer liable for the employee's tort only if the intentional tort is related to the employee *carrying forth the employer's business* (*i.e.,* the employee must have acted to further the employer's business interests). Also recall that if the employer is liable, the employer is liable only *civilly* (under respondeat superior) and not criminally, unless, of course, the employer participated in the act.

d. Omissions by Employee

If an employee's failure to act constitutes a tort, the employer may be held liable under respondeat superior just as if the employee had been guilty of some affirmative wrongful act. [Rest. 3d § 7.07, comment c]

e.g. **Example:** Railroad hires S as a switchman, and she is directed to throw a certain switch each day. S neglects to do as instructed, and this causes a train wreck. Railroad is liable for S's failure to act.

e. Employee's Personal Acts

An employer may be liable for injuries caused by an employee's personal acts (*e.g.,* smoking, eating, personal hygiene, etc.) if the act is ***incidental to the employee's performance of assigned work.*** Moreover, even a personal act performed off the employer's premises and while the employee is not engaged in work will be considered to be within the scope of employment if the ***employer exercises control*** over the employee's personal acts. [Rest. 3d § 7.07, comment d]

(1) Employer's Negligence

Even if smoking, etc., is considered to be outside the scope of employment, the employer will be liable for her own negligence in supervising the employee. That is, if the employer permits the employee to smoke (or fails to exercise reasonable care to prevent it) while aware of the risk created by smoking—*e.g.,* the employer observes the employee smoking around flammable liquids—and fails to put a stop to it, she will be liable for any injuries that result from the smoking. [20 A.L.R.3d 893]

f. Employee's Use of Employer's Vehicle, Equipment, Etc.

The mere fact that the employer has permitted the employee to use the employer's truck, machine, etc., is not sufficient to impose liability on the employer for injuries negligently caused by the employee in using the vehicle, machine, etc. For liability to attach, the use must be within the scope of employment; *i.e.,* the employer is liable only when the instrumentality is being used ***for the purpose of advancing the employer's business interests,*** rather than the employee's personal affairs. [**Keener v. Jack Cole Trucking Co.,** 233 F. Supp. 181 (W.D. Ky. 1964)]

e.g. **Example:** E hires S and provides her with a bicycle for use on the job. E also permits S to take the bicycle home at night for personal use. If S negligently injures someone while using the bicycle for recreational purposes, E is not liable.

e.g. **Example:** Railroad hires an engineer. For the sole purpose of scaring P, the engineer blows a train whistle, causing P's horse to bolt and injure P. Railroad is not liable. [**Chesapeake & Ohio Railway v. Ford,** 166 S.W. 605 (Ky. 1914)]

(1) Distinguish—"Permissive Use" Statutes as to Vehicles

Even when an employer is not otherwise liable under respondeat superior for the employee's negligent use of the employer's vehicle outside the scope of employment, some jurisdictions have "permissive use" statutes that impose limited liability on the owner of a vehicle for any damages negligently inflicted by a person driving it with the owner's permission. [*See, e.g.,* Cal. Veh. Code §§ 17150, 17151—registered owner liable for injuries inflicted by any person driving owner's vehicle with owner's express or implied consent] In such jurisdictions, if the employee was driving the employer's vehicle with consent, it is immaterial to the employer's liability whether the employee was within or outside the scope of employment when he acted tortiously.

EXAM TIP

If on the exam you encounter a situation where the employee was using the employer's vehicle or equipment, be sure to determine whether he was doing so in a manner that was *advancing the employer's business* and with the *employer's authorization.* If he was not using the instrumentality within the scope of employment (*i.e.,* he was using it for his own personal interest), then the employer will not be liable for any damages or injuries resulting from the use (unless a "permissive use" statute applies).

g. Employee's Use of Unauthorized Instrumentalities

A more difficult problem arises when the employee uses some vehicle, equipment, etc., in performing the employer's business and the employer has ***not authorized*** the use. The cases hold that if the instrumentality used is ***substantially different*** from that authorized, the use of the instrumentality must be deemed outside the scope of employment, and the employer cannot be held liable. What is "substantially different" is generally measured by determining whether ***any greater risk*** is involved in the instrumentality used. [**Spence v. Maier,** 59 A.2d 609 (N.J. 1948)]

e.g. **Example:** E tells his employee, D, to drive X into town, using E's car. D chooses to use E's pickup truck instead. Although the instrumentality used was different from that authorized, it probably would not involve any greater risk of harm. Thus, E probably would be liable for D's negligence in driving the truck.

cf. **Compare:** E hires M as a messenger, instructing him to use public transportation. However, M decides to drive his own car and negligently injures someone. The use of a private automobile is "substantially different" from the use of public transportation, and hence E probably would not be held liable. [**Barton v. McDermott,** 108 Cal. App. 372 (1930)] Note: If E had given M ***no*** instructions as to the means of transportation, E would probably be held liable.

h. Employee Going to and from Work

An employee's actions of going to and from work or meals is ordinarily considered outside the scope of his employment for purposes of respondeat superior. [Rest. 3d § 7.07, comment e; **Salmon v. Hinojosa,** 538 S.W.2d 22 (Tex. 1976)]

(1) Exception—"Special Errand Rule"

However, when the employee's going to or from work ***also*** involves some service or purpose for his employer, he may be held to be within the scope of employment. [**Boynton v. McKales,** 139 Cal. App. 2d 777 (1956)]

(2) Exception—Traveling Salespeople

Likewise, a traveling salesperson compelled by work to be away from home or business headquarters for long periods of time is generally regarded as within the scope of employment the entire time that he is away, even while not actually at work, as when he is returning home.

i. Acts of Employee Done Entirely or Partially on Own Behalf

When the employee temporarily departs from instructed duties and undertakes personal business, is he acting outside the scope of employment? *Example:* While delivering goods for E, D goes out of his way to visit a friend, and while en route back to work injures someone. Is E liable?

(1) Substantial Departure Required

Again, the cases turn on the ***degree*** to which the employee was serving his own interests: Only a ***substantial*** deviation or departure from the employer's business will take the employee outside the scope of employment. If the ***main purpose*** of the activity is still the employer's business, it does not cease to be within the scope of the employment merely because of incidental personal acts, slight delays, or deflections from the most direct route. [**Posin v. A.B.C. Motor Court Hotel, Inc.,** 344 N.E.2d 334 (Ohio 1976)]

Example: E directs S to sell E's goods in Middletown, but S proceeds instead to neighboring Clarksville because he believes he can sell more goods there. While there, P tampers with the merchandise in S's truck, and S uses unreasonable force in getting P away from the truck, causing injury to P. Notwithstanding the change of locale, the particular act causing the injury to P was directly related to S's duties for E, and E would therefore be liable.

Compare: S, while en route to the office after delivering a package for E, picks up a personal friend, drives her 50 miles ***past*** his office, and while there, negligently injures P. Because S actually reached ***and passed*** his business objective, this would probably be considered a substantial "departure" from the employment, relieving E of liability to P.

(a) Frolic vs. Detour

Courts sometimes use the term "*detour*" to indicate a minor deviation still within the scope of employment, and "*frolic*" to indicate a substantial deviation or abandonment that is outside the scope of employment. A frolic ends when the employee resumes performing work for the employer. [Rest. 3d § 7.07, comment e]

(2) "Mixed Motives"

In many cases, the employee may be acting partly for his own interests and partly for his employer. If any substantial part of the act was done for the purposes of the employer, that is generally sufficient to impose liability on the employer for all the consequences of the act. [Rest. 3d § 7.07, comment c]

Example: E instructs S to deliver goods in town, and S decides to transact some personal business en route. On the way to perform both tasks, S negligently injures P. E is liable for P's injuries.

e.g. **Example:** S, employed in driving a truck for E, gives a ride to a personal friend who is late for an appointment. To accommodate the friend, S drives the truck at an excessive rate of speed and injures P. E is liable for P's injuries. [**Cochran v. Michaels,** 157 S.E. 173 (W. Va. 1931)]

EXAM TIP

One of the most likely ways in which your professor will test scope of employment is to have an employee deviate from the employer's business and undertake personal business. While undertaking the personal business, the employee will commit a tort. You will need to determine whether the employer is liable for the employee's tort in this situation. Be sure to discuss whether there was a *substantial deviation* (frolic) or a *minor deviation* (detour) from the employer's business. The greater the employee's deviation is from the employer's business, the more likely it is that the employee's undertaking will be considered *outside the scope* of employment, and the employer will *not* be liable for the employee's tort.

j. Liability to Unauthorized Passengers of Employee

If the employee invites a third person to ride along with him in the employer's vehicle (or the third person is riding as a trespasser in the vehicle), and that person is injured through the employee's negligence, can the employer be held liable?

(1) Majority View

The general rule is that unless otherwise authorized by the employer, the employee's invitation to a third person to ride in the employer's vehicle does ***not*** constitute an invitation by the employer. The employee's invitation is held to be ***outside the scope*** of his employment, thereby relieving the employer of any liability for any injuries to the invitee. [**White v. Brainerd Service Motor Co.,** 232 N.W. 626 (Minn. 1930)]

(a) Note

This is true even though the conduct that causes the harm—the employee's operation of the vehicle—is within the scope of the employee's employment. [**Union Gas & Electric Co. v. Crouch,** 174 N.E. 6 (Ohio 1930)]

(b) And Note

The employer clearly is not liable to trespassers riding without an invitation from the employee.

(2) Minority View

California and several other states take the position that because the employer would be liable to a stranger on the street for the employee's negligent acts, she should be liable to an invitee or a trespasser ***within*** the vehicle as well. Under this approach, the employer would be liable if the employee's negligence occurs within the scope of employment—whether the injured person's presence was authorized is immaterial. [**Meyer v. Blackman,** 59 Cal. 2d 668 (1963)]

(3) Other Courts

Still other courts would hold the employer liable when injuries to the unauthorized passenger are sustained due to the "***wanton and willful misconduct***" of the employee. [*See, e.g.,* **Wilson v. Dailey,** 62 A.2d 284 (Md. 1948)]

DETERMINING SCOPE OF EMPLOYMENT	
ACT OF EMPLOYEE	**RULE**
AFFIRMATIVE ACTS	Within scope of employment ***if act advances employer's interest***
SPECIFICALLY FORBIDDEN ACT	Within scope of employment ***if employee is acting within scope of duties for which he was hired***
INTENTIONAL TORT	Within scope of employment ***if act is related to carrying on employer's business***
OMISSIONS	***Treated the same as affirmative acts***—within scope of employment if it advances employer's interest
PERSONAL ACTS	Within scope of employment ***if act is incidental to employee's performance of assigned work*** or ***employer exercises control over personal act,*** even if off work premises and times
USE OF EMPLOYER'S INSTRUMENTALITIES	Within scope of employment ***if use is for purposes of advancing employer's interests***
USE OF UNAUTHORIZED INSTRUMENTALITIES	Within scope of employment ***unless instrumentality is substantially different from that authorized***
GOING TO AND FROM WORK	Within scope of employment ***only if employee was on a special errand*** for employer or employee is on a ***business trip***
ACTS THAT DEPART FROM EMPLOYER'S BUSINESS	Within scope of employment ***if departure is minor*** (*i.e.,* a "detour")
ACTS WITH MIXED MOTIVES	Within scope of employment ***if any substantial part of the act was done for the purposes of employer***
RIDES TO UNAUTHORIZED PASSENGER	Generally ***not within the scope of employment*** unless employer ***authorized invitation to passenger***
GRATUITOUS ACTS	***Treated the same as other acts***—within scope of employment ***if it advances employer's interests***

k. Gratuitous Work of Employee

An employer can be held vicariously liable for the torts of an employee acting within the scope of employment ***even if the employee performed the work gratuitously.*** [Rest. 3d § 7.07(2)(b)]

4. "Fellow Servant" Exception to Respondeat Superior

An important exception to the doctrine of respondeat superior is the "fellow servant rule"—*i.e.*, that an employer is not liable for the injuries inflicted by one employee upon a fellow employee while engaged in the same general enterprise. [**Williams v. Dade County,** 237 So. 2d 776 (Fla. 1970)]

a. Definition

A "fellow servant" is any other employee who (i) serves and is controlled by the same employer, ***and*** (ii) is engaged in the "same general enterprise." Both requirements must be met for the rule to apply. [**McTaggart v. Eastman's Co. of New York,** 28 Misc. 127 (1899)]

b. Rationale for the Rule

The traditional theories advanced for the "fellow servant rule" are that each employee "assumes the risk" that he might be injured by another employee with whom he is employed, and that the employee is as able as his employer to know of and protect himself against any such danger or risk. [**Farwell v. Boston & Worcester Railroad,** 45 Mass. (4 Metc.) 49 (1842)]

(1) Criticism

Neither of these theories makes sense in large companies with thousands of employees where it is impossible for an employee to know who is likely to be careless and who is not.

c. Exceptions

(1) Employer's Negligence in Hiring

Note that the "fellow servant" rule does ***not apply*** when the employer has failed to exercise reasonable care in the ***hiring*** of employees. For example, if an employer hires a driver, knowing of the driver's record of careless driving, and the driver negligently injures a fellow employee, the employer could be held liable.

(2) Acts by Superior

Likewise, the rule does not apply if the employee is injured by a ***superior*** employee acting within his authority in supervising the inferior employee's conduct or protecting the employer's property. [8 A.L.R. 1432]

d. Effect of Workers' Compensation Statutes

Workers' compensation statutes—in effect in all states today—provide for a fixed compensation to insured workers or their dependents in case of industrial accidents. Where such statutes apply, no legal action is allowed against an employer for injuries sustained on the job and, thus, there is no need for the "fellow servant rule."

(1) Impact of "Fellow Servant Rule"

However, some workers' compensation statutes cover only major industrial occupations (and exclude domestic workers or laborers). Others exclude employees in shops employing fewer than a specific number of workers, or injuries caused by willful misconduct of the employer or fellow employees. In such cases the "fellow servant rule" is still significant.

(2) Distinguish—Scope of Employment

Workers' compensation statutes usually are limited to injuries sustained "in the scope of employment." However, this is construed much more liberally than in the case of respondeat superior (*supra,* pp. 107–114)—so that many accidents that would be ***outside*** the scope of employment for respondeat superior purposes will be covered under workers' compensation statutes. [*See* **Zenith National Insurance Co. v. Workmen's Compensation Appeals Board,** 66 Cal. 2d 944 (1967)]

(a) And Note

Because workers' compensation statutes cover injuries to "employees," but not to "independent contractors," courts are more inclined to find an injured worker to be an "employee" for workers' compensation purposes than for purposes of respondeat superior. [147 A.L.R. 828]

B. Liability of Principal for Torts of Agent—Outside Respondeat Superior

1. In General

Entirely aside from vicarious liability under the doctrine of respondeat superior, an employer or other principal is liable for the tortious acts of her employee or other agent if the principal was directly responsible for the tort. [Rest. 3d §§ 7.03, 7.04] In these cases, the principal herself is at fault, and her ***own*** wrongdoing is the proximate cause of the injury (even though inflicted through the agent).

2. Wrongful Act Directed or Authorized by Principal

If the principal directs, authorizes, or permits the agent to perform a tortious act, the principal is liable just as if she had committed the tort herself—the act being considered that of the principal done through the agent. [Rest. 3d §§ 7.03, 7.04; **Abell v. Nash County Board of Education,** 321 S.E.2d 502 (N.C. 1984)]

e.g. **Example:** E hires G and directs him to destroy machinery belonging to a competitor, T. If G does so, E is liable to T without regard to respondeat superior.

e.g. **Example:** The same result follows when the employer knows that the employee is acting recklessly and ***permits*** him to do so. Thus, if E observes G smoking around flammable liquids and fails to direct him to cease, E is liable for the consequences. (*See supra,* p. 110.)

a. Distinguish—Liability of Agent

In most cases the agent who commits a tortious act upon another is ***also*** personally liable to the injured party—even though he acted with actual or apparent authority or within the scope of employment, he did not benefit personally, and he did not personally intend to injure anyone. [Rest. 3d § 7.01 and comment b]

e.g. **Example:** E directs R to take possession of certain property. The property in fact belongs to another, and R's act constitutes a conversion. R, as well as E, may be held personally liable for the value of the property—it would be immaterial to R's liability that R believed E to be the rightful owner. [**Swim v. Wilson,** 90 Cal. 126 (1891)]

(1) Exception—Fraud or Duress

However, an agent who assists his principal in the commission of fraud or duress is not liable to the injured party if the agent had ***no knowledge*** of the fraud or duress; *i.e.,* the knowledge of the fraudulent principal is not imputed to the agent. [Rest. 3d § 7.01, comment d]

e.g. **Example:** P authorizes A to sell P's apartment building and gives A a falsely inflated statement regarding income from the building. A makes representations to prospective purchaser, T, in reliance on P's statement. If A had no reason to doubt the information given him by P, he is not liable to T for the misrepresentation. [**Provost v. Miller,** 473 A.2d 1162 (Vt. 1984)]

3. Ratification of Tortious Conduct by Principal

Similarly, a principal may be liable for injuries caused by the tortious conduct of one acting or purporting to act as her agent if she ***ratifies*** the conduct in question. By her ratification, the principal becomes liable for the acts ***as if they had been authorized by her*** at the time they were committed. [Rest. 3d §§ 7.03, 7.04]

a. Ratification Theory

Technically, a tort ***cannot*** be ratified. For example, if A negligently injures X, and B voluntarily tells X, "Don't worry . . . I'll take care of your damages and will be responsible for everything," this is ***not*** a ratification of A's conduct. B does not become a party to the tort and cannot be held in tort for the damages inflicted by A. (If anything, B may be liable in contract to the extent X relies on her statement, or to the extent she has otherwise agreed to indemnify A.) However, if the principal ***accepts benefits or advantages*** obtained from the acts of another, who was otherwise not authorized to act for her, she is deemed to have authorized the acts from their inception—and thereby becomes liable for any torts incident to the acts. [**Colonial Stores, Inc. v. Holt,** 166 S.E.2d 30 (Ga. 1968)]

b. What Acts May Be Ratified

Any act committed by an agent (or one purporting to act as such) that could have been authorized in the first place can be ratified. It is essential, however, that in committing the act, the agent ***intended to act on behalf of the principal,*** rather than on behalf of himself or someone else. [Rest. 3d § 4.03]

e.g. **Example:** A trades his own car in for a new one, misrepresenting the condition of his car to the dealer. A's employer, P, subsequently decides that A should use the new car on the job, and it is agreed that P will buy the new car for A's use and will be responsible for any statements made by A in connection with its purchase. Here, there is ***no ratification*** because at the time of purchase A was not intending to act on P's behalf.

c. What Constitutes a Ratification

For there to be a ratification, the principal must have ***accepted or retained benefits*** that were obtained for her through the wrongful act of the agent, ***with knowledge*** of all relevant facts. [Rest. 3d § 4.01, comments d, g; *see also* **O'Connor v. Central National Bank & Trust Co.,** 28 N.E.2d 755 (Ill. 1940)]

e.g. **Example:** P authorizes A to sell her house. A shows the house to several prospective purchasers, and in the course of so doing, falsely identifies certain paintings in the house as "Picassos." If one of the prospective purchasers offers to buy the paintings, and P accepts the offer knowing of A's misrepresentations, she is deemed to have ratified the previously unauthorized representation.

(1) Failure to Fire Employee Who Commits Tort

The courts have split on whether the employer's retaining an employee who commits a tort upon another is a ratification of the employee's act. The prevailing view is that this constitutes "some" evidence that the employer affirms or ratifies the wrongful act, but it is by no means conclusive. [**Edmunds v. Atchison, Topeka & Santa Fe Railway,** 174 Cal. 246 (1917)]

(2) Principal Must Know All Relevant Facts

There can be no effective ratification unless the principal had knowledge of ***all*** relevant facts surrounding the tortious conduct; *i.e.,* unless the principal knows (or is chargeable with knowledge) that the agent committed a tort incident to the acts in question, her affirmation of the transaction may be rescinded when she discovers the true facts. [Rest. 3d § 4.06; **Hirzel Funeral Homes v. Equitable Trust Co.,** 83 A.2d 700 (Del. 1951)]

e.g. **Example:** Without authority from P, A purports to sell P's property to T. In making the sale, A misrepresents the income and expenses attributable to the property. Unless P knew about the misrepresentations when she accepted the purchase price from T, she cannot be deemed to have authorized A's misrepresentations. Therefore, if P discovers A's misrepresentations ***after*** consummating the sale to T, she can avoid liability to T by rescinding the transaction and returning the purchase price.

(a) No Duty to Investigate Facts

The principal is generally under no duty to investigate whether the agent made any representations—*i.e.,* a ratification *cannot* be based on the principal's *negligence* or failure to exercise reasonable care to ascertain what may have been said to the other party. [**Hirzel Funeral Homes v. Equitable Trust Co.,** *supra*] On the other hand, the principal cannot "close her eyes" to apparent fraud by an agent.

e.g. **Example:** Suppose A brings P an unsolicited offer by T to purchase one of P's paintings for $50,000. If P *knows* the painting is not worth anywhere near this amount, she may be under a duty to inquire into the circumstances by which A obtained the offer. If P fails to do so, she "assumes the risk" and may be held to have ratified any misstatement made by A to obtain the offer. [**Wilder v. Beede,** 119 Cal. 646 (1898)]

d. Effect on Contractual Liability

Ratification has already been discussed (*supra,* pp. 56–66) in connection with the ***contractual*** liability of a principal for previously unauthorized acts by the agent.

4. Independent Duty Owed to Injured Party

a. Employer Negligence in Hiring, Training, or Supervising

When it appears that an employer cannot be held liable under respondeat superior, consider whether she may be liable for breach of her independent duty of due care in ***hiring, training, or supervising*** the person whose act caused the injury. If it appears that the employer ***knew or should have known*** that the person in her employ (employee, agent, ***or*** independent contractor) was not qualified to perform the duties assigned to him, or was likely to perform in a negligent or otherwise dangerous manner, the employer is probably liable for the consequences. [Rest. 3d § 7.05(1); *see, e.g.,* **Williams v. Feather Sound, Inc.,** 386 So. 2d 1238 (Fla. 1980)]

(1) Note

As noted previously, an employer generally is not liable for torts committed by employees outside the scope of their employment. However, if the employer knows or should have known that the employee was likely to commit such torts, she is chargeable nonetheless. Thus, an employer who continues to use a bartender with known vicious tendencies would be liable for an unprovoked battery inflicted on a patron, which was otherwise outside the scope of employment.

b. Employer Charged with Care of Third Persons

If the employer is charged with care of the injured person (*e.g.*, common carrier charged with care of its passengers), she is directly liable for any injuries the injured person sustains as a result of the tortious or criminal acts of the employee—even though the acts are clearly outside the scope of employment. [Rest. 3d § 7.05]

e.g. **Example:** P, a passenger on a train, was raped by a Pullman porter. The Pullman Co. was held liable, the court finding it immaterial that the porter's act was clearly outside the scope of his employment. [**Berger v. Southern Pacific Co.,** 144 Cal. App. 2d 1 (1956)]

c. Knowledge of Dangerous Condition Imputed to Employer

As discussed *supra* (p. 68 *et seq.*), an employer is charged with notice of all facts that her employee discovers in the course of his employment that pertain to the employment. [Rest. 3d § 5.03] Thus, whenever an employee acquires knowledge of some fact or condition that would require the employer to exercise a duty of care to third persons, the employee's knowledge of that fact is imputed to the employer, giving her notice of the fact so that she owes a duty of care to third persons—just as if she had actual knowledge of the fact or condition involved.

e.g. **Example:** E hires J as a maintenance person in E's apartment building. J discovers that a stair railing is loose but neglects to fix it or notify E of the danger. E is ***charged*** with notice of the condition and will be liable to any third person injured by it just as if E had actual knowledge of the condition.

(1) Limitation

It is essential, however, that the facts to be imputed are ***within the scope of employment.*** Thus, for example, a railroad is not charged with notice of a defective condition on its tracks if knowledge of the defective condition was held by a baggage room employee rather than a member of the "line department" charged with repairs. [**Comer v. Los Angeles Railway,** 66 Cal. App. 219 (1924)]

5. Defamation

An employer in the business of disseminating information (*e.g.,* a broadcasting company, or a credit reporting bureau) may be held liable for disseminating defamations uttered by one of its employees acting with apparent authority, even though the defamations were neither actually authorized nor within the scope of the employment. Again, liability is not based on respondeat superior, but rather on the employer's repetition of the defamations—which makes it directly liable. [Rest. 3d § 7.08, comment d]

EXAM TIP

Many students have had the doctrine of respondeat superior so drummed into their heads that that is all they look for on an exam. Regardless of whether you decide that the principal can be held vicariously liable under respondeat superior, always remember to check to see whether you can hold the principal *directly liable* for the tort. Ask yourself if the principal did something (or failed to do something) that makes her directly responsible for the agent's tort. (*See* chart, *infra.*)

NONRESPONDEAT SUPERIOR LIABILITY OF PRINCIPAL FOR AGENT'S TORTS	
AUTHORIZATION	A principal is liable for the tortious act of her agent if she ***authorized*** or directed the agent to perform the act.
RATIFICATION	A principal is liable for the tortious act of her "agent" if (i) at the time of the act, the agent ***purported to act*** on the principal's behalf, and (ii) the principal ***accepts*** the benefits of the act (iii) ***knowing*** all relevant facts.
INDEPENDENT DUTY	A principal is liable for the tortious act of her agent if the principal was ***negligent in hiring, training, or supervising*** the agent; the principal was ***charged with the care*** of the person injured by the agent's act; or the principal ***fails to exercise due care*** in handling a fact or condition of which the agent has knowledge and which knowledge is ***imputed*** to the principal.
DEFAMATION	A principal is liable for disseminating her agent's defamations if the principal is ***in the business*** of disseminating information.

C. Liability of Principal for Tortious Representations of Agent

1. Introduction

One of the most frequent problems involving vicarious tort liability of one person for the acts of another concerns the circumstances under which one person will be held liable for the misrepresentations of another. This problem generally arises when representations have been made by an ***agent,*** rather than merely an employee or independent contractor; but liability turns more on the ***authority*** than the status of the party making the representations.

2. General Rule

An employer or other principal is subject to tort liability for any loss sustained by third persons as a result of misrepresentations made by an employee or other agent ***whenever the making of representations was actually (expressly or impliedly) or apparently authorized.*** [Rest. 3d § 7.08, comment c]

a. Nature of Tort Liability

The tort of misrepresentation requires the showing of: (i) a false statement of material fact; (ii) scienter (*i.e.*, knowledge of the false statement or reckless disregard of truth); (iii) intent to deceive; (iv) justifiable reliance on the false statement; and (v) damages. (*See* Torts Summary.)

(1) Note

The agent's representations may ***also*** constitute defamation, trade libel, unfair competition, etc.; in effect, they may constitute ***any*** tort in which the wrongful act consists of statements or representations.

b. Status of Person Making Misrepresentation

In analyzing liability for representations, the crucial factor is whether the person making the statements was ***actually or apparently authorized*** to make ***any statement*** at all by the person who is sought to be held liable. While the status of the person making the representations (*e.g.*, agent, employee, independent contractor) is not controlling, that person's status may reflect on whether he had the authority to make representations. Authority to make representations is most frequently found when dealing with ***agents***—the creation of the agency relationship often implies certain authority to make representations. (*See* below.) However, an employee or independent contractor may be found to have authority to make representations as well.

e.g. **Example:** E hires D to demonstrate E's wares in a trade show and to answer any questions from potential customers. D recognizes a longtime enemy, X, in the audience, and falsely represents to X that E's product is safe for human consumption. X subsequently purchases and consumes the product in reliance on D's statements, suffering injury. Even though D was acting entirely for her own purposes in deceiving X, and was therefore outside the scope of employment, D had been given authority by E to make statements about the product. E is thus liable to X.

e.g. **Example:** E hires independent contractor I to develop and publish advertising copy for E's products. Because authority has been given to I to publish statements regarding E's products, E will be responsible for any misrepresentations made by I.

EXAM TIP

On an exam, if you have to determine whether a principal is liable for an agent's misrepresentations, your discussion should focus on whether the agent was *authorized to make representations* and not on the status of the agent (*e.g.,* employee, independent contractor), as you did to determine a principal's liability for an agent's torts under respondeat superior. *But note:* The status of the agent may be a factor to consider in determining whether the agent had authority.

---

c. Distinguish—Contract Liability

The examples above concern representations that expose the principal solely to tort liability. Frequently, however, an agent's misrepresentations are made in connection with a ***contract*** between the principal and a third party and, thus, the principal will be subject to contract liability.

e.g. **Example:** P authorizes A to sell his car for him. A turns back the mileage on the car from 50,000 miles to 500 miles and sells the car to an innocent buyer as a "low mileage" special. In such a case—and assuming the agent's representations were authorized (*see* below)—the buyer has a choice of remedies:

(i) The buyer ***can sue P for contract damages*** (the difference in value between what she actually received and what she would have gotten had the agent's statements been true); and/or

(ii) The buyer can sue to ***rescind the contract*** with P, on the ground of fraud or mistake.

[**Holland Furnace Co. v. Williams,** 295 P.2d 672 (Kan. 1956)]

3. Authority to Make Representations

Obviously, a principal rarely authorizes an agent to make false statements, and it is not necessary to show that he did. The injured party need only establish that the agent had authority to make ***statements concerning the subject matter involved.*** Such authority may be ***express*** or ***implied*** from the circumstances of the case, or based on the principal placing the agent in a position to deceive.

EXAM TIP

Don't be confused on an exam into thinking that the principal must actually authorize the agent's making of a false statement to be liable for it. It is important to remember that a principal will be liable for the agent's false statement if the agent had authority to make *any statements* about the matter involved.

a. Express Authority

An agent may be expressly directed by the principal to disseminate certain information to third parties. If this is the case, any misrepresentations made by the agent in the course of disseminating the information are deemed to have been "***expressly authorized***" by the principal.

e.g. **Example:** P engages auctioneer A to sell P's apartment building at a public auction. P provides A with detailed information regarding the income and expenses from the property and directs A to provide this information to all potential bidders. To get higher bids (and hence a higher commission for himself), A gives prospective purchaser X a figure for rental income that is falsely inflated. Because A was expressly authorized to disseminate information regarding rental income, his misrepresentation is deemed expressly authorized by P. Thus, upon discovery of the true facts, X can either sue P (or A) for damages or to rescind the purchase.

b. Implied Authority—"Incidental Representations"

When the principal authorizes another to deal on her behalf in transactions where representations about the subject matter are customarily made, she is deemed to have ***impliedly authorized*** all such representations unless that authority was specifically withheld; *i.e.*, the making of representations by the agent is considered "incidental" to his authority to deal in the transaction, and the principal will be liable for the agent's representations unless the third party knows (or should know) that the representations are unauthorized. [**Boehm v. Friedman,** 1 So. 2d 508 (Miss. 1941)]

(1) Attorneys

An attorney is generally regarded as an agent of his client concerning all matters on which he is retained to represent the client. He is deemed to have implied authority to make representations as to all such matters, even though the client never specifically authorized the attorney to make any statements at all on her behalf. [**Associated Indemnity Corp. v. Industrial Accident Commission,** 56 Cal. App. 2d 804 (1943)]

(2) Brokers and Factors

A typical example of implied authority is the employment of a broker or factor to sell property. A "broker" is a person employed by the owner of property ***to obtain a sale*** of the property (or possibly employed by a potential purchaser ***to find property to purchase***). A "factor" is a broker who is given possession of property with the authority to sell it and receive the proceeds on behalf of the owner. Whether the broker is considered the agent of the seller or an independent contractor (*see* below), he is deemed to have implied authority ***to make representations concerning the property involved***—this being "incidental" to his authority to sell—and the seller is therefore liable for any misrepresentations made by the broker whether or not express authority to make representations was given. [**Speck v. Wylie,** 1 Cal. 2d 625 (1934)]

(a) Misrepresentations by Broker or Factor

Under the prevailing view, a broker or factor is an *agent* of the person by whom he is engaged, because he is hired to perform a "legal act"; *i.e.,* to bind his principal in the purchase or sale of property to a third party. Hence, any misstatement by a broker or factor is imputed to the principal, so that any person relying on the broker's or factor's *misrepresentation* may rescind the transaction or sue the principal for fraud.

1) Minority View—Broker or Factor Is Independent Contractor

A minority view holds that the broker or factor is an ***independent contractor***—bargaining with the employer for a result (the sale of property), having his own organization, employing his own personnel, etc. Even under this view, however, the employer is ***still liable for the broker's or factor's representations.*** [**Connecticut Mutual Life Insurance Co. v. Carson,** 172 S.W. 69 (Mo. 1914)]

(b) Distinguish—No Power to Sell

The result may be different if the owner has *not conferred the power to sell* upon the agent (even if the agent is called a "broker" or "factor"). For example, if the only authority conferred was to advertise the property (*e.g.,* by listing it in a catalog or newspaper), there may be no authority to make representations as above. Under such circumstances, misstatements of pertinent information by the broker or factor would not be chargeable to the owner. Thus, the defrauded purchaser could sue the *agent* for fraud, but he could not rescind the purchase or sue the owner for damages.

(c) Effect of Contractual Provision Limiting Principal's Responsibility for Agent's Representations

To avoid liability for misstatements made by brokers, factors, etc., owners sometimes insist on "exculpatory" provisions in their contracts—*e.g.,* "Representations not contained herein are not part of our agreement, and shall be given no effect." Such provisions will normally absolve the principal from liability for *damages* for fraudulent statements made by her agent. However, *rescission* of the contract is usually still available to protect the purchaser. [Rest. 3d § 7.08, comment c(4); **Owen v. Schwartz,** 177 F.2d 641 (D.C. Cir. 1949)]

cf. **Compare:** Of course, if the principal *knew* of the agent's misstatements at the time the contract was executed, she may be liable for damages as well. *Rationale:* One cannot exculpate herself from the consequences of her own fraud. [**Herzog v. Capital Co.,** 27 Cal. 2d 349 (1945)]

c. Agent Placed in Position to Deceive

When the principal places the agent in a ***position*** to defraud, and third parties rely on the agent's apparent authority to make representations, the principal is liable even though the agent is acting for his own purposes and no express or implied authority can be found. The theory is that the agent's ***position*** facilitates the fraud—*i.e.,* from the point of view of the third party, the agent appears to be acting in the ordinary course of authority confided to him. In these situations, the principal may be held liable for the agent's false representations even though he receives no benefits from the transaction. [**American Bankers Life Assurance Co. v. Tri City Bank & Trust Co.,** 677 F.2d 28 (6th Cir. 1982)]

e.g. **Example:** P employs A as manager of P's bank and places him in a position to know the affairs of all borrowers at the bank. A falsely tells one of these borrowers that the bank will not renew his note unless he sells certain property to Y (a friend of A) at a certain price that is less than its reasonable value. P would be liable to the borrower for the loss sustained on his sale to Y.

cf. **Compare:** However, the result would probably be different if A were only a teller or clerical employee in the bank, because a reasonable person in the borrower's position would not conclude that A was acting within the ordinary scope of his authority in making the representations and any reliance would not, therefore, be justified.

EXAM TIP

The key to finding a principal liable for an agent's misrepresentations is finding that the agent was authorized to make representations. Recall that an agent will be considered to have authority to make representations for his principal if he is instructed by the principal to make representations (*express authority*), or if the agent has authority to deal with third parties for the principal in situations where representations are customarily made (*implied authority*). If you are unable to find express or implied authority, note that the principal may still be liable for the agent's misrepresentations if she has *placed the agent in a position to deceive.*

4. Effect of Innocent Misrepresentations by Agent

When the agent makes a misstatement innocently—believing it to be true, and with no intent to deceive—the principal generally is not liable in tort for any damages flowing from the misstatement. Tort liability requires scienter (*i.e.,* knowledge of falsity) and intent to deceive, and in the absence of these elements, neither the agent nor the principal can be held liable. [Rest. 3d § 7.08, comment c(*l*)]

a. Exception—Principal's Scienter

Of course, if the principal knows that the agent is not aware of the facts, but puts him in a position to innocently misrepresent the facts, and then fails to advise the third party of the error, the principal is deemed ***directly*** responsible for any damages sustained by the third party in reliance on the misrepresentation. [**Abbate v. Abbate,** 82 A.D.2d 368 (1981)]

b. Exception—Negligent Misrepresentations

Also, when the agent knows that third parties may rely on his statements (*e.g.,* accountant preparing financial statements knowing that third parties as well as employer may rely), many courts hold that the employer would be held responsible for negligence by the agent in the preparation of the statements. (*See* Torts Summary.) [Rest. 3d § 7.08, comment c(3)]

c. Effect on Contract Liability

If the misrepresentations are made in connection with a contract involving the principal and a third party, or as part of a warranty in the contract, the third party may sue to ***rescind*** on the ground of mistake—even though the misrepresentations were innocent. [**Lindlots Realty Corp. v. Suffolk County,** 278 N.Y. 45 (1938)]

Part Two: Partnership

Chapter Eight:

Nature and Formation of Partnership

CONTENTS	PAGE

Key Exam Issues

This chapter introduces you to the concept of partnership and includes a discussion of an issue that is one of the most common in examination questions: ***Has a partnership been formed*** under the given facts?

To determine whether a partnership has been formed, you should first remember the general definition of a partnership: an association of two or more persons to carry on as co-owners a business for profit. (Note that "intent to form a partnership" is ***not*** within the definition.) Then you will have to determine whether:

(1) The business is ***"for profit"***; if not, there is no partnership.

(2) The parties have ***agreed*** to form a partnership. Remember that a writing generally is not required—any agreement to run a for-profit business as co-owners will suffice. The agreement need not even be verbal; it can arise from the conduct of the parties. If there is an ***agreement to share profits***, it constitutes a presumption (prima facie evidence under the UPA) that the parties intended to form a partnership unless the sharing is to repay a loan, as payment of wages, constitutes rent, etc.

(3) The parties have ***capacity*** to contract.

An examination question might also touch on the ***nature of partnerships***. Remember that there are certain situations in which a partnership is not treated as an entity distinct from the partners (*e.g.*, under federal tax laws, a partnership is not a taxable entity; profits and losses flow through the partnership to the partners). But note that there are other situations in which a partnership is treated as an entity (*e.g.*, a partnership may sue or be sued in its own name and may own property in its own name).

A. Governing Law

1. In General

In 1914, the Commissioners on Uniform State Laws approved the ***Uniform Partnership Act*** ("UPA"), which was adopted by most states as the basis for their partnership law. However, in 1992, the Commissioners approved the ***Revised Uniform Partnership Act*** ("RUPA") in an attempt to clarify some ambiguities contained in the UPA and to align partnership law with contemporary business practices. The RUPA has been amended several times since its adoption in 1992, most recently in 1997. Because the majority of states have adopted the RUPA, this Summary is based on the RUPA, but the UPA provisions will be noted below where they differ substantially from the RUPA.

2. Statute vs. Agreement

It is well-settled that most provisions of the RUPA are default provisions; *i.e.*, they control ***unless the partners have agreed otherwise.*** However, the partners' ability to agree to different terms in some key areas is specifically limited. Partners generally may ***not*** (i) unreasonably restrict the right of access to books and records (*see infra*, p. 144), (ii) eliminate the duties of loyalty or of good faith and fair dealing (*see infra*, p. 143), (iii) unreasonably reduce the duty of care (*see infra*, p. 143), (iv) vary the power of a partner to dissociate by express will (*see infra*, p. 179), (v) vary the right of a court to expel a partner (*see infra*, p. 179), (vi) vary the requirement that the partnership be wound up when partnership business becomes illegal or a court finds that it should be wound up on application of the partners or an assignee of a partner (*see infra* p. 176), or (vii) restrict the rights of third parties under the RUPA. [RUPA § 103]

EXAM TIP

Even though you have studied one or both of the Uniform Partnership Acts, before you decide an exam issue based on those statutory provisions, first check to see if the partners have entered into an *agreement* concerning that issue. If so, remember that the agreement generally controls.

3. Relationship to Agency Law

Partnership law is akin to the law of agency in many respects. As discussed below, a partner is considered the agent of her co-partners for certain purposes. Also, the acts of a partner within the scope of the partnership relationship may be imputed to the other partners, and the agency concept of imputed notice likewise applies to partnerships.

B. Basic Nature of Partnership

1. Defined

According to the RUPA, a partnership is an ***"association of two or more persons to carry on as co-owners a business for profit."*** [RUPA § 202(a)] The RUPA goes on to state that this is so ***whether or not the parties intend to form a partnership.*** Thus, the parties need not have the intent to form a business entity called a partnership; they need only intend: (i) to form a for-profit business, and (ii) to own the business together.

EXAM TIP

An exam question will usually require that you determine whether a partnership has been formed before you can determine the rights and liabilities of the parties involved. Remember that you need to look only for evidence that two or more parties are *operating a business for profit.* You do *not* need to determine whether they actually intended that a partnership be formed. If two or more parties are operating a business for profit together as co-owners, then a *partnership exists even if that was not their intent.*

2. Distinguish—Agency

The primary distinction between a partnership and an agency relationship is that a partnership consists of ***co-owners.*** While an agent may sometimes receive a share of the profits of the principal's business as compensation for services, the agent is not an owner of the business.

3. Distinguish—Unincorporated Association

The RUPA specifically recognizes other types of associations formed under other acts or statutes and provides that such associations are not considered partnerships. [RUPA § 202(b)]

a. "Massachusetts" Trust

A "Massachusetts" trust is an unincorporated association in which the participants transfer property of the association to trustees who manage and control the property for the benefit of the participants. The interests of the participants are represented by transferable shares. The usual "Massachusetts" or business trust is not a partnership. [*See* **Goldwater v. Oltman,** 210 Cal. 408 (1930)] Note that a "Massachusetts" trust would be considered a partnership if the participants take over management and control from the trustees. [**Stitzinger v. Truitt,** 81 Cal. App. 502 (1927)]

b. Nonprofit Purpose

Whereas other types of unincorporated associations may be formed for non-profit as well as profit-making purposes, a partnership is an association of co-owners of a business ***for profit*** and hence cannot be formed for nonprofit purposes.

4. Distinguish—Joint Venture

A joint venture resembles a partnership in that its members associate together as co-owners of a business enterprise, agreeing to share profits and losses. However, a partnership ordinarily engages in a continuing business for an indefinite or fixed period of time (*see* below), whereas a joint venture is usually formed for a ***single transaction*** or series of transactions—thus being more limited in scope and duration. [138 A.L.R. 968]

a. Note

It is often difficult to distinguish between a joint venture and a partnership. What starts out as a joint venture (a single business transaction) may turn into more continuous activity and at some point become a partnership. This difficulty of classification, however, generally has no serious legal consequence, because the rights and liabilities of partners and joint venturers are the same in all important respects. Hence, the courts usually apply the provisions of the RUPA to joint ventures whenever appropriate. [*See* **Zeibak v. Nasser,** 12 Cal. 2d 1 (1938)]

C. Aggregate vs. Entity Characteristics of Partnership

1. Common Law View

At common law, a partnership was never regarded as a separate entity in itself. Rather, it was treated as an ***aggregate*** of the individual partners.

a. Lawsuits

Thus, for example, an action at common law could not be brought against the partnership in the partnership's name; each individual partner had to be sued. [**Dunham v. Shindler,** 20 P. 326 (Or. 1889)]

b. Title to Real Estate

Similarly, title to real estate could not be held in the partnership name. Partnership assets were deemed to be owned by the individual partners as "tenants in partnership," rather than by the partnership as a distinct entity.

2. UPA and RUPA—Aggregate and Entity Characteristics

a. Aggregate Characteristics

(1) Liability for Partnership Obligations

Under the RUPA, the most significant aggregate characteristic of a partnership is that partners are jointly and severally liable for partnership obligations (*see infra*, p. 154), regardless of whether the partnership itself can be sued (*see infra*, pp. 133–134).

(2) Partnership Property

Under the RUPA, partners are ***not*** co-owners of partnership property. The UPA, however, provides that partners are co-owners (tenants in partnership) of specific partnership property, but this term is misleading because a partner's rights in specific partnership property are extremely limited and any one partner is limited in transferring or encumbering specific partnership property; *e.g.*, a partner's right in specific partnership property is not assignable unless all partners are assigning their rights. (*See infra*, pp. 166–167.)

(3) Federal Income Tax Law Retains Aggregate Characteristic

For tax purposes, the income or losses incurred by a partnership are attributed to the partners individually. The partnership itself is not a ***tax-paying*** entity. [I.R.C. § 701] However, the partnership ***is*** a ***tax-reporting*** entity. It must file an "informational return" to establish the amount of income or loss that partners must include on their individual tax returns. [I.R.C. § 6031]

b. Entity Characteristics

The RUPA and other statutes treat a partnership as an ***entity*** distinct from its several members. [RUPA § 201(a)]

(1) Capacity to Sue or to Be Sued

The RUPA permits a partnership to sue or be sued in the name of the partnership. [RUPA § 307(a)] The UPA, however, does not address whether a partnership may sue or be sued in the name of the partnership. [*See* RUPA § 307, comment 1] This issue sometimes depends on federal and state court procedural rules.

(a) Federal Courts

In federal courts, a partnership can sue or be sued in the partnership name if the litigation involves a "federal question" (*see* Civil Procedure Summary). In all other cases (*e.g.*, diversity of citizenship actions), the partnership's capacity to sue or be sued is determined by the law of the state in which the federal court is located. [Fed. R. Civ. P. 17(b)]

1) Determining Diversity

If the case comes under diversity jurisdiction, the citizenship of ***all partners*** (even limited partners) is considered. [**Carden v. Arkoma Associates,** 494 U.S. 185 (1990)]

(b) State Courts

A majority of states, pursuant to their adoption of the RUPA, permit a partnership *to sue or be sued* in the partnership name. [*See, e.g.*, Cal. Civ. Proc. Code § 369.5]

A few states, however, continue to hold that a partnership can *be sued* as an entity (to facilitate jurisdiction and service in actions against it), but that it *cannot sue* in the partnership name—*i.e.*, partnership claims must be brought in the names of the individual partners.

(c) Effect of Judgment Against Partnership Only

A judgment against the partnership is not by itself a judgment against any partner; thus, the judgment may not be satisfied from a partner's personal assets *unless there is also a judgment against the partner.* [RUPA § 307(c)] Thus, good practice dictates the joinder of all partners individually. Of course, if the plaintiff sues both the partnership and its members, any judgment rendered must be consistent—*i.e.*, the partnership cannot be held liable if the individual partners are not.

e.g. **Example:** Plaintiff sues both the individual partners and the partnership on an alleged partnership debt. The partnership fails to respond, and Plaintiff thus obtains a default judgment against it. However, if the individual partners answer and successfully defend at trial, simultaneously disproving Plaintiff's claim against the partnership, the default judgment against the partnership would have to be vacated. The "entity theory" could not justify the inconsistent judgments. [*See* **Nicholls v. Anders,** 13 Cal. App. 2d 440 (1936)]

(2) Bankruptcy of Partnership vs. Partners Individually

Under federal bankruptcy law, the partnership is likewise treated as an entity, so that the adjudication of the partnership as a bankrupt does not constitute an adjudication that the partners are bankrupt. Nor does an adjudication of a partner as a bankrupt bring the partnership or its assets into bankruptcy. [11 U.S.C. § 723]

(3) Capacity to Convey Property

Also, a partnership can hold and convey title to ***real or personal property*** as an entity (*i.e.*, in the partnership name), without all partners joining in the conveyance. [RUPA §§ 204, 302; *and see* UPA § 8]

D. Formation

1. In General

It is implicit in the definition of a partnership (*supra*, p. 131) that it is a ***voluntary*** association of two or more persons. As such, a partnership must generally be based on the agreement of the partners; hence, a contract (express or implied) is ordinarily essential to the formation of a partnership.

2. Formalities

A written agreement is ***not*** ordinarily necessary to create a partnership. In fact, a partnership agreement can be implied from conduct. However, certain partnership agreements ***must*** be in writing in order to be effective:

a. Continuance for More than One Year

An agreement that provides for the mandatory continuance of the partnership for a period in excess of one year falls within the Statute of Frauds (as a "contract which by its terms is not to be performed within a year"), and therefore must be evidenced by a sufficient writing.

If partners agree to a term of more than one year and there is no writing to evidence the agreement, the partnership will be treated as a partnership at will (*i.e.*, one that may be rightfully dissolved by any partner at any time).

b. Dealing in Real Property

An agreement authorizing partners to deal in real property (or otherwise to enter into contracts within the Statute of Frauds) need not be in writing insofar as the rights of the partners among themselves are concerned. However, when a third person attempts to bind the partnership to such a contract, some courts hold that the authority of the partner executing the contract must be evidenced by a sufficient writing.

3. Capacity to Become a Partner

Any ***person*** having the capacity to contract has the capacity to become a partner.

a. Minors

Because a minor does not have capacity to make a binding contract, a partnership contract in which a minor is one of the partners is ***voidable*** and subject to disaffirmance by the minor. [**Latrobe v. Dietrich,** 78 A. 983 (Md. 1910)]

b. Partnerships

Under the RUPA, the definition of a "person" who may become a partner includes a partnership; thus, a partnership itself may be a partner in another partnership. [RUPA §§ 101(10), 202(a); *and see* UPA §§ 2, 6]

c. Corporations

Moreover, the RUPA includes corporations within the definition of persons who may become partners [RUPA § 101(10)], so that a corporation has the capacity to become a partner. However, whether becoming a partner is within the corporation's powers is a question of corporations law. Older corporations cases held that corporations had no implied power to be partners, but modern corporations statutes explicitly grant corporations the power to become a partner. [*See, e.g.*, Illinois Business Corporation Act 805 ILCS 5/3.10(q)]

d. Other Entities

Note that other entities, such as limited liability partnerships (*see infra*, p. 157), limited partnerships (*see infra*, p. 192), and limited liability companies (*see infra*, p. 214), are also included in the definition of persons who may become partners. [RUPA § 101(10)]

ANSWERS TO REVIEW QUESTIONS

If you have to determine if a partnership exists, remember that there must be at least *two persons* involved in forming a partnership; a partnership may not exist with only one partner. But also remember that a "person" may be a partnership, corporation, or other entity; thus, Partnership A and Corporation B can agree to form Partnership C.

---

4. Consent of Co-Partners

As a voluntary association of co-owners, it is essential that each and all of the co-owners agree on who will be a partner. Thus, the RUPA provides that "a person may become a partner only with the consent of ***all*** of the partners." [RUPA § 401(i); *and see* UPA § 18(g)]

REQUIREMENTS FOR PARTNERSHIP FORMATION
FOR A PARTNERSHIP TO EXIST THERE MUST BE:
☑ ***Agreement*** between partners to form a for-profit business; and ☑ ***Capacity*** of partners to contract (a "partner" may be a partnership or corporation). *Note:* No specific formalities ordinarily required (*i.e.*, usually agreement need not be in writing).

5. Rules for Determining Existence of Partnership

In many cases, there may be a dispute or uncertainty as to whether the parties intended to form as co-owners a business for profit. In such cases, the courts attempt to ascertain the intent of the parties as expressed by their acts or agreements. When attempting to ascertain the intent of the parties, courts consider the following factors, which ***may indicate the existence of a partnership***:

a. Joint Ownership of Property

Although joint ownership of property may be some evidence that the parties intended to form a partnership, a partnership is ***not*** established merely by the joint ownership of property (*i.e.*, joint tenancies, etc.). Also, the fact that the profits from the use of such property are shared between the owners is significant (*see* below), but likewise it is not conclusive. [RUPA § 202(c)(*l*); UPA § 7(2); 150 A.L.R. 1003]

b. Contribution of Capital

The contribution of capital to an enterprise does not by itself establish a partnership. Conversely, it is not essential to the existence of a partnership that all parties contribute capital. [**Whitley v. Bradley,** 13 Cal. App. 720 (1910)]

c. Sharing of Gross Income

Similarly, the sharing of ***gross*** income does not itself establish a partnership. This is true whether or not there is a joint interest in the property from which the income is derived. [RUPA § 202(c)(*l*), (2); UPA § 7(3)]

d. Sharing Profits from Business

The RUPA describes the sharing of profits from a business as raising a ***presumption*** of partnership, unless they were received as payment for, *e.g.*, debts, rent, wages, or retirement benefits. [RUPA § 202(c)(3); *see infra*, p. 136] Under the UPA, however, the sharing of profits from a business is ***prima facie evidence*** (*i.e.*, evidence sufficient to prove a particular fact unless contradicted and overcome by other evidence) that a partnership exists. [UPA § 7(4)] However, the legal effect of a presumption is the same as that of prima facie evidence, *see* above. [RUPA § 202(c)(3), comment]

(1) Exception

The sharing of profits will indicate a partnership relationship only when ***no other business reason exists*** for the sharing. [*See* **Martin v. Peyton,** 246 N.Y. 213 (1927)] For example, if it appears that profits are distributed as a debt, bonus or wages to an employee, rent to a landlord, annuity to a surviving spouse, interest on a loan, or consideration for the sale of the goodwill of a business or other property, the distribution will not be considered the sharing of profits. [RUPA § 202(c)(3); UPA § 7(4)]

e. Parties' Designation

While the parties' characterization of their relationship as a "partnership" or some other business form is entitled to some weight, it is not conclusive. *And note:* The parties cannot avoid partnership liability, even by an express stipulation negating the relation, if the evidence establishes the essential elements of a partnership. [**Streeter & Riddell v. Bacon,** 49 Cal. App. 327 (1920)]

E. Partnership by Estoppel

1. In General

A true partnership relation depends on a contract, express or implied, between the parties. However, parties who are ***not*** partners in that sense may—in certain circumstances—be bound as if they were partners in their dealings with third persons.

2. Liability of Purported Partner

If someone represents herself, by words or conduct, to be a partner in an actual or apparent partnership or consents to a representation that she is a partner, she is liable to any third person to whom the representation is made who extends credit in good faith reliance on the representation. [RUPA § 308; UPA § 16] The rule is one of ***equitable estoppel*:** One who knowingly permits another to believe that she is a partner and to extend credit in reliance on the representation cannot later be permitted to deny that she is a partner and escape liability.

a. Generally No Duty to Deny

The comments to the RUPA (section 308) make clear, and the comments to the UPA (section 16) suggest, that there is ***no duty to deny*** affiliation with a partnership when, ***without consent,*** one is held out by another as a partner. The comments were written in response to cases where, *e.g.*, without consent, A runs an ad or prints a brochure indicating that B is his partner. B has no duty to take out an ad or otherwise attempt to counter A's representations even if B discovers them. The comments, however, may not be taken to the extreme. For example, if A, B, and C are standing together and A tells C that he and B are partners, B must deny the affiliation or she will be held to have consented to the representation through conduct.

EXAM TIP

If an exam question asks you whether you can hold a person who is not a partner liable to a third person on a partnership debt, your answer will depend on whether the person did something to indicate that she was in fact a partner. Remember that a person who *represents herself* as a partner or *consents to a representation* that she is a partner is liable to a third person who extends credit to the partnership *in reliance* on the representation.

SUMMARY OF FACTORS INDICATING A PARTNERSHIP

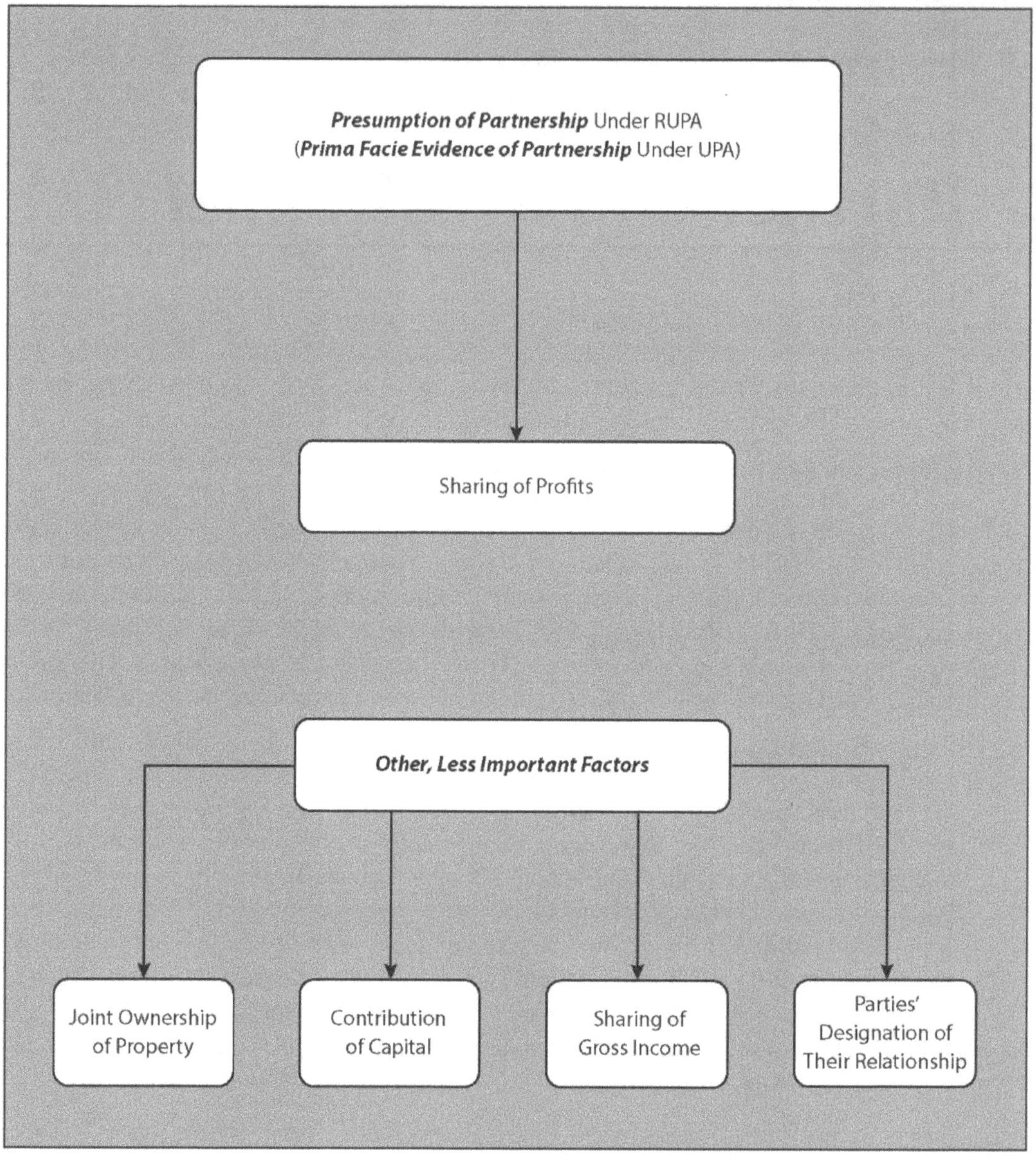

b. Extent of Liability—"Holding Out" Language

(1) RUPA

The RUPA provides that a person who ***relies on the representation*** of partnership made in a public manner can hold the purported partner liable "even if the purported partner is not aware of being held out as a partner to the claimant." [RUPA § 308(a); *see* **Reisen Lumber & Millwork Co. v. Simonelli,** 237 A.2d 303 (N.J. 1967)—if the holding out is in a public manner, the plaintiff need not prove that the purported partner specifically consented to having the communication made to the plaintiff]

(2) UPA

The UPA rule is the same as the RUPA rule: When a person represents himself as a partner or consents to another so representing him, he is liable to any person to whom the representation has been made, and if the representation was made "in a public manner," he is liable to such person, whether or not the representation has been made or communicated to that person giving credit by or with the knowledge of the apparent partner. [UPA § 16(1)]

3. Liability of Partners Who Represent a Third Person to Be a Partner

If an actual partner represents a nonpartner to be a member of the partnership, she constitutes that person as her agent with the power to bind her as though the person were in fact a partner. However, any resultant liability binds ***only those partners who made or consented to the representation.*** [RUPA § 308(b); UPA § 16(2)]

e.g. **Example:** A represents to the public that T is a partner in the A-B partnership, even though the only partners are A and B. If T enters into a contract on behalf of the partnership, the contract is binding on A, but ***not*** on B, unless B authorized or consented to A's representation.

a. Note

No actual partnership has been created by the representation. Thus, for example, T would have no right to manage the business, inspect the partnership books, etc.

Chapter Nine: Effect of Partnership Relationship

CONTENTS	PAGE

Key Exam Issues

Once you have established that a partnership relationship exists, you will be ready to address the heart of a partnership question: Who is liable to whom and for what? On your exam, you need to remember the following:

1. Partners as Among Themselves

Partners are fiduciaries and owe each other the duties of loyalty and due care and must act in good faith and with fair dealing. They must account to the partnership for any profits made from partnership-related activities. They may not compete with the partnership. Unless otherwise agreed, each partner has an ***equal*** right to participate in management and profits but is ***not*** entitled to any salary. The RUPA allows a partner to sue another partner at law or in equity to enforce certain rights, such as those under the partnership agreement or arising independent of the partnership relationship. Under the UPA, partners cannot sue each other at law for damages during the term of the partnership but can only seek an equitable accounting to determine what monies are owing to each partner.

2. Partners' Authority to Bind Partnership to Third Persons

Each partner is an agent for the partnership and has ***apparent authority*** to bind the partnership whenever apparently carrying on the business of the partnership in the usual way. A partner's ***actual authority*** can be granted in the partnership agreement or by a vote of the partners (majority vote for ordinary business; unanimous vote for extraordinary matters).

3. Notice and Knowledge

The rules regarding notice to and knowledge of the partnership are similar to those for agency. ***Under the RUPA***, a partnership has notice or knowledge of a fact if the individual conducting the transaction has notice or knowledge or would have had notice or knowledge of the fact had reasonable diligence been exercised. ***Under the UPA***, the partnership is deemed to have notice whenever it is communicated to any partner. Whether a partnership will be deemed to know what a partner knows depends on whether the partner was participating in the transaction and when the knowledge was acquired. If the partner was a participant, any knowledge acquired ***after*** becoming a partner will be imputed to the partnership, but knowledge acquired ***before*** becoming a partner will be imputed only if it was "present to her mind" at the time she was acting. If the partner was a nonparticipant, her knowledge will be imputed to the partnership only if she reasonably could have and should have communicated it.

4. Partners' Liability to Third Persons

Under the RUPA, partners are ***jointly and severally*** liable for ***all*** partnership obligations. Under the UPA, partners are ***jointly*** liable for all contract obligations to partnership creditors and ***jointly and severally*** liable for all other obligations owed by the partnership to third persons (*e.g.*, tort liabilities). An incoming partner is not liable for partnership obligations incurred before the partner joined the partnership (or the incoming partner's liability is limited to partnership assets under the UPA). A retiring partner remains liable on all partnership obligations incurred before giving notice of withdrawal.

A. Relations Between Partners

1. Fiduciary Duty

Under the RUPA, a partner owes to the partnership and the other partners the ***fiduciary duties of loyalty and care*** and must exercise those duties ***in good faith and with fair dealing.*** [RUPA § 404(a), (d)]

a. Duty of Loyalty

In exercising the duty of loyalty, a partner must: (i) ***account to the partnership*** and hold as a trustee for it any property, profit, or benefit derived by him in the conduct of or winding up of the partnership business or by his use of partnership property, including the appropriation of a partnership opportunity; (ii) ***refrain from dealing with the partnership on behalf of an adverse party***; and (iii) ***not compete*** with the partnership before dissolution. [RUPA § 404(b); *see also* UPA § 21; **Leff v. Gunter,** 33 Cal. 3d 508 (1983)—partner has no right to compete with partnership without consent of all partners]

(1) Exclusive Service

If a partner has promised to devote his ***full time*** and exclusive services to the partnership business, his time is considered to be a partnership asset. Hence, he may not render services to any other employer (even one that does not compete with the partnership) without the consent of all the other partners; if he does so, the salary obtained may be considered partnership income. [*See* **Weller v. Simenstad,** 127 N.W.2d 794 (Wis. 1964)]

b. Duty of Care

The duty of care requires that partners refrain from engaging in grossly negligent or reckless conduct, intentional misconduct, or a knowing violation of law in the conduct or winding up of partnership business. [RUPA § 404(c)]

c. Assets

A partner who purchases or holds partnership assets in his own name does so as trustee for the partnership and can be compelled to account to the partnership for the assets or their value. It is immaterial that the partner used his own funds in purchasing the property if it was the partners' intention that the assets would belong to the partnership. [44 A.L.R.2d 519; *and see infra*, pp. 162–166]

d. Transacting Business with Partnership

A partner may make loans to or transact other business with the partnership. Moreover, the fiduciary duties are not violated merely because a partner's actions further his own interest. [RUPA § 404(e), (f)]

2. Other Rights and Duties of Partners to Each Other

The rights and obligations of the partners are largely governed by the ***partnership agreement.*** However, in the absence of provisions to the contrary in the agreement, the ***law imposes*** the following rights and duties:

a. Management

"Each partner has equal rights in the management and conduct of the partnership business." [RUPA § 401(f); *and see* UPA § 18(c)] Note that unless the partnership agreement provides otherwise, the partners' management rights are equal, even though some partners may be entitled to a larger percentage of profits.

(1) Majority vs. Unanimous Vote

A majority vote of the partners is required to settle any difference arising as to a matter in the ordinary course of partnership business. A unanimous vote of the partners is required as to an act outside the ordinary course of partnership business and for an amendment to the partnership agreement. [RUPA § 401(j); *and see* UPA § 18(h)—ordinary matters associated with partnership business require majority vote and acts in contravention of partnership agreement require unanimous vote]

(2) Managing Partner

By agreement, one or more partners may assume a greater share of the management authority, or may even become the "managing partner" or "general manager" of the partnership. Such assumption of authority carries with it the obligation to deal fairly on behalf of all partners—so that secret dealings by which some partners are favored and others prejudiced by the managing partner's acts will be held invalid as to the nonconsenting partners. [**Application of Lester,** 87 Misc. 2d 717 (1976)—managing partner of law firm purported to bind firm to purchase interest of retiring partner on terms basically unfair to other partners, and of which they had no knowledge or opportunity to object]

b. Books and Records; Information

Each partner is entitled to access to the partnership books and records and may inspect and copy any of them. The books and records must be kept at the partnership's chief executive office. [RUPA § 403; *and see* UPA § 19] Moreover, partners must be given, ***without demand***, any information concerning the partnership that is reasonably necessary for the exercise of the partners' rights and duties. In addition, a partner must be given, on demand, any other information concerning the partnership business. [RUPA § 403(c)] The UPA approach is that partners are not obligated to provide information regarding partnership business ***unless a demand is made*** for such information. [UPA § 20]

EXAM TIP

Notice that the RUPA requires partners to be furnished with information necessary for them to carry on their duties (or exercise their rights) as partners, *even if they do not demand* this information. This is contrary to the UPA position, which requires partners to be furnished with information affecting partnership business *only on demand.*

---

(1) Deceased Partner

Upon the death of a partner, her personal representative has the same rights with respect to access and inspection of partnership books and records as the partner herself would have had. [RUPA § 403]

c. Profits and Losses

Each partner will share in the partnership profits and losses according to the partnership agreement. In the absence of an agreement, each partner is entitled to an equal share of the partnership profits, and must contribute to the partnership losses according to her share in the profits. [RUPA § 401(b); UPA § 18(a)]

e.g. **Example:** Alice, Becky, and Charles form a partnership. Their partnership agreement does not state how partnership profits and losses will be shared. In this case, Alice, Becky, and Charles will share profits equally, and losses according to profits; thus, they will share losses equally.

e.g. **Example:** If, in the above example, Alice, Becky, and Charles state in their partnership agreement that partnership profits will be shared 30% to Alice, 30% to Becky, and 40% to Charles, but do not state how losses will be shared, losses will be shared according to profits: Alice 30%, Becky 30%, and Charles 40%.

d. Distributions from Partnership

(1) Agreed upon Capital Contribution

Upon dissolution of the partnership, partners have a right to the return of the capital that they contributed to the partnership. [RUPA §§ 401 (a), 807(b); UPA §§ 18(a), 40; *and see infra*, pp. 177, 186] Under the UPA, no interest is due on account of the contribution until after the contribution should have been repaid. [UPA § 18(d)]

(2) Indemnification for Expenses; Advancements

A partnership must reimburse a partner for expenses and personal liabilities that the partner reasonably incurs while conducting partnership business. Similarly, a partner has a right to the return of any capital that the partner advances beyond the partner's agreed-upon contribution. In either case, the payments made by the partner constitute loans to the partnership and so accrue interest from the date the payments are made. [RUPA § 401(c)–(e); UPA § 18(b)–(c)]

(3) Remuneration

A partner generally has no right to remuneration for services performed for the partnership unless the partners agree otherwise. [RUPA § 401(h); UPA § 18(f)] Thus, a partner is not entitled to extra money even where her efforts have been the major factor creating the profits of the partnership. [*See* **Security-First National Bank v. Lutz,** 322 F.2d 348 (9th Cir. 1963)]

(a) Exception—Winding Up

A partner who winds up the partnership's affairs upon dissolution is entitled to reasonable compensation for her services rendered in winding up. [RUPA § 401(h); UPA § 18(f)]

SUMMARY OF RIGHTS OF PARTNERS	
MANAGEMENT—	Each partner has an ***equal right*** to participate in the management of the partnership unless the partnership agreement provides otherwise.
INSPECTION—	A partner has a right to inspect and copy the partnership books and records and receive information concerning the partnership.
DISTRIBUTIONS—	Partners have whatever rights are granted in the partnership agreement as to distribution of profits. If the agreement is silent, partners share profits ***equally***; upon dissolution, partners have a right to the return of their capital contributions.
INDEMNIFICATION—	A partner has a right to be indemnified by fellow partners for expenses and personal liabilities incurred on behalf of the partnership.
REMUNERATION—	Partners generally have ***no right*** to remuneration for their services to the partnership except for winding up the partnership business.

3. Actions Between Partners

a. Under the RUPA

The RUPA specifically allows partners to maintain actions against other partners for either ***legal or equitable*** relief, with or without an accounting, to enforce:

(i) ***A right under the partnership agreement;***

(ii) ***A right relating to sharing profits, participating in management, indemnification***, etc. [RUPA § 401], ***relating to obtaining partnership information*** [RUPA § 403], or ***relating to the standards of conduct*** [RUPA § 404];

(iii) ***Rights relating to dissociation or dissolution and winding up*** the business of the partnership; or

(iv) ***Any other right of the partner***, including rights and interests arising independently of the partnership relationship.

[RUPA § 405(b)] Partners have access to the courts during the term of the partnership to resolve claims against the partnership and the other partners, leaving broad judicial discretion to fashion appropriate remedies. [RUPA § 405, comments]

b. Under the UPA

(1) Dissolution

The principal remedy of a partner against co-partners is a suit in equity for dissolution of the partnership and an accounting of its assets. (*See* further discussion *infra*, pp. 180–181.)

(2) Accounting

In addition to the accounting in connection with dissolution proceedings, a partner has the right to obtain an accounting from co-partners as to the affairs of the partnership whenever: (i) he has been wrongfully excluded from the business; (ii) the partnership agreement gives him that right; (iii) any other partner is withholding any benefit or profits belonging to the partnership; or (iv) other circumstances "render it just and reasonable." [UPA § 22]

(3) No Action at Law for Damages

Since disputes between partners invariably involve conflicting claims requiring an accounting, there can generally be no action at law by one partner against another during the term of the partnership. A partner's sole remedy is an equitable suit for dissolution and/or an accounting.

(a) Rationale

If a partner were allowed to sue his partnership, he would be on both sides of the litigation because each partner is personally liable for all of the debts and obligations of the partnership (*see infra*, p. 154). Moreover, settlement of one partner's claim without a complete accounting and settlement of all of the partnership's affairs could result in needless piecemeal litigation.

(b) Exceptions

In a few situations, however, an action at law *is* permitted where:

1) ***The partnership has dealt with one partner as if he were a third person,*** and it is clear that the transaction is not to be reflected in the general partnership account (*e.g.*, a partner opens an account at the partnership-owned bank);

2) ***The suit is not related to the partnership business*** (*e.g.*, action on a loan from one partner to another) [**Estes v. Delpech,** 73 Cal. App. 643 (1925)];

3) ***The wrongful acts of one partner constitute fraud or a conversion of the partnership assets*** (since these are not really partnership transactions) [**Prince v. Harting,** 177 Cal. App. 2d 720 (1960)];

4) ***One partner is wrongfully excluded*** from the partnership, and the remaining partner converts the partnership assets (the wronged party may elect to seek damages rather than assert his partnership rights) [**Gherman v. Colburn,** 72 Cal. App. 3d 544 (1977)];

5) ***One partner negligently injures the person or property of another*** (the injured partner may maintain an action against the tortfeasor-partner) [**Campbell v. Campbell,** 162 A. 379 (Vt. 1932)]; or

6) ***Injury to a partner is caused by the negligence of an employee*** of the partnership (the traditional rule has been that the negligence of the employee would be imputed to the partnership and partners, thus barring suit; however, the modern trend is to ***permit the partner to sue***) [*See, e.g.*, **Smith v. Hensley,** 354 S.W.2d 744 (Ky. 1961)].

B. Relations as to Third Persons

1. Authority of Partner to Bind Partnership

Every partner is an agent of the partnership for purposes of the partnership's business. [RUPA § 301(1); UPA § 9(1)] Thus, the rules of agency apply in determining whether a partnership is bound by the dealings of one of its partners with a third party. [**Rice v. Jackson,** 32 A. 1036 (Pa. 1895)] Consequently, to bind the partnership, a partner must have either apparent or actual authority.

a. Apparent Authority

An act of a partner, including the execution of an instrument in the partnership name, ***for apparently carrying on in the ordinary course the partnership business or business of the kind carried on by the partnership*** binds the partnership ***unless:*** (i) the partner had ***no authority*** to act for the partnership in the particular matter, ***and*** (ii) the person with whom the partner was dealing ***knew or had received notification that the partner lacked authority.*** [RUPA § 301(1); *and see* UPA § 9(1)]

Example: Sara and Leigh form a partnership to operate a bakery. They agree that Sara will do the baking, and Leigh will manage the bakery (*e.g.*, order supplies, assist customers, etc.). One day Sara decides to order a week's supply of flour from Supplier. Supplier delivers the flour to bakery. Supplier knew that Sara and Leigh operated a bakery but neither knew nor received notification that Sara had no authority to purchase supplies. Because the purchase of the flour is apparently to enable the partnership to carry on in the usual way its business, Sara's act binds the partnership to Supplier.

Compare: If in the example above Supplier knew or received notification that Sara was the creative talent (baker) behind the bakery and had no authority to purchase supplies, the partnership would not be bound to Supplier for Sara's purchase.

(1) Act Unrelated to Partnership's Business

A partner's act that is not apparently related to the business of the partnership is not within her apparent authority. Therefore, the act does not bind the partnership unless the partner had the actual authority (*see* below) to act. [RUPA § 301(2); UPA § 9(2)]

Example: Baker Sara above purchases season tickets for the opera in the partnership name. This purchase does not seem related to the business, and therefore, the partnership would not be bound unless Sara and Leigh agreed to purchase the tickets and thus Sara had actual authority.

(2) Act Unrelated to Partnership's Business

A partner's act that is not apparently related to the business of the partnership is not within her apparent authority. Therefore, the act does not bind the partnership unless the partner had the actual authority (*see* below) to act. [RUPA § 301(2); UPA § 9(2)]

Example: Baker Sara above purchases season tickets for the opera in the partnership name. This purchase does not seem related to the business, and therefore, the partnership would not be bound unless Sara and Leigh agreed to purchase the tickets and thus Sara had actual authority.

APPROACH TO WHETHER PARTNER'S ACT BINDS PARTNERSHIP

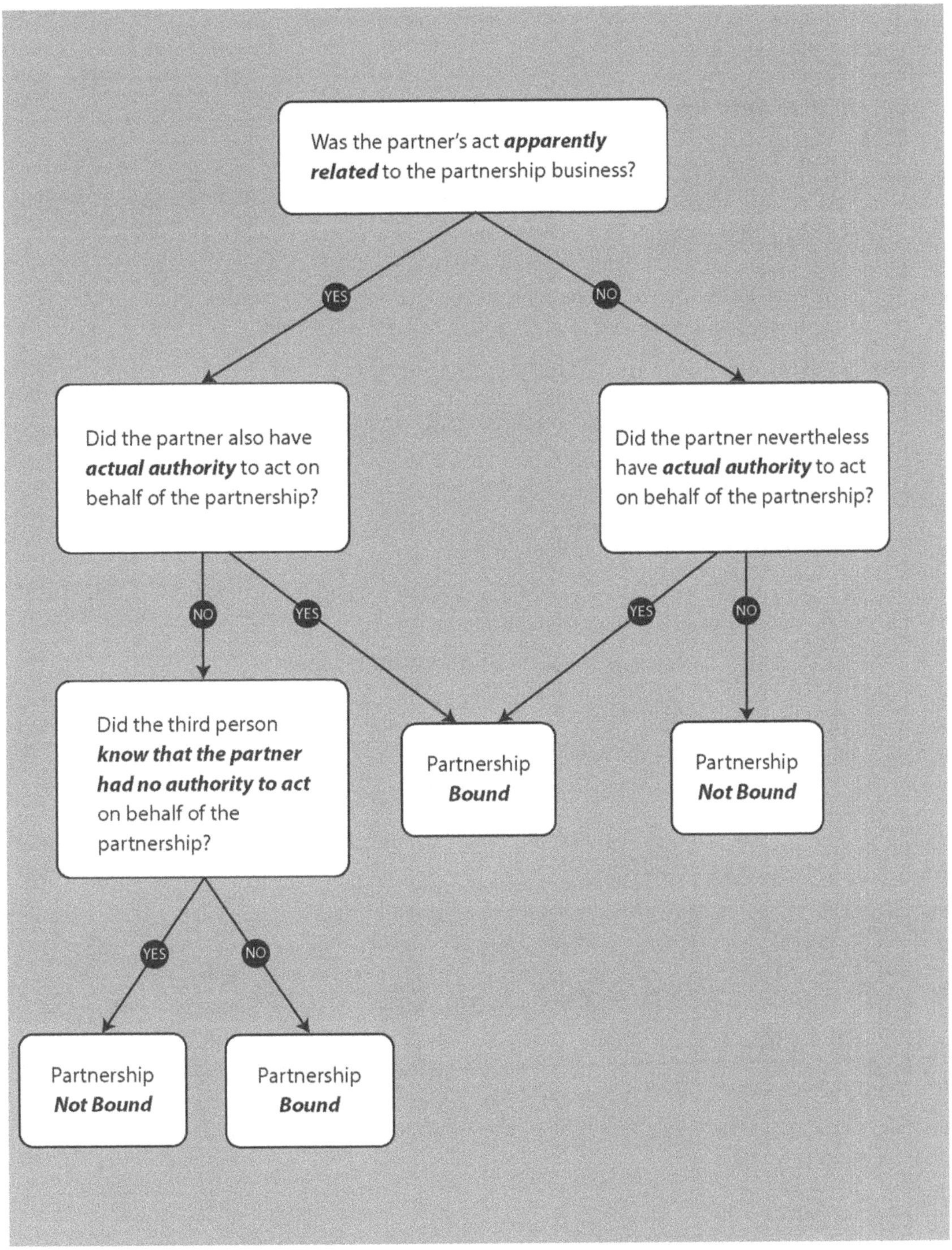

EXAM TIP

Remember that a partnership may be bound by an act of a partner even if the partnership did not give the partner the authority to act. For the partnership to be bound: (i) the partner's act must have been *apparently to carry on the partnership business,* and (ii) the person with whom the partner dealt must *have neither known nor received notification* that the partner acted without the partnership's authority.

b. Actual Authority

A partner's actual authority can be granted in the partnership agreement (*e.g.*, P shall have the power to make all purchasing decisions), or it can be granted by a vote of the partners.

(1) Majority Vote

A majority vote of the partners is sufficient to give a partner actual authority to carry on ***ordinary business.*** [RUPA § 401(j); UPA § 18(h)]

(2) Unanimous Vote

If the act to be done by a partner is ***outside the ordinary course of business,*** actual authority can be granted only by a unanimous vote of the partners, unless the partnership agreement provides otherwise. [RUPA § 401(j); *and see* UPA § 18(h)]

(a) Distinguish—UPA

Under the UPA, a unanimous vote of the partners is required for five specifically enumerated *extraordinary acts:*

(i) ***Submitting the partnership to arbitration***;

(ii) ***Assigning partnership assets*** for the benefit of creditors;

(iii) ***Confessing judgment*** against the partnership;

(iv) ***Disposing of the goodwill*** of the partnership; or

(v) ***Doing any act that would make it impossible*** to carry on partnership business. [UPA § 9(3)]

WHEN A MAJORITY OR UNANIMOUS VOTE IS NEEDED—EXAMPLES

ORDINARY BUSINESS REQUIRING MAJORITY VOTE	BUSINESS OUTSIDE ORDINARY COURSE REQUIRING UNANIMOUS VOTE
Hiring an attorney to represent the partnership in litigation	Undertaking a new business venture
Paying partnership bills	Amending partnership agreement
Borrowing money to run the partnership	Purchasing inventory unrelated to the business
Selling the partnership's inventory in the ordinary course of business	Obtaining an unnecessary business license

Doing any act necessary to carry on in the ordinary course the business of the partnership (*e.g.*, hiring employees, leasing office space)	

(3) Formalities

The cases are split on whether a partner's authority to convey real property other than in the ordinary course of business must be in writing in order to bind the partnership. The prevailing view is that a writing is ***not required***, the authority being inherent in the partnership relation. [**McGahan v. National Bank,** 156 U.S. 218 (1895)]

c. Statement of Partnership Authority

The RUPA allows a partnership to publicly file (with the office of the secretary of state) a statement of partnership authority. In the statement of authority, the partnership may expand or limit the authority of some or all of the partners to enter into transactions on the partnership's behalf. [RUPA § 303(a)(2)]

(1) Mandatory Contents

The statement of partnership authority must include:

(i) The ***name of the partnership***;

(ii) The ***address of the partnership's chief executive office*** and of an office within the state, if there is one;

(iii) The ***names and addresses of all partners*** or of an agent who has a list of such information; and

(iv) The names of the ***partners authorized to execute an instrument transferring real property*** held in the partnership name.

[RUPA § 303(a)(*l*)]

(2) Effect of Statement of Authority

The effect of the statement depends on whether it grants or limits a partner's authority.

(a) Grant of Authority

A statement of authority granting a partner authority to enter into a transaction is *conclusive evidence* of the partner's authority to enter into the transaction if the person who dealt with the partner gave value without notice that the partner did not have authority to act.

e.g. **Example:** A, B, and C are partners in a boat-building business. They file a statement of authority granting C the authority to sell the partnership's business equipment from time to time. Later, they orally agree that C must not sell any equipment without first obtaining permission from either A or B. After the oral agreement was made, C sells three of the partnership's desks to P at their fair market value without discussing the sale with A or B. If the partnership tries to void the sale, P can use the statement of authority as conclusive proof that C had the authority to sell the desks.

1) **Real Property**

For a grant of authority to transfer partnership real property to be conclusive, the statement of authority must be filed with the secretary of state, and a certified copy of the statement must be filed with the ***office for recording real property interests*** for that real property (and the transferee must have given value for the property without notice that the partner did not have the authority to act).

EXAM TIP

It is important to remember that *two* filings are required when dealing with a statement of authority containing a *grant of authority to transfer real property.* First, the statement of authority must be filed with the secretary of state. Second, a *certified copy* of the statement filed with the secretary of state must be filed with the office for recording real property interests.

(b) Limitation of Authority

A limitation on a partner's authority to enter into a transaction on behalf of the partnership may be contained in a statement of authority or may be contained in another filed statement. However, the mere filing of the limitation does *not* give third parties constructive notice of the limitation. Thus, unless the third party *knows* of the limitation, he is not bound by it.

e.g. **Example:** The boat builders above filed a statement limiting C from selling the partnership's boats. Despite the limitation, C sold a boat to P. If P did not know of the limitation, it is not effective against her because, as a partner of a boat-building business, C would normally have the authority to sell a boat.

1) **Exceptions**

The filing of a limitation of a partner's authority will be effective as constructive notice to third parties dealing with the partner when the limitation:

(i) ***Limits a filed grant of authority***; or

(ii) ***Limits a partner's authority to transfer real property***, and the limitation is filed with the secretary of state and the ***office for recording real property interests*** for that real property.

e.g. **Example:** If the boat builders filed a statement of authority providing that C had no authority to sell partnership real property, and C subsequently sells a lot owned by the partnership to P, the limitation is effective against P—even if she did not know about the limitation—if it was filed with both the secretary of state and the recorder of deeds.

(3) Statement of Denial

The RUPA also provides that a partner or person named as a partner may file a statement of denial, denying any fact, including denial of the person's authority or status as a partner. [RUPA § 304]

(4) Distinguish—Termination Under UPA

It is doubtful under the UPA that any single partner can terminate the authority of co-partners, short of dissolving the partnership.

(a) Two Partners

Some cases have held that a partner's notice to a creditor regarding nonliability for a co-partner's act is effective to limit that partner's liability—at least where only two partners are involved. [*See, e.g.*, **Bank of Bellbuckle v. Mason,** 202 S.W. 931 (Tenn. 1918); *but see* **National Biscuit Co. v. Stroud,** 106 S.E.2d 692 (N.C. 1959)—partner liable for co-partner's purchases of bread even though partner told seller of bread that he would not be personally liable for the co-partner's purchases]

(b) More than Two Partners

If more than two partners are involved, the majority vote of the partners governs all matters within the scope of the partnership business. Therefore, the partners in the minority *cannot refuse to be bound* by an approved act unless they *dissolve* the partnership *before* the act is done so as to terminate partners' actual authority, and provide notice of dissolution to any third parties involved in the transaction so as to terminate partners' apparent authority. [*See* UPA § 18(h); *and see infra*, p. 183]

1) But Note

No partner may act contrary to an ***agreement*** among the partners without the consent of ***all*** the partners. [UPA § 18(h)]

(c) Dissolution

Requirements for an effective dissolution are discussed *infra*, p. 175 *et seq.*

d. Admissions and Representations

The rules of agency also apply to charge the partnership with the admissions and representations of any partner concerning partnership affairs made within the scope of her actual or apparent authority. [*See* UPA § 11]

2. Notice and Knowledge

Notice or knowledge to any one partner of matters pertaining to the regular partnership business is ***imputed to the partnership*** under rules similar to those for agency.

a. RUPA Reasonable Diligence Test

The RUPA provides that a partnership will be deemed to have notice or knowledge of a fact when the individual conducting the transaction ***has notice or knowledge or would have had notice or knowledge of the fact had reasonable diligence been exercised.*** Reasonable diligence can be shown through maintenance and use of reasonable routines for communicating significant information. It does not require an individual to communicate a fact unless the communication is part of the individual's regular duties or the individual has reason to know of the transaction and that the transaction would be materially affected by the information. [RUPA § 102(e)]

b. UPA Rules

(1) Notice

Under the UPA, "notice" is a communication by a third person about a matter relating to partnership business. Unless otherwise required, notice need not be in writing but may be given orally to any partner. If a writing is required, it must be given to a proper person at the partner's office or residence. [*See* UPA § 3(2)]

(2) Knowledge

Under the UPA, "knowledge" refers to information that is known or reasonably should be known by an individual partner. In determining whether the partnership will be charged with a partner's knowledge, it is important to determine whether the partner is a participating partner and when the partner acquired the knowledge.

(a) Participant

If the partner is participating in the transaction in which the knowledge is relevant, whether her knowledge will be imputed to the partnership depends on whether she acquired the knowledge before or after she became a partner.

1) Acquired When Partner

If the knowledge was acquired by the partner while she was a member of the partnership, her knowledge ***will be imputed*** to the partnership.

2) Acquired When Not a Partner

If the knowledge was acquired when the partner was not a member of the partnership, her knowledge will be ***imputed*** to the partnership ***only if*** the knowledge is "present to her mind" at the time she is acting for the partnership. [UPA § 12]

(b) Nonparticipant

Information possessed by a partner who is not participating in a transaction will be imputed to the partnership *if*, under the circumstances, the partner "reasonably could and should have communicated it" to the participating partner. There is an exception to this rule where the partner is engaged in a fraud against the partnership (*see* below). [UPA § 12]

c. Fraud

Notice to or knowledge of a partner will not be imputed to the partnership if the partner is acting fraudulently or adversely ***to the partnership.*** [RUPA § 102(f); *and see* UPA § 12]

3. Partnership Liability to Third Persons

A partnership is liable to third persons for the wrongful acts of a partner committed within the scope of the partnership business or otherwise committed with authority. [RUPA § 305; UPA § 13]

4. Partner Liability to Third Persons

In general, partners are personally liable for all obligations of the partnership. Under the RUPA, all partners are ***jointly and severally liable for all obligations*** of the partnership unless otherwise agreed by the claimant or provided by law. [RUPA § 306(a)] Under the UPA, however, liability on contracts is ***joint***; while liability for obligations arising from torts is ***joint and several.*** [UPA § 15(a), (b)]

a. Joint and Several Liability

Under the RUPA, partners are jointly and severally liable for ***all*** partnership debts and obligations, not just torts and breaches of trust. Under the UPA, partners are jointly and severally liable only for ***torts and breaches of trust*** injuring third parties. [UPA § 15(a)] When liability is both joint and several, an action may be brought against any single partner ***without*** joining the others. But note that if an action is brought against only one of the partners, any judgment obtained against him is ***not*** res judicata against the other partners in subsequent suits against them. A partnership relationship does not establish the requisite privity to invoke res judicata, because the liability is several. [**Dillard v. McKnight,** 34 Cal. 2d 209 (1949)]

(1) Torts of Co-Partners

The liability of partners for the torts of their co-partners is analogous to the rules of agency. Instead of a respondeat superior theory, however, each partner is deemed to assume liability for any tortious act committed by a co-partner. [**Madsen v. Cawthorne,** 30 Cal. App. 2d 124 (1938)—partnership liable for injuries to guest caused by intoxication of partner-driver]

(a) Exception—Torts Requiring Malice or Intent

However, if the particular tort requires a showing of malice or wrongful intent, it must appear that *each* partner sought to be held liable possessed such intent. [88 A.L.R.2d 474]

(b) Fraud

Partners can be held liable for a co-partner's fraud on third persons only if the co-partner was acting within the scope of partnership business.

e.g. **Example:** P, a partner in a brokerage firm, accepts securities from a customer of the firm and, without knowledge of the other partners, indorses the securities, converts them to cash, and deposits the cash into his own bank account. The partnership is liable.

(2) RUPA Exhaustion Requirement

The RUPA specifically provides that a judgment against the partnership entity is ***not*** a judgment against an individual partner. A judgment may be satisfied from a partner's personal assets only if there is also a judgment against the partner (which may be sought in the same action as the action against the partnership). [RUPA § 307(b), (c)] Moreover, the partner's personal assets cannot be reached unless:

(i) ***A judgment*** on the same claim has been obtained against the partnership and has ***not been fully satisfied*** after execution on the judgment;

(ii) ***The partnership is a debtor in bankruptcy***;

(iii) ***The partner has agreed that the creditor need not exhaust partnership assets***;

(iv) ***A court grants permission*** to levy on the partner's assets because the partnership assets are clearly insufficient to satisfy the judgment, exhaustion of partnership assets would be excessively burdensome, or the grant is otherwise appropriate; or

(v) ***Liability is imposed*** on the partner by ***law or contract independent*** of the existence of the partnership.

[RUPA § 307(d)]

b. Joint Liability Under UPA

Under the UPA, partners are ***jointly*** (but not severally) liable on all partnership debts and contracts. [UPA § 15(b)] When the partners have only a joint liability to creditors, a contract creditor may not proceed against any single partner. If he does so, the partner sued can generally force the joinder of all other partners—*i.e.*, they are "necessary parties" within the rules of compulsory joinder. (*See* Civil Procedure Summary.)

(1) Action Against Partnership as Entity

Of course, a creditor can always proceed against the partnership by filing suit against the partnership in the partnership name, without the necessity of joining all the partners. (*See supra*, p. 133.)

EXAM TIP

Remember, in most entity states, if a creditor sues the partnership in the partnership name alone and obtains a judgment against the partnership, the judgment may be enforced *only against partnership assets;* the creditor cannot reach an individual partner's assets unless he obtains a judgment against that partner; *i.e.*, the partner must be named and served. (*See supra*, p. 133.)

(2) Joint Liability Bars Further Actions

If a creditor obtains judgment for less than the amount sought, satisfaction of that judgment is a ***bar*** to any further action against other partners or against the partnership. [170 A.L.R. 1180]

(3) Release

In some states, a release of ***one*** partner operates to release ***all*** partners, because their liability is joint rather than several. However, some jurisdictions do not follow this rule. [*See, e.g.*, Cal. Civ. Code § 1543; **Seafirst Center Limited Partnership v. Erickson,** 898 P.2d 299 (Wash. 1995)]

(4) Silent Partner

A partner's joint liability for partnership contracts does not depend on knowledge of his existence; a silent partner (*i.e.*, one whose identity is kept secret) is liable to the same extent as known partners. It is immaterial that the creditor dealt with the partnership without relying on the "silent partner." [**Nelson, Inc. v. Tarman,** 163 Cal. App. 2d 714 (1958)]

(a) Note

Silent partners' liabilities may differ from known partners' liabilities on dissolution. (*See infra*, p. 184.)

(5) Remedies

Partnership assets are subject to attachment and execution only upon ***partnership*** debts. Thus, an attachment or execution against partnership assets is void if the claim at issue is the debt of an individual partner. "A partner's right in specific partnership property is not subject to attachment." [UPA § 25(2)]

(a) Charging Order

Therefore, the only option of a creditor who is trying to recover against the partnership on an individual partner's debt is for the creditor to obtain a *charging order* against the debtor-partner's interest in the partnership. [UPA § 28; *see infra*, pp. 168–169]

c. Distinguish—Limited Liability Partnerships

Nearly all states have enacted laws permitting the formation of limited liability partnerships ("LLPs"). LLPs are treated as general partnerships and subject to the RUPA (or UPA); however, the liability of the partners is limited—*i.e.*, the partners are ***not personally liable*** for all partnership debts and obligations. Although state statutes vary, most states require an LLP to register with the state and to adopt a business name that indicates the partnership's limited liability status (*e.g.*, by including the letters "LLP" or something similar in the partnership name). Once an LLP has registered with the state, most state statutes provide that a partner in an LLP is ***not personally liable*** for the debts or obligations of the partnership arising from the negligence, wrongful acts, or similar misconduct (*i.e.*, torts) of her co-partners. Many states go further and shield a partner from personal liability for ***any*** partnership debts or obligations, whether arising in contract, tort, or otherwise. Note though that even if a partner in an LLP is not liable for partnership debts or obligations (whether arising in contract and/or tort), the partner remains liable for her own wrongful acts and for those committed by someone whom she directly supervises.

(1) State Variations

As noted above, LLP statutes vary by state. Some states limit the formation of LLPs to professional partnerships (*e.g.*, those comprising attorneys, doctors, or accountants). Some states even require an LLP to carry insurance against such acts protected by the LLP statute, usually in an amount between $100,000 and $1 million. And as discussed above, states vary as to the extent of a partner's limited liability protection, *i.e.*, whether a partner is shielded from liability only for partnership obligations arising in tort or also those arising in contract, tort, or otherwise.

(2) RUPA

Under the RUPA, a partner in an LLP is not personally liable for partnership obligations, whether arising in contract, tort, or otherwise, solely by being or acting as a partner. A partner, however, remains personally liable for her own misconduct. [RUPA § 306] The RUPA does not require an LLP to carry insurance, nor does it restrict the formation of LLPs to professional partnerships.

EXAM TIP

If on an exam you have to determine the liability of a partner in an LLP for a tort committed by a co-partner, recall that a partner's liability is usually limited; *i.e.*, the partner is *not personally liable* for partnership debts or obligations. But be sure to check to see if the partner *engaged in the tort*; if she did, she will not be shielded from liability.

---

5. Effect of Change in Partnership Membership

a. Liability of Incoming Partner

A person admitted into an existing partnership is ***not personally liable*** for any partnership obligation incurred ***before*** the person's admission as a partner. [RUPA § 306(b)]

EXAM TIP

To determine the scope of a new partner's liability for a partnership debt under the RUPA, remember that a new partner is liable only for partnership obligations incurred *after* admission as partner.

(1) Liability Under UPA

The UPA provides that a new partner is liable with the other partners for ***all debts*** of the partnership, whether incurred ***before or after*** his admission to the partnership. He is deemed to assume his share of the liabilities upon admission, and this cannot be avoided by agreement among the partners to the contrary. However, the UPA also provides that an incoming partner's liability for debts arising before his admission to the partnership must be satisfied only out of the partnership assets. [UPA § 17] Thus, in effect, the incoming partner's personal liability for old debts is ***limited to his partnership contribution***, unless he agrees otherwise. In effect, this is the same as the RUPA rule.

b. Liability of Retiring Partner

A retiring partner remains liable on all obligations incurred by the partnership while a member of the partnership, unless there has been payment, release, or novation. She can also be held liable for obligations incurred after retirement unless she gives a proper notice of withdrawal. (*See infra*, pp. 175, 183.)

6. Liability for Crimes

The mutual agency of partners generally is ***not sufficient*** to make a partner criminally responsible for the crimes of a co-partner, even if the crime was committed within the scope of partnership business, unless the partner participated in the commission of the crime with the co-partner.

7. Third Person's Liability to Partnership for Injuries to Partner

A partnership generally has ***no right*** to recover damages from a third person because of injuries inflicted on a member of the partnership; *i.e.*, a partner is not considered a "servant" or employee of the partnership. [**Sharfman v. State,** *supra*, p. 98]

COMPARISON OF A PARTNER'S LIABILITY TO THIRD PERSONS UNDER THE PARTNERSHIP ACTS	RUPA	UPA	RUPA-LLP
LIABILITY FOR CONTRACTS	Joint and several	Joint	Not liable
LIABILITY FOR TORTS	Joint and several	Joint and several	Not liable except for own misconduct
LIABILITY FOR CO-PARTNER'S CRIMES	Not liable	Not liable	Not liable

Chapter Ten: Partnership Property and Partners' Property Rights

CONTENTS	PAGE

Key Exam Issues

Sometimes in an exam question it will be necessary to determine if property is partnership property (*i.e.*, property belonging to the partnership) or the individual property of a partner that may have been loaned to the partnership. For example, when an action is brought against the partnership as an entity, it may be important to distinguish whether certain property is partnership property because any judgment against the partnership may be satisfied only out of partnership property. Similarly, the issue of whether property is partnership property may arise when a partner is sued on a personal obligation, because any judgment against the partner can be satisfied only out of that partner's individual property. To determine whether property is partnership property, consider the following, which tend to prove it is partnership property:

1. Was the property acquired ***in the name of the partnership?***
2. Was the property acquired ***in the name of a partner with any indication of partnership?***
3. Was the property ***purchased with partnership assets?***

Once you have decided that a certain asset is partnership property, you will probably have to discuss the partners' rights in that property. The RUPA grants partners ***no specific rights in partnership property***. Under the UPA, however, partners' rights in partnership property arise from the form of ownership known as ***tenancy in partnership***. This tenancy gives partners the right to possess the property only for partnership purposes. In any case, under either act, partners cannot assign their rights in partnership property or have partnership property attached to satisfy their personal debts. Upon death, a partner's rights in partnership property vest in the surviving partners and are not subject to dower or curtesy, etc.

A partner's interest in partnership property must be distinguished from his interest in the partnership, which is his right to his share in the partnership's profits, losses, and distributions. This right is assignable and can be attached by a charging order. However, the assignee receives only the right to receive the distributions the partner would have received; he receives no right to participate in management of the partnership.

A. Partnership Property

1. RUPA Rules

Generally, property acquired by a partnership is ***partnership*** property; it does not belong to the partners. [RUPA § 203] The RUPA provides four specific provisions for determining whether property is partnership property:

APPROACH TO DETERMINING WHETHER PROPERTY IS PARTNERSHIP PROPERTY UNDER THE RUPA

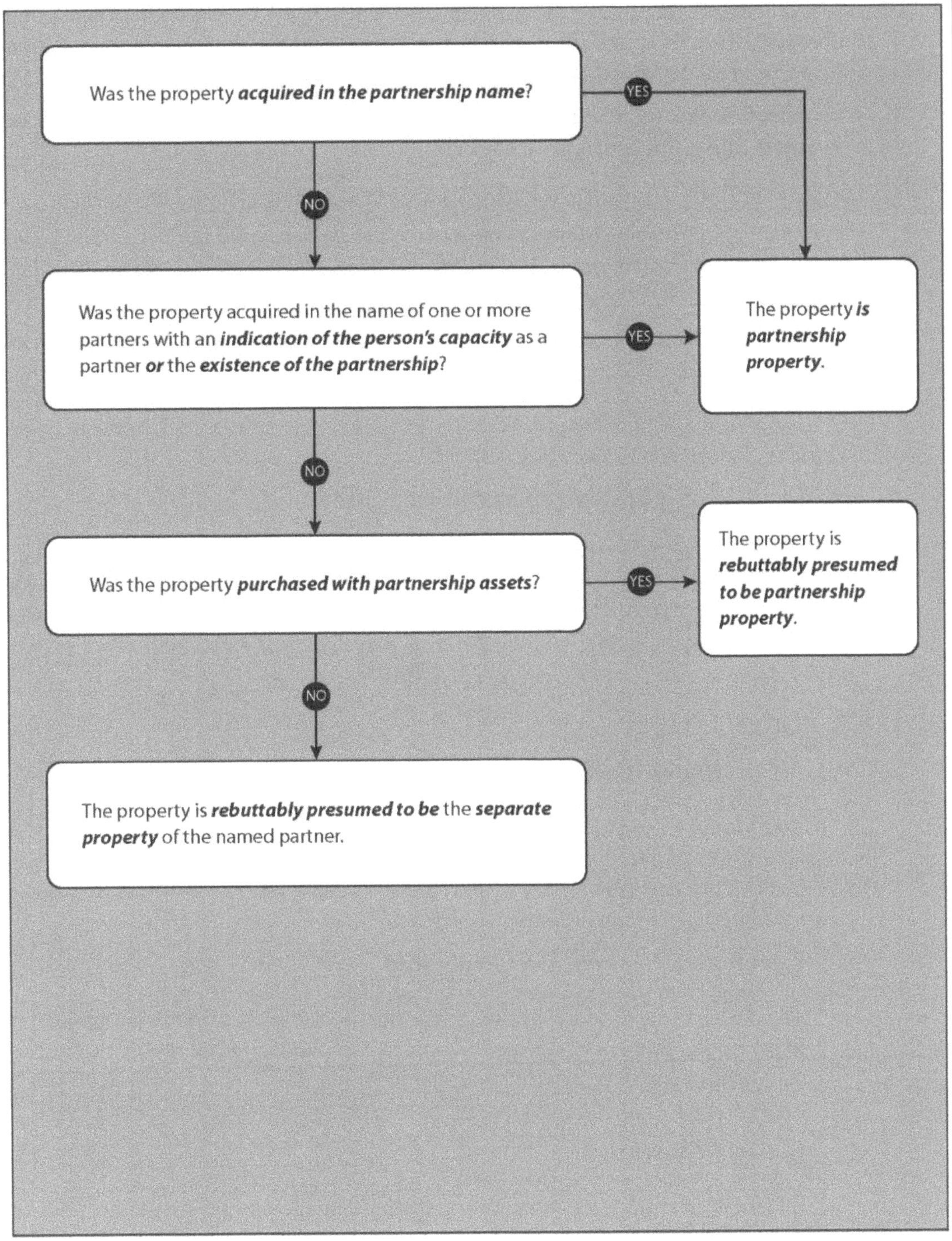

a. Acquired in Name of Partnership—Property Deemed to Be Partnership Property

If property is acquired in the name of the partnership, it is partnership property. [RUPA § 204(a)(*l*)] Property is considered to be "in the name of the partnership" not only when it is held in the actual name of the partnership, but also when it is held in the name of one or more partners in their capacity as partners ***and*** the instrument that transferred title ***indicates the name of the partnership.*** [RUPA § 204(b)]

b. Acquired in Name of Partner with Indication of Partnership—Property Deemed to Be Partnership Property

Property is also considered to be partnership property if it is acquired in the name of one or more partners and the instrument transferring title ***indicates the named person's capacity*** as a partner ***or*** the ***existence of the partnership***, but without an indication of the name of the partnership. [RUPA § 204(a)(2)]

c. Purchased with Partnership Assets—Property Presumed to Be Partnership Property

There is a rebuttable presumption that property is partnership property if it is ***purchased with partnership assets.*** [RUPA § 204(c)]

d. Distinguish—Separate Property Presumption

If property is acquired in the name of one or more partners and the instrument transferring title indicates neither the person's capacity as partner nor the existence of the partnership, ***and*** the property is purchased without use of partnership assets, there is a rebuttable presumption that the property is the ***separate property of the named partner*** even if it is used for partnership purposes. [RUPA § 204(d)]

2. UPA Rules

a. What Constitutes Partnership Property

In the absence of an agreement, there is no limitation or restriction on what can become the property of the partnership. Under the UPA, "all property originally brought into the partnership stock or subsequently acquired, by purchase or otherwise, ***on account of the partnership*** is partnership property." [UPA § 8(1)]

(1) Intention of Partnership Ownership

The chief criterion for determining whether something is partnership property is the intent of the partners to devote the property to partnership purposes. It must appear that the property was acquired with the intention that it be a partnership asset. If the partners' intentions are in doubt, the courts rely on the factors discussed below.

(2) Indicia of Intention

If there is no clear expression of the partners' intention as to ownership of the asset in question, the courts consider the facts and circumstances surrounding acquisition and ownership of the asset. However, no factor alone will be conclusive.

(a) Title

Under the UPA, the fact that the asset is acquired or held in the name of the partnership, rather than in the name of one of the partners, is *not* conclusive as to its ownership. The name in which property is held may be entirely a matter of convenience. Thus, although the status of title will be taken into account, the courts generally consider other factors as being more indicative of the partners' intentions. [*See, e.g.*, **Wilen v. Wilen,** 486 A.2d 775 (Md. 1985)]

(b) Purchase with Partnership Funds

The purchase of property with partnership funds may justify a conclusion that the asset belongs to the partnership. Indeed, the UPA provides that "*unless the contrary intention appears*, property acquired with partnership funds is partnership property." [UPA § 8(2)]

(c) Improvements by Partnership

The fact that partnership funds have been used to improve the asset in question is entitled to some weight, but is usually not determinative—particularly where the improvements are severable from the asset.

(d) Relation of Property to Business

The more closely the asset is associated with the business operations of the partnership, the more likely it will be held to be a partnership asset. This is particularly true when the dispute is between a partner and the partnership—the courts view the partner as a *trustee* for the partnership, and as such the partner has an obligation to purchase assets related to partnership operations on behalf of the partnership (rather than acquiring them for himself). [*See, e.g.*, **Secrest v. Nobles,** 223 P. 863 (Okla. 1924)]

(e) Use of Property

Use of an asset in the partnership business is not enough by itself to establish an intention that the partnership owns the asset—*e.g.*, it may merely be a loan of the asset to the partnership. However, such use may be relevant in conjunction with other factors tending to show partnership ownership (*e.g.*, purchase with partnership funds). [*See* **Strother v. Strother,** 436 So. 2d 847 (Ala. 1983)]

(f) Status in Partnership Books

The fact that property is listed as a partnership asset on the books and records of the partnership is given considerable weight, especially if all parties are shown to have knowledge of this fact. [**Robinson Bank v. Miller,** 38 N.E. 1078 (Ill. 1894)]

EXAM TIP

Unlike the RUPA, the UPA does not have specific provisions for determining whether property is partnership property. If you have to determine if property is partnership property under the UPA, you must first look to the *intent* of the partners. If the partners' intentions are unclear, then you will have to consider such factors as how title of the property is held, if partnership funds were used to purchase the property, how the property is used, etc. Remember, however, that *none of these factors alone* is conclusive evidence that the property is partnership property.

---

3. Real Property

a. Common Law

As noted previously, a partnership at common law was deemed to be merely an aggregate of individuals, and hence incapable of taking title to real property (*see supra*, p. 132). A grant of such property to a partnership was ineffective to pass title, and only an equitable interest passed to the partners. [**Donohoe v. Rogers,** 168 Cal. 700 (1914)]

b. RUPA and UPA View

However, both the RUPA and UPA clearly provide that any estate in real property may be acquired and held ***in the partnership name.*** [RUPA § 204; UPA § 8(3)]

4. Insurance Policies

Very frequently, partners purchase "cross-life insurance policies" on each other's lives.

e.g. **Example:** By agreement between the partners, an insurance policy is taken out on the life of partner A, on which B is shown to be the owner and beneficiary; a similar policy is taken out on B's life, with A as owner and beneficiary. Premiums are customarily paid out of the partnership funds, but are usually charged to the draws of each partner. The problem arises when a partner dies, and the benefits are paid to the survivor. Are these benefits partnership assets, which must be used to pay off the debts of the partnership, or are they the sole property of the surviving partner to be used as he pleases?

a. Agreement

Frequently, the problem is covered by an agreement between the partners—*e.g.*, a provision that insurance benefits paid on the death of one partner ***must*** be used by the other partner to ***buy out*** the interest of the decedent partner in the partnership.

b. No Agreement

In the absence of an agreement or other clear expression of intent, many courts hold that the benefits belong outright to the surviving partner who is shown as "owner" and "beneficiary." Thus, the fact that the premiums were paid with partnership funds, or that the partnership itself may be in need of funds to pay creditors, is disregarded. [83 A.L.R.2d 1347]

B. Partners' Property Rights

1. In General

The property rights of a partner are: (i) the rights in ***specific partnership property***, (ii) an ***interest in the partnership***, and (iii) the ***right to participate in the management*** of the partnership. [*See* UPA § 24]

2. Rights in Specific Partnership Property

a. RUPA Approach

Under the RUPA, a partner is not a co-owner of partnership property and has ***no transferable interest in partnership property.*** Therefore, he cannot ***voluntarily or involuntarily*** transfer partnership property. [RUPA § 501] This position is in keeping with the fact that the RUPA specifically treats a partnership as an entity (*see supra*, p. 133), and as such, partnership property is owned by the partnership and not the individual partners. Thus, adoption of the entity theory has the effect of protecting partnership property from a partner's personal creditors. [*See* RUPA § 501, comment] Also, the partner's spouse or family are not entitled to any rights in the partnership property. [RUPA § 501, comment]

b. UPA Approach

Under the UPA, a partner is a ***tenant in partnership*** with her co-partners as to each asset of the partnership. [UPA § 25(1)] The incidents of this tenancy are as follows:

(1) Possession

Each partner has an ***equal right*** with her co-partners to possess partnership property for partnership purposes, but has no right to possess it for any other purpose without the consent of her co-partners. [UPA § 25(2)(a)]

(2) Assignability

A partner's right in specific partnership property is ***not assignable***, except in connection with the rights of all of the partners in the property. [UPA § 25(2)(b)]

(3) Attachment of Specific Property

A partner's interest in specific partnership property is ***not subject to attachment*** or execution at the instance of her individual creditors. It ***is*** subject to attachment or execution on a claim against the partnership. [UPA § 25(2)(c)]

(4) Death

Upon a partner's death, her rights in partnership property vest in the ***surviving partners*** (or in the executor or administrator of the last surviving partner). [UPA § 25(2)(d)] Thus, partnership property is not a part of a deceased partner's estate when determining the value of the decedent's interest in the partnership (*see* below; *and see infra*, pp. 182–183).

(5) Family Interests

A partner's right in partnership property is ***not subject to family allowances, dower, curtesy***, etc. [UPA § 25(2)(e)] Neither is it community property. [**Estate of Grivel,** 10 Cal. 2d 454 (1937)]

3. Interest in Partnership

A partner's interest in the partnership is his share of the profits and losses, and the right to receive distributions. This interest is treated as ***personal*** property. [RUPA § 502; and *see* UPA § 26]

a. Importance of Classification

The classification of a partner's interest as personal property could be important for ***inheritance*** purposes. For example, if any distinction is made in a partner's will (or under the laws of intestate succession) as to inheritance of his "personal" as opposed to "real" property, his interest in the partnership is treated as personalty. And this is true even where all of the partnership's assets are real property. [**Comstock v. Fiorella,** 260 Cal. App. 2d 262 (1968)]

(1) Equitable Conversion

The personal property classification of a partner's interest in the partnership is an application of the doctrine of equitable conversion (*see* Remedies Summary); *i.e.*, a partner's rights are ***equitable*** in nature, and the partnership itself holds full legal title to the property.

b. Assignment of Interest

A partner's interest in the partnership is assignable unless there is an agreement to the contrary. Such an assignment will not itself cause the partner's dissociation or dissolve the partnership. [RUPA § 503(a)(*l*), (2); UPA § 27(1)]

EXAM TIP

Notice the difference between the assignment of a partner's interest in the partnership and the assignment of a partner's right in specific partnership property: A partner's *interest* in the partnership *is* assignable, whereas a partner's right in *specific partnership property* is *not* assignable.

(1) Rights of Assignee

The assignee is merely entitled to receive the distributions to which the assigning partner would have been entitled. The assignee does ***not become a partner***; and he is not entitled to interfere with management of the partnership or to exercise any rights with respect to its affairs. [75 A.L.R.2d 1036; RUPA § 503(a)(3), (b); UPA § 27(1)]

(a) Rights at Dissolution

If the partnership dissolves, an assignee of a partner's interest is entitled to whatever the partner would have received. The assignee may require an accounting only from the date of the last accounting agreed to by all of the partners. [RUPA § 503(b), (c); UPA § 27(2)]

1) Note

The RUPA also gives the assignee the right to seek a judicial determination that it is equitable to wind up the partnership business. [RUPA § 503(b)(3)]

(2) Rights of Assignor

Generally, the assignor retains all rights and duties of a partner other than the interest in distributions that was transferred. [RUPA § 503(d); UPA § 27] The assigning partner also remains liable on all partnership debts.

(3) Effect of Assignment

Under the RUPA, a partner who transfers all or substantially all of his partnership interest may be expelled by the other partners, and the partner would thereby be dissociated from the partnership (*see infra*, p. 173). [RUPA § 601] Under the UPA, an assignment of all of a partner's interest in the partnership will not result in a dissolution of the partnership unless the partner ceases performing his partnership duties.

c. Rights of Creditors of Individual Partners

A creditor of an individual partner has no right to execute or attach partnership assets or property; hence any such attachment or execution is void and ineffective. [**Taylor v. S & M Lamp Co.,** 190 Cal. App. 2d 700 (1961)]

(1) Charging Order Remedy

The creditor's sole remedy is to prosecute her claim to ***judgment*** against the debtor-partner, and thereafter to obtain a ***charging order*** against the debtor-partner's interest in the partnership. The partnership is thereby impressed with a lien in favor of the creditor, who is entitled to all future distributions otherwise flowing to the debtor-partner until the judgment is satisfied. (The debtor's partnership interest may also be sold under court order, in appropriate cases.) [RUPA § 504; UPA § 28]

d. Death

The rights of a deceased partner's estate in the decedent's partnership interest are discussed in detail *infra*, pp. 173–174, 182–183.

e. Family Rights

The partner's interest in the partnership ***is*** subject to family allowance, and is generally treated as community property in community property jurisdictions. [*See* **Wood v. Gunther,** 89 Cal. App. 2d 718 (1949)]

EXAM TIP

If you encounter a fact pattern in which a partner dies and there is a dispute as to whom his share in the partnership passes, remember that his share in the *partnership interest* is subject to family allowance. *Specific partnership property*, however, does not pass to the partner's spouse or family, but remains in the partnership.

4. Right to Participate in Management

As discussed in the previous chapter, each partner has an ***equal*** right to participate in the management of the partnership (*see supra*, p. 144).

COMPARISON OF A PARTNER'S PROPERTY RIGHTS

IN SPECIFIC PARTNERSHIP PROPERTY	IN PARTNERSHIP INTEREST
A partner has an equal right with co-partners to possess partnership property for partnership purposes (UPA)	A partner has a right to share in the partnership's profits and losses
An individual partner has **no right to assign** partnership property	A partner has a right to assign her partnership interest
A partner's individual creditor **may not attach** partnership property	A partner's individual creditor may obtain a charging order against the partner's interest in the partnership
A partner's right in partnership property is **not subject** to family allowance	A partner's interest in the partnership is subject to family allowance

Chapter Eleven: Dissociation, Dissolution, and Winding Up of a Partnership

CONTENTS	PAGE

Key Exam Issues

Often, an exam question will involve a situation where a partner leaves the partnership, requiring you to determine the status of the partnership and the rights and liabilities of the parties. Be sure you understand the difference between dissociation and dissolution.

Dissociation: The RUPA adopts a modern approach that recognizes that it is common for partners to leave the partnership and the partnership to continue. The RUPA uses the term "dissociation" to denote the change in the relationship caused by a partner's ceasing to be associated in the carrying on of the business. Dissociation terminates the partner's right to participate in the business and the partner's duty to refrain from competing with the business, but it ***does not necessarily terminate the partnership***. The ***dissociation*** of a partner occurs when, *e.g.*, a partner is expelled, a partner notifies the partnership of intent to withdraw, or a partner dies. If the dissociation does not result in dissolution (*see* below), the partnership must buy out the interest of the dissociated partner. The dissociated partner remains liable on partnership obligations incurred before the dissociation, unless the creditor releases the dissociated partner from liability. Note that the UPA does not recognize dissociation—the partnership is dissolved whenever a partner leaves the partnership.

Dissolution: Dissolution refers to the process of terminating and winding up the partnership. The events giving rise to dissolution differ under the RUPA and UPA; however, the procedure for terminating the partnership is substantially similar. The actual authority of the partners to act as agents for the partnership is terminated, except for winding up the partnership's business. Note that under the UPA, dissolution occurs whenever a partner leaves the partnership. If dissolution is proper, all partners have a right to wind up the partnership's affairs. If it is wrongful, the partners may have an action for damages against the wrongful partner, and may be able to purchase the wrongful partner's interest. If dissolution is caused by the death of a partner, the surviving partners may wind up and must account to the deceased partner's estate for the value of her interest; however, they are entitled to compensation for winding up. After dissolution, the assets of the partnership are generally converted into cash, and the cash must be distributed to creditors and partners.

A. Dissociation Under RUPA

1. Introduction

Under the UPA, when a partner leaves a partnership, the partnership is dissolved, even if the remaining partners want to continue the partnership business (in which case, a new partnership is formed among the remaining partners). The RUPA recognizes that in modern partnerships it is common for a partner to leave and for the partnership to continue. Rather than consider every such change in membership a full dissolution, the RUPA has bifurcated the UPA dissolution concept into two separate components: dissociation and dissolution. A partner's leaving the partnership is a ***"dissociation."*** If the partnership goes on after a dissociation, the partnership is not dissolved. The term ***"dissolution"*** is used to signify the process for actually ending the partnership.

a. Effect of Dissociation

Dissociation terminates a partner's right to participate in the business, and the partner's duty to refrain from competing with the business. [RUPA § 603]

(1) But Note

Dissociation does not necessarily terminate the partnership. The RUPA spells out the situations in which the partnership must be dissolved and wound up (*see infra,* p. 176 *et seq.*), but if one of those situations does not occur, the partnership can continue; however, the partnership must buy out the dissociated partner's interest in the partnership (*see infra,* p. 174 *et seq.*).

b. Events Causing Dissociation

The RUPA provides that a partner will become dissociated from the partnership upon:

(i) ***The partnership's receipt of the partner's notice to withdraw*** from the partnership;

(ii) ***The happening of an event agreed to in the partnership agreement*** as a cause of dissociation;

(iii) ***The partner's expulsion pursuant to the partnership agreement;***

(iv) ***The partner's expulsion pursuant to a unanimous vote of the partners*** where it is unlawful to carry on the business with that partner, substantially all of the partner's interest in the partnership has been transferred, or the expelled partner is either a corporate entity that has given up or lost its right to do business in the corporate form or a partnership that has dissolved;

(v) ***Judicial determination of the partner's expulsion*** on application of another partner or the partnership because the partner engaged in wrongful conduct that adversely and materially affected the partnership, the partner willfully breached the partnership agreement or statutory standard of conduct, or the partner is engaged in conduct that makes it impracticable to carry on the partnership business with the partner;

(vi) ***The partner's bankruptcy, assignment of assets for the benefit of creditors, or acquiescence to the appointment of a trustee, receiver, or the like*** to take substantially all of the partner's property, or failure to have an appointment of such person vacated within 90 days;

(vii) ***The death*** of the partner, ***appointment of a guardian or conservator*** for the partner, or ***judicial determination that the partner has become incapable of performing his duties*** to the partnership;

(viii) ***If the partner is a trust, distribution of the trust's interest in the partnership*** (except merely to substitute a successor trustee);

(ix) ***If the partner is an estate, distribution of the estate's interest in the partnership*** (except merely to substitute a personal representative); or

(x) ***Termination of a partner who is not an individual, partnership, corporation, trust, or estate*** (*e.g.,* limited liability company).

[RUPA § 601]

c. Wrongful Dissociation

A partner who wrongfully dissociates is liable for any damages caused by the wrongful dissociation. A partner's dissociation will be deemed wrongful if: (i) it is in ***breach of an express provision of the partnership agreement;*** **or (ii)** the partnership is for a ***definite term or particular undertaking,*** and the partner ***withdraws, is expelled, or becomes bankrupt*** before the end of the term or accomplishment of the undertaking. [RUPA § 602]

2. Effect of Dissociation Where Business Not Wound Up

a. Purchase of Dissociated Partner's Interest

If a partner's dissociation does not result in a dissolution of the partnership, the partnership must buy out the dissociated partner's interest in the partnership. The buyout price is equivalent to the greater of the amount that would be distributable to the partner if, on the date of dissociation, partnership assets were sold at their liquidation value or their value if the partnership were sold as a going concern without the dissociated partner. [RUPA § 701 (a), (b)]

(1) Liabilities Offset

Damages for wrongful dissociation and all other amounts that the dissociating partner owes must be offset against the buyout price. [RUPA § 701(c)]

(2) Interest

Interest must be paid on the buyout price from the date of dissociation to the date of payment. [RUPA § 701(b)]

(3) Indemnification

The partnership must indemnify the dissociated partner against all partnership liabilities except liabilities incurred by the dissociated partner's acts after dissociation that bind the partnership (*see infra,* p. 174). [RUPA § 701(d)]

(4) Where Partner Disputes Value

If the dissociated partner disputes the value of his partnership interest, and an agreement cannot be reached as to value within 120 days after the dissociated partner demands payment in writing, the partnership must pay the dissociated partner the value of his interest based on what the partnership estimates to be the buyout price and accrued interest. [RUPA § 701(e)]

(a) Action Against Partnership

If the dissociated partner disagrees with the buyout price, offsets, etc., the partner may bring an action against the partnership within 120 days after the partnership has tendered payment or an offer to pay, or within one year after the partner's written demand if there has been no payment or tender. The court may assess attorneys' fees and costs against a party that the court finds to have acted not in good faith. [RUPA § 701(i)]

(5) Dissociation Before Expiration of Term or Completion of Undertaking

A partner who dissociates before the expiration of a partnership term or completion of a partnership undertaking is not entitled to payment of the buyout price before the expiration of the term or completion of the undertaking, unless the partner can prove that payment will not harm the partnership. [RUPA § 701(h)]

b. Dissociated Partner's Power to Bind Partnership

Under the RUPA, a partnership will be bound by any act of a dissociated partner done within ***two years*** after the dissociation if:

(i) ***The act was within the partner's apparent authority;***

(ii) The ***other party reasonably believed the dissociated partner was still a partner;*** and

(iii) ***The other party did not have notice or knowledge of the dissociation.***

[RUPA § 702(a)] Of course, the partnership can hold the dissociated partner liable for losses it incurs as a result of the dissociated partner's conduct. [RUPA § 702(b)]

c. Dissociated Partner's Liability to Others

A dissociated partner remains liable on partnership obligations incurred before the dissociation. [RUPA § 703(a)] The dissociated partner can also be held liable on partnership obligations incurred within ***two years*** after dissociation if the party dealing with the partnership reasonably believed the dissociated partner was still a partner and did not have notice or knowledge of the partner's dissociation.

(1) Release

Of course, the creditor may agree to release the dissociated partner from liability. [RUPA § 703(c)] A release will also occur if the creditor knows of the dissociation and agrees with the partnership to materially alter the nature or time of payment of the obligation without the dissociated partner's consent. [RUPA § 703(d)]

d. Constructive Notice Through Statement of Dissociation

To limit liability after dissociation, the dissociated partner or the partnership may file with the state a statement of dissociation. Nonpartners will be deemed to have notice of the dissociation ***90 days*** after the statement of dissociation is filed. [RUPA § 704]

PARTNERSHIP LIABILITY FOR ACTS OF DISSOCIATED PARTNER
A PARTNERSHIP WILL BE BOUND BY THE ACT OF A DISSOCIATED PARTNER IF:
☑ The act occurred within ***two years*** of the partner's dissociation
☑ The act was within the partner's ***apparent authority***
☑ The third party ***reasonably believed*** that the dissociated partner ***was still a partner***
☑ The third party ***did not have notice* or knowledge of the partner's dissociation***
**Note:* A third party will be deemed to have notice of a partner's dissociation 90 days after a statement of dissociation is filed.

e. Continued Use of Partnership Name

Continued use of the partnership name, even if it includes the dissociated partner's name, does not alter the liabilities discussed above. [RUPA § 705]

B. Dissolution

1. Introduction

Dissolution does ***not terminate*** the partnership. It is merely a change in the legal relationship of the partners. It does not mean that business has ended or that any assets have been distributed to partners. The partnership continues until the winding up of partnership affairs is completed. [RUPA § 802; UPA § 30] Thus, even after dissolution has occurred, the partnership relationship continues.

e.g. **Example:** In an action against the partnership after dissolution but before the final winding up of affairs, service on one partner is sufficient to obtain jurisdiction over the partnership. [136 A.L.R. 1071]

2. RUPA Approach

Under the RUPA, dissolution connotes the process that leads to termination of the partnership.

a. Events Causing Dissolution and Winding Up

A partnership is dissolved and its affairs must be wound up upon:

(i) ***Receipt by a partnership at will of notice*** from a partner, other than a dissociated partner, of an ***express will to withdraw***;

(ii) ***In a partnership for a definite term*** or particular undertaking: (a) within 90 days after a partner's death, bankruptcy, or wrongful dissociation, the ***express will of at least half the remaining partners*** to wind up; (b) the express will of ***all*** partners to wind up; or (c) the ***expiration of the term or accomplishment of the undertaking***;

(iii) ***Occurrence of an event that the partnership agreement states will cause dissolution,*** unless ***all*** partners agree to continue the business;

(iv) ***Occurrence of an event that makes it unlawful to carry on the partnership business*** (unless cured within 90 days);

(v) ***Judicial determination, on application of a partner***, that the economic purpose of the partnership is likely to be unreasonably frustrated, that another partner has engaged in conduct that makes it not reasonably practicable to carry on the partnership business, or that it is otherwise not reasonably practicable to carry on the partnership business; or

(vi) ***Judicial determination, on application of a transferee*** of a partner's interest, that winding up is equitable (if the partnership was for a definite term or particular undertaking at the time of transfer, a judicial dissolution cannot occur until the term expires or the undertaking is accomplished).

[RUPA § 801]

b. Right to Wind Up

Any partner who has not ***wrongfully*** dissociated may participate in winding up, or the legal representative of the last surviving partner may wind up. The RUPA specifically allows the person winding up to run the business ***as a going concern for a reasonable time.*** [RUPA § 803] After dissolution, the partnership will be bound by any partner's act appropriate for winding up or, if the other party does not know of the dissolution, any act within the partner's apparent authority. [RUPA § 804] However, a partner who binds the partnership to an act not appropriate for winding up is liable to the other partners for any loss that is caused by the act. [RUPA § 806]

c. Statement of Dissolution

After dissolution, a partner who has not wrongfully dissociated may file a statement of dissolution. The statement is sufficient to cancel any additional authority granted under a filed statement of authority. A nonpartner will be deemed to have notice of the dissolution 90 days after the statement of dissolution is filed. [RUPA § 805]

d. Distribution of Assets

Under the RUPA, when a partnership is formed, an account is established for each partner. The account is credited with the money and value of property contributed by the partner to the partnership, plus any profits due the partner. The account is charged with any distributions made to the partner and with the partner's share of any losses. [RUPA § 401] On dissolution, after all creditors (including partners who are creditors) are paid, positive balances in the partners' accounts are paid to the partners; any partner with a negative balance must contribute that amount to the partnership. [RUPA § 807(a), (b)]

EXAM TIP

Notice that in the distribution of assets under the RUPA, there is no distinction between creditors who are partners and creditors who are not partners: All creditors, *including partners who are creditors*, are paid first. This differs from the UPA, which provides that assets are first distributed to creditors who are *not* partners and then to creditor partners.

---

(1) Where Partner Fails to Contribute to Losses

If a partner fails to contribute her share of the losses, the other partners must pay that share in the proportion in which they share losses, but they have a cause of action against the noncontributing partner. [RUPA § 807(c)]

(2) Deceased Partner

The estate of a deceased partner is liable for the partner's obligation to contribute to the partnership. [RUPA § 807(e)]

3. UPA Approach

Under the UPA, "the dissolution of a partnership is the change in the relation of the partners caused by any partner ceasing to be associated in the carrying on, as distinguished from the winding up, of the business." [UPA § 29]

a. Note

Older cases often use the term "dissolution" as a synonym for "winding up" and "termination," which are different concepts under the UPA. (*See infra*, pp. 184, 188.)

b. Causes of Dissolution

Dissolution may be caused in any of three ways: (i) by act of the partners, (ii) by operation of law, or (iii) by court decree.

(1) By Act of the Partners

(a) Per Partnership Agreement

If the partnership agreement provides that the partnership is to last for a specific period of time (*e.g.*, one year), or until a certain project is accomplished (*e.g.*, until certain property is sold), the expiration of the period or accomplishment of the objective dissolves the partnership. [UPA § 31(1)(a)]

1) Note

Even when the partnership is for a fixed term or particular undertaking, any partner can effectively terminate the partnership relationship ***prior*** to the expiration of the term or accomplishment of the undertaking by express will. (*See* discussion below.)

2) **Distinguish**

Conversely, the partners ***can***—at the expiration of the partnership term or accomplishment of the particular partnership undertaking—***continue*** the partnership business, in which case they become partners at will. In this situation, the rights and duties of the partners remain the same as they were at the expiration of the partnership term or accomplishment of the particular partnership undertaking, to the extent this is consistent with a partnership at will. [UPA § 23]

(b) **By Will of Partner**

The partnership relation is personal and cannot be specifically enforced in equity; *i.e.*, a person cannot be forced to become a partner, or to remain a partner, when he does not wish to do so. Thus, any or all of the partners can effect a dissolution of the partnership *at any time*, merely by expressing their will to dissolve the relationship. [**Zeibak v. Nasser,** *supra*, p. 132]

1) **Partnership at Will—No Violation of Agreement**

If the partnership is at will (*i.e.*, no definite term or particular undertaking specified), the partner's election to dissolve is not in violation of the agreement. His right to dissolve at any time is deemed implicit in a partnership at will, and even if his dissolving the partnership results in a loss to the other partners, he cannot be held responsible for that loss. [UPA § 31(*l*)(b)]

a) **Good Faith Limitation**

However, this assumes that the right to dissolve is exercised in good faith. If a partner acts in bad faith—as by attempting to appropriate personally some special advantage or opportunity that was coming to the partnership—this would be treated as a ***wrongful*** dissolution, and his rights on dissolution would be affected accordingly (*see* below). In other words, a partner cannot use his right to dissolve to exclude his co-partners from a business opportunity that rightfully belongs to the partnership. [**Page v. Page,** 55 Cal. 2d 192 (1961)]

2) **Partnership for Fixed Term or Particular Undertaking—Violation of Agreement**

If the partnership is for a fixed term or particular undertaking, dissolving the partnership prior to the term's expiration or accomplishment of the undertaking ***is a violation*** of the agreement. A partner still has the power (albeit not the right) to dissolve in this situation [UPA § 31(2)], but he may be liable for any losses caused by the dissolution. (*See infra*, p. 182.)

3) **What Constitutes Will to Dissolve**

For a partnership to be dissolved at the will of a partner, the partner must have evidenced an intention to discontinue the partnership relation.

a) **Assignment of Partnership Interest**

A partner's assignment of his interest in the partnership is some evidence of his intention to dissolve, but it is not conclusive. "A conveyance by a partner of his interest in the partnership does not of itself dissolve the partnership." [UPA § 27]

b) **Levy of Charging Order**

Similarly, the levy of a charging order on the interest of a debtor-partner [UPA § 28; *and see supra*, p. 169] does not of itself dissolve the partnership.

c) **Right of Assignee to Obtain Dissolution**

The ***assignee*** of the partnership interest (or holder of the charging order) can obtain a ***judicial dissolution*** of the partnership after expiration of the partnership term or accomplishment of a particular partnership undertaking, or, in a partnership at will, whenever he acquires the interest or the charging order is levied. [UPA § 32(2)]

EXAM TIP

Remember that every partner has the *power* to dissolve the partnership by *express will* at any time, even if the dissolution is in violation of the partnership agreement; however, if a partner dissolves the partnership by express will in contravention of the partnership agreement, that partner may be liable to the partnership for any losses that result because of the dissolution.

(c) **Mutual Assent of Partners**

As indicated above, persons cannot be forced to be partners. Thus, a partnership may be dissolved by the mutual assent of all of the partners who have not assigned their interests or had them charged for their separate debts. [UPA § 31(*l*)(c)]

1) **Note**

Such a dissolution is rightful even if a specified term has not terminated or a specified undertaking has not been accomplished.

(d) **Expulsion of Partner**

The expulsion of a partner will also cause a dissolution of the partnership. If the expulsion is bona fide and pursuant to a power reserved in the partnership agreement, there is no violation of the agreement and the expelling partners are not liable for any resulting losses. (The result would be contra, however, if the expulsion were made in bad faith, or without any right to expel reserved in the partnership agreement.) [UPA § 31(1)(d)]

(2) **By Operation of Law**

(a) **Illegality**

Dissolution of partnership also results on the occurrence of any event making it unlawful for the partnership to continue in business. [UPA § 31(3)]

1) **Note**

Although the illegality of the partnership business may be a ground for dissolution, the partners may thereafter decide to change their business and continue the partnership relation.

(b) **Death of Partner or Bankruptcy of Partner or Partnership**

A partner's credit and services are deemed to be an integral part of his contribution to the partnership. Thus, in the absence of an agreement to the contrary, the partnership is dissolved upon the death of a partner or bankruptcy of the partnership or of any partner. [UPA § 31(4), (5)] In this situation, the surviving (or nonbankrupt) partners have the right to wind up the partnership affairs. (*See* below.)

(3) **By Decree of Court**

Any of the acts or events enumerated above is sufficient in itself to dissolve the partnership. However, certain other acts or events may also lead to a dissolution, provided there is an appropriate ***judicial declaration.***

(a) **Grounds for Judicial Dissolution**

The UPA provides that on application of a partner, a court "shall decree" a dissolution of the partnership in the following situations:

1) **Incompetency of Partner**

If a partner has been declared incompetent in any judicial proceeding, or otherwise shown to be of unsound mind [UPA § 32(*l*)(a)];

2) **Incapability of Partner**

If a partner is or has become incapable of performing his part of the partnership contract [UPA § 32(*l*)(b)] (*but note:* illness or incapacity does not in itself justify a dissolution; however, if it appears that the incapacity is permanent and will materially affect the partner's ability to discharge the duties assumed by him under the partnership agreement, a court decree of dissolution is proper [**Raymond v. Vaughan,** 21 N.E. 566 (Ill. 1889)]);

3) **Improper Conduct of Partner**

If a partner has been guilty of conduct tending to prejudice the carrying on of the business, or otherwise constituting a breach of the partnership agreement (*e.g.*, if the partner is acting to further his own interests rather than those of the partnership, or is wrongfully excluding his co-partners from the business) [UPA § 32(1)(c), (d)];

4) **Partnership Loss Inevitable**

If the business can be carried on only at a loss [UPA § 32(*l*)(e)]; or

5) **Dissolution Equitable**

If there are other circumstances "rendering a dissolution equitable" [UPA § 32(*l*)(f)].

(b) Nature of Proceeding

A suit for dissolution is equitable in nature, and the court therefore generally considers all the facts and circumstances in granting or withholding relief. [**Bates v. McTammany,** 10 Cal. 2d 697 (1938)—court could refuse decree of dissolution if it would result in substantial loss to innocent partner]

(c) Accounting

The judicial action is generally for dissolution and an accounting, since the court has to determine the credits and debits to each partner in order to provide for distribution of the partnership assets. (*See supra*, p. 147.)

CAUSES OF DISSOLUTION UNDER THE UPA—A SUMMARY		
ACT OF THE PARTNERS	**OPERATION OF LAW**	**DECREE OF COURT**
• Per ***partnership agreement***	• ***Illegality***	• ***Incompetency*** of partner
• By ***will of partner***	• ***Death*** of partner	• ***Incapability*** of partner
• ***Mutual assent*** of partners	• ***Bankruptcy*** of partner	• ***Improper conduct*** of partner
• ***Expulsion*** of partner		• ***Business operating only at a loss***
		• Circumstances rendering ***dissolution equitable***

c. Rights of Partners in Dissolution

(1) When Dissolution Does Not Violate Partnership Agreement

If the cause of dissolution is not a violation of the partnership agreement (*e.g.*, a dissolution upon expiration of partnership term), no partner has a claim or cause of action against any other partner for any loss sustained in the dissolution. Each partner has the right to have the partnership assets applied to the discharge of partnership liabilities, and the balance distributed to the partners in accordance with their respective interests. [UPA § 38(1)]

(a) And Note

In this situation, no partner can appropriate the partnership assets for herself, nor can one partner be forced to pay the other the appraised value of any asset (as is the case when dissolution violates the agreement; *see* below). [**Pluth v. Smith,** 205 Cal. App. 2d 818 (1962)]

(2) When Dissolution Violates Partnership Agreement

If the dissolution is caused by an act in violation of the partnership agreement (*e.g.*, a partner's electing to dissolve a partnership for a fixed term prior to the expiration of the term), the other ("innocent") partners are accorded certain rights in addition to those listed above:

(a) Right to Damages

The partnership agreement is a contract, and even though a partner may have the *power* to dissolve, she does not necessarily have the *right* to do so. (*See supra*, p. 178.) Therefore, if the dissolution she causes is a violation of the agreement, she is liable for any damages sustained by the innocent partners as a result of the wrongful dissolution (*e.g.*, loss of profits due to interruption of business). [UPA § 38(2)]

(b) Right to Purchase Business

The innocent partners also have the right to continue the partnership business in the partnership name, provided they pay the partner causing the dissolution the value of her interest in the partnership (less any damages recoverable).

1) Bond

Alternatively, the partners wishing to continue the business may post a bond in an amount approved by the court and institute appropriate proceedings for a determination of the dissolving partner's interests and any damages to be charged against her. [UPA § 38(2)(b)]

a) Failure to Pay

If the partners fail to pay or post bond within a reasonable time, the partner causing the dissolution is entitled to compensation for the use of her partnership assets in the continuing business measured in the same way as if she had died or retired. [*See* UPA § 42; *and see infra*, p. 182]

2) Continuing Services

Should the dissolving partner be requested by the remaining partners to continue any services for the partnership, she is entitled to reasonable compensation for such services. [**Vangel v. Vangel,** 45 Cal. 2d 804 (1955)]

(c) Right to Wind Up Partnership Affairs

If the partners decide not to purchase the wrongdoer's interest, the innocent partners have the right to wind up the partnership affairs and arrange for distribution of assets (*see infra*, p. 184 *et seq.*). [UPA § 37]

(3) Rights and Duties of Surviving Partner(s)

On the death of a partner, the surviving partner is entitled to possession of the partnership assets and is charged with the winding up of partnership affairs. [UPA § 37]

(a) Fiduciary

The surviving partner acts as a fiduciary in liquidating the partnership, and he must account to the estate of the deceased partner for the value of the decedent's interest in the partnership. [**Sibert v. Shaver,** 111 Cal. App. 2d 833 (1952)]

1) **Continuing Business Without Consent**

The surviving partner is under a duty to settle the partnership affairs without delay. If he continues the business ***without the consent*** of the deceased partner's estate, the surviving partner is liable for interest on the amount which he is found to owe the decedent's estate, ***or*** an appropriate share of any profits earned by the surviving partner through use of partnership property following the decedent's death, whichever is greater. [UPA § 42; 55 A.L.R.2d 1391]

2) **Result of Delay**

If an unjustified delay ***diminishes*** the value of the partnership business, the surviving partner may be held accountable for the value of the deceased partner's interest ***at the date of death***, rather than the value at the date of ultimate liquidation. [**Sibert v. Shaver,** *supra*]

(b) **Compensation**

The surviving partner is entitled to compensation for his services in winding up the partnership, as well as to reimbursement for any costs incurred or expended in winding up. [UPA § 18(f)]

d. **Effects of Dissolution**

(1) **General Rule—Termination of Actual Authority**

As a general rule, the dissolution of a partnership ***terminates the actual authority*** of any partner to act as an agent for either the partnership or the other partners, except for the purpose of winding up the affairs of the partnership (unless the partnership agreement or partners provide that the business shall be continued). [UPA § 33]

(a) **When Effective**

In general, a partner's actual authority to bind the partnership terminates only if and when he acquires knowledge of the dissolution. Thus, in a partnership between A, B, and C, if A notifies B of his election to dissolve, and before this information is communicated to C, C enters into a contract with a third party, the contract is binding on all partners.

(b) **Termination of Apparent Authority**

Even though a partner's actual authority is terminated by dissolution, he still has apparent authority as to all who knew of the partnership prior to its dissolution. Such apparent authority can be terminated only by proper notice.

1) **Prior Creditors**

Those who were creditors at the time of dissolution or who had extended credit to the partnership prior to dissolution must be given ***actual notice*** (*e.g.*, a letter) in order to terminate apparent authority.

2) **Others**

Apparent authority as to other third parties who have had dealings with the partnership or anyone who simply has knowledge of the partnership prior to its dissolution can be terminated by notice published in a newspaper of general circulation in the area where the partnership carried on its business (constructive notice).

3) Silent Partners

The liability of a partner for post-dissolution transactions when notice was not given is ***limited to partnership assets*** if the partner was unknown or so inactive in partnership affairs that credit to the partnership was not based on the partner's personal credit, and the creditor in fact did not know that the partner was a partner.

a) Distinguish

In predissolution transactions, a silent partner's liability is the same as a known partner's liability. (*See supra*, p. 156.)

(2) Liability for Existing Partnership Debts

A dissolution in no way affects each partner's liability for the partnership debts. The partners' joint liability ***remains*** until the debts are discharged. [**Faricy v. J.S. Brown Mercantile Co.,** 288 P. 639 (Colo. 1930)]

(a) Novation

However, there may be a *novation*—creditors agree to look only to certain of the partners for payment, and by doing so release the others. [UPA § 36(3)]

(3) Liability of Partners Continuing Business

If, after a dissolution, there is a change in the composition of the partnership (*e.g.*, death or retirement of a partner, or admission of a new partner) and the business continues, the new partnership remains liable for all of the debts of the previous partnership. The creditors of the first or dissolved partnership are also creditors of the partnership continuing the business. [UPA § 41; *and see* **Blumer Brewing Corp. v. Mayer,** 269 N.W. 693 (Wis. 1936)]

(a) Incoming Partners

Note, however, that an incoming partner's liability is limited to her interest in the partnership. [UPA § 17; *see* discussion *supra*, p. 158]

e. Winding Up

(1) In General

Under the UPA, after dissolution, absent an agreement to the contrary, the partnership business must be wound up. "Winding up" is the process of settling partnership affairs after dissolution. During the winding up process, actual authority exists to carry out the necessary acts to wind up the business. However, generally ***only transactions*** designed to ***terminate***, rather than to carry on, the business are within the scope of a partner's actual authority. In short, "old business" can be wrapped up; if "new business" is entered into, the partner who continues to carry on business on behalf of the partnership with knowledge of the dissolution assumes sole liability for her actions (unless partnership liability arises from failure to give notice as described above). If losses result, she alone will bear them.

EXAM TIP

If you are presented with a situation on an exam that results in the dissolution of the partnership, remember that under the UPA, a *winding up of the partnership business must occur*, absent an agreement to the contrary.

(2) "Old Business" vs. "New Business"

After dissolution but ***before termination***, the liquidating partners can bind the partnership in transactions ***winding up old business***, but not in transactions constituting new business.

(a) Old Business

The following are old business:

(1) ***Assigning claims***;

(2) ***Selling partnership assets***;

(3) ***Performing contracts made prior to dissolution***;

(4) ***Collecting debts due***;

(5) ***Compromising claims***;

(6) ***Paying off creditors*** (*see* below); and

(7) ***Distributing the remainder of the business's assets*** (*see infra*, p. 186 *et seq.*).

(b) New Business

The following are new business:

(1) ***Extending time*** on a debt;

(2) ***Entering into new contracts;*** and

(3) ***Increasing any obligation*** of the partnership, even by one cent—***except necessary contracts*** such as hiring an accountant to help wind up the business.

EXAM TIP

To determine on an exam if a partner is liable for entering into a transaction after the partnership is dissolved, you must examine the transaction and decide if it constitutes old business necessary to wind up the partnership or new business that will carry on the partnership. Recall that a partner will *not* be liable for engaging in a transaction constituting *old business*, such as selling assets or paying off creditors.

(3) Who May Wind Up

(a) All Partners

If all partners agree to a dissolution of the partnership, or if the partnership term expires or the particular partnership undertaking is accomplished, then all the partners have the right to wind up the affairs of the partnership.

(b) **Remaining Partners**

If a partner dissolves the partnership by bankruptcy, the remaining partner(s) have the right to wind up the partnership's affairs.

(c) **Surviving Partners**

If a partnership is dissolved by the death of a partner, the surviving partner(s) have the right to wind up partnership affairs.

(d) **Executor**

If the partnership affairs have not been wound up when the last surviving partner dies, the executor or administrator of the last survivor's estate has the right to wind up the partnership's affairs. [U.P.A. § 37]

(e) **Distinguish—Partner Wrongfully Dissolving Partnership**

A partner who *wrongfully* dissolves a partnership is *not entitled to wind up* the affairs of the partnership.

f. **Distribution of Assets—Final Accounting**

(1) **Order of Distribution**

After a partnership is dissolved and its assets reduced to cash, the cash must be used to pay the partnership liabilities in the following order under the UPA (section 40):

(a) **Outside Creditors**

Outside creditors (*i.e.*, creditors who are not partners) are paid first.

(b) **Partners**

The remaining cash is distributed to the partners in the following order:

1) **Partner Creditors**

If any partner has contributed more than the capital provided for in the partnership agreement, she is entitled to a return of that additional capital, plus any accrued interest.

2) **Capital Contributions**

Next, partners are entitled to a return of any contribution that they have paid into the partnership.

3) **Profits or Surplus**

Finally, any cash remaining is distributed to the partners according to their share of the profits or surplus.

(2) **When There Are Losses**

If there is no surplus, and partnership assets are insufficient to pay all of the partnership liabilities (including repayment of capital contributions), the shortfall is a loss, and each partner must contribute his share of the loss—usually in the same proportion as his share of the profits. [UPA § 18(a); *and see supra*, p. 145]

APPROACH TO ORDER OF DISTRIBUTION OF ASSETS

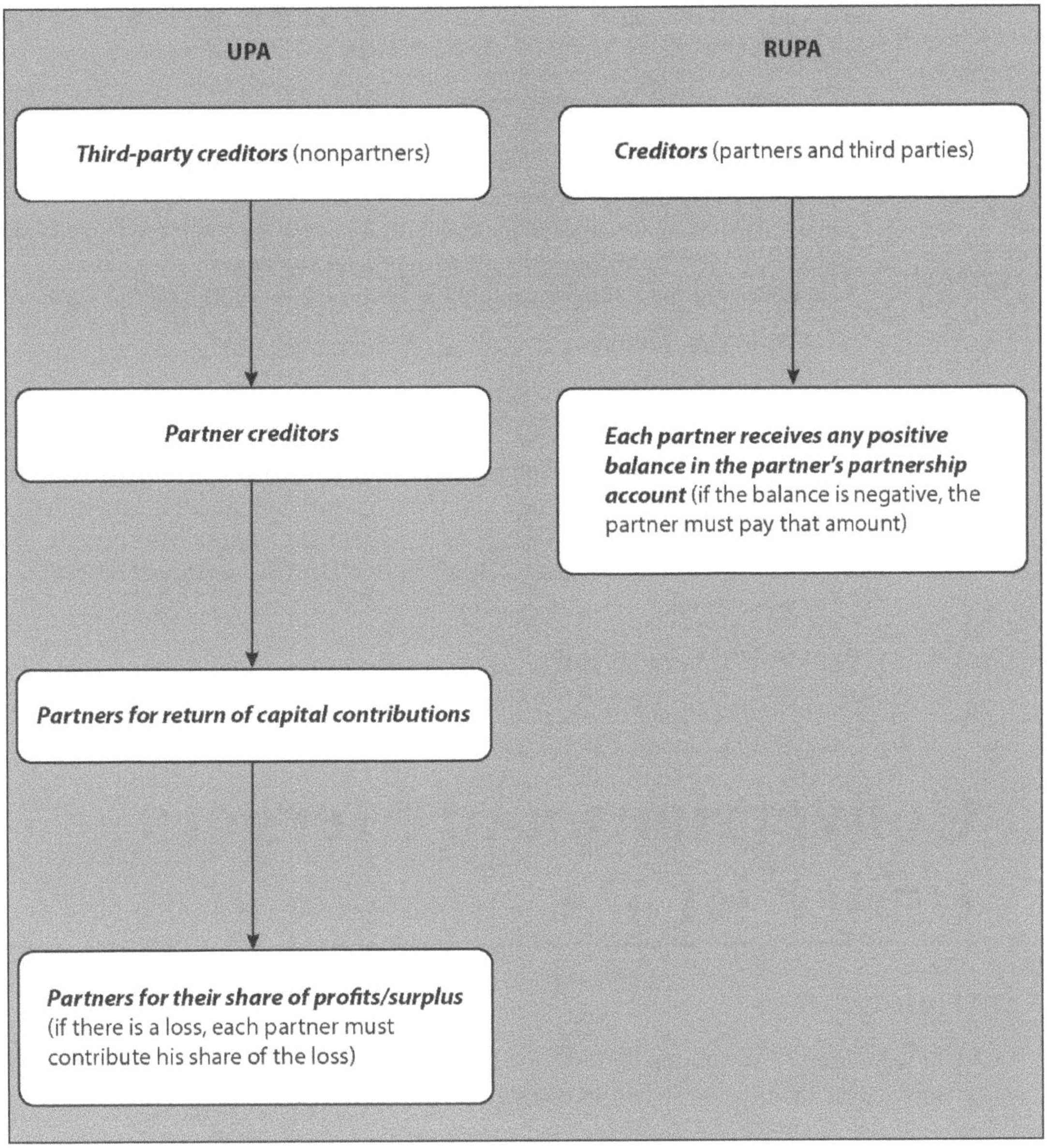

e.g. **Example:** A, B, and C are partners who contributed $10,000, $5,000, and $2,000, respectively. They share profits and losses equally. Only $5,000 remains after winding up the partnership. The total capital investment was $17,000; so there is a $12,000 loss. Each partner's proportionate share of the loss is $4,000. Therefore, A is entitled to receive $6,000 as a partial return of his capital contribution ($10,000–$4,000), B will receive $1,000 ($5,000–$4,000), and C must contribute $2,000 ($2,000–$4,000).

(a) If Partner Insolvent or Refuses

If one of the partners is insolvent or refuses to contribute his share of the losses, the remaining partners must make up his share proportionately. They will then have a right of action against the defaulting partner to enforce his contribution (which can also be enforced by an assignee for the benefit of creditors or by a bankruptcy trustee if the partnership has become insolvent). [UPA § 40(d)–(f)]

1) Dual Insolvency

Under bankruptcy law, if both a partnership and a partner are insolvent, partnership creditors have priority in partnership assets and parity with the partner's separate creditors with respect to the partner's individual assets. [11 U.S.C. § 723(c)] Under the UPA, partnership creditors have priority in partnership assets, and the partner's separate creditors have priority in the partner's individual assets. However, the UPA ***is preempted*** in bankruptcy proceedings.

(3) Termination of Partnership

A partnership is terminated when all of the partnership affairs have been wound up (including the liquidation and distribution of any assets).

C. Conversions and Mergers Under RUPA

1. Introduction

In addition to the provisions for dissociation and dissolution, the RUPA provides rules for converting a partnership into a limited partnership, converting a limited partnership into a partnership, and for merging partnerships.

2. Conversion of Partnership to Limited Partnership

A partnership may be converted to a limited partnership upon the ***unanimous consent*** of the partners (or by such vote as is specified in the partnership agreement) by filing a certificate of limited partnership with the state. [RUPA § 902(b), (c)]

a. Contents of Certificate

In addition to the other mandatory provisions (*see infra*, p. 194), the certificate must include the partnership's former name, a statement that the partnership was converted to a limited partnership, and the number of votes cast for and against conversion, which vote can be less than unanimous if the partnership agreement so provides. [RUPA § 902(c)]

b. Liability

A general partner who becomes a limited partner as a result of a conversion remains liable as a general partner on obligations incurred before the conversion. A limited partner has no personal liability on obligations incurred after a conversion except for obligations incurred within 90 days after the conversion if the other party reasonably believed that the limited partner was a general partner. [RUPA § 902(e)]

3. Conversion of Limited Partnership to Partnership

A limited partnership may be converted to a partnership only upon the consent of ***all partners*** (notwithstanding a contrary provision in the limited partnership agreement). Conversion is accomplished by canceling the certificate of limited partnership. A limited partner who becomes a general partner as a result of a conversion remains liable only as a limited partner for obligations incurred by the partnership before the conversion, but is liable as a general partner for all post-conversion obligations. [RUPA § 903]

4. Merger

A partnership may merge with one or more partnerships or limited partnerships upon approval of a merger plan: (i) if the party is a partnership, by all partners or the number set in the partnership agreement; or (ii) if the party is a limited partnership, by the vote required by statute, or if there is none, by the consent of ***all*** partners, notwithstanding a contrary provision in the partnership agreement. [RUPA § 905(c)]

a. Contents of Plan

The plan must state: (i) the name of each partnership or limited partnership that is a party to the merger; (ii) the name of the surviving entity, its status as a partnership or limited partnership, and the status of each partner; (iii) the terms and conditions of the merger; (iv) the basis for converting the interests of each party into interests in the surviving entity; and (v) the street address of the surviving entity's chief executive office. [RUPA § 905(b)]

b. Liabilities

A partner of the surviving partnership is liable for: (i) all obligations of the merging entity that the partner was liable for before the merger; and (ii) to the extent of partnership property, all other obligations of the surviving entity incurred before the merger, and all obligations of the surviving entity incurred after the merger takes effect (but such obligations may be satisfied only out of property of the entity if the partner is a limited partner). [RUPA § 906(a)–(c)]

Chapter Twelve: Limited Partnerships

CONTENTS PAGE

Key Exam Issues

A limited partnership is a hybrid business organization that offers a management and tax structure similar to that of a partnership, but allows some investors (*i.e.*, the limited partners) to have limited liability like shareholders of a corporation.

Exam questions concerning limited partnerships often focus on formation issues. It is important to remember that unlike a partnership without limited partners ("general partnership"), ***formation of a limited partnership requires certain formalities***. A written certificate of limited partnership must be filed with the secretary of state. If a certificate has not been filed, there is no limited partnership. Formation also requires that there be at least one general partner, *i.e.*, a person personally liable for all partnership obligations. A limited partnership cannot be formed in which all partners will have limited liability.

An exam question also might focus on the difference between limited partnerships and general partnerships concerning the ***sharing of profits***. Profits in a limited partnership are not divided equally as in a general partnership, but rather are divided in proportion to the partners' contributions.

Another common exam issue involves ***management*** of the limited partnership. Under the Revised Uniform Limited Partnership Act ("RULPA"), day-to-day management of a limited partnership is in the hands of the general partner(s). Limited partners generally are not allowed to participate in the management of the partnership business except to vote on extraordinary matters. A limited partner ***who participates in management or control*** of the partnership ***may lose her limited liability*** as to a partnership creditor who dealt with the partnership under the erroneous belief that the limited partner was a general partner. Note that the Uniform Limited Partnership Act of 2001 ("ULPA") view is that a limited partner does ***not compromise limited liability*** status if he participates in the management or control of the partnership.

Finally, an exam question might deal with the ***dissolution*** of a limited partnership. A limited partnership can be dissolved judicially or whenever a certain event occurs *(e.g.*, on the partners' written consent or on the occurrence of the time or event stated in the certificate of limited partnership). When a limited partnership is dissolved, it must be wound up and its assets must be distributed first to creditors, including partners who are creditors, and then to partners for (i) interim distributions and distributions on withdrawal, (ii) return of contributions, and (iii) share of the profits. The ULPA sets forth the same basic provisions for dissolution as the RULPA. However, under the ULPA the withdrawal of a partner can be treated as a ***dissociation***, which does not necessitate dissolution of the partnership.

A. In General

1. Nature

Limited partnerships are hybrid business organizations that offer partners a business structure similar to that of a partnership, but provide the limited partners with limited liability similar to that of a shareholder in a corporation. They were developed to facilitate commercial investments by those who wanted a financial interest in a business but did not want all of the responsibilities and liabilities of partners. They have become popular under current laws because they allow profits and losses to flow directly to the partners—thus avoiding the "double tax" on corporate profits—and, unlike S corporations, they are not limited in size. (*See* Taxation of Business Entities Summary.)

a. Limited Liability Rationale

The limited liability of a limited partner is rationally supported by two attributes of the limited partnership structure. First, at least one person in the limited partnership is personally liable for all partnership debts—the general partner. Second, because it is difficult to justify immunity from debt for persons who actively create the debt, limited partners are not allowed to participate in the management or control of the limited partnership. Both of these topics will be discussed in greater detail below.

2. Governing Law

Limited partnerships did not exist at common law. They are entities created by statutes. In 1916, the original Uniform Limited Partnership Act was adopted. The 1916 Act was completely revised by the National Conference of Commissioners on Uniform State Laws in 1976. This Revised Uniform Limited Partnership Act ("RULPA") was amended in 1985. Almost every state in the United States has adopted the 1976 RULPA, and a majority of those states have also adopted the 1985 amendments. The Commissioners again completely revised the RULPA and named this revision the Uniform Limited Partnership Act of 2001 ("ULPA"). However, as of press time, the RULPA as amended in 1985 remains majority law. Thus, this Summary discusses the RULPA as amended in 1985 but highlights provisions of the 2001 act where the distinctions are significant.

a. Note

Where the RULPA does not provide an applicable rule for a limited partnership, the rules of the jurisdiction's general partnership act will govern. [RULPA § 1105] The ULPA, on the other hand, is a stand-alone act that is de-linked from any general partnership act. [ULPA, Prefatory Note]

3. Structure

A limited partnership is a partnership formed by two or more persons, having as its members one or more general partners and one or more limited partners. [RULPA § 101; ULPA § 102(11)]

a. General Partner

A general partner is a partner who assumes the management responsibilities of the partnership and full personal liability for the debts of the partnership. [RULPA §§ 101, 403] Under the ULPA, general partners are ***jointly and severally liable.*** [ULPA § 102(8)] A general partner is similar to a partner in a general partnership, and may be a natural person, partnership, limited partnership, trust, estate, association, or corporation. [RULPA § 101(11)]

b. Limited Partner

A limited partner is a partner who makes a contribution (*e.g.*, cash) to the partnership and obtains an interest in the partnership's returns, but who is not active in the partnership's management and generally is not liable for partnership debts beyond her contribution. A limited partner may be a natural person or any of the entities listed above for a general partner. [RULPA § 101(11)]

4. Permitted Activities

The RULPA does not contain any limitation on the activities in which a limited partnership may engage, although many jurisdictions forbid the undertaking of certain activities by a limited partnership (*e.g.*, banking and insurance). The ULPA states that a limited partnership can be formed for ***any lawful purpose.*** [ULPA § 104]

B. Formation of Limited Partnership

1. Certificate of Limited Partnership

To form a limited partnership, a certificate of limited partnership must be signed by all of the general partners and filed with the secretary of state. [RULPA §§ 201(a), 204(a); ULPA §§ 201, 204] The limited partnership comes into existence at the moment of filing if there has been substantial compliance with the requirements regarding content and execution of the certificate. [RULPA § 201(b); ULPA § 201(c)] Absent substantial compliance, all partners may be held liable as general partners for partnership obligations.

EXAM TIP

It is important to remember that a limited partnership is a creature of statute and thus can exist *only on compliance with the limited partnership statute.* Watch out for an exam question that sets up facts where one partner wants limited liability and the other partner tells him that he can be a limited partner, but there is no filing with the secretary of state. Because there is no statutory compliance, a limited partnership is *not created,* and all partners are subject to full liability.

a. Contents

The information required in the certificate of limited partnership is minimal; it need only include: (i) the name and address of the limited partnership; (ii) the name and address of an agent for service of process; (iii) the name and address of each general partner (***not*** the limited partners); and (iv) the latest date upon which the limited partnership is to dissolve. The ULPA also requires the certificate to state whether the limited partnership is a limited liability limited partnership. (*See infra*, p. 203.) [RULPA § 201(a); ULPA § 201(a)]

(1) Distinguish—Partnership Agreement

The RULPA recognizes that the document that truly governs the limited partnership is the ***partnership agreement***, not the certificate of limited partnership, and that creditors should and do look there for information on the nature and financing of the partnership. Thus, the RULPA requires the following information to be kept in the partnership agreement or other record: (i) the amount of cash or agreed value of all property or services contributed (or agreed to be contributed) by each partner; (ii) the times or events upon which future contributions are to be made; (iii) any right of a partner to receive distributions (including a return of the partner's contribution); and (iv) any events that will cause dissolution of the partnership. [RULPA § 105(a)(5); *and see* ULPA § 111(9)]

b. Amendment of Certificate of Limited Partnership

If there are errors in the certificate or significant changes concerning information required to be kept in the certificate (*e.g.*, change in general partners or time for dissolution), an amendment must be filed. [RULPA § 202; ULPA § 202] The amendment must be signed by ***at least one general partner*** and, if the amendment reflects the admission of an additional general partner, the ***additional general partner*** must sign the amendment. Note that the responsibility to amend the certificate rests with the general partner(s); a limited partner will not be liable for failure to amend. [RULPA §§ 202(c), 204(a); ULPA § 202] However, not even a general partner will be liable for preamendment information if an amendment is filed within 30 days after the event necessitating the amendment.

(1) Cancellation of Certificate

The certificate of limited partnership is cancelled upon dissolution of the limited partnership. A certificate of cancellation must be filed with the secretary of state. [RULPA § 203; *and see* ULPA § 203]

c. Liability for False Statements

Anyone who suffers a loss by relying on a false statement in the certificate of limited partnership (or any amendment) may recover damages for the loss from (i) any person who signed the certificate (including agents) ***knowing*** that it contained a false statement, and (ii) any general partner (whether or not he signed) who ***knew or should have known*** that the certificate contained a false statement. [RULPA § 207; *and see* ULPA § 202, comment]

2. Records Office

A limited partnership is required to maintain a records office with records of, *inter alia:* (i) the names and addresses of all partners; (ii) copies of the partnership's tax returns and partnership agreements for the three most recent years; and (iii) the information mentioned on p. 194, *supra.* [RULPA § 105; ULPA § 111]

C. Name of Limited Partnership

1. Requirements

The RULPA requires that the name of a limited partnership (i) include the words "limited partnership"; (ii) not be the same as or deceptively similar to the name of any corporation or limited partnership licensed or registered in the state; and (iii) not include the name of a limited partner unless (a) it is also the name of a general partner, or (b) prior to the time the limited partner became such, the business had been carried on under a name in which the limited partner's name appeared. [RULPA § 102]

2. Liability for Use of Limited Partner's Name

A limited partner who ***knowingly permits*** her name to be used in the partnership's name contrary to the Act's provisions is liable, as a general partner, to creditors who extend credit to the limited partnership without knowledge that she is not a general partner. [RULPA § 303(d)]

3. ULPA View

Unlike the RULPA, the ULPA ***allows a limited partnership to use the name of any partner in its name.*** The ***name chosen should be distinguishable*** from the name of other business entities unless authorized by the secretary of state. Under the ULPA, the name of the limited partnership must contain the words "limited partnership" or the abbreviation "LP" or "L.P." The name of a limited liability limited partnership must contain the phrase "limited liability limited partnership" or the abbreviation "L.L.L.P." or "LLLP." [ULPA § 108]

D. Changes in Membership

1. Admission of Additional General and Limited Partners

An additional general or limited partner may be admitted to the partnership (i) in any manner provided in the ***partnership agreement***; or (ii) if the partnership agreement does not so provide, upon the ***written consent of all partners.*** [RULPA §§ 301, 401]

EXAM TIP

If an exam fact pattern has an additional *general* partner admitted to the limited partnership, don't forget that a certificate of *amendment* must be filed with the secretary of state to reflect the admission of the new general partner. Also recall that the certificate must be signed by at least one existing general partner and the new general partner (*see supra*, p. 194).

a. Admission of Additional Limited and General Partners Under ULPA

An additional ***limited partner*** may be admitted as provided in the partnership agreement, as the result of a conversion or merger, or with the consent of all of the partners. [ULPA § 301] An additional ***general partner*** may be admitted in the same manner and also after the dissociation of the last general partner. [ULPA § 401] Note that under the ULPA the consent of the existing partners ***does not*** need to be in writing.

2. Assignment of Partner's Interest

A partner has an interest in the partnership that may be assigned in whole or in part, although the RULPA specifically permits the partnership agreement to alter this rule. The assignment by a partner of his interest does not dissolve the partnership. However, unless otherwise provided in the partnership agreement, a partner ceases to be a partner upon the assignment of ***all*** of his interest. [RULPA §§ 701, 702]

a. But Note

If a ***general*** partner assigns all of his interest, the assignment can be of significant consequence to the partnership because it would constitute an "event of withdrawal" which may require the partnership to be dissolved and wound up. (*See infra*, p. 197.)

b. Assignee's Rights

An assignee of an interest in a limited partnership, unless she becomes a substitute partner, is entitled to receive only the share of profits or return of contribution to which her assignor would be entitled. [RULPA § 702; ULPA § 702] The assignee does not have the other rights of a limited partner. (*See infra*, p. 199 *et seq.*)

c. Creditor's Right to Charge Partner's Interest

A creditor of a partner does not have the right to become a partner, but may charge the partner's interest. [RULPA § 703; ULPA § 703] In effect, the creditor becomes an assignee of the partner's interest.

3. Death, Incompetency, or Withdrawal of a Partner

a. Limited Partners

The death, incompetency, or withdrawal of a limited partner does ***not*** dissolve the partnership. If a limited partner dies or becomes incompetent, her legal representative may exercise all of her rights for the purpose of settling her estate and administering her property. [RULPA § 705; ULPA § 704]

(1) Right to Withdraw

A limited partner may withdraw at the time or upon the happening of the events specified in the written partnership agreement. If no time or event is specified, a limited partner may withdraw on six months' prior written notice to each ***general*** partner. [RULPA § 603]

b. General Partners

Under the RULPA, the death, incompetency, or withdrawal of a general partner constitutes an "event of withdrawal" that dissolves the partnership unless (i) there is at least one other general partner, and the partnership agreement permits the business to be carried on by the remaining general partner; or (ii) within 90 days after the event of withdrawal, all partners consent in writing to continue the business and to appoint a general partner if necessary. [RULPA §§ 402, 801] If a general partner dies or becomes incompetent, his legal representative may exercise all of his rights for purposes of settling his estate and administering his property. [RULPA § 705]

(1) Right to Withdraw

A general partner may withdraw from the partnership at any time by providing written notice to the other partners; however, if the withdrawal is in violation of the partnership agreement, the partner will be liable to the partnership for damages caused by his breach of the agreement. [RULPA § 602]

(2) Other "Events of Withdrawal"

Not only are the death, incompetency, and withdrawal of a general partner "events of withdrawal" that may cause the dissolution of the partnership, but also there are other events that are considered "events of withdrawal" that may cause the partnership to be dissolved, including the bankruptcy of a general partner and the assignment by a general partner of all of his partnership interest. [RULPA § 402]

4. Dissociation Under ULPA

The ULPA uses the term ***"dissociation"*** when discussing the withdrawal of a limited or general partner from the partnership. Dissociation can be voluntary or involuntary.

a. Dissociation of a Limited Partner

A limited partner has ***no right to voluntarily dissociate*** before the termination of the limited partnership but in most cases still has the power to do so (although it would be considered wrongful). [*See* ULPA §§ 601(a), 601(b) and comment] ***Involuntary dissociation*** of a limited partner can occur in several instances (*e.g.*, pursuant to an event agreed to in the partnership agreement or by expulsion). [ULPA § 601(b)]

b. Dissociation of a General Partner

Like a limited partner, a general partner has ***no right to voluntarily dissociate*** before termination of the partnership, but has the *power* to do so at any time. [ULPA § 604(a)] If the dissociation is ***wrongful*** (*e.g.*, it occurs before the termination of the limited partnership), the partner may be liable to the limited partnership for damages caused by the breach. [ULPA § 604] ***Involuntary dissociation*** of a general partner can occur for a variety of reasons, such as bankruptcy or for wrongful conduct leading to expulsion by court order. [ULPA § 603]

c. Continuation of Limited Partnership After Dissociation

The dissociation of a general partner ***does not automatically dissolve the partnership.*** If at least one general partner remains, there is no dissolution unless within 90 days after the dissociation partners owning a majority of the rights to receive distributions consent to dissolution. If no general partner remains after the dissociation, dissolution occurs after 90 days unless the limited partners consent to continue and admit at least one new general partner. [ULPA § 801] Under the RULPA, dissolution occurs automatically upon the withdrawal of a general partner (*see supra*, p. 197). [RULPA §§ 402, 801]

E. Nature of Partner's Contribution

1. In General

A partner's contribution to the partnership may be in cash, property, or services, or a promise to contribute such in the future. [RULPA § 501; ULPA § 501]

2. Liability for Unpaid Contribution

A partner is obligated to perform any promise to contribute cash or property or to perform services; the partner is obligated to do so even if he is unable to perform because of death, disability, or other reason. Moreover, if a partner does not make a promised contribution of property or services, the partnership may hold the partner liable for the cash equivalent of the promised contribution. [RULPA § 502(b); ULPA § 502]

a. But Note

A ***limited*** partner's promise to contribute to the partnership is not enforceable unless it is set out in a writing signed by the limited partner. [RULPA § 502(a)]

3. Compromise of Liability

A partner's obligation to make a contribution may be compromised by the consent of ***all*** of the partners. However, even when there has been a compromise, it does not affect a creditor of the partnership who extends credit after the partner signs a writing that reflects the obligation and before the amendment of the writing to reflect the compromise. [RULPA § 502; *but see* ULPA § 502(c)—partnership creditor not affected if he extends credit or acts in reliance on an obligation and without notice of the compromise]

4. Liability for Return of Contribution

a. Rightful Returns

As a general rule, a partner may not receive the return of any part of his capital contribution unless sufficient assets remain to pay the partnership's liabilities, excluding liabilities owed to partners on account of their partnership interests (*e.g.*, profits). Thus, even if the return is rightful (*i.e.*, does not violate any provision of the certificate of partnership, the limited partnership act, or the partnership agreement), the receiving partner may be held liable for the returned contribution for one year to the extent necessary to discharge prereturn creditors. [RULPA § 608(a)]

b. Wrongful Returns

If a return of contribution is wrongful, the partner is liable to the partnership for the return for six years. [RULPA § 608(b); *and see* ULPA § 509—liability extends for two years]

F. Rights and Liabilities of Partners

1. Rights of General and Limited Partners

a. Right to Share in Profits and Losses

A partner is entitled to his share of the profits and losses specified in the partnership agreement. If the partnership agreement is silent as to the division of profits and losses, profits and losses are allocated on the ***basis of the value of the contributions*** made by each partner. [RULPA § 503]

EXAM TIP

Note that the RULPA rule for partners' sharing profits and losses—*i.e., according to contributions*—is different from the RUPA rule that, absent an agreement to the contrary, partners share profits and losses *equally.* Be careful on an exam not to confuse the two rules. Additionally, remember that the *ULPA* has no provision for allocating profits and losses. Under the ULPA, the partners have *distribution rights.*

(1) ULPA View

Unlike the RULPA, the ULPA has no provision governing allocation of profits and losses among the partners. Instead, it apportions the right to receive ***distributions***. [ULPA § 503, comment] A distribution by a limited partnership must be shared among the partners on the basis of the value, as stated in the required records when the limited partnership decides to make the distribution, of the contributions the limited partnership has received from each partner. [ULPA § 503] In other words, distributions are apportioned in relation to the value of contributions without regard to whether the limited partnership has returned any of those contributions.

b. Right to Distributions

Besides addressing how profits and losses are to be shared by the partners, the RULPA also contains a number of provisions regarding when and how the partnership is to make distributions. The RULPA provides that the partners may agree in the partnership agreement to allocate distributions of cash or other assets on any basis, including a basis different from the partners' shares of the profits and losses. However, if no provision is made, distributions are made on the basis of the value of the partners' contributions (same as for profits). [RULPA § 504]

(1) Interim Distributions

The RULPA provides that the partnership agreement may set times for interim distributions; *i.e.*, distributions to be made before withdrawal or dissolution. [RULPA § 601]

(2) Creditor Status

When a partner becomes entitled to a distribution, he obtains the status of a creditor with respect to the distribution. [RULPA § 606; ULPA § 507] Thus, he is entitled to any remedy that a nonpartner creditor may obtain.

(3) Solvency Limitation

A distribution cannot be paid unless partnership assets are sufficient to satisfy all partnership liabilities, other than those arising on account of the partners' interests in the partnership. [RULPA § 607; ULPA § 508]

(4) ULPA View

As stated *supra*, p. 199, under the ULPA a distribution by a limited partnership must be shared among the partners on the basis of the value of the contributions the limited partnership has received from each partner. [ULPA § 503] A partner has no right to any distribution (i) before the dissolution and winding up of the limited partnership ***unless the partnership decides to make an interim distribution***, or (ii) upon dissociation (*see infra*, p. 201). [ULPA §§ 504, 505]

c. Right to Transact Business with the Partnership

A partner has the right to transact business with and make loans to the partnership to the same extent as a person who is not a partner. Thus, the creditor-partner can share pro rata with the nonpartner-creditors in the assets of the partnership in the event of a claim on those assets. [RULPA § 107; ULPA § 112]

d. Right to Assign Interest

As discussed earlier, a partner has an interest in the partnership and has the right to assign his interest. (*See supra*, p. 196.)

e. Right to Withdraw

A partner has a right to withdraw from the partnership. (*See supra*, p. 197.)

(1) Right to Distributions on Withdrawal

When a partner withdraws, he has the right to receive in cash any distribution for which the partnership agreement provides. If the partnership agreement does not so provide, the partner is entitled to receive the value of his interest in the partnership as of the date of withdrawal based on his right to share in the distributions of the partnership. The partnership may return property in kind, but it cannot force the withdrawing partner to accept an asset that exceeds the value of his share of the distributions. [RULPA §§ 604, 605]

EXAM TIP

If on an exam a partner withdraws and the partnership owes the partner a distribution, remember that the partnership cannot pay the withdrawing partner the distribution unless it is *solvent* (*see supra*, p. 200).

f. Right to Dissociate Under ULPA

As discussed above (*see supra*, pp. 197–198), a limited or general partner has a right to dissociate from the partnership. A partner who dissociates has no right to receive a distribution on account of dissociation [ULPA § 505] and is treated as a transferee of his own transferable interest (*e.g.*, he has no voting rights, etc.) [ULPA §§ 602(a)(3), 605(a)(5)].

2. Rights Specific to General Partners

a. RULPA "Catch-All" Provision

Except as provided by statute or in the partnership agreement, a general partner of a limited partnership also has all of the rights and powers of a partner in a general partnership. [RULPA § 403] One of the most important rights of a general partner in a limited partnership is the right to manage the limited partnership. (*See supra*, p. 193; *and see infra*, p. 203, for consequences of a limited partner's management of the partnership.)

b. Right to Compensation

The RULPA does not specifically address a general partner's right to compensation. Thus, the provisions of the RUPA apply, and under that Act, a general partner is ***not*** entitled to compensation beyond his share of the profits for services rendered to the partnership, unless otherwise agreed.

c. Rights of General Partners Under ULPA

The ULPA generally provides the same rights to general partners as the RULPA, with a few distinctions: Under the ULPA, general partners have explicit ***rights to information*** without having any particular purpose for seeking the information, and the Act imposes an obligation on the limited partnership and other general partners to volunteer certain information. [ULPA § 407] Additionally, general partners have the right to maintain a ***derivative action to enforce the partnership's rights*** if the person first makes a demand on the general partners requesting to bring an action to enforce the right and the general partners do not do so within a reasonable time, or if a demand would be futile. [ULPA § 1002] Note that this differs from the RULPA, which gives the right to maintain a derivative action only to limited partners. (*See infra*, p. 201.)

3. Rights Specific to Limited Partners

a. Right to Bring a Derivative Action

The RULPA grants a limited partner the right to bring a derivative action to enforce the partnership's rights when the general partners refuse to do so or when an effort to cause those partners to do so is not likely to succeed. The limited partner must have been a limited partner when the transaction she is complaining of occurred or her interest must have devolved upon her from one who was a limited partner at the time of the transaction. [RULPA §§ 1001, 1002]

b. Right to Information

In a limited partnership, there are two concerns relating to information: the need of the limited partners to ***access*** information and the need of the partnership to ***protect*** confidential information. General partners are obligated to protect information through their duties of loyalty and care. Each limited partner has the right to:

(i) ***Inspect and copy any partnership records*** required to be maintained (***see supra***, p. 195); and

(ii) Obtain from a general partner, upon reasonable demand, full ***information regarding the state and financial condition of the partnership business***, the partnership's income tax returns, and other information concerning the partnership's affairs that is just and reasonable.

[RULPA § 305]

c. Right to Vote

The RULPA provides that a limited partner who participates in control of the limited partnership can be held personally liable as a general partner for the partnership's obligations. (*See infra*, p. 203.) However, the RULPA allows limited partners to vote on certain issues (generally regarding fundamental changes in the partnership) without being deemed to have participated in control of the business. [RULPA §§ 302, 303; *and see infra* p. 203]

(1) ULPA View

Note that although the ULPA does not include the rule that a limited partner who participates in control of the partnership is liable as a general partner, it specifically gives limited partners the right to be asked for consent to undertake fundamental changes, such as the admission of a new partner [ULPA §§ 301(3), 401(4)], the amendment of the partnership agreement [ULPA § 406(b)(*l*)], or with respect to dissolution [ULPA § 801(2)].

RIGHTS OF LIMITED PARTNERS
A LIMITED PARTNER HAS THE RIGHT TO:
☑ Share in partnership ***profits and losses*** and receive ***distributions***
☑ ***Transact business with the partnership***
☑ ***Assign*** her interest
☑ ***Withdraw*** from the partnership
☑ ***Dissociate*** from the partnership (ULPA only)
☑ Bring a ***derivative action***
☑ ***Inspect and copy partnership records*** and obtain from a general partner information concerning the state and financial condition of the partnership
☑ ***Vote on*** (or "consent to" under ULPA) ***limited issues*** (*e.g.,* fundamental partnership changes)

4. Liabilities of General Partners

Just as a general partner of a limited partnership has all of the rights and powers of a partner in a general partnership, he also has all of the liabilities of a partner in a general partnership.

[RULPA § 403; ULPA § 404(a)] Thus, a general partner is ***personally*** liable for the limited partnership's debts. (*See supra*, p. 193.)

a. Limited Liability Limited Partnership Under ULPA

Under the ULPA, a limited partnership may opt for limited liability limited partnership status by a statement in the certificate of limited partnership. In a limited liability limited partnership, the general partners typically are not personally liable for the partnership's obligations, like the limited partners. [ULPA §§ 102(9), 201(a)(4), 404(c)]

5. Liabilities of Limited Partners

The general rule is that a limited partner, as such, is not liable for the debts of the partnership beyond her contribution. [RULPA § 303]

a. Exceptions to General Rule

However, there are four exceptions to the general rule:

(i) The limited partner ***signs the partnership certificate knowing of a falsity*** in the certificate (*see supra*, p. 195);

(ii) The limited partner ***knowingly permits her name to be used*** in the partnership's name contrary to the RULPA (*see supra*, p. 195);

(iii) The limited partner ***is also a general partner*** (*see supra*, p. 193); and

(iv) The limited partner ***participates in control*** of the business.

The first three exceptions have been detailed in the sections indicated. The fourth exception will be discussed in greater detail below.

b. Participates in Control

Under the RULPA, a limited partner is liable as a general partner if she participates in control of the business, ***and the person dealing with the limited partnership reasonably believes***, based on the limited partner's conduct, that the limited partner is a general partner. [RULPA § 303(a)]

(1) Note

Before the 1985 amendments, the RULPA provided that a creditor could hold a limited partner liable as a general partner if he had ***actual knowledge*** of the limited partner's controlling acts regardless of whether the creditor reasonably believed the limited partner to be a general partner. [RULPA (1976) § 303(a)] A number of states have retained this rule.

(2) "Safe Harbors"

The RULPA does not define what constitutes "participation in control of the business," but it does list certain activities that a ***limited partner may engage in*** without being found to have participated in control of the business, including:

(i) ***Being an employee, agent, or independent contractor*** for the partnership or of a general partner, or being an officer, director, or shareholder of a corporate general partner;

(ii) ***Consulting with and advising a general partner*** with respect to the business of the partnership;

(iii) ***Acting as surety*** for the partnership or guaranteeing or assuming one or more specific partnership obligations;

LIABILITY OF A LIMITED PARTNER TO THIRD PARTIES—RULPA

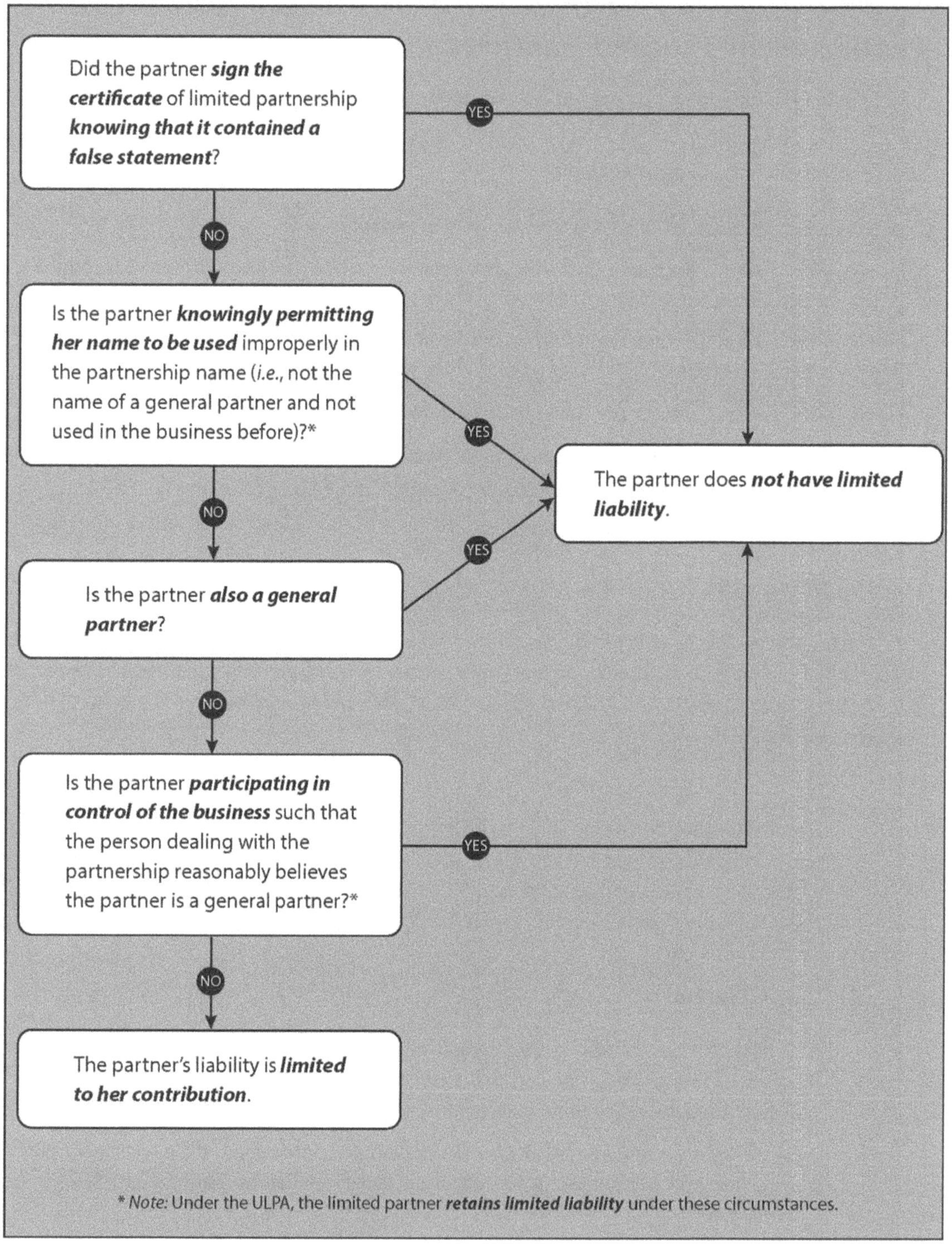

(iv) ***Approving or disapproving an amendment*** to the partnership agreement or the certificate of limited partnership;

(v) ***Requesting or attending a meeting*** of the partners and/or voting on a fundamental change in the partnership (*e.g.*, removing or adding a partner, dissolving the partnership, etc.); and

(vi) ***Winding up*** the limited partnership.

[RULPA § 303(b)] Note that the statutory list of safe harbors is not exclusive; whether other activities constitute "exercising control" is determined on a case-by-case basis.

EXAM TIP

A very common question covering limited partnership law is whether a limited partner *participated in control of the business.* This question is significant because under the *RULPA* a limited partner who participates in control of the business may be liable *beyond her contribution* to a third party who transacts business with the partnership and reasonably believes the limited partner to be a general partner (the ULPA attaches no such liability). Under the RULPA, in determining whether a limited partner participated in control of the business, you must examine the limited partner's conduct. Remember that if the limited partner's conduct involves one or more of the activities considered to be a "safe harbor" under the RULPA (*e.g.,* consulting with or advising a general partner or winding up the business), the limited partner will *not* be liable to a third party beyond her contribution.

---

(3) ULPA—No Similar Rule

In light of the emerging popularity of LLPs, LLCs, and LLLPs, the ULPA does away with this so-called control rule and provides a ***full liability shield for limited partners.*** Thus, an obligation of the limited partnership, whether arising in contract, tort, or otherwise, does not become the obligation of a limited partner. A limited partner is not personally liable, by way of contribution or otherwise, for an obligation of the limited partnership solely by reason of being a limited partner, ***even if the limited partner participates in the management and control of the limited partnership.*** The full shield provided by the ULPA protects only against ***liability for the limited partnership's obligations and only to the extent that the limited partner is claimed to be liable on account of being a limited partner.*** Thus, a person who is both a general and a limited partner could be liable as a general partner for the partnership's obligations. A limited partner could also be liable to another partner or the partnership for breach of a duty or to a third party for his own wrongful conduct which results in injury of that third party. [ULPA § 303 and comment]

EXAM TIP

If you get a "control question," remember that the RULPA and ULPA provide differing views on the issue of liability of a limited partner who participates in the management or control of the limited partnership. Under the RULPA, such a limited partner *is liable* as a general partner if the person with whom the partnership was dealing reasonably believed that the limited partner was a general partner. Under the ULPA, however, the limited partner *does not lose limited liability* status solely by participating in the management or control of the partnership.

G. Rights of One Erroneously Believing Herself to Be a Limited Partner

1. General Rule—Not Liable as General Partner

A person who makes a contribution to a business enterprise and ***erroneously***, but in good faith, believes that she has become a limited partner as a result can avoid being held liable as a general partner if, on ascertaining the mistake, she:

(i) ***Causes an appropriate certificate of limited partnership or certificate of amendment to be filed with*** the secretary of state; or

(ii) ***Withdraws from future equity participation*** in the enterprise (thus retaining a right to any then-current interest in the partnership) by filing with the secretary of state a certificate declaring withdrawal.

[RULPA § 304(a); ULPA § 306(a)]

2. Exception

A person who erroneously believes herself to be a limited partner will be liable as a general partner to third parties who (i) reasonably believe the person to be a general partner, ***and*** (ii) transact business with the enterprise before the person withdraws or before her true status is reflected in the certificate. [RULPA § 304(b); ULPA § 304(b)]

H. Dissolution and Distribution

1. Methods of Dissolution

A limited partnership can be dissolved nonjudicially or judicially.

a. Nonjudicial Dissolution

A limited partnership will be dissolved whenever any of the following occurs:

(i) ***The occurrence of the time or events of dissolution specified in the certificate*** of limited partnership (or partnership agreement);

(ii) ***All of the partners consent in writing*** thereto; or

(iii) ***A general partner withdraws*** (or dissociates under the ULPA) and no provision is made for continuation, and the partners do not consent to continue (*see supra*, p. 197).

[*See* RULPA § 801; ULPA 801]

b. Judicial Dissolution

Any partner can have the limited partnership judicially dissolved whenever it is not reasonably practicable to carry on business in conformity with the partnership agreement. [RULPA § 802; ULPA § 802] Dissolution is most commonly granted where the general partner is guilty of misconduct such as neglect or self-dealing. [*See, e.g.*, **Wood v. Holiday Mobile Home Resorts, Inc.,** 625 P.2d 337 (Ariz.), *cert. denied*, 454 U.S. 826 (1981)]

2. Winding Up of Partnership Affairs

Once the partnership has been dissolved, its affairs must be wound up. The winding up process is similar to that of a general partnership. (*See supra*, pp. 174, 184–186 *et seq.*) Any general partner who has not wrongfully dissolved the partnership can wind up the partnership's affairs. If no such general partner is available, the limited partners may wind up (or appoint a person to oversee winding up under the ULPA). The RULPA also provides that upon application of a partner or his assignee, the court may wind up. [RULPA § 803; ULPA § 803(d)]

3. Distribution of Assets

Upon the winding up of the limited partnership, the partnership assets will be distributed in the following order:

(i) ***To creditors, including general and limited partners who are creditors***, in satisfaction of liabilities of the limited partnership other than liabilities for distributions to partners upon withdrawal or for interim distributions;

(ii) Except as provided in the partnership agreement, ***to general and limited partners and former partners in satisfaction of liabilities for interim distributions*** and to former partners to satisfy distributions owing them upon the partners' withdrawal; and

(iii) Except as provided in the partnership agreement, ***to general and limited partners first for the return of their contributions and second for partnership profits and property***, in the proportions in which the partners share in distributions.

[RULPA § 804]

a. ULPA

The ULPA's method for distribution of assets upon winding up is more specific than the approach under the RULPA. Under the ULPA, the assets of the limited partnership must be applied to satisfy the limited partnership's obligations ***to creditors, including partners who are creditors.*** If a limited partnership's assets are insufficient to satisfy all of its obligations, each person who was a general partner when the obligation was incurred must contribute to satisfy the debt. Any surplus remaining after the obligations are paid will be paid ***to the partners as a distribution.*** [ULPA § 812] Under the ULPA, creditors have ***five years from the date of publication of dissolution*** to bring their claims or they are barred. [ULPA §§ 806, 807]

4. Cancellation of Certificate

Upon the dissolution and winding up of the limited partnership, a certificate of cancellation must be filed with the secretary of state. [RULPA § 203] Under the ULPA, the limited partnership may amend its certificate to indicate dissolution and ***may*** file a statement of termination indicating that winding up has been completed. [ULPA § 803(b)]

MAJOR DIFFERENCES BETWEEN A GENERAL PARTNERSHIP AND A LIMITED PARTNERSHIP		
REQUIREMENTS	GENERAL PARTNERSHIP	LIMITED PARTNERSHIP
WRITING REQUIRED?	No	Yes (certificate of limited partnership)
RECORDS OFFICE REQUIRED?	No	Yes
SPECIAL NAME REQUIRED?	No	Yes (must include words "limited partnership")
LIABILITY LIMITED?	No	Yes (for limited partners)
PARTNERS HAVE MANAGEMENT RIGHTS?	Yes	No (for limited partners under RULPA)
PARTNERS SHARE PROFITS AND LOSSES?	Yes (equally)	Yes (according to value of contributions)

I. Conversions and Mergers Under ULPA

1. Conversions

An organization other than a limited partnership may convert to a limited partnership, and a limited partnership may convert to another organization. [ULPA § 1102(a)] In a statutory conversion, an existing entity changes its form, the jurisdiction or its governing statute, or both. Thus, a conversion involves only one entity. [ULPA § 1105(a)] A plan of conversion must be consented to by all of the partners. [ULPA § 1103(a)]

2. Mergers

In contrast to a conversion, a merger involves at least two separate entities. A limited partnership may merge with one or more other constituent organizations. [ULPA § 1106(a)] When a merger becomes effective, the surviving organization continues or comes into existence and each constituent organization that merges into the surviving organization ceases to exist as a separate entity. [ULPA § 1109(a)] A merger requires the consent of the partners. [ULPA § 1107(a)]

J. Foreign Limited Partnerships

1. In General

The RULPA provides that a foreign limited partnership may register with the secretary of state to do business in the state. The law of the state of organization governs the partnership's internal organization. Note that a foreign limited partnership cannot maintain an action in court until it registers with the state; however, the partnership may defend an action or suit filed against it in the state notwithstanding its failure to register. [RULPA §§ 901, 902, 907; ULPA §§ 901–903]

Part Three: Limited Liability Companies

Chapter Thirteen: Limited Liability Companies

CONTENTS	PAGE

Key Exam Issues

A limited liability company ("LLC") is a hybrid business organization designed primarily to be ***taxed like a partnership*** yet offer owners the ***limited personal liability that shareholders*** of a corporation enjoy. LLCs are creatures of statute, and the statutes vary considerably from state to state.

An exam question may ask you to consider an LLC as an alternative to the formation of a partnership or limited partnership. Exam questions concerning LLCs generally focus on formation issues and the basic characteristics of such an organization. Remember that an LLC is formed by ***filing articles of organization*** and that the majority of states allow an LLC to have ***one or more members***. An LLC is distinct from its members, who are not personally liable for the obligations of the LLC. Members have the right to manage the LLC themselves or they can appoint managers. The following discusses general LLC principles and highlights the issues most likely to be tested.

A. Introduction

1. History

In 1977, the Wyoming legislature adopted a law permitting the formation of a type of business organization available in a number of civil law countries but previously not provided for in the United States—the limited liability company or "LLC." LLCs combine some of the characteristics of corporations, partnerships, and limited partnerships. Since 1977, every state has adopted an LLC statute. There is quite a bit of variance among the states regarding LLC details. A small but growing number of states have adopted the Revised Uniform Limited Liability Company Act ("RULLCA"), a uniform LLC act approved by the National Conference of Commissioners on Uniform State Laws and revised in 2006. The major highlights of state statutes and the RULLCA will be discussed in this Summary.

2. Main Features

An LLC is a tax-driven entity designed to provide its owners (called "members") with two main features: (i) the ***limited liability that shareholders of a corporation enjoy*** (*i.e.*, owners are not liable for obligations of the entity), and (ii) the ***tax advantages that partners enjoy*** (*i.e.*, profits and losses flow through the entity and are treated as the owners' personal profits and losses, unlike profits of a corporation which are taxed at the corporate level and again when distributed to the shareholders in the form of a dividend).

3. Controlling Law—Statute vs. Operating Agreement

Although LLCs are governed by statute, LLC statutes generally provide that LLC members can adopt an ***operating agreement*** with provisions different from the LLC statute, and generally the operating agreement will control. [*See, e.g.*, 805 Ill. Comp. Stat. § 180/15–5] A majority of states require such an agreement to be in writing.

B. Formation

1. Filing Articles

An LLC is formed by filing articles of organization with the secretary of state. (This document is called a "certificate of organization" under the RULLCA and in some states.) In most states and under the RULLCA, an LLC may have ***one or more members.*** [*See, e.g.*, 805 Ill. Comp. Stat. § 180/5–1; Mass. Gen. L. ch. 156C, § 2(5); RULLCA § 201(a)] However, there are some states that require an LLC to have ***at least two members.***

a. Contents of Articles

Many states require the articles of organization to include the following:

(i) ***The name of the LLC***, which must include an indication that it is an LLC;

(ii) ***The street address of the LLC's registered office***, and the name and street address of its registered agent;

(iii) If the LLC is a term company, ***the specified term***;

(iv) ***If management is to be vested in managers***, a statement to that effect;

(v) ***Whether any member or members are to be liable for all or certain debts of the LLC***; and

(vi) ***Any other provisions*** that the members elect to include.

(1) RULLCA

Under the RULLCA, only (i) and (ii) from the list above are required to be included in the certificate. Also, if the LLC will have no members at the time of filing, the certificate must include a statement to that effect. (An LLC formed without members is called a "shelf" LLC, and these are allowed only in certain states.) [RULLCA § 201(b)]

2. Capital Contributions

All states allow a member's capital contribution to be in cash, property, or services already performed, and many also permit promissory notes and other binding obligations to contribute cash, property, or services. [*See, e.g.*, 805 Ill. Comp. Stat. § 180/20–1; RULLCA § 402]

C. Basic Characteristics of an LLC

1. Distinct Legal Entity

An LLC is treated as an entity distinct from its members. Thus, it may hold property in its own name, sue or be sued, etc. **Although some statutes require the LLC to have a *business purpose* [*see, e.g.*,** Tenn. Code Ann. § 48–249–104**], other statutes and the RULLCA allow an LLC to be formed for *any lawful purpose*, regardless of whether for profit [*see, e.g.*, Fla. Stat.** § 605.0108; **RULLCA** § **104(b)].**

a. Power to Carry Out Activities

Unless the articles provide otherwise, an LLC generally has the same power as a corporation to do whatever is necessary or convenient for carrying out its activities. [*See, e.g.*, 805 Ill. Comp. Stat. § 180/1–30*l*; RULLCA § 105] For example, an LLC may buy and sell real and personal property, make contracts, incur liabilities, borrow money, and transact business in any state.

2. Taxation

Under federal taxation law, an LLC is automatically taxed as a ***partnership*** unless it makes an election on its federal income tax return to be taxed as a corporation. Note though that although many states allow the formation of a single-member LLC (*see supra*, p. 215), the United States Treasury Department has determined that partnership tax treatment is not allowed for a single-member LLC. A single-member LLC will be disregarded as an entity separate from its owner, and it will be treated as a sole proprietorship. [Treas. Reg. § 301.7701–3]

EXAM TIP

If asked on your exam about the tax treatment of an LLC, recall that an LLC with *at least two members* does not have to do anything to be taxed as a partnership; taxation as a partnership is *automatic.* But remember that an LLC can elect ("check the box") on its federal income tax return to be taxed as a corporation.

3. Fiduciary Duties

Most statutes provide that members owe duties of loyalty and care to each other. In some states, the duty of care is to refrain from grossly negligent or reckless conduct, intentional misconduct, or knowing violation of law. [*See, e.g.*, Mont. Code Ann. § **35–8–310]** Under the RULLCA, members owe each other the duty of ordinary care and have the benefit of the business judgment rule (*i.e.,* they cannot be liable for making good faith business decisions that turn out poorly). [RULLCA § 409(c)]

a. Effect of Operating Agreement

Many statutes provide that the duties of loyalty and care may not be eliminated in the operating agreement, although the agreement may prescribe standards for measuring the performance of the obligation if ***not manifestly unreasonable***. [*See, e.g.*, 805 Ill. Comp. Stat. § 180/15–5] Under the RULLCA and other statutes, the operating agreement may eliminate these duties (but may not authorize intentional misconduct or knowing violations of law) as long as the elimination is not manifestly unreasonable. [RULLCA § 110]

4. Distributions

Under most statutes, unless the articles or an operating agreement provides otherwise, distributions of an LLC are allocated to the members ***on the basis of the value of the members' contributions***. [*See, e.g.*, Fla. Stat. § 605.0404] However, other statutes and the RULLCA provide that distributions are to be ***shared equally*** by the LLC members. [*See, e.g.*, RULLCA § 404(a); Mont. Code Ann. § 35–8–503]

a. Profits and Losses

Statutes generally provide that profits and losses of an LLC are allocated among members on the same way as distributions. However, the RULLCA and some states are silent on the allocation of profits and losses on the basis that many LLCs will choose to allocate profits and losses in order to comply with tax, accounting, and other regulatory requirements. [RULLCA § 404, comment]

5. Management

An LLC can be managed by the members, as in a partnership, or management may be centralized in one or more managers, as in a corporation. There is some variance among the state statutes in determining who is to manage. The RULLCA and many state statutes presume that the members will manage unless the articles provide otherwise. [*See, e.g.*, Mass. Gen. L. ch. 156C, § 24; RULLCA § 407] Other statutes require the articles to specify who will manage the LLC—members or managers. [*See, e.g.*, Mont. Code Ann. § 35–8–202]

a. Apparent Authority to Bind LLC

If the members are managing the LLC, each member is an agent of the LLC and has the power to bind the LLC by acts apparently for carrying on the business of the LLC. If management is by managers, the members do not have the power to bind the LLC, but the managers do. [*See, e.g.*, Mont. Code Ann. § 35–8–301; Fla. Stat. § 605.04074]

(1) RULLCA View

The RULLCA rejects the concept of "statutory apparent authority" and provides that a member has no power to bind the LLC solely because of her status. Instead, the principles of agency law will determine whether a member may bind the LLC. *Rationale:* An LLC's status as member-managed or manager-managed is not apparent from an LLC's name; a third party must check a public record to make this determination. [RULLCA § 301 and comment] To provide notice of a member's authority (or lack thereof), an LLC may file statements of authority with the secretary of state. [RULLCA § 302]

b. Voting

(1) Manager-Managed LLC

In a manager-managed LLC, each manager generally is entitled to one vote, and a ***majority vote*** of the managers is ordinarily required to approve most decisions affecting the LLC. [*See, e.g.*, RULLCA § 407(c)]

(2) Member-Managed LLC

In a member-managed LLC, all members have a right to participate in management decisions, but the voting strength of the members (*i.e.*, how a majority vote of the members is calculated to approve an LLC matter) generally follows how profits and losses are shared. Thus, if profits and losses are shared according to contributions, a member's voting strength is based on his percentage of ownership interest in the LLC—not one member, one vote. In this case, a vote of a majority in ***interest*** will be required to approve an LLC matter. [*See, e.g.*, Fla. Stat. § 605.04073] However, if profits and losses are shared equally, each member is entitled to one vote regarding an LLC matter, and a majority vote of the ***members*** will be required to approve an LLC matter. [*See, e.g.*, RULLCA § 407(b)]

e.g. **Example:** A, B, and C form an LLC. A makes a contribution of $20,000, B makes a contribution of $20,000, and C makes a contribution of $60,000. A and B each have a 20% ownership interest in the LLC, and C has a 60% ownership interest in the LLC. The LLC is formed in a state where the LLC statute provides that profits and losses of the LLC are shared according to contributions, unless the members provide otherwise. A, B, and C did not provide in the articles or the operating agreement how profits and losses would be shared. The LLC members now have to vote on whether to buy expensive equipment for the LLC. A and B vote in favor of buying the equipment, and C votes against buying the equipment. Even though A and B voted in favor of buying the equipment, their votes do not constitute a majority in interest because they own only 40% of the capital; consequently, the vote of C (whose ownership interest is 60%) will control, and the LLC will not be authorized to purchase the equipment.

cf. **Compare:** If in the above example the LLC were formed in a state where the LLC statute provides that profits and losses are shared equally, the votes of A and B would be sufficient to approve the buying of the equipment because each member would be entitled to one vote.

6. Limited Liability

Members of an LLC are not personally liable for the obligations of the LLC merely by virtue of their ownership in the LLC. Similarly, if an LLC is run by a manager (*see above*), the manager is not personally liable for the LLC's obligations either. In this way, members and managers are similar to shareholders and directors of a corporation. Of course, members and managers can contract to become personally liable for the LLC's obligations. Similarly, like any other person, a member or manager is liable for his own torts performed in the course of working for the LLC. [*See, e.g.*, Mont. Code Ann. § 35–8–304; RULLCA § 30]

a. Exception—Piercing the Veil

Generally, courts will "pierce the veil" of an LLC and impose personal liability on its members to prevent fraud or other inequity (*e.g.*, when an LLC is formed to avoid existing personal obligations of the members). Note, however, that while lack of the observance of formalities is sometimes held to be a ground for piercing the veil of a corporation, because LLCs can be run with fewer formalities than a corporation, lack of formalities generally is not a ground for piercing an LLC. [*See, e.g.*, RULLCA § 304(b); Fla. Stat. § 605.0304]

7. Transfer of Ownership

A member may assign (in whole or in part) his interest in the LLC. An assignment only transfers the member's ***right to receive distributions*** (*e.g.*, profits or on dissolution); management rights are not transferred. An assignee can become a member (*i.e.*, management rights can be transferred) only with the consent of ***all*** members. [*See, e.g.*, Mass. Gen. L. ch. 156C, §§ 39, 41; RULLCA § 401(d)] Thus, transfer of ownership in an LLC is similar to that in a partnership.

SUMMARY OF THE BASIC CHARACTERISTICS OF AN LLC	
ENTITY STATUS	An LLC is an entity distinct from its members.
TAX TREATMENT	An LLC is generally taxed as a partnership, unless its members elect to be taxed as a corporation.

PROFITS AND LOSSES	In most states, members share profits and losses of the LLC according to the value of their contributions.
MANAGEMENT	An LLC may be managed by members or managers.
LIABILITY OF MEMBERS	A member is not liable for the LLC's obligations but is liable for her own torts.
TRANSFER OF OWNERSHIP	A member may assign her interest in the LLC but the assignment transfers only the member's right to receive distributions; management rights are not transferred.

8. Information Rights

Each state statute grants members certain access to the LLCs books and records. Generally, each member of an LLC is entitled to inspect and copy the books and records of the LLC during regular business hours. [*See, e.g.*, Mont. Code Ann. § 35–8–405; Mass. Gen. L. ch. 156C, § 9] Some statutes require the member to make an advance demand for certain records that are not related to the member's rights and duties under the operating agreement. [*See, e.g.*, Fla. Stat. § 605.0410; RULLCA § 410]

9. Derivative Action

Most state statutes and the RULLCA permit members to bring derivative actions on the LLC's behalf based on a breach of fiduciary duties. A member may bring a derivative action if she first makes a demand on the controlling members or managers to enforce the right and they do not bring an action within a reasonable time, unless demand would be futile. [*See, e.g.*, 805 Ill. Comp. Stat. § 180/40–1; RULLCA § 902]

10. Withdrawal of Members

Generally, the events that will cause dissociation of a partner in a partnership (*see supra*, p. 173) will also cause dissociation of a member of an LLC. Under most statutes and the RULLCA, a member has the power to dissociate as a member of an LLC at any time by expressing the will to withdraw, although a wrongfully dissociating member may be liable to the LLC for damages. [*See, e.g.*, Fla. Stat. § 605.0601; RULLCA § 601] However, some statutes provide that a member may withdraw only at the time or upon the happening of events specified in the operating agreement. [*See, e.g.*, Mass. Gen. L. ch. 156C, § 37]

a. Obligation to Buy out Interest

Following the rule for general partnerships (*see supra*, p. 174), some statutes provide that an LLC is obligated to buy out the interest of a dissociating member. [*See, e.g.*, 805 Ill. Comp. Stat. § 180/35–55] To provide LLCs with greater stability, the RULLCA and other statutes have declined to impose such an obligation. [*See, e.g.*, Fla. Stat. § 605.0601; RULLCA § 601]

11. Events Causing Dissolution

The events giving rise to dissolution vary widely among the states. Under the RULLCA and many statutes, an LLC will be dissolved upon: (i) the occurrence of an event or circumstance that the operating agreement states causes dissolution; (ii) the consent of all the members; (iii) the passage of 90 consecutive days during which the LLC has no members; or (iv) a judicial decree or administrative order dissolving the LLC. [RULLCA § 701(a)]

a. Grounds for Judicial Dissolution

The grounds for judicial dissolution vary by state. The RULLCA provides that an LLC may be dissolved by a court upon application by a member when: (i) the conduct of all or substantially all of the LLC's activities is unlawful; (ii) it is not reasonably practicable to carry on the company's activities in conformity with the certificate of organization and the operating agreement; or (iii) the managers or controlling members have acted, are acting, or will act in a manner that is illegal or fraudulent, or have acted or are acting in a manner that is oppressive and directly harmful to the member applying for dissolution. [RULLCA § 701(a)]

12. Review of Testable Limited Liability Companies Issues

1. Defined: A HYBRID BETWEEN A CORPORATION AND PARTNERSHIP IN WHICH THE OWNERS WHO ARE CALLED MEMBERS HAVE LIMITED LIABILITY AND ALSO THE BENEFITS OF PARTNERSHIP TAX TREATMENT.
2. Formation Requirements: ORGANIZERS MUST FILE ARTICLES OF ORGANIZATION AND MAY ADOPT AN OPERATING AGREEMENT.
3. Control: OWNERS (MEMBERS) CONTROL, BUT MAY DELEGATE TO A TEAM OF MANAGERS.
4. Limited Life: THE COMPANY WILL DISSOLVE UPON UNANIMOUS CONSENT OF MEMBERS OR AS PROVIDED IN ARTICLES OF ORGANIZATION OR OPERATING AGREEMENT.
5. Limited Liquidity: A FULL MEMBERSHIP INTEREST MAY NOT BE TRANSFERRED WITHOUT UNANIMOUS CONSENT OF ALL MEMBERS, OR AS PROVIDED IN THE OPERATING AGREEMENT.
6. Therefore: LLCs= LIMITED LIABILITY + LIMITED LIFE + LIMITED LIQUIDITY+ LIMITED TAX

Mini-Review, Review Questions, and Answers

Mini Review

Agency Law

1. **Principal's Liability for Agent's Torts**
   (a) Assent, Benefit, Control plus Scope
   (b) No Vicarious Liability for Independent Contractor's Torts
2. **Principal's Liability for Agent's Contracts**
   (a) Express Authority—Oral, Except for Land
   (b) Implied Authority—Necessity, Custom, or Prior Dealings
   (c) Apparent Authority—Principal Cloaks and Third Party Reasonably Relies
   (d) Ratification: Knowledge plus Acceptance of Benefits
   (e) Authorized Agents Are Not Liable for Principal's Contracts, Unless There Is an Undisclosed Principal
3. **Duties Agent Owes Principal**
   (a) Care,
   (b) Obedience, and
   (c) Loyalty

Partnership Law

1. **Formation**
   (a) There Are Generally No Required General Partnership Formalities
   (b) Definition: Association, 2 Persons, Carrying On, Co-Owners of a Business for **Profit**
2. **Liabilities to Third Parties**
   (a) General Partners Are Liable for All Partnership Obligations
   (b) Estoppel—Representers Are Liable as if General Partners
3. **Relations Between Partners**
   (a) Fiduciaries, Which Gives Rise to an Action for Accounting and Disgorging for Profits
   (b) Only the Share of Profits Is Liquid, Personal Property
   (c) Absent Contract, Equal Control, No Salary, Profits Shared Equally and Losses Shared Like Profits
4. **Dissolution**
   (a) Priority
      (1) All Creditors, (2) All Capital, (3) Profits, if Any, Shared Equally in the Absence of an Agreement
   (b) Distribution Rule

      Each Partner Must Be Repaid Their Loans and Capital, plus Their Share of Profits, but Minus Their Share of Losses

5. Alternative Unincorporated Business Organizations

Limited Partners, Registered Limited Liability Partners, and LLC Members All Have Limited Liability

Review Questions

FILL IN ANSWER

1. Indicate whether each of the following statements is true or false: ______________

   a. A principal is ***disclosed*** only if the third party knows that the agent is acting for a principal and knows the identity of the principal. ______________

   b. A special agent is authorized to conduct a ***series of transactions*** involving a ***continuity of service***. ______________

   c. An agency agreement must be based on the mutual consent of the purported principal and agent. ______________

2. At a local bar, Leslie overhears Yolanda say, "I certainly would like to find a good Picasso for my study." Unbeknownst to Yolanda, Leslie contacts collector Pierre and purchases one of his Picasso paintings "as Yolanda's agent." Can Yolanda refuse to pay for the painting? ______________

   a. If Pierre has relied on Leslie's statements in selling her the Picasso for Yolanda, can he allege an apparent agency against Yolanda? ______________

3. A minor may be an agent, but she cannot be a principal. True or false? ______________

4. The relationship between principal and agent must be supported by consideration in order for the agent's acts to bind the principal. True or false? ______________

5. Randy telephones Alicia and asks her to sell his ranch "for any price more than $200,000" and deposit the proceeds in his account. Alicia signs a purchase agreement with Bessie, who contracts to buy the ranch for $250,000. Can Bessie enforce the contract against Randy? ______________

   a. Would the result be different if Randy had negotiated the sale with Bessie and instructed Alicia by telephone to sign his name to the agreement? ______________

6. Jackie meets Truman at a party and offers to find a publisher for Truman's new book "solely as a friend." Jackie promptly forgets the matter and makes no attempt to find a buyer for the manuscript. Is Jackie liable to Truman for her failure to perform? ______________

7. Manufacturer hires Otis as a marketing agent. May Otis properly handle marketing for Manufacturer's competitors as well? ________________

   a. As part of the job, Otis is authorized to rent warehouse space on Manufacturer's account. Otis rents space from a landlord, Wendy, who unbeknownst to Manufacturer agrees in return to give Otis a reduced rental on Otis's apartment. Has Otis breached his fiduciary duty to Manufacturer? ________________

8. Anita is engaged to find and purchase "suitable farming property" for her principal, Paul. While searching for such property, Anita discovers a small apple orchard for sale and purchases the orchard for herself. Has Anita breached her fiduciary duty to Paul? ________________

   a. Anita's uncle Raphael is attempting to sell his farm and promises Anita a commission if she can find a buyer. Anita then arranges for Paul to purchase the farm from Raphael. Assuming that the sales price represents the fair market value of the property, can Paul rescind the sale? ________________

9. An agent is responsible to the principal for acts by subagents hired by him, whether or not the hiring was authorized by the principal. True or false? ________________

10. Bob hires Cathy as an engineer to maintain Bob's automated assembly line. While repairing a portion of the line, Cathy discovers a new method of lubricating certain moving parts which would not work for Bob's plant but would have wide applicability in other industries. Does Bob have any rights in Cathy's discovery? ________________

11. A principal has a right to indemnification for any loss sustained as a result of his agent's improper acts, but an employer has no similar right against his employee. True or false? ________________

12. Marvin hires Bill as his exclusive sales agent to sell Marvin's new line of widgets. After Bill has developed a substantial market for the product, Marvin enters the field to sell directly to customers. Does Bill have an action against Marvin for the profits on Marvin's sales? ________________

    a. Would the result be different if Marvin had subsequently retained Carol as a sales agent to compete with Bill? ________________

13. Penny hires Adam on commission to sell Penny's boat. Adam in turn engages Sally on the same basis to help him find a buyer. Sally induces Brad to purchase the boat. Is Penny liable for Sally's commission on the sale? ________________

14. Phil hires Archie to transport a load of steel ingots across the state, and Archie (with Phil's consent) engages Tad, who owns

a truck, to help him on the trip. En route, the ingots slide off Tad's truck and injure Denise, the driver of a passing car.

a. If Denise obtains a judgment against Archie for her damages, is Archie entitled to indemnification from Phil? ______________

b. Assuming Denise's judgment is against Tad rather than Archie, would Tad be equally entitled to indemnification from Phil or Archie? ______________

c. Suppose instead that Phil changes his mind for no apparent reason and engages another agent to haul his steel. If Archie has turned down an alternative job to make the trip, can he obtain specific performance of his agreement with Phil? ______________

15. As a general rule, courts will construe grants of authority containing extravagant phrases broadly, in order to protect the interests of third parties dealing with the agent. True or false? ______________

16. Phoebe authorizes Anna to sell her boat for $5,000. Chris offers to pay $50 for a right of first refusal on the boat. Does Anna have the authority to accept Chris's offer? ______________

17. Paula tells Alex, "Please try to collect this overdue account from Tamyra. You may have 20% of what you collect as your fee." Does Alex have authority to settle with Tamyra for less than the full amount owed? ______________

18. Pete engages Arnold, a real estate broker, to sell his house. Does Arnold have the authority to negotiate and conclude a sale with Dean, a prospective buyer? ______________

a. Suppose Arnold appoints fellow broker Edith as his agent to help secure a buyer for Pete's house. Edith produces the highest bidder on the house, who signs a purchase contract with Pete. If the appointment of brokers as subagents is customary in the area, can Edith recover compensation from Pete for her services? ______________

b. Does Arnold have the power to warrant the structure of Pete's house "sound against any and all defects"? ______________

19. Opie decides to open a store and hires Bea as his general manager. Before leaving on a sailing trip, Opie tells Bea not to spend more than $2,000 on "noninventory items" while he is away. Shortly after Opie's departure, Bea receives a call from a city official indicating that certain rewiring in the store must be completed within 24 hours in order to avoid losing its business permit. If the rewiring will cost $3,000 to complete in that period, does Bea have authority to have it done? ______________

a. While Opie is away, someone tells Bea that several people have been living on Opie's remote mountain property for some time. Bea neglects to mention this fact to Opie, and thereafter the "squatters" claim title to the land by adverse possession. Is Bea's knowledge imputed to Opie in resolving the claim? _______________

b. Shortly before her employment by Opie, Bea managed a similar store and became familiar with the Fair Employment Act hiring requirements. If such requirements are significant in her present position, will Bea's knowledge be imputed to Opie? _______________

20. Louise gives Stephen her power of attorney to purchase for her certain pieces of sculpture upon Stephen's representation that he is an art expert with considerable experience. Stephen then contracts with Dennis for several expensive items on Louise's account. If Louise subsequently discovers that Stephen has no art expertise, can she rescind the sale? _______________

a. Would the result be different if Louise discovered Stephen's misrepresentations prior to the sale by Dennis? _______________

21. Elmer writes to Graham, authorizing Graham to act as his agent for the sale of Elmer's car. Elmer then mails a copy of the letter to Hector, whom Elmer believes to be a prospective buyer. Does Graham have apparent authority to sell the car to Hector? _______________

a. Would the result be different if Hector instead had spotted a notation on Elmer's desk, "Contact Graham regarding the sale of the car"? _______________

b. Assuming Elmer mailed to Hector a copy of the above letter written to Graham, can Elmer avoid liability to Hector by expressly revoking Graham's authority in writing, prior to any agreement with Hector? _______________

22. Suppose Elmer in the question above tells Graham, "You're authorized to sell my car, but ***only*** during the next 30 days." At the same time, Elmer—who is leaving the country for several months—signs over the title to the car to Graham, it being clearly understood that this is solely for purposes of the agency. If Graham sells the car to Francine 90 days later, can Francine enforce the sale against Elmer? _______________

23. Claudia borrows Don's lawnmower and then offers to sell the mower to Ned. Ned mentions the offer to Don, who merely says, "I think it's a good mower, alright." Ned pays Claudia for the mower, and Claudia moves to another town after returning the mower to Don. Can Ned obtain the mower from Don? _______________

24. Pat engages broker Alan to purchase a summer home for her in the Woodland Glen subdivision. Five years elapse without further communication between Pat and Alan, and Alan discovers a prospective property. Is Alan authorized to proceed with a purchase? _______________

a. Shortly after he is hired by Pat, Alan learns that the area around the Woodland Glen subdivision is being rezoned to permit logging and heavy industry. Can Alan proceed to purchase a home there on Pat's behalf? ______________

25. Oscar engages Agatha to sell his collection of antique guns. Thereafter, she enters into a purchase agreement with Sam and receives payment for the collection. Unbeknownst to Agatha or Sam, Oscar has died in the interim. Can Sam enforce the sales contract against Oscar's estate? ______________

    a. Would the result be different if Oscar had hired Agatha to sell the guns as a means of discharging a loan from Agatha to Oscar? ______________

26. Brandon hires Chuck as exclusive agent to sell his estate for a period of six months. The agreement between the two provides that the agency is irrevocable during that period. Two weeks later, Brandon writes Chuck a "letter of termination" and engages Daphne to sell the property. Can Chuck obtain specific performance of the agreement against Brandon? ______________

    a. Would the result be different if Chuck's employment was a means of discharging a debt owed by Brandon to Chuck? ______________

27. The apparent authority of an agent can never terminate until proper notice of the termination is given to third parties. True or false? ______________

28. Purporting to act on Linda's behalf (but without authority), Jackie agrees to purchase Stacey's skis and bindings for $200. Elizabeth then gives Jackie $10 for an assignment of rights under the agreement and tenders the $200 contract price to Stacey. Is Stacey free to rescind? ______________

29. Teddy steals Omar's television set and, posing as Omar, purports to sell it to Xavier. Feeling guilty about the theft, Teddy informs Omar, who decides that the sale would be advantageous and ratifies it. Can Omar enforce the purchase agreement against Xavier? ______________

    a. Suppose instead that Teddy forges Omar's name to a gambling wager, intending that the proceeds will go to Omar if he wins. Can Omar later ratify and enforce the wager? ______________

30. Without authority, Anne purports to sell Penelope's rare violin to Theo. When informed of this, Penelope says, "I was thinking of selling it anyway, and Anne would certainly be the one to handle it for me. Fine." If the agreed price were $25, can Theo enforce the contract by tendering that amount to Penelope? ______________

31. Acting without authority, Jack purports to sell Lucy's farm to Paul. If Lucy later telephones Paul to say that she ratifies the sale, can Paul enforce the purchase agreement against her? ______________

    a. Suppose that the agreed sales price between Jack and Paul is $200,000. Subsequently, and without knowledge of the above agreement, Lucy contracts to sell the farm to her neighbor for $150,000. When Lucy learns of Jack's agreement, she promptly ratifies it in writing. Can Paul then enforce the contract? ______________

32. Without authority, Abby hires Tom to install a new roof on Priscilla's house. Tom arrives and, informing Priscilla of the agreement, installs the roof. Does Tom have an action against Priscilla for the price agreed upon by Abby? ______________

    a. Would the result be different if Priscilla were out of town when Tom arrived to install the roof? ______________

33. Without authority, Steve purports to sell Richard's collection of antique automobiles to Betsy. Before Richard learns of the agreement, Betsy dies. Can Richard subsequently ratify the sale? ______________

34. Although he has no authority, Adam agrees to sell Eve's house to Moses "as agent for Eve." Adam believes in good faith that he is authorized to sell the house, but Eve does not ratify the sale. Is Adam liable to Moses? ______________

    a. Suppose instead that Eve authorized Adam to sell the house. In negotiating with Moses, Adam (without authority) contracts to sell the house *and* an adjoining shop in a "package deal." Moses makes the agreed down payment. Eve learns of the unauthorized additional terms and repudiates the contract. Does Moses have any rights against Eve? ______________

35. Smith Company authorizes Jones to purchase a new generator for the company plant. Jones enters into an agreement to purchase a generator from Omega Corporation and executes the agreement, "Smith Company, by its agent, Jones." Can Omega Corporation enforce the agreement against both Smith and Jones? ______________

    a. Is extrinsic evidence admissible to show who the parties actually intended would be liable on the contract? ______________

36. Ponch authorizes John to purchase a mountain cabin for him. John discovers that Wayne has a cabin for sale and signs a purchase agreement with Wayne, in his own name and without mention of his role as agent.

a. Wayne conveys title to the cabin to John, but Ponch does not pay as required in the agreement. Can Wayne sue John to enforce the contract? ____________

b. After signing the purchase agreement, Wayne learns that John was actually an agent for Ponch. Can Wayne sue both Ponch and John on the contract? ____________

c. Suppose instead that John pays the purchase price to Wayne, but Wayne refuses to convey title to the cabin. Can Ponch sue Wayne on the contract? ____________

d. Would the result in the preceding hypothetical be different if Ponch knew that Wayne would never sell the cabin to him? ____________

e. Assume that Ponch gives John sufficient funds to purchase the cabin, but John leaves the country with the money. Can Wayne sue Ponch for the purchase price? ____________

37. Nelson engages Kristin to hire a tutor to teach him French. Kristin contracts with Marie for this purpose, but fails to inform Marie that Nelson will be her student. Can Nelson enforce the contract? ____________

38. Barney authorizes Fred to sell an inventory of his spare parts. Fred enters into an agreement with Yogi to purchase the parts, which Fred signs "as agent." Barney's identity is not revealed; Yogi pays Fred for the parts. If the parts are not delivered, can Yogi sue Fred on the contract? ____________

a. Would the result be different if Yogi knew that Fred was Barney's agent, even though Fred had never mentioned his identity? ____________

39. Indicate whether each of the following statements is true or false:

a. Under the doctrine of respondeat superior, the employer alone is liable for the tortious acts of her employee. ____________

b. An employer may avoid vicarious liability if she expressly contracts that the employee assumes full responsibility for his actions. ____________

c. An employer may be liable for the acts of her employee even though the employee is exonerated from liability. ____________

d. An employer is not vicariously liable for an employee's torts if she has no right to control the physical acts of the employee. ____________

e. A minor who hires an employee and has the right to control the acts of the employee can be held vicariously liable for the employee's torts. ______________

40. Tim is walking through Mac's warehouse to meet a friend when he sees several workers trying to lift a large box. Although not an employee, Tim offers to assist them, and negligently drops the box on Mac's customer, injuring him. Could Mac be held vicariously liable for Tim's acts? ______________

a. Suppose instead that the box falls on one of Mac's employees. Can Mac recover for injuries to his employee? ______________

41. Mario's sporting goods store advertises that Kermit, a noted gymnast, will formulate personalized exercise programs at the store. During a demonstration, Kermit negligently injures Lincoln, a customer at the store, while adjusting an exercise device on Lincoln's arms. The agreement between Mario and Kermit gives Mario no right to control Kermit's actions during demonstrations. Could Mario be held vicariously liable to Lincoln? ______________

a. Would the result be different if Lincoln had entered the store to purchase some ski wax and, while waiting at the sales counter for his purchase, was injured by Kermit's negligently thrown barbell? ______________

42. Porgy hires Bess to drive a truckload of wheat from Kansas to Los Angeles. Bess in turn hires Sanford to help her as a relief driver. While Sanford is driving en route, he negligently collides with a car, injuring its driver. Is Porgy vicariously liable to the injured driver? ______________

43. Marcus, a heavy equipment contractor, leases a scoop-shovel tractor and a skilled operator, Seth, to Taggert to excavate a standard sewer line at Taggert's home. In the process of digging, Seth negligently severs an electric line, which falls on and injures Taggert's neighbor, Raul. Can Marcus be held vicariously liable to Raul? ______________

a. Would the result be different if the electric line was severed while Seth was making a special excavation ordered by Taggert that required Seth to excavate a hole for a pond? ______________

44. Sonny is a truck driver hired by Cher to transport construction materials. In determining whether Sonny is an employee or an independent contractor, would it be helpful to know whether Sonny drives one of Cher's trucks? ______________

45. Alex falls and injures himself while staying at Bessie's resort.

Bessie calls Dr. Wiley, a physician employed by the resort, to treat Alex. Dr. Wiley negligently wrenches Alex's back, aggravating the injury. Is Bessie liable to Alex for the aggravation? ______________

a. Would the result be different if the aggravation were due to the fact that Dr. Wiley was intoxicated at the time he treated Alex? ______________

46. David hires independent contractor Iman to spray his alfalfa crop. Iman uses all reasonable care in spraying, but a certain amount of gas is blown onto Cindy's land, killing two of her sheep. Is David liable to Cindy? ______________

47. Delilah, a department store owner, hires Samson as a sales clerk in the book department. Although he is instructed never to wait on customers in the adjoining sporting goods department, Samson nevertheless does so and injures a customer while demonstrating how to fire a spear gun. Is Delilah liable to the customer? ______________

a. Would the result be different if Samson had been employed in the sporting goods department but was instructed never to demonstrate spear guns? ______________

48. Ace Bar & Grill employs Walker as a dishwasher. Shortly thereafter, Walker hears Zeke, a customer in the establishment, whistling off key and asks him to stop. When Zeke refuses, Walker takes a baseball bat from under the bar and hits Zeke over the head, severely injuring him. Is Ace vicariously liable to Zeke? ______________

a. Would the result be different if Walker had been employed in a railroad dining car and the same incident had ensued? ______________

b. Suppose instead that Walker is taking a smoke break when he carelessly flips his cigarette into a corner. A fire ensues, which injures two customers in the Ace Bar & Grill. Is Ace liable to the injured customers? ______________

c. During a lull in business, Walker decides to clean his bicycle chain in the Ace dishwasher. This causes the washer to explode, injuring customer Nancy. Is Ace vicariously liable to Nancy? ______________

d. Walker is asked to clean grease off a stove top in the Ace kitchen. Walker uses gasoline to cut the grease, which promptly ignites and burns a customer. Is Ace vicariously liable to the injured customer? ______________

49. When an employee acts partly on his own behalf and partly for his employer, the employer is vicariously liable only for that

conduct designed to further the employer's business. True or false? ________

50. Archie is hired by Phil to deliver newspapers in Phil's truck. While on the delivery route, Archie (without authority) invites a friend, Trish, to ride along. Archie then negligently collides with a car, injuring Trish. Is Phil liable to Trish? ________

    a. Suppose Trish were an employee of Phil hired to unload papers from the truck. Would Phil be liable to Trish for the injuries she sustained due to Archie's negligent driving? ________

51. Usury Loan Company hires Acme Collection Agency to collect a debt owed by Daphne and instructs Acme to "repossess the car" if Daphne refuses to pay. Acme takes possession of a car from Daphne's garage, but he takes Sasha's car instead of Daphne's. Can Sasha hold both Usury and Acme liable? ________

    a. Suppose that Usury merely tells Acme to collect Daphne's debt, but Acme (without authority) takes the car that actually belongs to Sasha and delivers it to Usury. Can Sasha hold Usury liable if she discovers the car in its possession? ________

    b. Would the result be different if Acme took the car for its own purposes, but inadvertently delivered it to Usury? ________

52. Sam hires Diane as manager of his apartment building. Diane notices a loose step on the stairwell of the building, makes a note to repair it, but does not mention it to Sam. Woody, a tenant in the building, falls through the step and breaks his leg. Can Woody hold Sam liable? ________

    a. Would the result be different if Diane were Sam's bookkeeper instead of his manager? ________

53. Unless all of the essential elements for misrepresentation are proved, an employer (or principal) cannot be held liable in tort for the statements of his employee (or agent). True or false? ________

54. While an employer can be liable for false statements made by employees or agents, he cannot be held liable for the statements of an independent contractor. True or false? ________

55. Burns hires Allen to sell his art collection and provides Allen with recent appraisal information for prospective buyers. To induce a higher sales price, Allen actually gives Doris an inflated appraisal figure, and Doris buys the collection. Can Doris hold Burns liable for Allen's false statements? ________

    a. Would the result be different if Burns had given no appraisal information to Allen? ________

b. Would the result be different if Burns had engaged Allen merely to advertise his collection? ______

56. Lester engages Vanessa to sell his car, and tells Vanessa that the car has been driven 50,000 miles (the present setting on its odometer). In fact, Lester knows the car has been driven 150,000 miles. Upon Vanessa's representation of the lower mileage, a buyer purchases the car. Can the buyer sue Lester? ______

 a. Would the result be different if neither Lester nor Vanessa were aware of the true mileage on the car? ______

57. A partnership must always consist of co-owners carrying on a business for profit. True or false? ______

58. For purposes of determining rights and liabilities, a partnership is always treated as an aggregate of the individual partners. True or false? ______

59. Indicate whether each of the following statements is true or false:

 a. A partnership is equally effective whether formed by oral or written agreement of the partners. ______

 b. A corporation has the capacity to become a partner. ______

 c. No person may become a member of a partnership unless all partners consent. ______

 d. The sharing of gross income is more likely to establish a partnership relation than the sharing of profits from the business. ______

 e. If an actual partner represents that a nonpartner is a member of the partnership, the nonpartner can bind the partnership as though he were a partner. ______

 f. In the absence of a contrary agreement, the management rights of a partner in the partnership are proportional to his agreed share in partnership profits. ______

 g. As a general rule, a partner cannot be reimbursed for his services to the partnership unless all partners agree. ______

 h. Under the Revised Uniform Partnership Act ("RUPA"), any action by one partner against another involving partnership business must be brought in equity rather than at law. ______

60. Partner Mary signs a loan agreement with Bank to borrow $500,000 for the partnership. Unbeknownst to Bank, the partnership agreement provides that no single partner may borrow for the partnership without the written consent of all of

the partners. Is the agreement enforceable against the partnership? ______________

a. After hearing about the loan, partner Rhoda notifies Bank that she will not be liable on any subsequent partnership debts. Is this notice effective under the UPA to relieve Rhoda of further liability? ______________

61. Marcus joins the business partnership of Steele and Wool as a new partner. Shortly thereafter, Acme, a contract creditor of the partnership, sues for partnership debts incurred before Marcus became a member. Does Marcus have any liability for the debts? ______________

a. Can Acme sue Steele alone on the claim? ______________

b. On a business trip for the partnership, Marcus negligently runs his car onto a sidewalk, injuring Shelby. Can Shelby recover from Wool alone for Marcus's tortious conduct? ______________

c. Suppose instead that Steele is the person injured by Marcus's negligence. Can Marcus be held liable to Steele? ______________

62. Kato and Darva form a limited liability partnership ("LLP") to house-sit for wealthy people while they are on vacation. The Kato and Darva LLP is hired to house-sit for Orenthallius while he is on a one-month vacation. Orenthallius tells Kato and Darva that as part of their house-sitting duties, one of them must be present at the house at all times, they may use his pool, sauna, etc., but they must clean up after themselves. One day while Kato is house-sitting at Orenthallius's house and is relaxing on the patio he drops a glass. He decides that he is hot and will go for a swim and then clean up the glass. Meanwhile, Orenthallius's gardener comes to do his weekly gardening and is watering plants on the patio when he steps on the glass, injuring himself.

a. Is Darva personally liable to the gardener for his injuries? ______________

b. Is Kato personally liable to the gardener for his injuries? ______________

63. Partner purchases a warehouse with her own money but puts title to the building in the name of the partnership. Is the warehouse partnership property? ______________

64. One of several partners in a fast-food restaurant incurs heavy personal debts that she is unable to pay. Can her creditors attach her interest in the restaurant premises to satisfy their claims against her? ______________

a. Can the creditors proceed against the partner's interest in the partnership? ______________

65. When a partner is ***dissociated*** from the partnership under the RUPA, the partnership is automatically dissolved and must be wound up. True or false? ____________

66. Tanya, Jeff, and Nancy form a partnership under the ***RUPA*** to operate an ice skating rink for two years. After one year, Nancy decides she no longer wants to be associated with Tanya and Jeff and notifies them that she is withdrawing from the partnership.

    a. Does Nancy's withdrawal result in the dissolution of the partnership? ____________

    b. Would your answer to the preceding question change if the partnership were an "at will" partnership? ____________

    c. If Tanya and Jeff decide to continue the business after Nancy's withdrawal, can Nancy be held liable to a creditor who sells ice skates to the partnership one year after her withdrawal? ____________

    d. Would your answer to the preceding question change if Nancy had filed a statement of dissociation with the secretary of state 30 days after her withdrawal? ____________

67. Indicate whether each of the following statements is true or false under the ***UPA***:

    a. If a partnership is one for a specified period of time (*e.g.*, two years), the partners cannot continue the partnership relation beyond that period without a new agreement. ____________

    b. Any partnership may be dissolved at any time at the express choice of any partner. ____________

    c. The fact that the partnership business can be carried on only at a loss is sufficient per se to dissolve the partnership. ____________

    d. When there are net partnership losses upon dissolution, these are divided equally among all partners. ____________

68. Lucy, Desi, and Ethel form a partnership under the ***UPA*** for a three-year period to produce chocolates. Six months later, Desi elects to dissolve the partnership.

    a. Is Desi liable to Lucy and Ethel for any damages resulting from the dissolution? ____________

    b. After Desi's election to dissolve the partnership, Lucy and Ethel continue to operate the business in the partnership name. Can Desi sue Lucy and Ethel for compensation accruing after he withdrew from the partnership? ____________

c. Would the result in the preceding situation be different if Desi had died six months after the formation of the partnership? ________________

d. If Lucy and Ethel continue the business after Desi withdraws, can Desi be held liable for debts of the partnership incurred while he was a partner? ________________

69. Chris, Debbie, and Laurie agree to form a limited partnership to run a funeral home with Chris as general partner and Debbie and Laurie as limited partners. Chris executes a certificate of limited partnership but forgets to file it with the secretary of state. Chris subsequently enters into a contract with Mortuary Supplies to purchase formaldehyde.

    a. Have Chris, Debbie, and Laurie formed a limited partnership? ________________

    b. Are Debbie and Laurie personally liable on the contract with Mortuary Supplies for the purchase of the formaldehyde? ________________

70. Jerry, Elaine, George, and Kramer form a limited partnership to manufacture latex gloves. Jerry and Elaine are general partners, and George and Kramer are limited partners. George wants to name the partnership George's Gloves Galore. May George's name appear in the name of the limited partnership under the ***RULPA***? ________________

    a. Would your answer to the preceding question change if Jerry, Elaine, and Kramer had formed the limited partnership with Jerry as general partner and Elaine and Kramer as limited partners prior to George becoming a limited partner, and the partnership was named George's Gloves Galore? ________________

71. Cindy, Jan, and Marsha decide to form a limited partnership under the ***RULPA***, with Cindy as general partner and Jan and Marsha as limited partners.

    a. Can Jan assign her interest in the partnership to Greg without the approval of Cindy or Marsha? ________________

    b. If Marsha dies, will her death dissolve the partnership? ________________

    c. Would the result be different if Cindy had died? ________________

    d. Can Jan's and Marsha's contribution to the partnership be a promise to contribute services to the partnership? ________________

    e. Are Jan and Marsha personally liable for the debts of the partnership? ________________

72. In the absence of an agreement to the contrary, partners in a limited partnership share profits and losses equally. True or false? __________

73. An LLC is formed by filing an operating agreement with the secretary of state. True or false? __________

74. Jeff forms an LLC, and he is the only member. Can the LLC receive partnership tax treatment? __________

    a. Would the result be different if Jeff and Tracy formed an LLC? __________

75. Lisa, Michelle, and Roger form an LLC to operate a grocery store. Steve, a nonmember, manages the LLC. One day Lisa goes into the grocery store and sees that it is running low on produce. Lisa places an order for more produce with the store's produce supplier. Is the LLC liable to the supplier for Lisa's order? __________

    a. Assume that Steve had placed the order with the supplier. Is Steve, Lisa, Michelle, or Roger personally liable to the supplier? __________

Answers to Review Questions

1. a. **TRUE** A principal is disclosed if the third party knows that the agent is acting for a principal ***and*** the third party knows the principal's ***identity***. [p. 5]

   b. **FALSE** It is a general agent who conducts a series of transactions involving a continuity of service. A special agent is authorized to conduct only a ***single transaction*** or series of transactions ***not*** involving a continuity of service. [p. 5]

   c. **TRUE** Consent may be either express or implied from the conduct of the parties. [p. 8]

2. **NO** A person can bind another to a contract with a third party only if the person has agency power. Generally, creation of an agency requires the consent of both the principal and the agent. Here, it appears that Leslie consented to act as Yolanda's agent, but Yolanda never asked Leslie to be her agent. Thus, no agency was created, and Yolanda will not be bound. [p. 8] There are a few circumstances in which a person can be bound despite the lack of a true agency relationship (*e.g.,* through estoppel or ratification), but nothing in the facts supports binding Yolanda under either of these theories. [pp. 8–9]

   a. **NO** An apparent agency must be based on statements by the alleged ***principal***—not the agent—which create the appearance of an agency. [p. 9]

3. **TRUE** A principal must have the capacity to perform the act he delegates, which usually requires the capacity to contract, and a minor generally does not have the capacity to contract; thus, a minor cannot be a principal. However, an agent needs only minimal mental capacity (which a minor has); therefore, a minor may be an agent. [p. 10]

4. **FALSE** An agent may act gratuitously, and a gratuitous agency can impose liability on the principal. [p. 10]

5. **NO** Because a contract for the sale of land is involved, Alicia's authority to sell must be in ***writing*** to make the contract enforceable against Randy. (Note, however, that the agreement can be enforced ***by*** Randy, if he so chooses.) [pp. 10–11]

   a. **YES** Written authority by the principal is usually not required for purely ***mechanical*** acts performed by the agent (such as signing the principal's name). [p. 11]

6. **DEPENDS** Jackie is generally not liable for her failure to perform because her promise did not give rise to an enforceable contract. However,

if Jackie's failure to act can be classified as a tort she can be held liable for tort damages. And if Truman ***detrimentally relied*** on Jackie's promise (*e.g.,* did not arrange for another agent to find a publisher), Truman may recover contract damages suffered due to Jackie's failure to perform. [p. 15]

7.	**DEPENDS**	An agent must not compete with his principal or act on behalf of a party in competition with his principal ***unless the principal consents***. [p. 16]
a.	**YES**	The arrangement constitutes a breach of Otis's fiduciary duty of loyalty—anything that an agent obtains by virtue of his employment belongs to the principal. Here, the reduced apartment rental is in effect a "rebate" to Otis on the commercial rent paid by Manufacturer, and absent consent by Manufacturer, Otis's retention of the rebate violates his fiduciary duty. [p. 17]
8.	**DEPENDS**	If Anita knows that Paul would be interested in acquiring the orchard for himself (as "suitable property"), she owes Paul the right of first refusal before purchasing it on her own account. [p. 18]
a.	**YES**	Anita is acting as a "dual agent" for both Raphael and Paul, and the sale is therefore voidable by Paul (unless Paul knew of the arrangement in advance and consented to it). The fairness of the price paid is immaterial (though it might reduce any damages against Anita were Paul to sue her for fraud). [p. 19]
9.	**TRUE**	Authority to hire a subagent will affect the principal's liability to third persons (and the subagent's liability to the principal), but the agent remains responsible to the principal for the subagent's conduct whether or not the agent was authorized to hire a subagent. [pp. 19–20]
10.	**PROBABLY**	While this is a close situation, Bob could probably argue that he has an irrevocable right to use Cathy's discovery under the "shop right" doctrine—since it was developed on the job and as a result of Bob's business (although not specifically applicable to his business). [p. 22]
11.	**FALSE**	Both a principal and an employer have a right to indemnification. [pp. 22, 95]
12.	**SPLIT OF AUTHORITY**	Some courts would allow Bill to recover against Marvin, on the ground of Marvin's prevention of performance by Bill. Others, however, hold that Marvin ***can*** compete with his own agent. [p. 22]
a.	**YES**	Assuming Marvin retained Carol without Bill's consent, all courts would allow Bill an action against Marvin for prevention of Bill's performance by hiring a competing ***agent***. [p. 22]
13.	**DEPENDS**	Penny is not liable unless Adam was authorized to hire ***additional agents*** on the same commission basis. If Adam was not, Sally must look solely to Adam for her compensation. [p. 23]

14.	a.	**DEPENDS**	Archie cannot be indemnified for unauthorized acts that do not benefit Phil, or acts that are the result of his own negligence. Thus, for example, if Archie or Tad negligently loaded the truck, Archie may not be entitled to indemnification. [pp. 24, 25]
	b.	**YES**	Assuming indemnification is otherwise proper (*i.e.,* no unauthorized or negligent act), Tad—as an authorized subagent—can recover against ***either*** Phil or Archie. [p. 25]
	c.	**NO**	While Archie may be entitled to damages against Phil for breach of contract, the agency agreement ***cannot*** be specifically enforced. [p. 25]
15.		**FALSE**	Courts generally ***limit*** extravagant phrases to what appears to be the business intended by the parties. [p. 31]
16.		**YES**	Anna has implied actual authority to do all acts ***reasonably necessary*** to accomplish her given objective of selling the boat for $5,000. Chris's offer is not inconsistent with Anna's authority to sell, and actually represents a gift of $50 to Phoebe because Chris is merely purchasing the right to match any other offer made. [p. 31]
17.		**PROBABLY**	Ordinarily, authority "to collect" a debt would not authorize an agent to compromise the debt. But Paula's additional reference to a fee based on "what you collect" probably ***implies*** authority in Alex to settle the debt for a lesser amount. [p. 31]
18.		**PROBABLY NOT**	A mere authority "to sell," without specification of terms, generally does ***not*** give a real estate broker the power to negotiate and conclude a sale (even if the broker has an exclusive agency). [p. 34]
	a.	**SPLIT OF AUTHORITY**	Even if Arnold had the ***power*** to delegate his authority to a subagent, Edith is not a party to the Pete-Arnold agreement and cannot sue Pete on the agreement. However, some courts would allow Edith to recover from Pete in quasi-contract for the reasonable value of her services. [p. 36]
	b.	**PROBABLY NOT**	An agent has the power to make all warranties implied by law or customary in the community as to the property he is selling. However, this power to warrant is ***narrowly*** construed by the courts, and a warranty of "absolute structural soundness" is probably outside the scope of Arnold's powers. [p. 33]
19.		**PROBABLY**	Despite Opie's statements, it may be assumed that he would have intended that such an emergency expenditure be made (particularly where it appears to be in his best interests). [pp. 32, 37]
	a.	**PROBABLY NOT**	As Opie's store manager, Bea probably had no authority to receive notification of facts concerning Opie's personal affairs, and the facts are not within the scope or subject matter of her

		position as manager; thus, Bea's knowledge will not be imputed to Opie. [pp. 69, 70, 71]
b.	**PROBABLY**	Generally, knowledge gained by the agent ***prior*** to her employment is not imputed to the principal, but an exception is made when there is a close connection between the two situations. (The Restatement imputes ***any*** knowledge of the agent if she had it in mind when it became relevant to her present work.) [p. 70]
20.	**NO**	Louise clearly intended to authorize Stephen's purchase of sculpture for her—even though her grant of authority was induced by Stephen's fraudulent misrepresentations about his qualifications. Hence, Louise is bound by the contract with Dennis. [p. 36]
a.	**YES**	Louise can rescind Stephen's authority (even if otherwise irrevocable) because of the fraud—***provided*** she does so ***prior to*** any agreement effected by Stephen. [p. 36]
21.	**YES**	Graham has actual authority to sell the car to anyone (because of Elmer's letter to him), but Elmer's manifestations ***to Hector*** give Graham apparent authority as to him, as well. [p. 37]
a.	**PROBABLY**	Apparent authority requires ***reasonable reliance*** by the third party upon manifestations by the principal. It is doubtful that a reasonable person would interpret Elmer's note as authorizing Graham to sell the car on Elmer's behalf. [p. 39]
b.	**NOT NECESSARILY**	The revocation will terminate Graham's ***actual*** authority, but ***unless communicated to Hector,*** Graham's apparent authority continues and is binding on Elmer. [p. 41]
22.	**YES**	Elmer has clothed Graham with both possession ***and*** apparent ownership of the car. Elmer will be estopped to assert the invalidity of Graham's dealings against an innocent purchaser. [p. 42]
23.	**PROBABLY**	Don's statement to Ned could be interpreted to mean that Claudia had authority to sell the mower, and hence Claudia would have ***authority by estoppel***—so that Don could not prevent Ned from obtaining what he paid for (even though Don never received payment). [p. 43]
24.	**PROBABLY NOT**	Even though no time is specified for Alan's agency, a reasonable time period is implied—and five years is probably beyond that period (considering the lack of communication between Pat and Alan, possible change in Pat's purposes, etc.). [p. 45]
a.	**PROBABLY NOT**	The change in zoning represents a sufficient change of circumstances to terminate Alan's authority (unless Pat knew of the rezoning when she engaged Alan). [p. 46]
25.	**SPLIT OF AUTHORITY**	Under the majority view, the death of the principal ***automatically*** terminates the agent's authority—whether or not the agent or third

		parties have knowledge of the principal's death. Thus, Sam could not enforce the sales contract against Oscar's estate. However, some states hold that the termination is not effective against a third party until he receives notice of the death. Thus, in those states, Sam would be able to enforce the sales contract against Oscar's estate. [p. 46]
a.	**YES**	In this case, Agatha's agency is given as security for the loan. Such agencies are irrevocable and do not terminate on the principal's death. Therefore, Sam can enforce the sales contract against Oscar's estate. [pp. 49–50]
26.	**NO**	Unless an agency is given as security or the agent has paid to become the agent, agencies are revocable. Either party can terminate a revocable agency relationship at will—despite a specified time period and a provision asserting that it is irrevocable for that period. However, Brandon may be liable in damages to Chuck for breach of contract. [pp. 49]
a.	**YES**	In this case, Chuck holds an agency power given as security for the loan, and he ***can*** obtain specific performance of his agreement with Brandon. [pp. 49–50]
27.	**FALSE**	While a third party must generally receive notice of the termination of authority, most states hold that the termination is ***automatic*** in the case of the death or incapacity of the principal. [p. 51]
28.	**SPLIT OF AUTHORITY**	Most courts would say that Stacey is free to rescind, on the ground that an "offer" rather than a contract existed until ratified by the purported principal, Linda. However, a minority of courts would not excuse Stacey from performing if she receives the contract price and incurs no additional burdens. [pp. 56, 58]
29.	**NO**	Teddy was not intending to act on Omar's behalf when he agreed to sell the set to Xavier; thus, Omar cannot subsequently ratify the act. [p. 58]
a.	**DEPENDS**	Here, Teddy purported to be acting for Omar by signing Omar's name. Thus, ratification is possible. However, the validity of the ratification will turn on whether the wager itself was a legal act (and therefore capable of being authorized). [p. 61]
30.	**PROBABLY**	As a general matter, a ratification is not effective unless the principal ***knows all the material facts*** concerning the transaction. However, Penelope assumes the risk of lack of knowledge when she ratifies without inquiring about the terms; thus, Theo can probably enforce the contract. [p. 62]
31.	**PROBABLY NOT**	A ratification must be in the same form required for an original authorization. An oral ratification of a sale of real property would, therefore, be insufficient under the Statute of Frauds or an "equal dignities" statute. [p. 63]

a.	**NO**	The neighbor has acquired rights in the farm prior to the ratification. Thus, Lucy's subsequent ratification of the contract between Jack and Paul does not "relate back." The neighbor can compel specific performance of his agreement with Lucy, and Paul may also be able to recover damages from her. [p. 57]
32.	**YES**	Priscilla will be deemed to have ratified Abby's acts, both because of her retention of benefits from Tom and her failure to repudiate the unauthorized agreement. [p. 64]
a.	**YES**	Unless Priscilla knew of the agreement when she failed to repudiate it, her "retention" of the benefits is involuntary and could not be deemed a ratification. [p. 64]
33.	**NO**	The death or incapacity of the third party terminates the purported principal's power to ratify. [p. 65]
34.	**YES**	Unless Moses knew that Adam had no authority (and thus could not be said to have relied on a warranty of authority from Adam), Adam is liable to Moses for breach of the warranty of authority regardless of his good faith belief. [pp. 74–75]
a.	**YES**	Although Moses cannot enforce the contract without Eve's ratification, he can sue Eve in quasi-contract for the value of the benefit conferred (*i.e.,* the down payment). [p. 77]
35.	**NO**	Jones's signature clearly indicates that he signed the contract only as Smith Company's agent. Thus, only Smith Company is liable on the contract. [p. 78]
a.	**NO**	Extrinsic evidence is generally admissible only to resolve an ***ambiguity*** in the contract. Here, there is no ambiguity because the agreement on its face indicates that Jones acted solely as Smith Company's agent; consequently, extrinsic evidence of the parties' intent is inadmissible. [pp. 78–80]
36. a.	**YES**	Under the objective theory of contracts, the agent of an undisclosed principal is liable to a third party contracting with him. (Of course, John would also have a ***right of indemnification*** against Ponch for any amounts collected by Wayne.) [pp. 80]
b.	**SPLIT OF AUTHORITY**	Once Ponch's identity is known, Wayne has a right to sue him, and most courts permit Wayne to sue ***both*** Ponch and John (requiring an election only prior to judgment if either Ponch or John objects). However, some courts require Wayne to make an election ***before*** filing suit—*i.e.,* to sue ***either*** Ponch or John, but not both. [pp. 81]
c.	**YES**	Even though the principal is undisclosed, he is deemed the assignee of all the rights in the contract entered into by his agent. Hence, he may sue the third party to enforce the contract. [p. 82]
d.	**DEPENDS**	If John ***fraudulently represented*** to Wayne that he was contracting on his own behalf, Wayne would have a ***right to rescind*** the purchase agreement; thus, Ponch could not enforce it

against Wayne. Courts are split as to whether an agent must make an affirmative misrepresentation for the third party to rescind. Some courts would allow Wayne the right to rescind the agreement even though John never stated that he was ***not*** acting for Ponch because John was aware that Wayne would not sell to Ponch. [p. 82]

	e.	**YES**	The weight of authority holds an undisclosed (but subsequently discovered) principal liable on the agent's contract in this situation—on the ground that because Ponch created John's authority, he must assume the risk of John's dereliction of duty. [p. 84]
37.		**PROBABLY NOT**	This would probably be considered a personal services contract, allowing Marie to rescind. [p. 84]
38.		**PROBABLY**	This is an unidentified principal situation, and unless the parties had agreed that Fred would not be bound (as to which parol evidence is admissible), Yogi ***can*** hold Fred liable on the contract. [pp. 85, 87]
	a.	**YES**	When the principal's identity is known to the third party, the principal is "disclosed" even if his name does not appear on the contract—and the agent is no longer considered a party to the contract. [p. 78]
39.	a.	**FALSE**	An injured person can proceed against ***both*** the employee (who is directly liable) and the employer (who is vicariously liable). [p. 93]
	b.	**FALSE**	Respondeat superior imposes strict liability on the employer that cannot be "contracted away." [p. 94]
	c.	**TRUE**	If the employer was herself guilty of negligence or other breach of duty toward the injured party (or where the employee is ***immune*** from liability), the employer may be liable even though the employee is not. (Generally, however, exoneration of the employee relieves the employer of liability as well.) [pp. 94–95]
	d.	**TRUE**	Respondeat superior depends on the right to control—which means that the employer generally is not liable for the torts of agents or independent contractors. [p. 96]
	e.	**FALSE**	An employer must have the ***capacity to contract,*** and a minor does not have the capacity to contract. Therefore, a minor cannot assume the position of employer (although he can certainly be hired as an employee). [pp. 96–97]
40.		**DEPENDS**	The employer-employee relationship is consensual, but mutual consent can be implied from the circumstances. If Mac had no knowledge of Tim's actions, he could not be held vicariously liable; however, if he ***knew*** Tim was assisting the employees and did not intervene, he would probably be deemed to have consented (and be subject to vicarious liability). [p. 97]

a.	**NO**	Even assuming that Mac knew nothing of Tim's attempts to assist (and cannot be said to have consented to the attempts), he cannot recover for ***negligent*** (as opposed to intentional) injuries to his employee by a third person. [pp. 97–98]
41.	**PROBABLY**	If the advertising gave the impression that Kermit was Mario's employee, and if Lincoln relied on the advertisement in requesting an exercise program, there is an ***employment by estoppel***—and Mario would be vicariously liable for Kermit's actions despite his lack of control over Kermit. [p. 98]
a.	**YES**	Here, Lincoln's injury was not sustained in reliance on Kermit's purported employment; therefore, there is no ostensible employment. [p. 98]
42.	**DEPENDS**	If Porgy had authorized Bess to hire a relief driver, he may be liable (assuming a right to control, etc.). If Porgy had not authorized such employment, he would be liable only if Sanford had been hired in an ***emergency*** (*e.g.,* Bess's illness en route, perishability of load, etc.). [pp. 99, 100]
43.	**PROBABLY**	A lessor renting equipment with an operator is presumed to retain the right to control the operator and would—absent a showing that the operator was required to take orders from the lessee—be liable to persons injured by the operator's tortious acts. [p. 100]
a.	**YES**	In this case, Taggert will be liable for Seth's act even if Marcus retained a primary right to control because Taggert ***directed*** Seth's act. [p. 100]
44.	**YES**	Truck drivers who drive their own trucks on specific jobs are usually independent contractors, whereas those driving their employers' trucks are more likely to be employees (*i.e.,* greater control by employer over their conduct). [p. 104]
45.	**PROBABLY NOT**	Most courts hold that physicians are independent contractors, even when employed on a retainer basis. Thus, Dr. Wiley alone would be liable for the negligent act. [p. 104]
a.	**DEPENDS**	If Bessie was aware of Dr. Wiley's drinking habits, she might be found negligent in her hiring of Dr. Wiley—in which case she would be ***directly liable*** to Alex even though Dr. Wiley remained an independent contractor. [p. 105]
46.	**YES**	Crop-spraying is considered a highly dangerous act imposing ***strict liability*** on the party contracting for the work—irrespective of whether the actor is an independent contractor ***or*** whether her conduct was negligent. [p. 105]
47.	**PROBABLY NOT**	Although it is a matter of degree in each case, Samson's forbidden act appears to deviate sufficiently from his assigned duties of book salesman that it is outside the scope of employment—and thus relieves Delilah of liability. [p. 108]

48.	**PROBABLY NOT**	Control of patrons was probably not related to Walker's duties, and his action appears to have been personally motivated. Thus, Ace would not be liable to Zeke under respondeat superior for the intentional tort of its employee. [pp. 108]
a.	**YES**	A common carrier is held to a higher standard of care and thus is liable for ***any*** tortious acts inflicted by employees on passengers—whether or not the tortious acts are within the scope of employment. (Note, however, that this is ***direct*** liability, not an application of respondeat superior.) [p. 119]
b.	**PROBABLY**	An employer might be liable for the personal acts of an employee if the employer is negligent in supervising the employee, even if the act is outside the scope of employment. Ace is liable for negligently allowing the employee to smoke in the restaurant. [p. 110]
c.	**NO**	Washing the bicycle chain is outside the scope of Walker's employment and does nothing to further the interests of Ace. The fact that Walker was permitted to use the dishwasher in his job will not impose vicarious liability on Ace. [p. 110]
d.	**PROBABLY**	If Walker was given no instructions on what solvent to use, Ace is probably liable for Walker's negligent use of gasoline. (*Note:* In each of these examples, Ace might be liable for negligence in ***hiring*** Walker.) [p. 111]
49.	**FALSE**	If ***any*** substantial part of the employee's act was done for the employer, the employer is liable for ***all*** the consequences of the act. [p. 112]
50.	**SPLIT OF AUTHORITY**	Under the general rule, Phil would ***not*** be liable to an unauthorized invitee of his employee, the invitation being outside the scope of his employment. However, some courts would hold Phil liable if Archie's misconduct were "wanton and willful"; others would hold Phil liable if Archie's ***negligent acts*** (as distinguished from the unauthorized invitation) were within the scope of employment. [p. 113]
a.	**PROBABLY NOT**	Unless Phil was shown to have been negligent in ***hiring*** Archie, the "fellow servant rule" would relieve Phil of any liability to Trish for Archie's conduct. [p. 115]
51.	**YES**	Usury ***ordered*** Acme to "repossess the car"—the tortious act—and thus is ***directly liable*** to Sasha. Likewise, Acme is liable for committing the tortious act even though acting with authority and without an intent to convert Sasha's car. [p. 116]
a.	**DEPENDS**	Usury can become liable if it ratifies Acme's unauthorized conduct—*i.e.,* by accepting benefits from the conduct ***with knowledge of the relevant facts***. In this situation, liability may turn on the number of accounts Acme was handling for Usury: If only Daphne's debt was involved, Usury would probably be held to know that the car was improperly obtained and thus be accountable to Sasha. [p. 117]

	b.	**YES**	Usury cannot ratify this act because it was not done on behalf of the loan company. Thus, Usury would not be liable to Sasha. [p. 117]
52.		**YES**	Sam is charged with notice of the dangerous condition because Diane's knowledge of the dangerous condition was in the scope of her employment, and thus is imputed to Sam. Consequently, Sam is liable to Woody just as if he had personally observed the defective step. [p. 119]
	a.	**PROBABLY**	Only those facts known to the employee ***and*** within the scope of employment are imputed to the employer. It is unlikely that a bookkeeper would be involved with building maintenance; thus, Diane's knowledge of the defective step would not be imputed to Sam if Diane were Sam's bookkeeper. [p. 119]
53.		**FALSE**	While misrepresentation is one type of tortious statement, an employer would ***also*** be liable if the employee's statements constituted defamation, trade libel, etc. [p. 121]
54.		**FALSE**	The false statements of an independent contractor can also make the employer liable, provided the independent contractor had the requisite authority to make statements. [p. 121]
55.		**YES**	Allen had ***express*** authority to disseminate appraisal data to buyers, and any misrepresentations by her in the course of such dissemination are imputed to Burns. [p. 122]
	a.	**PROBABLY NOT**	An agent has ***implied*** authority to make customary statements about the subject matter, and the appraisal value of an art collection would certainly appear to be such a statement (*i.e.,* "incidental" to her authority to sell the collection). [p. 122]
	b.	**PROBABLY**	Under these circumstances, Allen would probably have no authority to make statements concerning the appraisal value (unless Burns had specifically given her such information for use in the advertisements). [p. 123]
56.		**YES**	Although Vanessa's misrepresentation may have been innocent, Lester had the necessary scienter and thus would be liable to the buyer. [p. 124]
	a.	**NOT NECESSARILY**	Lester could be liable for negligent misrepresentation, and in any case, the buyer could seek rescission of the sale based on ***mistake***. [p. 125]
57.		**TRUE**	These characteristics distinguish a partnership from an agency (not co-owners) and unincorporated associations (which can be organized for nonprofit purposes). [pp. 131–132]
58.		**FALSE**	This was true at common law, and even under the Uniform Partnership Act ("UPA"), a partnership is viewed as an aggregate for most purposes. However, for certain purposes—*e.g.,* capacity

to sue or be sued, conveyance of title, etc.—a partnership is considered an ***entity***. Note that the Revised Uniform Partnership Act ("RUPA") treats a partnership as an entity, but retains some aggregate characteristics (*e.g.,* joint and several liability). [pp. 132–134]

59.	a.	**FALSE**	Certain partnership agreements—*e.g.,* those for a mandatory period of one year—***must*** be in writing to be effective. [p. 134]
	b.	**TRUE**	The UPA and RUPA include corporations within the definition of "persons" who may become partners. [p. 135]
	c.	**TRUE**	Each and all partners must agree on who will be a partner because the partnership is a voluntary association of co-owners. [p. 135]
	d.	**FALSE**	While neither factor is conclusive, a sharing of profits ***will*** establish a prima facie partnership (presumption of partnership under the RUPA), unless other business reasons exist for the profit sharing. Income sharing, however, is not prima facie evidence of a partnership. [p. 136]
	e.	**FALSE**	The nonpartner can bind only those partners who ***made or consented*** to the representation that he was a partner. [p. 139]
	f.	**FALSE**	Each partner has ***equal*** management rights (regardless of their agreed share of the profits), unless there is a provision to the contrary. [p. 144]
	g.	**TRUE**	Absent an agreement to the contrary, a partner has no right to be reimbursed for work performed on the partnership's behalf; there is one exception to this rule—a partner who winds up partnership affairs is entitled to reasonable compensation for his services rendered in winding up. [p. 145]
	h.	**FALSE**	Under the RUPA, a partner may maintain an action against another partner, at law or in equity, to enforce certain rights. Note that under the UPA, the action must be brought in equity, with a few exceptions (*e.g.,* personal disputes between partners, fraud, or conversion of partnership assets) that do not really involve partnership transactions. [pp. 146–147]
60.		**PROBABLY**	A partner has apparent authority to sign contracts on behalf of the partnership and related to its business. Thus, unless the loan would make it impossible to carry on business, the agreement is binding on the partnership. [p. 148]
	a.	**DEPENDS**	If Mary and Rhoda are the only partners, some cases would hold this notice effective. In any other situation, however, Rhoda will be bound unless she ***dissolves*** the partnership before the debts are incurred. [p. 153]
61.		**NO**	A new partner is not personally liable for any partnership obligation incurred before he became partner. [p. 158]

a.	**DEPENDS**	Under the RUPA, Acme can sue Steele alone because partners are ***jointly and severally*** liable for *all* partnership debts and obligations, and when liability is joint and several, a creditor can sue any single partner without joining the others. However, under the UPA, Acme cannot sue Steele alone on the claim because partners are ***jointly*** liable for ***contract*** obligations of the partnership, and when liability is joint, a creditor may not proceed against any single partner. Because Acme is a contract creditor, it must sue all partners or the partnership itself. [pp. 154, 156]
b.	**YES**	Under the RUPA, partners are ***jointly and severally liable*** for ***all partnership debts and obligations,*** including torts and breaches of trust. When liability is joint and several, an action may be brought against any one partner; therefore, Shelby can proceed against Wool alone. [p. 155]
c.	**YES**	One partner may maintain an action against another for injuries negligently inflicted on him. [pp. 146, 147]
62. a.	**NO**	A partner in an LLP is not personally liable for partnership obligations arising from the wrongful acts of a co-partner. [p. 157]
b.	**YES**	A partner in an LLP is not shielded from personal liability for his own wrongful acts. [p. 157]
63.	**DEPENDS**	Under the RUPA, the warehouse would be considered partnership property because the warehouse was ***acquired in the name of the partnership***. Under the UPA, property is partnership property if it is acquired ***on account*** of the partnership, and while record title is relevant, it is by no means determinative. Therefore, if Partner purchased the warehouse on account of the partnership, it is partnership property. [pp. 162–164]
64.	**NO**	Under the RUPA, a partner is not a co-owner of partnership property and has no interest in the property that can be attached by her personal creditors. Under the UPA, as to each partnership asset, a partner is a tenant in partnership with her co-partners, but her rights in the partnership property still are ***not*** subject to attachment for her personal debts. [pp. 166–167]
a.	**YES**	The partner's interest in the partnerships—*i.e.,* her right to a share in the partnership profits or surplus—is her ***personal*** property. Thus, a judgment creditor can obtain a lien against this interest (the effect being that the partner's share in the profits, or some portion of those profits, goes to the creditor). [pp. 167, 169]
65.	**FALSE**	Dissociation terminates a partner's right to participate in the business, but it does not necessarily result in the dissolution and winding up of the partnership. [p. 172]
66. a.	**DEPENDS**	Upon Nancy's notice of withdrawal to Tanya and Jeff, she is dissociated from the partnership. Nancy's dissociation is wrongful because Nancy has withdrawn before the partnership

term has expired. Nancy's wrongful dissociation will result in the dissolution of the partnership if within 90 days after her dissociation ***at least half of the remaining partners agree to wind up the partnership***. [pp. 173, 176]

b. **YES** A partnership at will (no term or particular undertaking specified) is dissolved and must be wound up on receipt by the partnership of a partner's notice to withdraw. [p. 176]

c. **DEPENDS** If the creditor extended credit to the partnership within two years of Nancy's withdrawal (dissociation), which is the case here, she can be held liable to the creditor for the partnership's ice skate purchase if the creditor ***believed that she was still a partner*** and ***did not have notice or knowledge of her dissociation***. [p. 175]

d. **YES** A dissociated partner can limit her liability for partnership obligations incurred after her dissociation by filing a statement of dissociation. Nonpartners will be deemed to have notice of the dissociation 90 days after the filing of the statement. Nancy's filing of the statement of dissociation 30 days after her withdrawal (dissociation) was effective to give nonpartners notice of her dissociation 120 days after her dissociation; the creditor extended credit one year after Nancy's dissociation—well past when he was deemed to have notice of her dissociation, and thus Nancy would not be liable to him for the partnership's purchase of the ice skates. [p. 175]

67. a. **FALSE** If the partners continue the partnership business beyond the period, they are deemed ***partners at will*** with the same general rights and duties that existed at the expiration of the partnership term. [p. 177]

b. **TRUE** The partnership relation is personal and cannot be enforced in equity. Thus, under the UPA any partner can dissolve the partnership at any time. Unless a partnership at will is involved, however, the dissolution may violate the partnership agreement and subject the partner to liability (since a ***power,*** rather than a right, is involved). [p. 178]

c. **FALSE** The partnership is not per se dissolved if the partnership business can be carried on only at a loss. This situation will, however, support ***a judicial decree of dissolution***. [p. 180]

d. **FALSE** Unless otherwise agreed, each partner must contribute to the loss according to her share of the profits. [p. 186]

68. a. **YES** Desi's dissolution violates the agreement, and the "innocent" partners (Lucy and Ethel) have a right to any damages sustained as a result. [pp. 178, 182]

b. **PROBABLY** If Lucy and Ethel fail to pay Desi for his partnership interest (or post a bond for it), Desi is entitled to compensation for the use of his partnership assets in the continuing business. [p. 181]

	c.	**NO**	The estate of a deceased partner is likewise entitled to compensation for the decedent's interest in the partnership, and if there is undue delay in paying the estate, the surviving partners are liable for an appropriate share of any profits earned, or interest on the value at death (whichever is greater). [pp. 182–183]
	d.	**YES**	A partner remains liable for debts incurred by the partnership while the partner was a member until the debts are discharged or the creditor releases the partner from liability. [p. 184]
69.	a.	**NO**	To form a limited partnership, a certificate of limited partnership must be signed by the general partners and ***filed with the secretary of state***. Chris executed the certificate but did not file it with the secretary of state; therefore, Chris, Debbie, and Laurie did not form a limited partnership. [p. 194]
	b.	**YES**	Because a limited partnership was ***not*** formed, Debbie and Laurie are liable to Mortuary Supplies as ***general*** partners. [p. 194]
70.		**NO**	Under the RULPA, a limited partner's name may ***not*** appear in the name of the limited partnership. If the partnership were formed under the ULPA, George's name could appear in the name of the partnership. [p. 195]
	a.	**YES**	Under the RULPA, a limited partner's name may appear in the name of the limited partnership if the partnership had been carried on under the limited partner's name prior to the limited partner becoming a partner. [p. 195]
71.	a.	**YES**	A partner has an interest in the partnership that may be assigned in whole or in part; thus, Jan has a right to assign her interest in the partnership without the consent of Cindy or Marsha. Greg, the assignee, is entitled to receive Jan's share of profits or return of contribution. However, Greg is ***not*** entitled to inspect the books or vote on the limited issues on which Jan is permitted to vote, unless all partners agree to admit Greg as a substitute limited partner. [p. 196]
	b.	**NO**	The death of a limited partner does not dissolve the partnership. Instead, the decedent's executor is given the rights of the limited partner. [p. 197]
	c.	**YES**	The death of Cindy, the general partner, ***does*** dissolve the limited partnership unless within 90 days of Cindy's death, Jan and Marsha agree to continue the business and appoint a general partner. [p. 197]
	d.	**YES**	A partner's contribution to the partnership may be in cash, property, or services, or a promise to contribute such in the future. [p. 198]
	e.	**NO**	Generally, limited partners are not liable for the debts of the partnership beyond their contributions. Because Jan and Marsha are limited partners, their liability is limited to their respective

investments in the partnership unless they do something to lose their limited liability (*e.g.,* participate in control of the business). (Remember that under the ULPA, limited partners are not liable, even if they participate in the management and control of the business.) [pp. 203–205]

72. **FALSE** In the absence of an agreement to the contrary, partners in a limited partnership share profits and losses according to the ***value of their contributions***. [p. 199]

73. **FALSE** An LLC is formed by filing ***articles of organization*** or a certificate of organization with the secretary of state; the articles must include such information as the name of the LLC, address of the LLC's registered office, etc. An operating agreement is an agreement adopted by the members of an LLC that controls the affairs of the LLC. [pp. 215]

74. **NO** The Treasury Department treats a single-member LLC as a ***sole proprietorship***. [p. 216]

a. **YES** An LLC with at least ***two*** members is ***automatically taxed as a partnership*** unless it elects to be taxed as a corporation. [p. 216]

75. **NO** If management of the LLC is vested in managers, the members do not have the power to bind the LLC, only the managers do. Therefore, Lisa's purchase of the produce does not bind the LLC to the supplier because Lisa, as a member of a manager-managed LLC, had no power to bind the LLC. [pp. 217]

a. **NO** Members and managers of an LLC are not personally liable for the LLC's obligations by virtue of their ownership/management of the LLC. Here, the manager, Steve, had the power to bind the LLC to the supplier for his produce order; thus, the produce order is an LLC obligation, and neither the members nor the manager are personally liable. Note that they can, however, contract to become personally liable. [p. 218]

Exam Questions and Answers

QUESTION I

Hannigan owned and operated a route for the sale and delivery of bakery products. Hannigan, desiring to take a vacation, made a contract with Rest, who agreed to take over the bakery route during Hannigan's absence. Hannigan took Rest over the route for two days' training, and then Rest assumed the operation of the route for six weeks. Since Rest did not have a truck, Hannigan allowed Rest to use his truck without charge for the six-week period. During this time, Rest purchased and paid for the bakery products which she sold on the route. She retained the entire proceeds from the sales she made.

During the six-week period, Rest was involved in a collision with an auto being driven by Jackson. As a result of the collision, Jackson was severely injured. Subsequently, he brought an appropriate action against Hannigan to recover for damages suffered as a result of the collision.

What decision? Explain.

QUESTION II

Milton, a meat processor, employed Sylvester to purchase livestock for him. Sylvester, from the beginning of his employment by Milton, purchased beef cattle from Thomas, who operated a stockyard. Thomas would bill Milton, who then forwarded his check in full payment. Milton had instructed Sylvester that he was not to purchase any sheep from Thomas. For the last four years, Sylvester bought over 5,000 head of cattle for Milton's account. On February 12 of this year, Milton discharged Sylvester, refusing to pay severance pay, to which Sylvester thought he was entitled. Sylvester, upset over his discharge, told Thomas, on February 14, to forward 100 sheep to Milton. Milton refused delivery of the sheep and refused to pay on the grounds that (a) he had expressly ordered Sylvester never to purchase sheep from Thomas, and (b) he had discharged Sylvester on February 12.

What decision? Explain.

QUESTION III

Carlton, a contractor, was building a multi-story building. Carlton had ordered materials for the construction, to be shipped by rail. The carrier was Diamond Railway Company. This railroad owned a large crane that was used for loading and unloading heavy articles from cars.

Heracles, the crane operator, was a regular employee of the railroad. Peters, an employee of Carlton, was helping with the unloading of the materials. The railroad permitted Carlton to use the crane without cost to assist in unloading. During the unloading, Heracles followed suggestions given him by Carlton.

Because of Heracles's negligent operation of the crane, Peters was injured. Peters subsequently brought an action against Diamond Railway Company to recover damages for his injuries. At trial, it was shown that Diamond Railway Company might have called Heracles to some other job and also could have told him exactly how to use the crane.

May Peters recover for his injuries from the railroad? Explain.

QUESTION IV

Roberta Rich was the owner of a racehorse named "Herald," which had won more than $500,000 from races run prior to being retired to stud. On June 1, Rich, wishing to sell "Herald," executed and delivered to Terry Siegel, a broker of horses, the following power of attorney:

> I hereby authorize Terry Siegel to act as my agent with authority to sell my horse "Herald," for the price of $150,000, all cash. Siegel shall not be entitled to receive from me a commission for making the sale, but is authorized to retain from the purchaser any sum paid by the latter in excess of $150,000.
>
> /s/ Roberta Rich

On October 15, Siegel met with Arthur Champion, praising the qualities of "Herald," and on showing Champion the written power of attorney, Champion agreed to buy "Herald" for $160,000, to be paid on the following day on delivery of the horse. On October 16, when Champion and Siegel were on their way to deliver the purchase price and turn over the horse, they learned, to their surprise, that on September 20, by proper judicial proceedings, Rich had been adjudicated incapacitated and that her cousin Bill had been duly appointed guardian of her person and property. When Champion and Siegel asked Bill to accept payment on behalf of Rich and to authorize delivery of "Herald," Bill refused, saying that he thought the horse could be sold for more than the $160,000 tendered. Champion now consults you and inquires what rights of action, if any, he has against Bill acting for Rich.

How should you advise Champion?

QUESTION V

Ardmore sold goods to Bobolink, in good faith believing him to be a principal. Bobolink, in fact, was acting as agent of Casper, within the scope of his authority. The goods were charged to Bobolink, and on his refusal to pay, he was sued by Ardmore for the purchase price. While this action was pending, Ardmore learned of Bobolink's relationship with Casper and filed suit against Casper as well.

May Ardmore proceed to judgment against both Bobolink and Casper?

QUESTION VI

Cornelius and Robert were partners in a fairly large widget business. The assets of their business had a market value of $200,000. Lacking in business experience, Cornelius and Robert allowed the business to become overextended, so that the partnership had obligations of $300,000. Realizing the desperate nature of their situation, Cornelius and Robert persuaded Veronica to invest $50,000 in the capital of the partnership and to become a full partner, assuring her that her financial contribution would be instrumental in allowing the partnership to overcome its difficulties.

One year after Veronica became a partner, the financial situation of the partnership remained in the same woeful state. In fact, the partnership was now further in debt. This led to a suit to wind up the partnership affairs.

In regard to this suit, answer the following questions:

(a) Is Veronica's $50,000 contribution available for payment of creditors who had claims against the partnership prior to her entry into the partnership?

(b) Would the answer to (a) be different if Veronica, upon her entry into the partnership, had agreed with Cornelius and Robert that the $50,000 would be exempt from such debts?

(c) Is Veronica personally liable for the partnership debts that existed prior to the time she became a partner?

QUESTION VII

Bobby, Cassidy, Shelby, and Tracy form a partnership to rehab houses and sell them for a profit. They agree that the partnership will continue for 10 years. After three years, Shelby tires of the business, gives notice to the other partners that she is leaving, and moves out of state.

(a) Under the Revised Uniform Partnership Act ("RUPA") what effect does Shelby's departure have on the partnership and/or Shelby, and what rights do the remaining partners have after her departure?

(b) What would the result be under the Uniform Partnership Act ("UPA")?

QUESTION VIII

Phil, Bob, and Louise form a limited partnership by properly executing and filing a certificate of limited partnership. Among other things, the certificate sets forth a designation that Phil and Bob are general partners and Louise is a limited partner. Their business, which consists of manufacturing furniture, prospers beyond their wildest expectations. Eventually, they reach a point where Louise, due to her extensive past managerial experience, is required to devote extensive time to the actual management of the business.

Two months after Louise began participating in the management of the partnership, Louise purchased lumber on credit for the partnership from Lumber Unlimited. Lumber Unlimited was unaware that Louise was a limited partner.

After Louise's purchase of the lumber from Lumber Unlimited, the partnership began to experience financial hardship, and it did not have sufficient funds to pay Lumber Unlimited for the lumber it purchased.

Is Louise personally liable to Lumber Unlimited?

QUESTION IX

Debbie and Emil form a limited liability company ("LLC") to own and operate a bookstore. They decide that Brigette, Joe, and Tammy will manage the bookstore.

Several years later, the bookstore is not doing well financially—customers are not visiting the bookstore. Brigette, Joe, and Tammy meet and decide that the bookstore needs a new, modern look to draw in customers, so they all agree to purchase new furniture and lighting for the bookstore.

The next day, Tammy purchases new bookshelves, couches, tables, and lighting fixtures on the LLC's credit. The purchases arrive the next week. Debbie and Emil visit the bookstore and notice the purchases. They are irate that Brigette, Joe, and Tammy would have made such purchases, and they indicate that the LLC will not pay for them.

(a) Is the LLC liable for the purchases?

(b) Are Brigette, Joe, and Tammy personally liable for the purchases?

QUESTION X

Jackie, Linda, and Stacey decide that they want to form a business. Jackie and Stacey do not want to be subjected to personal liability for the debts or obligations of the business. Also, Jackie demands that she be able to participate in the management of the business.

Analyze the various business entities that Jackie, Linda, and Stacey may form, and decide which, if any, would best accommodate their needs.

ANSWER TO QUESTION I

Hannigan should win. The first issue is whether Rest was an employee or an independent contractor. Under respondeat superior, an employer is liable for the torts of his employees, but not for those of independent contractors. The test for determining whether a person is an employee or independent contractor is whether the employer has the ***right to control*** the person's conduct in performing the work. Factors to consider in determining the status of the person include the agreed extent of control, the method of payment for the work performed, the length of time for which the person is employed, etc. The facts indicate that Rest worked without supervision, Rest purchased and paid for the bakery products, Hannigan did not pay Rest a salary—Rest retained the proceeds from the sales she made, and Rest was hired to take over Hannigan's route temporarily while he was on vacation. Thus, it appears that Hannigan did not have the right to control Rest's performance and so Rest is not an employee. Consequently, Hannigan is not liable for Rest's conduct under respondeat superior.

However, it is also necessary to consider whether Rest's use of Hannigan's truck will subject Hannigan to liability. An employer will be liable for the torts of an independent contractor if the work performed is of a ***highly dangerous nature***. If the truck were to be considered a dangerous instrumentality, then Rest's independent contractor status might not relieve Hannigan of liability. Whether the truck was a dangerous instrumentality is a question of fact, and there appears to be nothing in the statement of facts indicating that the truck was such an instrumentality—*i.e.*, it was not to be used to transport explosives, dangerous chemicals, etc., nor was it apparently in need of repair to make it safe.

Finally, it is necessary to examine if Hannigan was negligent in hiring, training, or supervising Rest. An employer will be liable for the torts of an independent contractor if the employer was negligent in hiring, training, or supervising the independent contractor. There is nothing in the facts to indicate that Hannigan's selection of Rest to operate his bakery route was in any way negligent. Also, there are no facts to indicate that Rest was a known poor driver, drug abuser, etc. Therefore, Hannigan should not be liable for the torts committed by Rest acting as an independent contractor.

ANSWER TO QUESTION II

Milton prevails. The issue here is whether Sylvester had the authority to bind Milton to the sheep purchase. Sylvester did not have the actual authority to purchase the sheep. Actual authority is authority that the agent reasonably believes he has based on the principal's dealings with him. In this case, Milton specifically discharged Sylvester on February 12, so Sylvester could not reasonably believe that he had the actual authority to purchase the sheep on February 14—in fact, it appears that he purchased the sheep out of spite. Consequently, it is necessary to examine whether Sylvester had apparent authority to purchase the sheep.

There is apparent authority if Milton held Sylvester out as having the authority to enter into such a contract, and Thomas ***reasonably relied*** on this holding out by Milton. Here, Sylvester had been an agent with actual authority to purchase cattle for four years, and thus it can be argued that he would appear to have authority to make this contract. Also, on the facts given, Milton did not take adequate steps to apprise those with whom Sylvester had dealt that Sylvester was no longer in Milton's employ—*i.e.*, he did not give notice of Sylvester's discharge to third parties to terminate Sylvester's apparent authority. Thus, the only ground upon which Milton may be able to rely is the fact that Sylvester could not be viewed as having the apparent authority to purchase sheep. The fact that Milton had given express orders not to purchase sheep is not persuasive if Thomas could have reasonably believed that Sylvester was also authorized to make sheep purchases. This is a fact question, but because, in the four years that he dealt with Thomas, Sylvester had never purchased sheep, it seems that Thomas could not reasonably believe that Sylvester had the authority to do so. Thomas should probably have called Milton before relying on Sylvester's order. Thus, Milton is not liable to Thomas for Sylvester's purchase of the sheep.

ANSWER TO QUESTION III

Peters should be able to recover damages for his injuries from Diamond Railway Company. The general rule is that an employer will be liable for the torts of his employee under the doctrine of respondeat superior. An employer-employee relationship exists whenever one person has the right to control the manner and method in which a task is performed by another. In this case, the facts are clear that Heracles was an employee of Diamond; however, the issue is whether the railroad has transferred its right to control over Heracles to Carlton.

This question involves a borrowed employee situation. In such a situation, the original employer (here, the railroad) remains the employer and is liable for the torts of its employee unless there is clear evidence of a transfer of the right to control. There is no question that Heracles is normally an employee of the railroad, and there seems to be insufficient evidence that Diamond, in fact, transferred the primary right to control Heracles's actions to Carlton. The mere fact that Heracles followed some of Carlton's suggestions, or that the railroad allowed Heracles to use the railroad's crane to unload the construction materials, does not constitute a transfer of the primary right to control. The railroad was always in a position to tell Heracles exactly how to operate its equipment and could have pulled him off the Carlton job at any time. Such facts indicate that control over Heracles was not transferred to Carlton and that as the employer, Diamond Railway Company remained liable for the torts of its employee Heracles under the doctrine of respondeat superior.

The fellow servant rule may not be raised, as Peters was an employee of Carlton while Heracles remained an employee of Diamond Railway Company. For the foregoing reasons, Peters should recover damages from Diamond for the injuries caused by Heracles's negligence.

ANSWER TO QUESTION IV

Champion has no rights against Bill. Under majority law, when a principal is adjudicated incapacitated, the agent's authority to act on the principal's behalf is ***automatically*** terminated. Notice of the principal's incapacity need not be given to anyone. Therefore, even though neither Siegel nor Champion knew of Rich's incapacity and both were acting in good faith, the contract would not bind Rich because Siegel's authority was automatically terminated on Rich's adjudication of incapacity. (Note that some jurisdictions follow the minority view that the termination of authority is not effective against the agent or third party until notice of incapacity is received. In such a jurisdiction, the contract to sell "Herald" to Champion would be enforceable.)

An exception to the rule that the incapacity of the principal terminates the agent's authority exists if the agency is a power given as security, but this is not the case here. A power given as security is an agency created for the benefit of the agent (or a third party). It requires that (i) the agent's authority be granted to secure performance of a duty to, or to protect the title of, the agent (or a third party); and (ii) the authority be given and supported by consideration at the time the duty or title was created. If these requirements are met, the agency will not terminate with the incapacity of the principal.

Here, the authority to sell "Herald" was given not for the benefit of the agent, but for the benefit of the principal. Siegel had no interest in the sale of the horse. He was not given the authority to sell the horse to secure any duty owed to him nor did he give any consideration for the agency. Also, the fact that Champion was willing to pay more than Rich's price does not make this a power given as security. Siegel's interest ($10,000) is merely in the proceeds of the sale, and he has no beneficial interest in the subject matter of the agency. Therefore, the agency was revocable, it was revoked by Rich's incapacity, Siegel had no authority to sell the horse, and Champion has no rights against Bill.

Note that the power of attorney Rich gave to Siegel was not a "durable" power of attorney. A durable power of attorney is a power given to an agent in writing that ***specifically*** indicates that the power will not be affected by the principal's incapacity and thus continues after the principal's incapacity. Here, the power of attorney Rich gave to Siegel was in writing, but it did not specifically indicate that it was to continue if Rich became incapacitated. Consequently, Siegel's authority to act on Rich's behalf terminated when Rich was adjudicated incapacitated, and Champion has no rights against Bill.

ANSWER TO QUESTION V

Yes, Ardmore may proceed to judgment against both Bobolink and Casper. When Ardmore's relationship with Bobolink began, Casper was an undisclosed principal (*i.e.*, both Casper's identity and the fact that an agency relationship existed were undisclosed). The undisclosed principal situation remained through the filing of suit against Bobolink. During the existence of an undisclosed principal situation, the remedy of the third party (here, Ardmore) is to bring suit against the agent. (Should a judgment be rendered against the agent, the agent ordinarily has a right to indemnity against the principal.)

Once the principal's identity (and her place in the agency relationship) is disclosed, the third party may file suit against the principal as well if a judgment has not been rendered and satisfied against the agent. However, if either the principal or the agent objects to the third party filing suit against both parties, the third party must elect ***prior to judgment*** which party he wishes to hold liable. In this case, the facts do not indicate that either Bobolink or Casper objected to Ardmore filing suit against both of them; thus, Ardmore may proceed to judgment against both parties. However, Ardmore is ***not*** entitled to satisfaction of judgment from both parties.

ANSWER TO QUESTION VI

(a) Veronica's contribution is available to satisfy claims which arose prior to her participation in the partnership. The essence of a partnership is the sharing of rights and responsibilities. When Veronica entered the partnership, she assumed her share of such rights and responsibilities. A new partner (here, Veronica) is jointly liable with the other partners for all partnership debts. This includes debts that were incurred by the partnership prior to the new partner's admission. Upon admission, the partner is deemed to have assumed her share of the partnership liabilities.

    As applied to this case, the above principles mean that Veronica's contribution of $50,000 is available for payment of partnership creditors, even the creditors whose claims against the partnership arose prior to Veronica's entry into the partnership.

(b) Because the sharing of responsibilities goes to the essence of the partnership relationship, the partners may not exempt one partner from partnership liability by agreement. (The limited partnership form of doing business is an exception to this, but those designated as limited partners generally do not participate in management of the business.) Thus, Veronica's $50,000 contribution may be reached by prior creditors despite any agreement to the contrary by the partners. Such agreement is voidable by the partnership's creditors and will not be enforced in Veronica's favor against them.

(c) Veronica is ***not*** personally liable for the preexisting debts. Although all partnership property—including that contributed by Veronica—may be reached by preexisting creditors, her personal assets may not. Veronica is personally liable only for partnership debts that accrued after her entry into the partnership. Only partnership property (and the personal assets of Cornelius and Robert) are available to satisfy debts that accrued prior to Veronica's becoming a partner.

ANSWER TO QUESTION VII

(a) Under the Revised Uniform Partnership Act ("RUPA"), Shelby's departure will cause Shelby to be ***dissociated*** from the partnership. A partner will be dissociated from the partnership on the partnership's receipt of the partner's notice to withdraw. Thus, when Shelby provided notice to the other partners that she was leaving the partnership, she was dissociated from the partnership.

    In a partnership for a definite term where a partner has wrongfully dissociated from the partnership, the partnership will continue after the partner's dissociation unless at least half of the remaining partners agree to wind up the partnership. Here, the partnership was for a definite term, and Shelby wrongfully dissociated by leaving the partnership before the end of the term. Thus, the partnership will continue unless at least half of the partners agree to wind up the partnership. If the partnership continues, then the partners must purchase the dissociated partner's interest in the partnership and may offset any damages caused by the partner's wrongful dissociation. If at least half of the remaining partners agree to wind up the partnership, then the partners who have not wrongfully dissociated from the partnership (Bobby, Cassidy, and Tracy) have the right to wind up the partnership affairs and distribute any assets.

(b) Under the Uniform Partnership Act ("UPA"), Shelby's departure will cause a ***dissolution*** of the partnership. A dissolution of the partnership occurs when any partner expresses a will to dissolve. A will to dissolve will be shown where the partner evidences an intention to discontinue the partnership. Here, Shelby expressed an intention to dissolve the partnership by giving notice of her departure and moving out of state; therefore, she effected a dissolution of the partnership.

Once the partnership is dissolved, the partners have rights in dissolution. If the dissolution is in violation of the partnership agreement, the nondissolving partners have a right to damages from the dissolving partner for any damages sustained because of the partner's dissolution. In this case, Bobby, Cassidy, and Tracy would be entitled to any damages caused by Shelby's dissolving the partnership because her departure was in violation of the partnership agreement. The partnership agreement provided that the partnership was to continue for 10 years, and Shelby left the partnership after only three years.

Moreover, Bobby, Cassidy, and Tracy have the right to continue the partnership. The nondissolving partners have the right to continue the partnership if they pay the dissolving partner the value of her interest in the partnership. If Bobby, Cassidy, and Tracy do not agree to continue the business, they have the right to wind up the partnership affairs and distribute any assets. Shelby does not have the right to wind up—only partners who have not wrongfully dissolved the partnership have the right to wind up partnership affairs and distribute any assets.

ANSWER TO QUESTION VIII

Under the Revised Uniform Limited Partnership Act ("RULPA"), Louise is personally liable to Lumber Unlimited as if she were a general partner. A limited partnership is a partnership formed by two or more persons, having as members one or more general partners and one or more limited partners. Such a partnership is formed by filing a certificate of limited partnership with the state. Under the provisions of the RULPA, those designated in the certification as limited partners (here, Louise) are normally not personally liable for the obligations of the limited partnership. The liability of a limited partner is usually limited to the amount she has invested in the limited partnership.

However, under the RULPA a limited partner who ***participates in the control of the business*** is liable as a general partner to any creditor who extends credit to the partnership reasonably believing that the limited partner is a general partner. Here, Lumber Unlimited could have reasonably believed that Louise was a general partner when it extended credit to the partnership because it was Louise who dealt with Lumber Unlimited in purchasing the lumber, and Lumber Unlimited was unaware that Louise was a limited partner. Therefore, under the RULPA Louise is personally liable to Lumber Unlimited for the purchase of the lumber. Note that the result is different under the Uniform Limited Partnership Act of 2001 ("ULPA"). Under the ULPA, a limited partner who participates in the management or control of the business retains her limited liability. Thus, under the ULPA, Louise is not personally liable.

ANSWER TO QUESTION IX

(a) The LLC is liable for Tammy's purchases. Management of an LLC may be vested in the members, or the members may choose to have the LLC managed by managers. Here, the members, Debbie and Emil, chose to have the LLC managed by managers, Brigette, Joe, and Tammy.

If management is vested in managers, the managers have the right to run the LLC, and they also have the power to bind the LLC for acts apparently related to carrying on the LLC's business. In this case, however, Tammy's purchases were actually authorized by the managers. A majority vote of the managers is ordinarily required to approve most decisions affecting the LLC. Here, all managers agreed to the purchases; thus, Tammy had the authority to make the purchases on the LLC's behalf, and, thus, the LLC is liable for Tammy's purchases.

(b) Brigette, Joe, and Tammy are ***not*** personally liable for the purchases. Generally, neither the members of an LLC nor its managers are personally liable for the LLC's obligations. Tammy's purchases were for the LLC and approved by the managers; therefore, Brigette, Joe, and Tammy are not personally liable.

ANSWER TO QUESTION X

Jackie, Linda, and Stacey can also form a limited liability partnership ("LLP"). An LLP is similar to a regular partnership (*e.g.*, all partners may participate in the management of the partnership, see below); however, the partners are not personally liable for the obligations of the partnership. In an LLP, Jackie can participate in the management of the business, and Jackie and Stacey would have their limited liability; thus, an LLP would be an appropriate entity for Jackie, Linda, and Stacey to form.

Jackie, Linda, and Stacey may also form a limited liability company ("LLC"). An LLC is a hybrid organization that provides its owners, called "members," with limited liability like shareholders in a corporation, but offers a business structure similar to that of a partnership. In an LLC, all of the members may manage the LLC, or the members may choose managers to manage the LLC. In an LLC, Jackie and Stacey again would have their limited liability, and Jackie would be able to participate in the management of the LLC; consequently, an LLC would also be an appropriate business entity for Jackie, Linda, and Stacey to form.

Jackie, Linda, and Stacey should not form a partnership. A partnership is an association of two or more persons to run a business for profit. Here, there would be more than two persons, and the business is to operate for profit. Each partner in the partnership has the right to manage the partnership, so Jackie's requirement that she participate in management would be satisfied. However, partners of a partnership ***are personally liable*** for the partnership's debts and obligations. Jackie and Stacey do not want to be personally liable for the partnership's debts and obligations; thus, a partnership would not be an appropriate entity for them to form.

Neither should Jackie, Linda, and Stacey can form a limited partnership if they are in a state that has adopted the RULPA, but they could if they are in a state that has adopted the ULPA. A limited partnership is comprised of one or more general partners, and one or more limited partners. The general partner manages the partnership and is personally liable for the partnership's debts and obligations. Under the RULPA, the limited partners are not personally liable for the partnership's obligations unless they participate in the management of the partnership (note that under the ULPA, the limited partners are not personally liable even if they participate in the management or control). Here, Jackie and Stacey want limited liability. They would be limited partners, and Linda would be the general partner. However, Jackie has required that she be able to participate in the management of the partnership. If a limited partner participates in the management of the partnership, then under the RULPA she may be personally liable to third parties who extend credit to the partnership believing the limited partner is a general partner. Consequently, if Jackie were a limited partner and participated in the management of the limited partnership, she may lose her limited liability. Thus, a limited partnership is not the best entity to accommodate the requests of Jackie, Linda, and Stacey (unless the partnership is formed under the ULPA, in which case Jackie would retain limited liability).

Table of Cases

Index